222/240

WITHDRAWN

OCT 0 1 2013 CO

D1452839

A THRILLING NARRATIVE OF INDIAN CAPTIVITY

Edited by CARRIE REBER ZEMAN AND KATHRYN ZABELLE
DEROUNIAN-STODOLA | *Foreword by* GWEN N. WESTERMAN

A THRILLING NARRATIVE

DISPATCHES FROM

OF INDIAN CAPTIVITY

THE DAKOTA WAR

Mary Butler Renville

UNIVERSITY OF NEBRASKA PRESS | LINCOLN AND LONDON

© 2012 by the Board of Regents of
the University of Nebraska. Untitled
poem by Simon J. Ortiz © 2009 by
Simon J. Ortiz, reproduced with
permission. Maps © 2011 by the
Pond Dakota Heritage Society,
reproduced with permission. All
rights reserved. Manufactured in
the United States of America.

This project has been made possible in
part by the Arts and Cultural Heritage
Fund through the vote of Minnesotans
on 4 November 2008. Administered
by the Minnesota Historical Society.

Library of Congress
Cataloging-in-Publication Data
Renville, Mary Butler, 1830–1895.
A thrilling narrative of Indian
captivity: dispatches from the
Dakota War / Mary Butler Renville;
edited by Carrie Reber Zeman and
Kathryn Zabelle Derounian-Stodola;
foreword by Gwen N. Westerman.
p. cm. Originally published: 1863.
Includes bibliographical
references and index.
ISBN 978-0-8032-3530-4
(cloth: alk. paper)
1. Dakota Indians—Wars, 1862–1865—
Personal narratives. 2. Renville,
Mary Butler, 1830–1895. 3. Indian
captivities—Minnesota. I. Zeman,
Carrie R. II. Derounian-Stodola,
Kathryn Zabelle, 1949– III. Title.
E83.86.R46 2012
973.7—dc23   2011047920

Set in Charis by Kim Essman.
Designed by Nathan Putens.

For Alan R. Woolworth,
generous colleague and friend

For Katie, Claire, Lilly, and Joy,
from their mother, Carrie:
"Learn wisdom from the past and
lay broad the platform of Justice,
Morality and Truth."

For Bob, from his wife, Zabelle

CONTENTS

ILLUSTRATIONS

FOREWORD

If we know anything about ourselves as human beings, it is that we know the power of a good story. And publishers know the power of a tantalizing title to attract readers and to increase profits. However, when a colleague gave me a copy of *A Thrilling Narrative of Indian Captivity* in 1995, my reaction to the title was cynical: here was another bodice-ripper that would reinforce every negative stereotype of Indigenous people ever conceived. The book found a place on a high shelf in my office and was not disturbed again. Yet such assessments are rarely as simple as they first appear.

It is often tempting to look back and make judgments on the actions of historical figures or ancestors, judgments made with what we think are keen eyes sharpened by current research, new facts, and our own experiences. We scan every letter, court document, and journal for meaning and for explanations of the choices those people in our past have made. To justify our interpretations, we extrapolate answers couched in current theories of literary criticism or historiography. But without explicit records, will we ever *definitively* know the answers to the questions we have about our history?

During her life among Dakota people, Mary Butler Renville witnessed a significant, pivotal period of cultural, political, and historic change, of which *A Thrilling Narrative of Indian Captivity* represents but a small part. However, her observations of a tumultuous time in American history reveal the almost immeasurable complexities of nineteenth-century Dakota-white interactions and the indelible mark left by Christian missionaries.

This new edition provides contemporary readers with a comprehensive critical analysis that contextualizes Renville's 1863 narrative and offers a broader picture of events that forever changed the Dakota people and the landscape of Minnesota.

Supported by Carrie Reber Zeman's detailed historical framework, we are better able to understand Renville's reflections about life as the wife of John B. Renville, a Dakota man who would become the first ordained "Sioux" minister in 1865. Her love for her husband is obvious, as is his dedication to serve and live among his own community. What is also obvious is how their positions as teachers and missionaries complicated their relationships with their peers as well as with many of John Renville's Dakota relatives, for whom Mary served as an amanuensis during her "captivity."

Throughout her journal, Mary Renville's Christian devotion is revealed in her language and in her earnest belief that God will deliver the captives from the dangers they faced during the Dakota-U.S. War in the late summer of 1862. She makes a distinction between "friendly" Indians and "Christian" Indians, one that is often blurred today in contemporary discussions of Dakota and Minnesota history. She spares no fury for the "rebels" and "demons" responsible for attacks on the Indian agencies and surrounding settler villages. Yet the identity of those "rebels" or "demons" is not always clear to her, or to us as readers, because of the movements of all factions among the villages or at the battle sites. Hers was an existence of conflict between her love for her husband and her fear of Dakota people.

Renville's narrative was originally published in serial form as "The Indian Captives: Leaves from a Journal," but someone at the Atlas Company's Book and Job Printing Office opted for the more sensational title. While it would be easy to condemn Renville's words from our vantage point or to dismiss the value of a nineteenth-century captivity narrative, Kathryn Zabelle Derounian-Stodola offers a discussion of the literary value of this volume and opens up new areas of conversation about women's roles in writing history.

While not written from a Dakota perspective, Renville's little notebook is important in that it records the experiences of Dakota people during a time of war and great upheaval. This new edition of *A Thrilling Narrative of Indian Captivity* includes for the first time English translations of John Renville's letters written in Dakota while Mary Renville's "The Indian Captives: Leaves from a Journal" was being prepared and printed in the *Berlin City Courant*. These letters, Renville's journal, and the accompanying literary and historical essays open more windows—among thousands of windows—from which to view the events of 1862. And with multiple perspectives on a story, we can come closer to knowing the answers to those questions we have about our shared history.

Henana epe kte. Wiŋuna de miye.

Gwen N. Westerman, PhD
Mankato, Minnesota
February 2011

PREFACE

HISTORICAL CONSIDERATIONS, BY CARRIE REBER ZEMAN

In "Historical Perspectives on *A Thrilling Narrative of Indian Captivity*" I have privileged primary sources, quoting them sometimes at length rather than simply providing the citation. Both practical and philosophical concerns suggested this approach. Because the primary text, *A Thrilling Narrative of Indian Captivity*, until now has been obscure, almost no secondary work has been done on the text (before my coeditor addressed it in 2009) and very little has been done on its authors. Thus the historical work this project posed was not the refinement or the reinterpretation of previous work (other than my own as-yet-unpublished work on the Sioux Agency) but the raw, preliminary sifting of the primary-source literature to see what turned up.

Therefore, my historical work in this volume rests heavily on primary sources. The exceptions are discussions of subjects like interracial marriage and the Underground Railroad movement, where an existing body of analytical work contextualizes elements of the Renvilles' story. In a few instances, like my discussion of the causes of the 1862 war, I have chosen to largely ignore the secondary literature in order to foreground period arguments in the fresh context of this story.

A philosophical concern undergirds these practical considerations. The secondary literature on the Dakota War of 1862 is so vast and varied that scholars can posit and seemingly support just about any assertion that suits their dialectic fancy. Because many primary sources are not readily accessible to those who live distant from major repositories, general readers may be unaware of the depth and breadth of the primary literature that has yet to be mined in this century by scholars. My intent is to challenge readers to wrestle with the sources themselves, not simply my own or anyone else's interpretation of them.

Readers should also be aware that I am not Native but European American, which posed challenges for a story heavily dependent on Dakota-authored sources. The primary author of *A Thrilling Narrative*, Mary Butler Renville, was the only person of my own ethnicity to spend the entire war in the Upper Camp. The secondary author, John Baptiste Renville, and every other Peace Party leader who appears in this story, was Dakota. Several conscious choices help mitigate this problem of a non-Dakota author approaching a Dakota story. I have chosen to privilege period Dakota sources as primary evidence and to privilege those sources' interpretations of their own narrative, even where it differs from the received (secondary, European American) story. While some readers may find this approach unbalanced, my intent in this volume is to tell a little-known *part* of the larger story of the 1862 war. The wider body of literature on this subject details the non-Native aspects. Therefore, privileging Dakota perspectives is a natural extension of my and my coeditor's resolve to bring *A Thrilling Narrative* back into print. In addition, my coeditor and I have sought out the meaningful participation of modern Dakota scholars since the earliest days of this project, and we are grateful for their help and perspectives, particularly in interpreting their own history and ethnography and representing the Dakota language.

Last, I approach this story as a Christian in the Reformed theological tradition, a worldview that holds much in common with the Presbyterians in this story. I do not excuse the missionaries' obvious ethnocentrism, which has never been part of the Gospel and was, unfortunately, bound up in the missiology of their day. Yet as Mary Butler Renville's and John Baptiste Renville's biographer I have done my best to faithfully represent their theological perspective to allow readers to understand and evaluate the worldview the authors brought to the story.

LITERARY CONSIDERATIONS, BY
KATHRYN ZABELLE DEROUNIAN-STODOLA

In "Literary Perspectives on *A Thrilling Narrative of Indian Captivity*" I approach the material from the vantage point of captivity narrative studies, a field to which I have contributed for the past thirty years. Therefore I situate *A Thrilling Narrative* within the extensive scholarship on captivity narratives in general and U.S.-Dakota War captivity narratives in particular. Additionally, I contextualize John and Mary Renville's search for a home base through the growing amount of literature on what might be termed home studies. Native American scholars, including Simon J. Ortiz and N. Scott Momaday, have contributed some of the most exciting and extensive reflections on home, and I refer to them in my introduction. Finally, preparing this edition has special significance for me since it is the last book I will publish before retirement in 2012. That, and the fact that I am an expatriate Englishwoman for whom England will always be home, may account for the tone of my literary introduction, described by one of the manuscript's external reviewers as "an almost lyrical meditation on the meaning of home, homeland, and the connection between place and identity."

ACKNOWLEDGMENTS

JOINT ACKNOWLEDGMENTS

First, we must thank Raymond J. DeMallie and Mary Lethert Wingerd, the external readers to whom the University of Nebraska Press sent our manuscript. Their encouragement and feedback have made the project much stronger. Walt Bachman, Lois Glewwe, and Gwen Westerman also read the entire manuscript with meticulous, helpful eyes for detail.

We are extremely grateful for the help and expertise offered by Dakota scholars Glenn Wasicuna and Gwen Westerman, the language advisors and translators for this project. Together they painstakingly decoded John B. Renville's holograph letters, written in old, irregular Dakota, and have brought his thoughts to life for modern readers in Dakota and English. Gwen also very generously offered to write the foreword, despite her many other commitments. Gwen's and Glenn's perspectives, counsel, and contributions have added immeasurably to the worth of this edition.

Stephen Osman, Tom Shaw, Florestine Kiyukanpi Renville, and Marcia Loudon all read and commented on portions of the manuscript. For research assistance we thank Lisa Elbert, Beth Brown, Steve Misener, Elden Lawrence, Corinne Marz, and Scott W. Berg. We are indebted to Butler family genealogist Marcia Loudon, who shared her extensive research on Mary Butler's family of origin. For their expertise and help in their respective collections, we thank: Darla Gebhard at the Brown County Historical Society, New Ulm, Minnesota; June Lynne at the Chippewa County Historical Society, Montevideo, Minnesota; Amanda Jenson at the Center for Western Studies at Augustana College, Sioux Falls, South Dakota; Sue

Gates at the Dakotah Prairie Museum, Aberdeen, South Dakota; Matthew Reitzel and Virginia Hanson at the South Dakota State Historical Society, Pierre, South Dakota; Peg Dilbonne of the Steuben County Historical Society, Fremont, Indiana; Betsy Dorris and Mary McAndrew of Knox College, Galesburg, Illinois; Andrew Prellwitz of Ripon College, Ripon, Wisconsin; and MaryFrances Morrow at the National Archives, Washington DC. At the Minnesota Historical Society Patrick Coleman and Debbie Miller offered assistance at many stages of the project.

There are several organizations and individuals to thank for production assistance. We thank Matt Bokovoy and the University of Nebraska Press for supporting this project. The Newberry Library generously donated a digital version of their copy of *A Thrilling Narrative of Indian Captivity*. We are also indebted to the Board of the Pond Dakota Heritage Society for supporting this project by sponsoring a Legacy Grant. As a result, the photographs and maps in this volume are made possible in part by the Arts and Cultural Heritage Fund through the vote of Minnesotans on 4 November 2008, administered by the Minnesota Historical Society. The maps were created by Philip Schwartzberg of Meridian Mapping, Minneapolis, Minnesota. Finally, we thank Southern Cheyenne artist Merlin Little Thunder for allowing us to use his painting *They Always Prefer the Old Ways* on the cover of this book and Bill Wiggins, who owns the painting.

CARRIE REBER ZEMAN'S ACKNOWLEDGMENTS

Two teachers influenced this work at a distance of two decades: Thomas Becknell, who opened my eyes to the literature of the oppressed, and Natalie Kusz, who taught me to write about complex truth.

To Glenn Wasicuna and Gwen Westerman: I am humbled and blessed that I happened to be the next Wašiçuŋ scholar who knocked at your door. Thank you for your hospitality, stories, questions, and understanding.

I am grateful to Alan Woolworth for his encouragement and for the loan of papers from his private collection, including Minnesota Indian captivity narratives; and to Walt Bachman, for a decade of almost daily collaboration in the trenches of primary-source research.

I am intellectually indebted to several historians whose work helped crystallize my understanding of this story. Conversations with Mary Wingerd and Kirsten Delegard during their work on *North Country: The Making of Minnesota* seeded key ideas at a formative stage in this project. More recent conversations have helped refine it. Susan Sleeper-Smith's work on the bicultural Potawatomis who persisted on their Indiana homelands post-removal helped me understand what I found in the bicultural Dakota literature. Linda K. Kerber's early work exploring the connections between the abolition and the Indian Reform movements was critical for my understanding of Mary Butler Renville's family of origin. My coeditor, Zabelle, opened my eyes to the Indian captivity narrative genre and to the treasures buried in my own backyard. I am indebted to each of you and regret I did not have room in this volume to give your ideas space commensurate with your influence on my work.

Last, I must acknowledge that this story is a gift. I do not deserve the privilege of telling it and am grateful to God for the opportunity.

KATHRYN ZABELLE DEROUNIAN-STODOLA'S
ACKNOWLEDGMENTS

I first encountered Carrie while working on my book *The War in Words: Reading the Dakota Conflict through the Captivity Literature*, published by the University of Nebraska Press in 2009. Partly because I was so focused on the narratives as literature, I was initially naïve about the historical dimensions of the U.S.-Dakota War. But I soon realized that I had better get my history right since so much information and misinformation about this war have been exploited in the past 150 years. As an independent historian specializing in the context of the U.S.-Dakota War, Carrie set me straight on many details so that historical accuracy underlaid my critical analysis, even if it could not always resolve ambiguity. In the course of our many e-mail exchanges, she mentioned an obscure but important narrative that was published in 1863 but then fell out of print: *A Thrilling Narrative of Indian Captivity*. I was grateful to Carrie for drawing my attention to this text, and I discussed it briefly in *The War in Words*. But we both agreed that it warranted republication, and eventually we decided to coedit it. This edition is the happy result.

I also owe thanks to my colleague Bill Wiggins, who offered advice on choosing cover art from his huge collection, the Dr. J. W. Wiggins Contemporary Native American Art Collection, housed at the Sequoyah National Research Center at the University of Arkansas at Little Rock. And I am most grateful to Simon J. Ortiz for allowing me to quote his poem on "home" in my literary introduction. Last, I am so pleased to have spoken to and exchanged e-mails with Florestine Kiyukanpi Renville (a descendent of John Renville's cousin Gabriel Renville), who read and commented on a portion of this manuscript, and to have felt a family connection to the Renvilles through her.

A NOTE ON EDITORIAL PROCEDURE

In this edition we use a variety of sources for the three sets of texts: *A Thrilling Narrative of Indian Captivity*, the letters in appendix A, and the letters in appendix B. Each of these sections requires specific adaptations of basic editorial procedure. But generally we try to make as few changes as possible while balancing readability with retention of existing textual markers.

A THRILLING NARRATIVE OF INDIAN CAPTIVITY (MINNEAPOLIS: ATLAS COMPANY'S BOOK AND JOB PRINTING OFFICE, 1863)

We use as copy-text the reserve copy of *A Thrilling Narrative of Indian Captivity* housed at the Minnesota Historical Society. According to the WorldCat library network, there are five surviving copies of this text: three have fifty-two pages (those at the Minnesota Historical Society, the Newberry Library, and Oberlin College) and two have forty-seven pages (those at Yale and the Wisconsin Historical Society/University of Wisconsin–Madison), meaning that they lack the five pages devoted to "H. D. Cunningham's Statement" in the fuller editions.

We preserve most accidentals; for example, we have not corrected any errors in the placement of apostrophes or other punctuation, except to remove some stray periods. Brackets [ ] in the text are ours, parentheses ( ) in the text are from the original, and in the two cases where the original uses square brackets, we change them to curly brackets { }. We silently correct a few typesetting errors we found by comparing the *Berlin City Courant* newspaper version with the Atlas book edition as well as obvious spelling mistakes (for example, we change "buiscuit" to "biscuit" in chapter 4 and "vp" to "up" in chapter 6). Otherwise, original spelling and paragraphing remain unchanged. For ease of reference, we have changed the original roman numeral chapter numbers to words, so, for example, "Chapter X" is now "Chapter Ten."

APPENDIX A

Appendix A compiles the extant correspondence between Dakota camps and federal authorities during the 1862 war. In the absence of holograph originals we reproduce the letters as they appear in the earliest known source, as cited in the annotations. We include the "lost" letters recovered in *A Thrilling Narrative* in appendix A to allow readers to consider the full sweep of the conversation without having to flip between the text and the appendix. Again, we preserve most accidentals. Brackets [ ] in the text are ours; parentheses ( ) are from the original. We silently correct a few typesetting errors but otherwise retain the sources' spelling and paragraphing (for example, we leave "Lake quiparle" in one of the letters instead of regularizing it to "Lac qui Parle").

APPENDIX B

Appendix B reproduces selected writings of John Baptiste and Mary Butler Renville. This is the only part of the edition where some of the reproduced texts come from unpublished holographs. In the case of letters that come from printed sources, we adhere to the same criteria as mentioned above for appendix A. For holograph letters we silently remove errant punctuation (a stray comma or period, for example) but we add missing and needed punctuation in brackets [ ]. Regarding sentence constructions, we place punctuation within brackets [ ] if the lack of it could cause confusion (some of the holograph letters were written hastily) but leave some run-on sentences where they do not affect comprehension or meaning.

For example, in the interest of readability, if there is no period at the end of what should be a sentence but a capital letter begins the word in the next sentence, then we make the correction since the writer signaled his/her intention to end one sentence and begin a new one.

OTHER CONVENTIONS

We would like to add a note on the Dakota language as reproduced in this text. The orthography, or written representation, of the Dakota language has been evolving for almost two centuries as English speakers have tried to subdue sounds that are not native to the English language. In this century the orthography continues to evolve in the hands of Dakota people themselves. Because its literature is embodied in the oral tradition of its people, modern efforts to revitalize the language focus on training people to understand, speak, and read Dakota. We have chosen to use the standard orthography developed at the University of Minnesota in the 1990s, Dakota Iapi (Mdewankanton), and have included a pronunciation key following this section.

After deliberating the merits of several possibilities, we chose to update the historical spellings of Dakota personal names to match their meanings, where the meanings are known. (An exception is Wambdiokiya, who wrote his own name with that spelling.) The meaning of a name is significant in Dakota culture, and historical familiarity seemed insufficient reason to perpetuate meaning-obscuring misspellings. For example, we have spelled Mazamani's name (Iron Walker) that way, not "Mazomani." Catherine "Totedutawin" is now Catherine Tatidutawiŋ (Her Scarlet House), and her son is Lorenzo Towaŋiteton (Face of the Village) Lawrence. Where necessary, the multiple historical misspellings are called out in a note. However, when the meaning of a name is not known we have chosen to retain the most often used spelling rather than guess. "Tokanne" is one example. It is not a Dakota name. But in the absence of more information, using "Tokanne" at least preserves a historically discrete identity for Mary Tokanne Renville, John Baptiste Renville's mother. We have retained the period spellings of place-names and bands.

As the editors of this volume, we have attempted to adhere to the editorial conventions of our disciplines, which include using the title attached to the work we are reprinting, *A Thrilling Narrative of Indian Captivity*. But given the title's sensationalism and the existence of an earlier title used in the newspaper version, "The Indian Captives: Leaves from a Journal," we did not make this decision lightly. While we suspect the book's title was changed by the publisher in 1863 to make the book more salable, we have not found direct evidence supporting the idea. Therefore, we observe the conventions governing reprints and retain the published title, despite its cultural insensitivity.

In terms of the introductory material to this edition we decided to draw on our own individual strengths and backgrounds to furnish two separate introductions. Hence, Carrie wrote "Historical Perspectives on *A Thrilling Narrative of Indian Captivity*" and Zabelle wrote "Literary Perspectives on *A Thrilling Narrative of Indian Captivity*." We exchanged drafts for comment, but in the end we respected each other's right to interpret the text as she saw it, especially as some of the material is genuinely ambiguous. Therefore, while we agree on major points of interpretation, we do not always agree on more minor ones. We hope readers concur that preserving such alternative readings adds to the interpretive richness of the texts under consideration.

PRONUNCIATION GUIDE
FOR DAKOTA IAPI

a	as in *wash*	m	as in *moon*
aŋ	as in *awn*ing	n	as in *noon*
b	as in *boy*	o	as in *open*
c	*ch* sound, but soft, almost like a *j*	p	soft *p*, almost like a *b*
		p	hard *p*, as in *pop*
ç	*ch* sound, but hard, as in *chalk* and *chop*	p'	*p* sound with a pause (glottal stop); used before a vowel
c'	*ch* sound with a pause (glottal stop); used before a vowel	s	as in *simple*
		s'	*s* sound with a pause (glottal stop); used before a vowel
d	as in *dog*	ṡ	*sh* as in sharp
e	as in *stay*	ṡ'	*sh* sound with a pause (glottal stop); used before a vowel
ġ	guttural *g* sound		
g	used only when *k* is contracted, e.g., Waŋyaŋka to wayag	t	soft *t* as in *storm*, almost like a *d*
h	as in *help*	ṭ	hard *t* as in *top*
ḣ	guttural *h* like *ch* in German (machen)	t'	*t* sound with a pause (glottal stop); used before a vowel
I	as in *pizza*	u	as the *oo* sound in *loop*
iŋ	as in *pink*	uŋ	as the *oo* sound in *tune*
k	soft *k*, almost like a *g*	w	as in *water*
ḳ	hard *k* as in *kite*	y	as in *yellow*
k'	*k* sound with a pause (glottal stop); used before a vowel	z	as in *zap*
		ż	as the *s* sound in *pleasure*

Adapted from "Daḳota Alphabet, Sounds and Orthography," in *550 Dakota Verbs*, ed. Harlan Fontaine and Neil McKay (St. Paul: Minnesota Historical Society Press, 2004), 5–6.

A THRILLING NARRATIVE OF INDIAN CAPTIVITY

HISTORICAL PERSPECTIVES ON
A THRILLING NARRATIVE OF
INDIAN CAPTIVITY

Carrie Reber Zeman

In 1863, when *A Thrilling Narrative of Indian Captivity* first appeared in print, its authors, Mary and John Renville, were too poor (they had lost everything in the U.S.-Dakota War of 1862) and too disenfranchised (as an interracial couple) to afford to do more than publish their story as an inexpensive pamphlet printed at the local newspaper's job office. The yellow paper cover, unadorned by illustration, was also devoid of John's name, and therefore his Dakota identity. But the cover of the small book was dressed up nonetheless: with a sensational title, *A Thrilling Narrative of Indian Captivity*, that both literally and figuratively covered the story's original designation, "The Indian Captives: Leaves from a Journal." However, the cover ploys failed to secure notoriety for the book because the story had a more fundamental problem: its sympathetic humanization of the Dakotas who opposed the Dakota War of 1862 was unwelcomed in postwar Minnesota. Marginalized by multiple circumstances, *A Thrilling Narrative* fell into obscurity, virtually unknown even among scholars for almost 150 years.

When the booklet first came to my attention in the form of the reserve copy owned by the Minnesota Historical Society, I dismissed it as a primary source on the Dakota War, returning it to the librarian after only a few minutes' reading, as put off by the melodrama in the opening paragraph as I was by the title. But years later, when I discovered that John B. Renville, the youngest son of Joseph and Mary Tokanne Renville of Lac qui Parle, was rumored to have married his English teacher, a white woman named

Mary Butler, I was intrigued. In that sensational little booklet with Mary Butler Renville's name on the cover, had she not claimed that "we"—that *both* of them—had come from Illinois to teach Indian children on the Minnesota frontier? How could John Renville come *to* the frontier? Was that place not his home and were the students he came to teach not his people?

Those questions led me back to the reserve copy of *A Thrilling Narrative*. But this time I read beyond the first page and became lost in the story of the formation and intrigues of the Dakota resistance movement I had known only vaguely as the "Peace Party," whose opposition to the war, marginalized by attribution to a handful of Christians, garnered mere sentences of space in most histories of the 1862 war. Even more remarkable, Mary Butler Renville managed to tell the whole story without ever letting on that her husband was Dakota. Was he not? Who was she to turn her back on her own white privilege to marry an Indigenous man?

This historical introduction is my attempt to answer those questions and dozens of others raised by the Renvilles' story, contextualizing *A Thrilling Narrative of Indian Captivity* for a modern audience. I approach the seven-decade sweep of the authors' lives in three parts. Part 1, "Borderlands," is set on the multiple geographical and social frontiers that shaped John Baptiste Renville and Mary Adeline Butler into the married couple we meet in the opening pages of the story reprinted in this volume. For part 2 I have borrowed the story's original title, "The Indian Captives," because it both captures and interrogates the complicated truths at the heart of *A Thrilling Narrative*: that in 1862 Dakota people simultaneously *took* captives, were held *as* captives, and were rebelling *against* cultural captivity imposed by outsiders and by their own kin. Part 3, "Afterwords," explores how *A Thrilling Narrative* came into being in the form reproduced in this volume, privileging the period words written by John and Mary and written about them by others to discover what became of their elusive "we" during the decades when their little yellow book plummeted into obscurity.

"No one's story," one of my former college professors, Daniel Taylor, reminds us, "exists alone. Each is tangled up in countless others. Pull a thread in my story and feel the tremor half a world and two millennia away."[1] In the case of *A Thrilling Narrative,* tug on the snag of Mary Butler Renville's "we" and unravel a story that begins in a place called Mde Ia Udan on what was then mapped by whites as the St. Peter's River in Wisconsin Territory almost two centuries ago.

PART I: BORDERLANDS

Mde Ia Udan (Lac qui Parle), 1834

Jean Baptiste was four years old the winter the white men came to Mde Ia Udan, bringing their odd language, strange smells, peculiar clothing, and weak womenfolk into the tipi village outside the stockade walls. Jean had plenty of time to observe the strangers because his father, Joseph Renville, who had invited them to Lac qui Parle, gave them a home inside the stockade: a log building on the north side of the Renville compound. Before Jean was born that storehouse had been stacked to the rafters with furs and pelts each spring. But for winters past it stood empty. Almost daily, the oldest of the strangers came into Jean's house, bearing the faint scent of old muskrat on his clothes. There, in front of the great hearth, in the considerable light cast from burning six-foot logs, the Waŝiҫuŋ spoke to Jean's father in stilted, halting French, sometimes rifling a small book he pulled from his pocket, running his finger over the page before speaking a word.

Jean, like the other boys at Lac qui Parle, knew what a book was. His father kept several, much bigger than the one The Doctor carried in his pantaloons. When one of Jean's relatives came to his father for traps or fishhooks, a clerk wrote in a big book. When the relative came again moons later bearing fat bundles of animal skins, the clerk counted them out—beaver, otter, muskrat, mink—and made writing in the book canceling out the traps and fishhooks. Jean thought the drawing called "writing" ingenious. Letters and numbers trapped information in the book called "Ledger" as surely as traps caught the rats whose skins were counted in the dark water called "ink." Jean's father worked for faraway Waŝiҫuŋ whose minds, like The Doctor's, were as leaky

*as an untended canoe. Books helped them remember things Ikće Wićasta—
Dakota people—held in memory.*

*Jean's father owned another, even bigger, book. Its hard wooden sides
and curved spine were covered in the finest tanned skin Jean had ever seen.
It contained ota paper so fine he could see through the page, the fire lighting
up the rows of marks the clerk called "words." Words looked like footprints
in the snow, the tiny tracks of many mysterious animals who crowded the
pages in the night and disappeared when the sun rose, leaving behind messages
only the clerk, like a shaman, could cipher and speak. Jean's father said it
was Wowapi Wakaŋ, the book of sacred words. The clerk was afraid of this
book and did not like to take it down off its shelf to read the messages the
animals scratched on its pages. Jean was not surprised. On fire-lit winter
evenings, out of the corner of his eye, Jean sometimes saw the sacred book
dance while his father related stories: the man who understood whiskey, the
captive warrior rescued by his wife, the Dakotas who had gone home rather
than eat the American soldier in the last war with the British.*

*One night when Jean fell asleep in his place on the bench along the wall,
his back turned to the room out of courtesy, a dream came to him. A great,
gnarled hand lifted the sacred book from its shelf and threw it on the fire. The
book exploded like a dry cob of popping corn tossed into the flames. Bits of
paper flew up like birds, the words migrating, multiplying, until they covered
the world.*[2]

"I will tell you in what manner we are related."
—Wambdiokiya to Joseph Nicollet, ca. 1839

In 1789 John (Jean) Baptiste Renville's mother, Tokanne, was born at
Kaposia, on the Mississippi River below Imnizaskadan, the White Bluffs,
which would become known as St. Paul, Minnesota.[3] As significant as
Tokanne's place in life were her people. She was born into the Little Crow
line, historically one of the most illustrious of the Mdewankanton Dakota
bands. The hereditary Little Crow chieftainship passed down through
Tokanne's male relatives: from her grandfather Centaŋwakaŋmani, to her

mother's brother Wakiŋyaŋṭanka, to her cousin Taoyateduta, the Little Crow of 1862.⁴ French-Dakota fur trader Joseph Renville married Tokanne in 1806 and again in the Catholic Church in 1829, where she took the English name Mary. Her brother Chatka (Left Hand), one of Little Crow's "principal men," married Catherine Tatidutawiŋ, who became a second mother to John after Mary Tokanne's death in 1840, when John was nine.⁵

On his father, Joseph Renville's, side John traced his lineage back to the De Rainville clan of Basse Normandie (Lower Normandy), France.⁶ Seven generations before John was born, his ancestors immigrated to North America and settled in modern-day Quebec. They were among the first three hundred settlers in French Canada, established by a French investment firm granted a royal monopoly on the fur trade.⁷ The Canadian branch of the family shortened the name to "Rainville."⁸

Within two generations of setting foot on the North American continent, Rainville men began marrying Native women. Given the family's long connection with the fur trade, it is quite possible that Native women entered the Rainville family generations before the first name on record: Miniyuhe, a young Mdewankanton woman from the Kaposia village at Mille Lacs.⁹ Miniyuhe was John's paternal grandmother.¹⁰ According to Renville family history her grandmother was a white woman, making Miniyuhe an early Wašiçuŋ çiŋça, or Dakota mixed-blood. The story came down through Wambdiokiya, John's father's cousin, a warrior in the Soldiers' Lodge at Lac qui Parle. Wambdiokiya, too, was descended from the mysterious white woman. He told the story to Joseph Nicollet, a French geographer mapping the Mississippi River watershed who visited Lac qui Parle in 1838 and 1839. In traditional Dakota fashion Wambdiokiya sought to establish whether there was a kin relationship between himself and the person to whom he was speaking.

"I will tell you in what manner we are related," Wambdiokiya said to French immigrant Nicollet,

and from what nation we are sprung I will relate to you.

A white woman married a Sioux, and they had a son, who grew up to manhood, and took a wife. He became the father of a son and in addition his wife gave birth to more children. After that the woman died, and left two children, the one a female, the mother of Rainville; the other, a male who is our father.

This is a correct account of our parentage, which shows us to have derived our origin partly from Whites, partly from the Sioux.[11]

In this translation by Raymond J. DeMallie, the identity of the mysterious woman is translated "white." But the story was told in Dakota and recorded in French. While Wašiçuŋ is generally translated as the Dakota word for "white person," it originally meant "French person."[12] Two other clues indicate that Miniyuhe's "white" grandmother was French: the fact that Wambdiokiya explicitly declared kinship with Nicollet, and the generations reported in the story. The "mother of Rainville" and the "male who is our father" were grandchildren of the "white woman [who] married a Sioux." Miniyuhe's grandmother would have been born around 1700, a date that fits the swell in French immigration to Canada driven by the fur trade in the last half of the seventeenth century.[13] Intermarriage in the Renville family, then, was historically egalitarian; in an era when white men had just begun marrying Dakota women, a white woman married a Sioux, so they said.

When Joseph Renville, John's father, was born to Miniyuhe in 1779, he inherited French and Dakota ancestry from both lines of his father's family and Dakota ancestry from his mother's. Miniyuhe left Joseph Rainville for a Dakota man when their sons, Joseph Psin Çinça and Victor Ohiya, were young. Rainville went to Canada and Miniyuhe and her husband raised the boys.[14] For the first decade of his life Joseph Renville was immersed in the intricate ethos of kinship that defined traditional Dakota culture. But in 1789, the year Joseph turned ten, his childhood abruptly ended when Rainville reappeared and took him away to Canada for French-language western education. When Rainville died, Joseph was taken in by British fur trader Robert Dickson. Several years later, in 1806, fully engaged in the fur trade himself, Joseph, now styling his surname "Renville," married Tokanne, the cousin of Little Crow. On 1 October 1831 their ninth and last child was born, a son they named Koda Mitawa, or "My Friend."[15] He was baptized Jean Baptiste Renville in the Presbyterian church founded by the missionaries at Lac qui Parle and grew up to be John B. Renville, the second Dakota man in his family to marry a white woman.

Mde Ia Udan: The Lake that Speaks

The sense of the extraordinary has vanished from translations of Mde Ia Udan since Joseph Nicollet first transliterated it into French as "Lac qui Parle" in 1838. The residents told Nicollet the lake was named not because the waters babbled at the banks of this broad stretch of the Minnesota River but because a long time ago the Great Spirit spoke to a man there.[16] Eight years later Presbyterian missionary Thomas S. Williamson recorded his conviction that the Holy Spirit had been brooding over the waters of Lac qui Parle, preparing the way for the Christian Gospel years before the first missionary arrived.[17] Mde Ia Udan was the birthplace of the Dakota Mission of the American Board of Commissioners for Foreign Missions (ABCFM).[18] It was a *wakaŋ*, or sacred place, an auspicious place to call home.

Joseph Renville settled at Lac qui Parle around 1824, about fifteen years before John was born. In the century and a quarter since Renville's ancestors had helped bring the fur trade into the region, the supply of prime furs had diminished. Renville was a pragmatist who for years had encouraged his relatives to enlarge their communal fields and to raise domestic animals as a hedge against hunger. These agricultural pursuits supplemented Renville's fluctuating trade income. Yet the example Renville set in this regard was quite different from that of the missionaries he invited to Mde Ia Udan. Instead of using the fruits of his work to insulate his nuclear family from want, Joseph Renville was a generous giver in the best Dakota tradition. When Renville had plenty, his family and his relatives feasted on the bounty of his flocks and fields. When his relatives were hungry, Renville's family went hungry, too, because he had shared so much.[19] Exceeding generosity was a Dakota virtue, and despite the decade Joseph Renville spent in Canada learning western ways, his adult life reflected his formative years in Dakota culture.

Bicultural men like Joseph Renville played a significant role on the local political scene because their influence appealed to Dakotas who disagreed over the viability of traditional lifeways in changing times. Missionary Stephen Riggs, who lived at Lac qui Parle in this era, recalled that acculturation to western ways was viewed by Dakotas as "the embodiment of principles diametrically opposed to the customs and religion of their fathers. The Dakota gods were in the opposition" to significant cultural change.[20] Renville's Soldiers' Lodge was an asset in this environment, composed of tipi-dwelling hunter-warrior relatives like Wambdiokiya and his brother, Mazakutemani, who honored Renville (when it suited them) as if he was their hereditary chief. Renville's soldier-enforcers were middlemen, supporting Renville's progressive agenda via traditional roles and lifeways.[21] They were also the first Dakotas at Mde Ia Udan to succumb to the written word. Missionary Thomas S. Williamson, their teacher, later told the story.

> The first school for learning to read and write Dakota was begun at Lac qui Parle in December, 1835. The schoolroom was a conical Dakota tent, fully twenty feet in diameter and about the same in height. It was the property of Mr. Renville, the trader, and was used as a mess-house for about twenty men, whom he called his soldiers. . . . These soldiers were the pupils. . . . When it was first proposed to teach them to read and write, they objected that their language was not like that of the white men, and the words could not be represented by marks. With the assistance of Mr. Renville I persuaded them to make the attempt.[22]

Using a few slates, chalk, and the blackened lid of a dry goods box for a blackboard, in about three months' time "several had made so much progress that they began to write each other on scraps of paper and of birch bark. These epistles were brief, and not elegant, but intelligible."[23]

While these earliest letters are not extant, a slightly later set of Dakota letters written from Lac qui Parle between 1837 and 1839 was preserved in the papers of missionaries Samuel and Gideon Pond, translated in the 1930s by Ella Deloria, the premier Dakota translator of the twentieth century. The epistles show Renville's soldiers using their new literacy

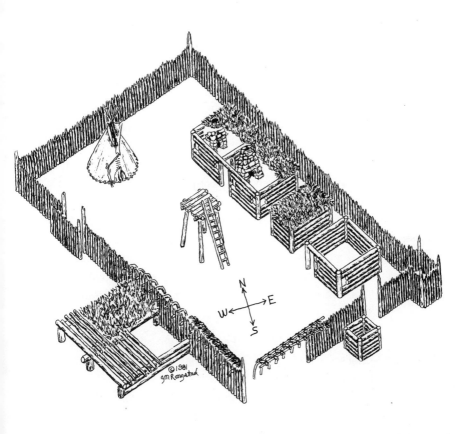

Fig. 1. Fort Renville, Lac qui Parle, ca. 1835. Courtesy of the Chippewa County (Minnesota) Historical Society. Based on a 1981 drawing by G. M. Rongstad created from archeological data and period sources. The original caption reads, "Stockade enclosed an area 130 x 85 feet made of six to ten inch, round logs six to ten feet high. Loop holes for musket fire helped discourage invasion from neighboring Chippewa Indians. Canoe port with sod roof facing river. Center of stockade: a raised platform and ladder used to overlook the area. East wall of stockade lined with three buildings. Northernmost Renville's home and place of business: two rooms, both with fire hearths of hand hewn logs, sod roof, dirt floor. Second building with sod roof use: armory, gunpowder stores. Third cabin 20 x 20 feet dirt floor/roof use as: quarters for visitors."

skills for their own ends: reminding others of kinship obligations, carrying on feuds with Renville, and working out their nascent fictive kinship ties with their missionary teachers, who needed remedial instruction in how to be Dakota.

The missionaries, of course, had their own agenda for teaching literacy. They believed "the word of God was the power of salvation unto those who believe" and understood that the Bible they were translating would be a medium of grace for those Dakotas who could read it.[24] Renville's soldiers, however, had different reasons for learning. During long, snowbound winters writing became a way of telling stories to hearers afar. Some letters were written to relatives hundreds of miles away who were learning literacy from missionaries Gideon and Samuel Pond near Fort Snelling; others were written between villages near Lac qui Parle.[25] Thus writing became another means for Dakotas to be good relatives. Wambdiokiya explained his own reasoning when he complained to the missionaries in an 1838 letter:

> When you first settled here and taught us writing, and you said you were going to teach us everything, at that time, I alone listened to all you said. But you have never heeded anything I have said to you. . . . I supposed that because you taught me writing, therefore what I asked would be granted, and so I bent every effort towards learning, and lo, from that time to this, I am even worse off. . . . I want you to be kind to me, but you are not, that is why I haven't come for a long time. What I wanted was for you to give a little pig to my mother.[26]

With his father's blessing, Jean Baptiste, who was five the winter written words came, sat in on the lessons in the Soldiers' Lodge and learned to read and to write his native language. The missionaries made headway with their Christian message inside Joseph Renville's nuclear family. In fact, given the missionaries' rudimentary grasp of the language, the Renvilles' reception of the Gospel was so remarkable that Williamson credited it to the work of the Holy Spirit. Joseph Renville's Christian convictions had arisen from exposure to Catholic doctrine and his clerk's reading aloud from a French Protestant Bible. John's mother, Mary Tokanne, said her own conversion to Christianity predated the missionaries' arrival.[27] John was the first Dakota child baptized in the Presbyterian church at Lac qui Parle, and most of his siblings became members upon their own professions of faith, although the circumstances were in some cases irregular.

Try as they might to create good New England–style presbyters at Mde Ia Udan, the missionaries could not rid the Renville family's Christianity of elements that made it a uniquely Dakota form of the faith. They were troubled that Joseph Renville's understanding of Christianity was more about personal conviction and less about accepted external evidence of regeneration like abstaining from travel on the Sabbath. The Dakota Mission refused Renville's recommendation of church membership for any man with more than one wife, even if the requirement that he divorce all but one brought undue hardship on the woman who was "set aside" and gravely injured his relationship with her kin.[28] The missionaries' conception of heaven as a place where babies would not need cradleboards and believers would not need blankets vied with the Dakota death rituals of burying loved ones with gifts. Yet the mission also opposed as wasteful the free giving away of a Dakota Christian's possessions after death.[29] While the missionaries recognized that they needed Renville's sanction and assistance to continue operating the mission at Lac qui Parle, privately they worried about the unorthodox nature of the Christianity rising up under Renville's tutelage.[30]

Others were troubled about Joseph Renville's racial identity. The prominence of Lac qui Parle and its "baron" on the frontier was predicated on the general understanding that Renville was of French and Dakota parentage. The presumed French quantum bought Renville a seat in the upper echelons of fur trade society, including the right to sit at Indian agent Lawrence Taliaferro's linen-spread dining table at Fort Snelling, where Renville ate with silver cutlery polished by the house slaves Taliaferro had brought with him from Virginia. It also bought Taliaferro the confidence to use Renville as an informant who kept him apprised of the rough-and-tumble trade on the western edge of the agency and on the critical border between Dakota and Ojibwe territory. But Taliaferro was disturbed when the commander of Fort Snelling repeated the rumor afoot that Joseph

Renville, whom Taliaferro had known for sixteen years, was actually a full-blood Native who had acquired facility in the French language in the fur trade. "But cannot solve the Mystery—as to his coulour [sic]," Taliaferro puzzled in his journal the day he heard the news. "[Renville] to suit his convenience or policy states to the whites that he is a half breed, and to his people that he is of unmixed blood, and that his interests are identified with theirs. Now as to his being either a half, or a whole blood I have yet to be more fully informed. [I]t would seem that he is, and that he is not a full Indian. I might say, that he is a full blood Sioux—as his colour has generally indicated—but his manners & intelligence are in opposition to this belief."[31] When the arrival of the missionaries at Lac qui Parle gave Taliaferro a choice, he made an unambiguously white man, Thomas S. Williamson, his informant instead.

The missionaries never doubted Renville's bicultural heritage, and as monogenist Christians they understood Renville to be their ethnic (if not cultural) equal.[32] Despite their egalitarian theology, the missionaries' sense of western cultural superiority caused chronic problems. Stephen Riggs, especially, seemed prone to falling into the trap of not showing Renville the kinship deference he commanded in the region.[33] The dynamic is clear in a story that also shows the extent to which Renville and most of the residents of Mde Ia Udan resisted acculturation via immersion education for their children, an idea that unfortunately remained on the Indian Reform agenda for another century.

John Baptiste remained at Lac qui Parle in June 1842 when his friends Waśicuŋtaŋka, Towaŋiteton, and Maḣpiyahdinape headed east with Stephen Riggs. The first edition of *Odowaŋ*, the Dakota hymnbook containing a dozen hymns written by Joseph Renville, was about to be printed in Boston, and Riggs had been designated to oversee the project. Renville had made his opinion clear: his children belonged at home; they would not be sent away to school.[34] So John stayed behind while his older friends, in traditional Dakota dress, boarded a steamboat at Traverse des Sioux and headed down the Minnesota River. Before the young men reached the Mississippi they received letters from Lac qui Parle pleading for them to return lest their mothers die of grief.[35] Riggs pressed on, writing from Galena, Illinois, that although "the boys were contented they had not yet put on their pantaloons."[36] The next stop was Brown County, Ohio, where the boys were placed on farms for a two-month immersion in European American culture and language under the tutelage of relatives of the missionaries.

When Riggs reached Massachusetts he learned that the boys' departure came as an unwelcome surprise at Lac qui Parle:

> I am sorry to know that our bringing on the boys was <u>even supposed</u> to have <u>caused</u> the killing of the [mission] cattle at Lacquiparle. A letter from Fanny Huggins . . . gives us a detailed account of the cattle-killing but does not even intimate that that was thought to be the cause or occasion but says that the Indians there are starving very badly which I supposed was reason enough.
>
> We left the boys with Mr. H[uggins]'s brothers and cousin near Sardinia. We received a letter from them since our arrival in Massachu-setts—they were then doing well. I wish you would say to any who are disposed to blame us in this matter that I told the boys time and again before we started on the steam Boat that if they wished to go back to go. And as it regards consulting Mr. Renville, I can say I had hardly time to consult myself and the brethren of the mission before leaving Lacquiparle. However I will write to Mr. Renville and perhaps heal any breach I may have made in <u>not honoring him as I ought</u> to have done. It seems that a person among the Sioux who wishes to do any thing, must consult every man woman and child in the nation before he has a right to do it. We must try and teach them better. . . . We shall prob-ably leave for the west in about two months.[37]

Two months turned into twelve. Printing delays and entreaties from friends detained Riggs in Massachusetts beyond navigation season on the rivers that led back to Minnesota. A full year after they left home the young men returned to Lac qui Parle bearing English names (Simon Waśicuŋtaŋka, Lorenzo Towaŋiteton, and Henok Maḣpiyahdinape) and wearing trousers. They made the last leg of the journey from Traverse des Sioux to Lac qui Parle on foot. News of their arrival traveled ahead of them and, unknown to the boys, some of their kin began walking downriver to welcome them home.

About five miles south of Lac qui Parle the Ohio party was surprised to encounter Anishinabe (Ojibwe or Chippewa) men painted for war. The Anishinabes leveled their guns at one of the young Dakota men, "but seeing that he was dressed in white man's clothes, someone prevented their shooting, whereupon they shook hands with him, and showed him the scalps they had just taken." Riggs finished the story:

> He did not until afterwards know that one was his own brother's, although he had reason to fear that was the fact. The war party passed homewards and as our party approached the Chippewa River, at the fording of which lay the bodies of the slain. . . . The news was quickly carried to the village by the wife of one of those who was killed, and the Indians came out greatly exasperated. As they met the teams not knowing what to do they shot one of the horses attached to the wagon. It was a horse we had brought from Ohio. . . . it will get well probably.[38]

And thus a journey that began a year before with the killing of cattle in the wake of the boys' departure ended in the deaths of relatives going out to greet their arrival home. To traditional Dakotas, who attributed misfortune to the caprice and displeasure of the spirit world, it was an inauspicious beginning to the experiment of sending out Dakota children to live in white families.[39]

Three years later, in March 1846, Joseph Renville died. The era of Mde Ia Udan as the locus of his family died with him. John Baptiste, then fourteen, was left in the care of Thomas S. Williamson, who soon received an invitation from Little Crow to establish a mission post at Kaposia, several hundred miles east of Lac qui Parle, south of St. Paul on the banks of the Mississippi River. The Kaposias were the band of John's ancestors, the people from whom his father had been wrenched and sent to Canada. At Kaposia John attended the school taught by Jane Williamson (Thomas's sister). Then John was placed out with a family to learn English by immersion.[40] Finally, between 1852 and 1855, when he was in his early twenties, John, with his cousin Daniel Renville, boarded a steamboat headed east to the United States for higher education in Galesburg, Illinois.

"So many, whose fathers were nothing, have come to be kings."
—Stephen Riggs to Alfred Riggs, 23 January 1862[41]

John was home for the summer from school in Galesburg, living with his brothers at Hazlewood, on 29 July 1856. After they finished the morning's work on their farms, Antoine, Michael, and John joined their Dakota neighbors in another session in an ongoing council on the subject of organizing an autonomous farmers' band on the Upper Reservation.

Three years before, in 1853, ratification of the Treaty of 1851 had signified substantial change for Sisseton and Wahpeton people in Minnesota. For the first time in their history they were assigned to a reservation, received cash annuities, and had a direct relationship with the federal government. They were learning from personal experience what their Mdewankanton and Wahpekute cousins had known since they had signed their first treaty in 1837: their "Great Grandfather," the president of the United States, suffered from chronic memory lapses and bureaucratic arthritis and could take decades to get around to fulfilling treaty promises.

Most Sissetons still made seasonal rounds into buffalo country from winter camps on or beyond the western fringe of the new reservation, as they had done for generations. Wahpeton bands had established semipermanent villages on reservation land on the upper Minnesota River. As the Treaty of 1851 had promised, the federal government used the treaty proceeds that had accrued to the Agriculture Fund to plow and plant communal fields that benefited all band members equally. But on the Upper Reservation the federal government had plowed three-acre fields for only seven of the twenty men who wanted to establish independent farms. The federal government had also failed to keep its promise to open schools.

The latter was a particularly sore point for the Dakotas from Lac qui Parle, whom the missionaries had taught to read and write twenty years earlier and who, for varying reasons, signed on to the Treaty of 1851, which promised to augment traditional Dakota education with "reading, 'riting and 'rithmatic" for their children. The first wave of Dakotas from Lac qui Parle settled around the Pejutazizi station when Williamson established it in 1852. A second wave followed Riggs to Hazlewood, just three miles north of Pejutazizi, in 1854. A third significant group of acculturationists, Cloud Man's band, had relocated to the neighborhood in 1852. Years later all still were waiting for the government to open treaty-funded schools.

The lack of education was a chronic problem for those Dakotas who viewed their future, and their children's futures, grounded in the soil of Mni Sota Makoçe. Farmers needed to be able to estimate seed needs, reckon crop yields, and know whether they were being offered a fair price. They needed to read almanacs and newspapers and, some hoped, Bibles. To become citizens—a fond hope the missionary-reformers held for their Dakota protégés—they needed to be able to understand the state constitution and to read a voter's ballot.[42] Thus the Dakota men who, with John, Michael, and Antoine Renville, gathered in Stephen Riggs's living room that morning in July 1856 felt pushed by the government's inadequacies and pulled by their desire to take their futures into their own hands. They assembled to debate the finer points of a consensus that had been building for months: to found their own community to advocate for their people to the federal government.

Although the subject at hand, constitutional government, was a new idea, the founders handled the proceedings in traditional Dakota fashion: all interested men were invited to council. In fact, Dakota men on the Upper Reservation had been discussing the same issues in councils going back at least to the previous fall. But that morning the conversation revolved around a written document that recorded the emerging oral consensus: a draft copy of the Constitution of the Hazlewood Republic. Thomas Riggs recalled, "The constitution was carefully explained. Each of its five sections was taken up in order by my father and talked over. Then every section already talked over was talked over again as if climbing a five-rung ladder."[43]

Stephen Riggs was ebullient over the result. "For several weeks past," he wrote to Selah B. Treat of the ABCFM, "the great theme of interest just about here has been the organization of a new Band on the principle of labor and the adoption of the customs and habits of white people. This has finally been accomplished. They adopted a written platform or Constitution."[44]

The circular nature of the councils is inherent in the republic's foundational principle. As paraphrased by Stephen Riggs: "[T]hey professed their faith in the one God as opposed to the many Gods of the Dakotas, and their desire to regulate their lives by the teaching of the Word of God."[45] Thus, unlike the Cherokee Nation, the Hazlewood Republic was founded as a theocracy. Its tenets were not to be drawn from democratic consensus or copied from tradition or the dominant culture but were to be based on God's law as revealed in the Bible. Each platform point must have elicited another round of discussion on what the Bible had to say on a range of subjects: education, acculturation, restitution, Christian orthodoxy, and submission to authority. Given the diversity of theological opinion in the Dakota Mission, as well as the several dozen Dakota men present who could read the portions of the Bible that had been published in their language, besides many others who were pro-acculturation but found little use for Christianity, it is understandable that consensus took months to emerge.

One of the signal components of most national constitutions, a geographic description of territory claimed, is missing from the Constitution of the Hazlewood Republic.[46] Instead the founders made a poignant plea to the U.S. president "to give us land and to put us individually in possession of a piece of land," asking for what the Office of Indian Affairs called "granting land in severalty."[47] Accepting individual homesteads of reservation land formerly held in community was the same process by which some eastern Native peoples had managed to persist on their homelands post-removal.[48]

Removal was a specter on the horizon for the Dakotas. The Minnesota Valley watershed was fertile agricultural land increasingly demanded by settlers. By a Senate amendment to the Treaty of 1851 the Dakotas occupied their reservation not by right of possession but at the pleasure of the president, who could change his mind at any time. Despite a provision in

17

the Treaty of 1858, ratified in 1860, Dakotas did not feel secure in their legal right to the land they lived on. This was an especially harsh reality for Dakota traditionalists. As Lower Chief Wabaśa told Bishop Henry Whipple just six weeks before the onset of the 1862 war, "You have said you are sorry to see my young men engaged still in their foolish dances. I am sorry. . . . [I]t is because their hearts are sick. They don't know whether these lands are to be their home or not. They have seen the red man's face turned towards the setting sun and feel afraid that many more long journeys are for themselves & children—This makes them weary and they never try to be different."[49] The men of the Hazlewood Republic were determined to see their families remain in Mni Sota Makoçe, even if traditionalists were forced west.[50]

Significantly, there is no evidence that the Hazlewood Republic sought to declare its independence from the Dakota nation. The signers asked to be recognized as "white men," yet they specifically requested to retain their treaty annuity rights. Rather, they sought recognition from the agent as a separate *band*, or in the words of their preamble, a "community."[51] By the nineteenth century the four Santee or eastern Dakota bands (the Mdewankanton, Wahpekute, Sisseton, and Wahpeton) were fairly fluid, interrelated via generations of exogamous (outside the band) marriage. Both anecdotal and annuity records show that individuals moved between bands over time as it suited them.[52] Administratively the federal government dealt with each band as a unit represented by a federally recognized chief. The Hazlewood Republic sought the right to elect and to be represented by leaders who were chosen not by hereditary claim (the Dakota custom) but by popularity via their ability to represent the band's unique intentions. By codifying these objectives in a Constitution, Hazlewood eliminated much of the political dissension that pitted pro- and anti-federal Dakotas against each other in elections for nonhereditary leadership positions like speaker.

Yet the theocratic nature of the Constitution virtually assured that the republic would never have enough members to operate as a political entity apart from the Dakota nation. Had independent nationhood been an objective, the founders might have recruited many more Dakota men by dropping the references to rule by biblical principles and the proscription of traditional Dakota spiritual practices—as did, later, the Farmers' Band at the Lower Agency. At the end of the day on 29 July 1856 only about seventeen Dakota and mixed-blood men signed on to the Constitution of the Hazlewood Republic. One-third of them were constitutional officers. Among the named founders were: Paul Mazakutemani (variously titled chief, governor, and president); Henok Maḣpiyahdinape (secretary); Simon Anawaŋgmani (judge); Antoine Frenier (judge); Lorenzo Towaŋiteton Lawrence; Joseph Kewanke; Enos Wasuhowaṡte; and Robert Hopkins Chaske. There were also at least four men surnamed Renville: John Baptiste, his brothers Michael and Antoine, and their cousin Gabriel Renville (judge).[53] Almost all the founders were Renville kin from Lac qui Parle.

The Hazlewood Republic never represented more than a fraction of the Dakota farmers on the Upper Reservation. While the republic grew, perhaps to as many as forty male members, the number of non-Christian farmers on the Upper Reservation grew faster, to about one hundred during the same period. Figuring an average of five to seven people per family, in 1861 there may have been about 200 to 280 Dakota men, women, and children associated with the Hazlewood Republic and an estimated 500 to 600 members of non-Christian farmers' families on the Upper Reservation.[54] These figures significantly revise the common understanding that "farmers" were "Christians" on the Sioux Reservation.

But it is hardly surprising given the persecution Hazlewood families faced, both from kin who found traditional ways threatened by Christianity and from the Yanktonai Dakotas who disputed the farmers' rights to the land they farmed.[55] In the fall of 1860 the harassment escalated dangerously. Dakota farmers stopped congregating outdoors after men gathering for a service at the Hazlewood church were fired upon by assailants concealed in the tree line. Shortly thereafter four Dakota farmers were murdered. Faced with this threat, most of the agency's first wave of converts to agriculture abandoned their farms, including, temporarily, those at Hazlewood.[56] But there is little evidence that the rumored dissolution of Hazlewood was permanent.[57] To the contrary: the men who honed their persuasive skills in the trenches of opposition to the Hazlewood Republic became the nucleus of the Peace Coalition, historically known as the Peace Party of 1862.

Her Name Was Adeline

Mary Adeline Butler, John B. Renville's future wife, was born white into a world on the brink of massive change for people of color in the United States. During the first decade of her childhood the Indian Removal Act, passed in May 1830, systematically removed most Native Americans from their homelands east of the Mississippi River, opening the Midwest to settlers like her family and clearing the South for settlers who owned slaves. The crackdown on slaves in the wake of the Turner Rebellion in Virginia in August 1831, when Adeline (as she was known) was ten months old, coming on the heels of Andrew Lloyd Garrison's radical call for the immediate and unconditional end of slavery in America, galvanized the nascent abolition movement. But perhaps most formatively, the adults in Adeline's family did not passively stand by and observe the winds of social change gusting around them. She was born into a family whose sense of social justice, rooted in the Second Great Awakening, committed its members to parlaying their racial privilege on behalf of the poor and oppressed no matter their color.

Lydia Weaver Butler was over forty years old when her last child, Mary Adeline, was born on 17 October 1830 in East Plattsburg, Clinton County, New York.[58] Lydia died shortly after her daughter's birth. Adeline's father, James Butler, forty-eight years old and with five or six children still living at home, probably remarried within the next few years.[59]

The Butlers had been in New England since an ancestor named Nicholas Butler immigrated from England in 1637 and settled on Martha's Vineyard, in the English colony of Massachusetts. One hundred and forty years later Adeline's grandfather, Benjamin Butler, a veteran of the Revolutionary War, exchanged his war-bounty scrip for land on the frontier: North Hero, Vermont, an island in the middle of Lake Champlain. In 1785 Benjamin named his first-born son James Butler. When the family home on North

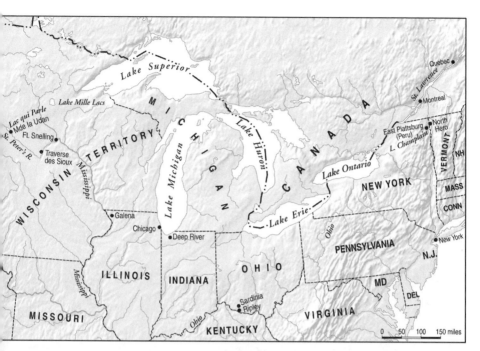

Map 1. Northeastern and Midwestern United States, 1835. Courtesy Pond Dakota Heritage Society.

Hero came under fire from the British in the War of 1812, James was part of the U.S. Army that defended it.[60] James Butler probably filed his own bounty scrip to claim land on the far side of Lake Champlain in Peru, Clinton County, New York, where all of his children, including Adeline (who was not known as Mary until she was in her twenties), was born.

By 1835, when Adeline was five, her oldest brother, Benjamin, had already left New York. Benjamin and his wife, Harriet Parsons Butler, settled at the edge of what was then the western frontier: the fledgling city of Chicago, Illinois, which was already big enough to support his trade as a tailor.[61] The following year, in 1836, James Butler followed his son Benjamin west, setting in motion the eventual migration of most of James's siblings and children to the western Great Lakes region.[62] James, with Adeline and her brothers, settled at the northwestern edge of Indiana,

21

at Deep River, Lake County, several hours from Chicago by horseback.[63] Adeline's only sister, Adelia, had married David Gilson Parsons (her sister-in-law Hannah's brother) in New York. David and Adelia followed Benjamin and Hannah west, settling a few hours away from Chicago in Dundee, Kane County, Illinois, where their children were born.[64]

With each remove west the Butlers, like thousands of American families before them, trod on the heels of the Indigenous peoples who had inhabited the land for millennia. Mere weeks before Adeline's family arrived in Indiana in 1836, four hundred Nishnabec (Potawatomi) traditionalists, reluctant to leave their homelands in the wake of a land-cession treaty, were driven west to a reservation in Kansas.[65] Another three hundred Nishnabecs who had married into the French fur trade community were given land grants to stay.[66] We can only speculate about what the Butlers found when they stopped in Deep Valley, Indiana. But Adeline's childhood home was not the "frontier" Hollywood has imagined. The dispossessed Nishnabecs left behind cabins with brick chimneys, outbuildings for stock, apple orchards, wagon roads, and hundreds of acres of fenced, cultivated fields.[67]

Adeline's uncles, Daniel, Loren, and Jesse Butler, followed her father west in 1838, settling around Salem Township, Steuben County, in northeastern Indiana. In the 1840 census James and his family were enumerated in Cedar Lake, Lake County, Indiana, only a few miles from Deep Valley, where they first settled. Adeline's brothers Russell, a farmer, and Loren, a stone mason, both came of age and left home between 1840 and 1850, settling in the fledgling town of Berlin in Marquette (later Green Lake) County, Wisconsin. Berlin was the site of a historic Mascoutin city and, at the time, was still the home of Hochunk (Winnebago) people.[68] Thus all of young Adeline's aunts, uncles, and cousins came to settle within a few days' journey of each other in the Midwest. Butler family tradition holds that sometime after 1840 James and Adeline, who by that time may have been the only child left at home, moved a few counties east to rejoin his brothers in Steuben County, Indiana. By 1850, when she was twenty, Adeline was living with her sister, Adelia Parsons, in Dundee, Illinois.[69]

In the Midwest, Adeline's father and uncles distinguished themselves on the sociopolitical frontier: the abolition of slavery in the United States.

After passage of the Fugitive Slave Act of 1850 Butler homes in Steuben County became stations on the expanding nexus of the Underground Railroad leading to Canada.[70] For the Butler family abolition was a cause born of proximity and conviction. Their hometowns in both Vermont and New York were on Lake Champlain, adjacent to Canada and on known routes of the early Underground Railroad. When the Butlers moved west, only the Ohio River separated their state, Indiana, from the slave state of Kentucky. Free blacks helped slaves cross the Ohio and passed them into the hands of Indiana conductors like Levi Coffin of Fountain City.[71] Within a few weeks of leaving Coffin's house, slaves fleeing toward Canada through the northeast corner of the state were aided on their way by the Butlers of Steuben County.

Adeline's cousin Marvin Butler, who was a teenager in the days his family operated a safe house in Salem Township, traced the family's involvement in the Underground Railroad movement to their abolition-ist roots. A generation before in North Hero, Vermont, their grandparents Benjamin and Perthia Butler had made the family's motto "As ye do unto the least of these, my brethren, ye do unto Me."[72] Benjamin Butler's "uncompromising and open hostility to slavery, the saloon, and the brothel . . . subjected him to severe criticism" for a time, even from those inside his church. Yet by the time of Benjamin's death in 1831 and his wife Perthia's in 1837, Marvin recalled, "they both were long remembered, loved, and honored, by a large community for their hospitality and kindness to the poor. . . . All their children inherited these sterling qualities of character from their parents." Marvin described Adeline's father and his own this way: "These two brothers [James Butler and Benjamin Butler Jr.] were very much alike, very positive in their character, both Methodists, and in their politics, old school Whigs, uncompromisingly anti-slavery, and ardently and bitterly opposed to the use of intoxicating liquor."[73]

In that milieu Adeline Butler grew to maturity: raised on successive western frontiers by a family whose humanitarian ideals superseded their rights to a good night's sleep or to a yard where the children could play unsurveilled by armed slave catchers. It may be no coincidence that as an adult known as Mary A. Renville, Adeline Butler lived in the trenches of the Indian Reform movement. "It was not merely by turn of the phrase

Map 2. Midwestern United States, 1858. Courtesy Pond Dakota Heritage Society.

that reformers so frequently compared the Indian question of the 1860s and 1870s to the abolition work of the 1840s and 1850s," Linda K. Kerber observes. "[B]oth were crusades for racial justice underwritten by a sense of guilt."[74]

Near the end of his life Marvin Butler considered his host of cousins and singled out two for special mention. One was James Butler Hickok of Troy Grove, Illinois, who, legend said, acquired precocious skill with guns while defending the family property from slave hunters. James grew up to become better known as "Wild Bill" Hickok of Wild West fame. Another of Marvin's cousins, "Adeline was for several years in the government, teaching in the Indian School in Minnesota. She and her school were captured by hostile Indians during the Civil War and expected brutal massacre. But before their captors could carry out their designs, they were recaptured by the U.S. Cavalry. She married one of her scholars, a half-breed Indian."[75]

"To form so unnatural an alliance."

—*St. Peter Statesman* on the Renvilles' marriage, 25 May 1860

The inscription on the flyleaf of a book places Mary Butler in Galesburg, Illinois, by April 1857, the first verified year of John Renville's residence there.[76] John and Mary are said to have met at Knox College, where (the story goes) he was a student and she, his teacher.[77] Finding the couple there would make sense; Knox was one of only a few institutions that would admit students of color like John. However, the records of Knox College and its preparatory school, Knox Academy, do not show John as a student or Mary on faculty.[78] Mary began teaching around the age of twenty and had five or six years' experience teaching in Wisconsin and Illinois by the time she met John in Galesburg.

John and his cousin Daniel Renville, who accompanied him to Galesburg, had gone east to advance their English-language education beyond opportunities available on the frontier. The virtual absence of John and Daniel from period ABCFM correspondence suggests that their education was privately funded, as had been the Ohio boys' education a decade before.[79] John boarded with a Presbyterian family and attended a Presbyterian church—yet another milieu in which John and Mary may have been introduced. While the outlines of the received story are possible, the details remain obscure.

In any case, by the spring of 1858 news of the couple's engagement had traveled back to the Minnesota frontier. On 1 March 1858 missionary Stephen Riggs mentioned to S. B. Treat of the ABCFM, "John B. Renville has made arrangements to bring back their teacher Miss Mary Butler as Mrs. Renville. This rather surprised us at first, but I hope it will work good. She is twenty five years old and has been engaged in teaching a good deal for the last six or seven. I hope they will make valuable auxiliaries in our missionary work."[80]

The announcement "rather surprised" the missionary community because, in their experience, interracial marriage was unusual. Whatever their belief about "elevating the Indian," the missionaries never took that idea so far as to consider a Native spouse suitable for their own children.[81] Even less common than an Indigenous woman marrying a white man—

a formula that was part of the history of the North American continent going back to the 1600s—was the idea of a white woman marrying a Native man.[82]

While uncommon, John's white great-great-grandmother's marrying a Dakota man in the early 1700s was not exceptional. Since settlers were first taken captive by Native people in North American Indian wars dating back to the seventeenth century, young female captives were adopted into many nations and grew up to marry Native men. Some chose to remain even when given the opportunity to return to their birth culture.[83] For example, Frances Slocum, taken captive as a child by Delawares in Pennsylvania in 1778, was discovered living in Indiana in 1839, less than one hundred miles from where Mary Adeline Butler (then nine years old) was growing up. Slocum had married a Miami chief, spoke that language fluently, and was a highly respected woman in the bicultural community of Miamis who remained in the region after their more traditional relatives were forced west.[84] Of course, Miniyuhe's grandmother may not have been a captive but rather the daughter of voyageurs or otherwise part of the trade community.[85] White-Native intermarriage fit Thomas Jefferson's idealistic vision of the future: "In truth, the ultimate point of rest and happiness for [Indigenous people] is to let our settlement and theirs meet and blend together, to intermix and become one people. Incorporating themselves with us as citizens of the United States, this is what the natural progress of things will of course, bring on, and it will be better to promote than retard it."[86]

Author Lydia Maria Child envisioned such a marriage in 1824 when she married Puritan Mary Conant to a Mohican man in the eponymous novel *Hobomok*, in one of the first publicly noted interracial marriages— albeit fictional—of the nineteenth century. However, attitudes in America were undergoing a radical shift toward polygenism, also called "scientific racism," which held that races evolved independently. In the polygenic worldview visible differences in skin color and physiognomy betrayed genetic incompatibility that threatened the integrity of an assumed racial hierarchy.[87] Thus the premise of *Hobomok* nearly ruined Child's budding career as a novelist.[88] An early review in the prestigious *North American*

Review moralized on Conant's marriage: "Now this is a train of events not only unnatural, but revolting, we conceive, to every feeling of delicacy in man or woman."[89]

As Child's novel was published two Yankee-Cherokee couples were about to move the subject of interracial marriage into the real world. Sarah Bird Northrup and John Ridge wed in 1825, and Harriett Gold married Ridge's cousin, Elias Boudinot, in 1826.[90] As Theresa Strouth Gaul found in her study of the Gold-Boudinot marriage, attitudes were not progressing toward Jefferson's interracial ideal but rather, with the ascendance of polygenism, were increasingly intolerant. When Gold informed her Connecticut family of her engagement, her brother "[a] few days later, in front of friends and neighbors on the village green . . . lit a fire that consumed his sister's effigy. He also wrote a letter . . . announcing the engagement to his siblings . . . 'The dye is cast, Harriett is gone, and we have reason to fear. Yes. She has told Mr Harvey that she was engaged to that Indian E. and that she is determined to marry him. Oh!! Dear!!!' "[91] Mary Adeline Butler, the future Mrs. John B. Renville, was born four years after the Gold-Boudinot wedding.

Despite hardening attitudes toward interracial marriage, a few women like Gold followed their heart to marry an Indigenous man. In 1833 Peter Jones (Kahkewaquonaby), the mission-educated son of Ojibwe parents, wed "Eliza his English-born wife." Seven years later, in 1840, Ojibwe George Copway (Kahgegagahbowh) married Elizabeth Howell, also born in England. In her discussion of the Jones and Copway marriages, LaVonne Ruoff quotes period newspapers echoing the *Hobomok* review. Interracial couplings were "unnatural . . . 'improper and revolting' " because "We believe that the Creator of the Universe distinguished his creatures by different colours, that they might be separate from each other, and we know of nothing in what we consider religion, to warrant any violation of his evident arrangement."[92]

Although contracted several decades earlier, these interracial marriages generally fit the pattern of Mary Butler and John Renville's relationship: an educated, Christian white woman wed an educated, acculturated, Christian Native man.[93] However, the Butler-Renville story suggests that simply

27

holding monogenist views of race did not make interracial marriage—specifically the pairing of a white woman with a Native man—expected or easily accepted. The initial surprise of the Dakota Mission community in response to news of John's engagement to a white woman is best understood in light of the interracial marriages with which the missionaries were familiar. There are only two known white-Dakota precedents in the region. In 1845 Mary Anne Dalton of Indiana married mixed-blood Antoine Joseph (Joe, A. J.) Campbell.[94] In 1858 John Otherday (Aŋpetutokeça), a full-blood farmer, returned from treaty negotiations in Washington DC with a white woman named Rosanne (or Roxanne), with whom he was cohabiting at the time the Butler-Renville engagement was announced.[95] The rumors about Mary Anne Campbell and Rosanne Otherday reveal what Minnesota frontier society thought of intermarriage. When Isaac Heard profiled the Campbell family in an 1865 newspaper story, he rationalized Dalton's willingness to marry Campbell by offering the rumor that she was secretly of Cherokee descent.[96] The rumors about Rosanne Otherday were more degrading; even the missionaries believed the prevailing gossip that Otherday had picked her up in a brothel.[97]

It is not surprising that character aspersions would dog Mary Butler Renville as well. The earliest example appeared in the *St. Peter Statesman* the year after she married John. On 25 May 1860 an anonymous reporter commented after a visit to the Upper Agency, "Mr. Renville, it appears, was for some time a pupil of Mrs. Renville in Illinois, and she came up some 18 months since for the purpose of marrying him. At first he seemed but little disposed to form so unnatural an alliance; but she persevered until the Indian yielded. . . . Her pretext for pressing the alliance was her desire to elevate the race . . . we do not fancy her style of 'elevation.'" Sixty years later the story was still alive. In 1918 Eli Huggins, a son of the Dakota Mission who had known John in Galesburg, told historian William Watts Folwell,

> J.B.R. was taken to Galesburg about 1855 by Dr. [Williamson] to board with a good Presbyterian family and went to school there for I think about two or three years. His teacher Miss Butler a strong masterful

woman, rather eccentric, "fell in love" with him, and married him. The story told—generally believed—is that he married her very reluctantly, that she courted him (he was younger than she) almost violently, and that while there had been no really criminal intimacy he felt in honor bound to marry her as he had permitted her to indulge in hopes and her life would be blighted if he deserted her. . . . Mrs. R. was past childbearing when she became his wife and neither of them has any posterity.[98]

Clearly the dominant society believed a woman who chose to marry an Indian fell quite short of ideal white womanhood: she must be of mixed blood, a prostitute, or "masterful." The latter word is telling. There was significantly less taboo attached to the frontier practice of white men marrying Native women. The reasons were deeply rooted in America's ongoing struggle to reconcile a paradox. The rising racial hierarchy that placed people of color beneath whites was at odds with the economic concerns that made an exception for white men marrying Indigenous women. The latter was tolerated on the frontier because it paved the way for transferring Native-controlled resources, like lands and treaty funds, into white control via mixed-blood children.[99]

Many of Mary's contemporaries must have struggled to understand her motivation. Socially, in the nineteenth century, her decision to marry a Native man carried a heavy penalty. John was, by blood quantum, slightly more than three-quarters Dakota. The Minnesota State Constitution granted mixed blood Natives automatic citizenship in May 1858, just seven months before John's and Mary's wedding. John Renville was technically a citizen of Minnesota, and his lifestyle at Hazlewood as a father and schoolteacher may not have been very different from that of the naturalized immigrant settlers living across the Minnesota River in Renville County. Even so, as events in the wake of the Dakota War would prove, "citizenship" could in no way be equated with "whiteness."[100]

Non-Native Minnesotans were relative newcomers to the state, and most brought racial baggage with them. Measured by the prevailing ideas about race enshrined in blood quantum standards in legal statutes elsewhere in the United States, John was clearly "colored." In this period Maine declared a person of mixed Native heritage to be "Indian" until he had one-eighth Native blood or less, at which point he became legally white.[101] In North Carolina Riggs would have been fined $100 for wedding Mary and John and their marriage would have been declared null and void.[102] Western states were not necessarily more tolerant. A Nevada law declared intermarriage between whites and Indians "a misdemeanor, punishable by 1–2 years in prison," and because such marriages were illegal, persons thus joined were "cohabiting in a state of fornication," which came with a "fine of $100 to $500 and/or 1 to 6 months in jail."[103] In the state of Washington the person performing an interracial wedding was fined $50–$500 and the marriage was declared void if a white married a person of one-half or more Native blood.[104]

In this social milieu in mid-nineteenth-century America white men especially struggled to find Mary Butler Renville's motivation for marrying a man who, by blood quantum, was irreconcilably Indian. The best they could do was posit she was driven by desperation to sacrifice white womanhood (and its corollary, the white birthright of her children) on the altar of her ideals.[105] If in Galesburg, Illinois, in 1858 Mary Butler had a passionate preoccupation with anything, it must have been with John himself (whom she affectionately called "Johnnie") and perhaps with her view of her personal mission, because she had not yet met significant numbers of the Dakotas among whom she would spend the rest of her life.

There is no direct evidence of anything besides John's and Mary's devotion to each other. Mary came to Minnesota in September 1858 and took up residence with the Riggs family at Hazlewood for four months before her marriage.[106] On 1 January 1859 Riggs performed their wedding in the Hazlewood chapel with white Christian friends from the Upper Agency neighborhood as matron and man of honor.[107] Three years later, at the outset of the Dakota War, when John was held captive, Mary chose to stay by his side rather than escape with the missionaries. In the wake of the war, while Otherday's white wife fled their marriage and Campbell deserted his wife, Mary Anne, Mary Butler Renville overcame her own trauma and dedicated herself to serving the people her husband called his own.[108]

I suppose *he* is not counted among the Indians now."
—Anna Jane Riggs to Alfred Riggs, 1 November 1859

One of the two extant photographs of the Hazlewood mission shows double fences: a common split-rail fence in the foreground keeping grazing stock out of planted fields and a starched white New England picket fence bounding the yards of missionary homes.[109] The picket fence, missionary Mary Ann Longley Riggs said early in her career on the Minnesota frontier, was to keep Dakotas *out* and her children *in*, lest they grow up to be "little Indians."[110] When Mary Butler arrived on the frontier in the fall of 1858, Stephen and Mary Riggs were veterans of more than two decades of Dakota Mission life and were expecting their eighth child.[111] Culture as reflected in lifestyle was as central to the Riggs's view of their Christian identity as it was to traditionalists' conceptions of being Dakota. But Mary Adeline Butler came to the frontier to bring a Dakota inside the picket fence, not as a beggar or a boarder but much more intimately, as her husband in a marriage that would, presumably, populate the yard inside the fence with Dakota children.

Most of what we know of the prewar years of Mary and John's marriage is filtered through the eyes of the Riggs women. History is fortunate on three counts: that the eldest son, Alfred Riggs, was away studying at Knox College, then at the Chicago Theological Seminary; that his mother, Mary Ann Riggs, required her children to write letters to their brother; and that because Alfred was away at school, his papers carrying reports from home on daily life in the Hazlewood neighborhood survived the 1862 war.[112] The letters written by the Riggs women tell us that the arrival of Mary Butler was disconcerting.

It was not every day that a white woman arrived at Hazlewood and vowed to stay a lifetime. Every few years an unmarried lady from the east arrived at the mission to spend a year or two teaching the missionary children before heading home to marry, as had Lucy Spooner Drake, confidant of Martha, the Riggs's second eldest daughter. Many of these young women were members of the missionaries' extended families or members of their churches back home. Any interpersonal friction was of short duration; when the teacher's term was up, she went home.[113]

Mary Riggs was dutifully resigned to her calling as the wife of a western missionary. Martha had been born on the frontier, felt stunted by "prairie" society, and longed to get out.[114] But Mary Butler, of her own free will, chose to come to Hazlewood and to stay.

Unlike the Riggs women, whose everyday dresses were made over from donations from a missionary barrel or styled in whatever example of "good dark calico 15 yds" came to the hand of their purchasing agent in St. Louis, Mary Butler's clothes were likely cut in the current fashion, in fabrics she had chosen to flatter her own figure and coloring, and finished with details that complemented the design, not with the good, serviceable, used buttons from the bottom of the barrel. Mary Butler also had an education that could not be obtained on the Minnesota frontier. She was a gifted vocalist and organist, could paint and draw, was an accomplished seamstress, and studied the Bible. Her love of learning and her winsome way with children made her a natural teacher.

Most painful to Martha Riggs was the fact that "Mrs. John B." (Martha never deigned familiarity with Mary's given name) was an extrovert who spoke her mind. Mary Butler believed that a person's destiny was not predetermined, except in a theological sense; opportunity and the desire to pursue it were all people needed to better themselves, whether slave, Dakota, or the daughter of frontier missionaries. Martha, whose educational and social opportunities were limited by her father's vocation, complained to Alfred just before her sister Anna Jane left for her turn at a female seminary:

> By the way, Mrs. John B. Renville is going to teach Drawing this winter—though she hasn't any Drawing boards or Paper or pencils or any other of the needful—I'd like to see her at it—I have felt very consequential and "stuck up" these last few days—I'll tell you why. Mrs. John B. called here last Saturday and gave Anna Jane some parting advice—as well as a fling at me—some would improve a great deal while gone as much as I have [been, in the east at school]—and a <u>little more</u>. Of course I've improved a vast deal and I <u>ain't</u> sociable one <u>single bit</u>—not at all—on the authority of Mrs. John B. Isn't that a great pity?

Well after all I should know but what it may do me some good after all.
. . . And I ought to be exceedingly grateful to Mrs. John B.[115]

Two months later Martha began teaching drawing to the Dakota girls who boarded with the Riggs family.

It also may have stretched the women of the Dakota Mission to have a working woman in their midst: Mary Butler Renville chose to work outside the home. The Riggs women seem to have borne up for the four months before the wedding when Mary lived under their roof and taught at the local government-sponsored day school for Dakota children. But after Mary and John moved into the house he and his brothers built, she continued to teach, even after they began adding children to their family. Within a few months of their wedding John and Mary had two Dakota children living with them: Anna Renville, the daughter of John's brother Joseph, and Isabel Renville Martin ("Belle"), daughter of John's sister Madeline. They also took in Lillie, the mixed-blood daughter of Nathaniel Brown, as a boarder.[116]

Martha admitted that Mary and John seemed to do well with the children, reporting to Alfred in January 1860,

By invitation, Mrs. John B. & family took tea with us on Sat. She has never before darkened our door, since that day when you [Alfred] said "must." She is apparently pleased with the prospect of being connected with the Government Boarding School. We had quite a pleasant chat— both she & her husband seemed to enjoy themselves, & without doubt the children were delighted. They have taken in a little girl of his sister Madeline's about the age of the one they took last summer of N. Brown's. They sang some little hymns in English & Dakota quite prettily.[117]

The birth of John and Mary's daughter, Ella, a few months later, on 20 March 1860, barely thawed the Riggs women's frosty relationship with Mary. Five days after the birth Mary Riggs commented, "Mr. & Mrs. John B. Renville have a daughter. She seems to feel very kindly just now—'the goodness of God leadeth to repentance' oftentimes even with those who are not God's children. Truly then, God's loving kindness & long forbearance with us, if we are his children will make us loving and forgiving."[118]

A month later Stephen wrote, "You will probably be interested to know that Mr. John B. Renville and family moved down to the Yellow Medicine to take charge of the Boarding School. They are each to have a teacher's salary and pay for their own board. Mrs. Renville stopped here and took dinner on her way down. Mr. Brown's family have not yet left the house— so Mr. & Mrs. Renville are domiciled in the [agency] office for the present, having one room upstairs."[119] In May 1860, when a reporter visited the Upper Agency curious to meet the two white women who had married Indians (by then John and Rosanne Otherday had legally wed), he did not find Mary Renville rocking newborn Ella or hanging her diapers out to dry. Instead, the reporter, who made no comment at all about the baby, found Mary Renville at work in the government boarding school:

> we first called upon Mrs. Renville, who has just commenced a manual labor school. A very interesting and affectionate scene transpired here. Four Indian girls, pupils of Mrs. R., were in the room, the two smallest of whom, only about five years old, sang the familiar song—"We wash our hands, we wash our hands, early in the morning;" "we wash our face," &c.; "we comb our hair," &c.; "we go to school," &c. at the same time making a practical application of the words in their actions—which was as touching a scene as we have ever witnessed. . . . we believe that manual labor schools, similar to the one she has opened, where Indian women are taught to cook, bake, wash, and perform all other domestic duties, while at the same time they are taught to read, write and speak the English language, is the only successful method of civilizing the Indian race.[120]

What did John Renville think of his unconventional wife? The reporter commented, "the two Indians who have white wives speak of the manner in which their household matters are managed with a great deal of apparent pleasure, and feel proud of their wives. Mr. Renville is about three quarters Indian."[121] While the reporter appraised John in terms of blood quantum, his marriage to a white woman had the opposite effect on the

Fig. 2. The Hazlewood Republic, Minnesota, 1860. Photograph by Alfred Hill, courtesy of the Minnesota Historical Society. On Monday, 21 July 1860, Stephen Riggs wrote to his son Alfred, "Saturday after I had written the above and was out hoeing rutabagas, Mr. Hill the artist, who has been here at Yellow Medicine since before the payment 'reaping golden honors' by making light pictures of almost every body, drove up with Mr. Frenier. He had come to take the likenesses of our mission premises. After trying from various points he finally placed his camera on the little mound back of Simon's. We gathered quite a company, perhaps too many, a mixed multitude, for the foreground. The wind blew considerably which was rather against the result. He tried several times. His first and his last negatives he thought tolerably good. He took one ambrotype which was beautiful of the buildings, the trees back of the church showing up very finely, but some of the crowd were rather blurred. It was half past two o'clock before we got ready to eat dinner." Letter in the Oahe Mission Collection, Center for Western Studies, Augustana College, Sioux Falls, South Dakota.

missionary community. Six months before the reporter visited Anna Jane Riggs told Alfred that most of their Dakota neighbors at Hazlewood had gone out on a fall hunt to the Big Woods—all except "Mr. John B. Renville. I suppose _he_ is not counted among the Indians now."[122]

John and Mary lived at the Upper Sioux Agency for only eight months. In November 1860 their house, the Federal Manual Labor School, burned down. With the election of Abraham Lincoln to the presidency, Joseph R. Brown, knowing a Republican would soon be appointed Sioux agent in his stead, did not rebuild the school and retired from the agency, leaving its debts, including the salaries he owed John and Mary, to his successor. With no home and no income, John and Mary moved back to Hazlewood and resumed teaching at the Hazlewood school.

In April 1861 Mary bought land in her own name in Renville County, becoming the first property owner on record in the fledgling township of Beaver Falls, which already had a population sufficient for John P. Williamson, the missionary son of Thomas S. Williamson and childhood friend of John B. Renville, to preach there once per month.[123] However, there is no indication that John and Mary moved off the reservation to the claim. At Hazlewood John became increasingly visible among the Christians in his role as elder in the Pejutazizi Church. Nearly four years after Mary arrived on the frontier, her independent spirit was still worthy of remark in the Riggs family. In June 1862 Anna Jane reported to Alfred, "Mrs. John B. Renville does not hear from her husband," who was absent in the east as a delegate to the Presbyterian General Assembly, "for the reason that, she would rather have him not write at all than to write in Dakota and she supposes he don't get time to write in English."[124]

PART II: THE INDIAN CAPTIVES

The first section in this second part recaps the Dakota War as it unfolded on the Upper Reservation, considering the diverse Dakotas who would come together to form the Peace Coalition and using _A Thrilling Narrative_ as its chronological spine. It also places that story in the context of the larger war by examining the letters written by both sides during the

Map 3. Southern Minnesota, 1862. Courtesy Pond Dakota Heritage Society.

conflict, supplying perspectives John and Mary glimpsed from the Upper Camp: the reasons of some for going to war and of others for opposing it and the diplomatic war in words exchanged between the Upper Camp, the Lower Camp, and federal authorities, leading to the release of the captives on 26 September 1862.

The Indian Captives (*A Thrilling Narrative*, chapters 1–3)

John and Mary were clearing supper dishes from the table in their home at Hazlewood on the evening of 18 August 1862 when they were interrupted by the arrival of John's brother, Antoine Renville, and Hazlewood Republic leader Paul Mazakutemani. John translated for Mary the story the two men told. They reported that fifty miles away at the Lower Sioux Agency Lower Dakota soldiers had killed the traders. In the communities across the river they were murdering settlers and taking captives. Lower warriors had decimated the command sent from Fort Ridgley to subdue them and were said to be killing bicultural Dakotas.[125]

In the three and half years she had been married to John, Mary had become as inured to Indian scares as any frontier veteran. Several times a year, especially in the summer, someone reported that the Indians threatened something dire. But except for the isolated murders of a few Dakota farmers on the Upper Reservation the winter after the Renvilles were married, the Minnesota frontier had been relatively quiet since the last major scare: the 1857 Spirit Lake attack in which thirteen settlers were killed and four women taken captive. So on that evening in August 1862 Mary and John shrugged off the rumors of unrest, finished their work, and gathered the children for evening family devotions.

Later that night Antoine and Mazakutemani returned. Whatever they said changed the Renvilles' minds. John went out to the stable and harnessed his horses. Mary had little time to plan. But knowing it was at least two days' journey to the nearest place of safety, Fort Ridgley, she hastily gathered into her trunk the necessities for prairie travel: her sturdy broadcloth skirt, spare dresses for Lillie and Ella, quilts, and a buffalo robe ground cloth. In the kitchen she packed her cast-iron frying pan and a few staple foods like salt, flour, baking soda, and lard.

John lugged the trunk outside. Mary had not fully recovered from childbirth two years before, so there was little she could do little to help load the wagon. Lillie climbed into the back of the open wagon box next to the trunk. Belle was away in St. Anthony attending school, so she was not home. John helped Mary climb up onto the board seat and settled eighteen-month-old Ella on her lap. The sun was sinking beneath the horizon as John untied the horses and the Renvilles turned their backs on home. A half mile east the road curved through the Hazlewood Mission Station, past the white frame church where they had been married. John and Mary were alarmed to see the lanes and footpaths of the mission peopled with Dakotas they did not know, wearing traditional Santee and

Yanktonai garb. Fearing the strangers, they left the main road and took a side track through the woods. They emerged from the timber into an open stretch of prairie scattered with log, frame, and brick houses and with tipis. Mary called the place "the Friendly Camp." They had fled for safety to the Hazlewood Republic. It was both a place—a neighborhood populated by Christian Dakota farmers—and a people—friends, family, those with whom they worshiped and worked, and parents of the children who attended their school.

By 2:00 a.m. on Tuesday, 19 August, having evacuated the Hazlewood Mission Station, the missionary families also arrived at the Republic. John and Mary joined their missionary and Dakota friends in a council about what the white families should do. Missionary Hugh Cunningham later summarized, "The Christian and Friendly Indians . . . offered to protect us all they could, but said they were but a few when compared to the others. We felt as though we didn't like to expose them, to protect us when the odds seemed so much against us. They all gave one voice, and that was to get to a place of safety."[126] Because only a few hours remained before sunrise and most of the escape route to Fort Ridgley led over open prairie, their friends hid the missionaries on an island in the Minnesota River to await escape under the cover of darkness that night.

John and Mary expected to be sent away with the missionary party. But the Hazlewood leaders prevented it. In Mary's words, "[T]hey were afraid of being pursued and thought it much safer that we should remain at the Camp."[127] For reasons she had not yet explained in the narrative, the Renvilles' presence endangered the others. So John, Mary, and their children remained at the Hazlewood Republic on Tuesday, 19 August, the second day of the war. About noon a trader's clerk who had been shot at Big Stone Lake wandered into camp, dazed from the loss of blood soaking his clothes. Mary helped clean and dress his gunshot wound, firsthand evidence that the swirling war stories contained truth. She was even more anxious to reach a safe haven. But an act of God intervened. Late that afternoon the missionaries decided to take advantage of a looming thunderstorm to leave the island and begin their escape before nightfall. Back at Hazlewood, John went to hitch the horses to their wagon and discovered the harness was missing. Mary was not strong enough to walk sixty miles to the fort. With the Dakota soldiers more interested in horses than tack, the missing harness was an anomaly. Had it been removed to prevent their leaving with the missionaries? The torrential thunderstorm broke, making it impossible for John to search for the missing harness and obscuring evidence of the missionaries' escape.

Mary and her friend Jane Williamson fled the storm, taking refuge in the unfinished house of a Dakota farmer. With the evacuation of the mission station and the Yellow Medicine Agency that same morning, Mary Renville, Jane Williamson (the unmarried sister of missionary Thomas S. Williamson), Margaret Williamson (Thomas's wife), and Sophia Huggins (who, living at outlying Lac qui Parle, was still oblivious to the war, which would lead to the murder of her husband, Amos, and her own captivity) were the only white women remaining on the Upper Reservation. The Williamsons, whose mission station was five miles southeast of Hazlewood, had evacuated their children that morning. Thomas, Margaret, and Jane had determined to stay, hoping in God to deliver them while they encouraged the Christian Indians.[128] But by Wednesday, 20 August, Thomas Williamson ceded to the collective wisdom of the Dakota elders of his church, including John B. Renville: the Williamsons, too, must leave.

John and Mary were prepared to flee with the Williamsons but again were thwarted. This time their Dakota friends elaborated,

> should we attempt to leave we would certainly be pursued, and thus endanger the lives of our whole party. This, it was said, was on account of the knowledge some of us had of the country, and the assistance we might render to the white settlements should we ever reach them. . . . We told them we had rather die than remain. They insisted that if we started we would share the fate of many others, a part being killed, the remainder being captives perhaps for life. . . .
>
> Paul advised us to remain in his tent, for so many were stealthily watching us, there was danger of our being shot.[129]

While Mary and John considered themselves adjuncts of the mission community on the Upper Reservation, the war crisis realigned primary identities. John was married to a white woman, was employed as a government schoolteacher, and served as an elder in the Presbyterian Church. While before the war traditionalists could socially ostracize and thus marginalize bicultural people like him as "whites," in this crisis it was John's Dakota heritage that was a liability. He had grown up in the region and knew the land intimately. He was a fluent first-language speaker of Dakota who also spoke English. Both factors made John a potentially powerful ally against the warring Dakotas should he reach federal lines. Aside from his fluency in English, John was not unique. Like hundreds of other bicultural Dakota men (mixed- and full-blood), John was a threat to the war from within and thus was targeted for containment: captivity for political purposes. While the missionaries could take their chances on escaping undetected, Lower soldiers had declared that every person of Dakota blood "fleeing toward the whites . . . was an enemy."[130] Believing that Mary and John's chances of survival were better if they remained, their Upper Dakota friends stopped the Renvilles' flight. There is no indication that Mary and John considered sending Mary alone away with the missionaries. The Renvilles chose to face their fate together as a family. Therefore, on Wednesday, 20 August, Thomas, Margaret, and Jane Williamson escaped without them.[131]

The men of Hazlewood counseled to determine what to do next. They had gently but persistently overruled Williamson and now, for the first time in the history of the Republic, met autonomous of any missionary influence. The needs of the *tiośpaye* (camp circle) were a priority. Their families were endangered by the Dakotas who had gone to war.[132] The Republic neighborhood, bounded by ravines, bluffs, and woods, was indefensible. Their consensus was as symbolic as it was strategic: to occupy the abandoned Hazlewood Mission Station. And so the men of the Hazlewood Republic rose to fill the roles previously retained by the missionaries—white men who, though well-intended, had tacitly, by their continued presence, undermined their Dakota protégés' ability to freely govern themselves.

The Hazlewood leaders selected the school boardinghouse as the mission station building best suited for defense.[133] Mary rose to the task by relocating their family yet again, trying to redeem the comfortable order of an earlier day from the chaos created by looting in the wake of the missionaries' departure. Retiring to a secluded room that hid her skin color from passing strangers, Mary said, "for the first time, we permitted our tears to flow, somewhat to the relief of our aching hearts."[134] Keenly aware that she might never see her family again, she opened a journal and penned the entry she later called the preface of her story:

> This little book, in the providence of God, may fall into other hands, for we are in jeopardy every moment, and are so closely watched that we scarcely dare use the pen for fear of being suspected of trying to get letters to friends at home. With a full sense of the danger we are in, we forthwith subscribe the names of our family and those of our friends. . . .
>
> Time hastens, night is coming on, and it may be the night of death to all of us; in view of which we will say farewell to the joys and sorrows of this life.[135]

The Peace Coalition Emerges (*A Thrilling Narrative*, chapter 5)

The next chapters of the Renvilles' story as related in their narrative unfurl out of chronological order. This is not a defect but rather an artifact of the composition process. Mary kept a journal during captivity. Sometimes she wrote entries daily. During other periods, waylaid by children, poor health, and her duties as amanuensis or scribe for Dakotas in the Upper Camp, she made no entries. After the war, in December 1862, Mary and John began reconstructing the gaps in her journal for a serial in their local newspaper, the *Berlin (WI) City Courant*. In this thirteen-part newspaper series, titled appropriately "The Indian Captives: Leaves from a Journal," they sometimes used an installment to flash back and fill in a gap in the journal's story line. In the book version, copyrighted in July 1863 as *A Thrilling Narrative of Indian Captivity*, the chapters substantially reprinted the newspaper installments in the order in which they were published.

The disjointed story line is also an artifact of the primary author. Mary Renville was not a political historian. She devoted more words to the stories of fellow captives like the Brown family, Julia LaFramboise,

Jannette DeCamp, Mrs. John Newman, Sarah Wakefield, and Harriet Adams (most of whom she did not fully identify) than she did to commentary on the political milieu of the war.[136] This makes sense. As a woman and a social extrovert, Mary was more personally concerned with the experiences of her fellow captives—especially those who spoke English—than with political infighting in the Dakota community. During her captivity, however, the war's outcome and the captives' fates were uncertain. So apparently Mary stretched beyond her personal concerns and used her journal to chronicle events she could not be certain any of the Upper Camp allies would live to tell. She recorded the names of her relatives in case the "leaves" (pages) of her journal outlived her and, in the same spirit, preserved copies of the letters she scribed and quite possibly council speeches John heard. Thus John and Mary became historians of events that, in importance, have outlived the experiences of individual captives and are, in fact, critical to modern conversations about what it meant to be Dakota in 1862. The result is that *A Thrilling Narrative* is a mix of captivity stories and the raw material of political history. While this is disconcerting for readers, it lends the text immediacy and authenticity that are missing in later, more consciously crafted stories of the war.

The stories of many individual captives are covered in depth in my coeditor, Kathryn Zabelle Derounian-Stodola's, *The War in Words: Reading the Dakota Conflict through the Captivity Literature*. For that reason, this overview of *A Thrilling Narrative* focuses on the emergence of the Peace Coalition, placing the extant information in chronological order and augmenting it with the recollections of two other captive eyewitnesses, John's cousins Paul Mazakutemani and Gabriel Renville.[137] As we will see, those Dakotas who actively sought peace were not a homogenous group of like-minded thinkers but a diverse coalition of men who, in times of peace, could vigorously oppose each other. However, for a brief time the war crisis created a remarkable unity of purpose that tells much about their mutual disdain for the war foisted upon them by others (Dakota and not) and about the power of kinship.

Mary Renville opened the story of the Peace Coalition with a flashback at the beginning of chapter 5, observing, "About the 25th of August Gabriel removed from Yellow Medicine, where he had been staying with his own and his sister's family a short time."[138] To understand the significance of that event in the formation of the Peace Coalition, it is necessary to go back even further, to 18 August, when news of the outbreak reached the Dakota farming communities of the upper Minnesota River Valley. At the time he first heard the news, John's cousin Gabriel Renville was probably at home on his farm on the north side of the Minnesota River, where he had taken land off the reservation in Renville County.[139] Gabriel, six years older than John, was the son of John's uncle Victor Renville Sr. When Victor was killed by Anishinabes around 1834, Joseph Renville adopted Gabriel, who grew to maturity as John's older brother (although John consistently referred to him by the more distant term "cousin"). As an adult Gabriel entered the fur trade like his uncle, working for Henry Sibley and J. R. Brown, among others.

Gabriel, who recorded an early, detailed chronicle of the war in Dakota, is an enigmatic figure in the period preceding it. In 1856 he was a founding member of the Hazlewood Republic, elected to the office of judge. As such, Gabriel pledged his belief in the Christian God, eschewed traditional Dakota ways, and vowed to regulate his life—and adjudicate his brothers' actions—by the Word of God. At that time he had only one wife, Mary Tuŋkaŋmani of the Scarlet Plume family. In 1857 Gabriel was enumerated as a farmer in Precinct 4 of Brown County (which included the Sioux Reservation).[140] But in 1858 he married Tuŋkaŋmani's sister Anna Tuŋkaŋ Tiyo Maniwiŋ, and in 1859 he took their sister Sophie Hu Tecawiŋ as his third wife. The Minnesota Census of 1860 found Gabriel at home on Hawk Creek, Renville County, next door to John's brothers Antoine and Michael Renville.[141] Gabriel's multiple traditional marriages seem to indicate that he lost interest in Christian religion about the same time he exercised his rights as a mixed-blood and took a homestead off the reservation. Further, his later stature as a chief on the Sisseton and Wahpeton Reservation indicates that Gabriel determined he did not need to abandon Dakota culture to become a leading homesteader. He seems to have fused subsistence agriculture with traditional lifeways.[142]

News of the outbreak may not have reached Gabriel at Hawk Creek until the morning of Tuesday, 19 August. Many of his family members lived on farms in the vicinity of the agency town of Yellow Medicine on the Upper Reservation. Gabriel first went there and determined that his mother was safe. He learned that his stepbrothers, though missing, were accounted for; they had gone to warn their stepsister Susan Frenier Brown, who lived off the reservation near Patterson's Rapids in Renville County.[143] About five that evening word came that the Browns had been taken captive. Gabriel and twelve Dakota friends, most of them full-blood relatives, spent the evening in council. They opposed the war, but their numbers were few. As bicultural Dakotas their lives and families were threatened if they did not join the war. Yet if they tried to escape, they could expect the same treatment as the Browns. So on Wednesday, 20 August, while some Lower Dakota soldiers were raiding outlying settlements and others were preoccupied with their first assault on Fort Ridgley, Gabriel Renville and his band of twelve men took a stand with their families in the fortified Sioux Agency buildings at Yellow Medicine.[144]

For the next few days the Lower soldiers were occupied inflicting damage on frontier settlements, while state authorities mounted a response. Lower soldiers were stationed on the Upper Reservation to surveil and to intimidate, but the Christian Dakotas holed up at Hazlewood and the Dakota farmers at the Upper Agency were generally left alone. But after that first week the tide of the war began to turn. The warring faction had succeeded in killing over five hundred settlers and in taking another three hundred people captive, but when they failed to take Fort Ridgley, they settled for placing it under siege.[145] They had also failed to take New Ulm, the first city in their plan to sweep the cities of the Minnesota River Valley all the way to the state capital of St. Paul. In that milieu Gabriel and Akipa (Tacaŋdupahotaŋka) marched down to the Lower Agency around 23 August and made a kinship demand: that Little Crow release the Brown family into their custody.[146] Little Crow agreed. Around 24 August Gabriel and Akipa returned to the Upper Agency with eleven members of the Brown family.

Besides the military defeats, Dakotas understood that the state's military response was finally underway. Governor Alexander Ramsey had appointed former Dakota trader and former state governor Henry H. Sibley commander of the state militia, which by 25 August had reached St. Peter.[147] That same day Little Crow retreated west toward Yellow Medicine with over two thousand Lower Dakota people and about three hundred white and mixed-blood hostages. When he arrived at the Upper Agency, he issued an ultimatum to Gabriel's band: "these houses are large and strong and must be burned . . . therefore you must get out of them and if you do not get out you will be burned with the buildings."[148] Gabriel, his compatriots, and their families, who with the addition of the Browns numbered 75–100 people, about 20 of them men of fighting age, headed north toward Hazlewood. When Gabriel arrived at Hazlewood, he found his cousin John Renville and family living in the mission school boardinghouse and set up his camp circle on the prairie just west of it.

The men of Hazlewood had been discussing the plight of the civilian captives held by the Lower Camp. Although they were now relocated to the Upper Agency, just a few miles east of Hazlewood, the Lower Dakotas still retained their hereditary identity and were held in deep suspicion by many Upper Dakotas, who, as subsequent events would show, had good reason to wonder where their loyalties lay. Significantly, the Upper Christian and non-Christian Dakota farmers were also uncertain about each other's loyalties and went into a council that likely extended over the next two days as they listened to each other and sorted matters out. The decision of men in both groups to turn to agriculture for subsistence is superficially misleading. Historically, Dakota people were resilient and over time adapted, when necessary, to significant changes in the environment. Small-scale communal farming had supplemented hunting and gathering for generations. Given increasing restrictions on these traditional subsistence activities in the reservation era following the Treaty of 1851, it is not surprising that growing numbers of Dakotas chose to adapt by turning to larger-scale, nuclear family agriculture to support their kin on their homelands. In their desire to stay in Minnesota, the Hazlewood Dakotas and the agency Dakotas were united. Most of them were long-time farmers. They had chosen this path for their family even before coercive financial incentives were brought to bear after the Treaty of 1858, and they understood that legislation was moving through Congress that would grant each man a title to the reservation land he homesteaded.[149]

However, their differences were deeply rooted and substantial. The Hazlewood group seems to have followed the white reformers' vision that the survival of Native people on the North American continent required assimilation into the dominant culture, a cultural conversion so thorough that (it was imagined) within a few generations people of Dakota descent would be as culturally indistinct from their settler neighbors as were the second and third generations of Swedish or German immigrants. As backward as it now seems to espouse cultural genocide as reform, in the nineteenth century this philosophy was viewed as the leading humanitarian alternative to outright extinction by any means, including calls for physical genocide.[150]

Assimilation was especially cherished by the Christian groups with whom the federal government increasingly partnered to administer Indian affairs. Thus the social reformers drawn toward working with Native Americans, like the Dakota missionaries, brought with them a dual cultural vision: for Christianization and assimilation. It makes sense that some Dakotas embraced both aspects of acculturation. Traditional Dakota lifeways and traditional Dakota spirituality were virtually inseparable, and Christianity offered a holistic worldview that was not linked to mode of subsistence or to the environment. However, even those Dakota men who found Christianity compelling did not advance as far or as fast in the direction their mentors hoped. Church leaders like Paul Mazakutemani (prominent throughout *A Thrilling Narrative*) were often reluctant to go along with the missionaries' cultural indoctrination.[151] For example, in the summer of 1856 Mazakutemani, along with Lorenzo Lawrence and the Ironheart family, removed their children from the mission school because, Stephen Riggs complained, "Dakota parents are very sensitive about the way in which their children are taken care of. We must clothe and feed and care for them far better than they could be attended to at home, and then if they are naughty and we correct them it makes quite a buzz in the community. Aunt Ruth Pettijohn is an admirable woman for the place she occupied but she has pretty scriptural notions in regard to the use of the rod which are not quite popular among these Native Americans."[152] The Hazlewood leaders withdrew their children and opened their own school, employing John B. Renville as its teacher. Although a devout Christian, John had more culturally appropriate ways of winning the cooperation and respect of his students. Over time initiatives like this one might have resulted in a theologically sound yet meaningfully indigenized form of Christianity at Hazlewood. But the endeavor has been historically obscured by the war that cut it short.

Many Dakotas, however, had chosen to walk a different path: selective acculturation. These Dakota men, like Gabriel Renville and his full-blood friends, while tolerant of Christianity, apparently did not find it personally compelling or necessary. To the contrary, they seem to have found some aspects of traditionalism, including spirituality, consistent with an agricultural lifestyle. In 1859 missionary Thomas S. Williamson described this trend to the ABCFM:

> Conversing with those who have had their hair cut and dress like white men they will generally admit that they ought to worship the White man's God; but very few of those who have changed their dress attend worship with us more than formerly. At first the general opinion was that all who changed their dress must change their religion and Little Crow the most celebrated Chief assigned this as his reason for doing neither saying he would not give up his Medicine sack, Gourd shell, and armor, because he wished when he died to go to the same place where his fathers are. To this Superintendent Cullen replied that he might retain all these and worship what, and how he pleased, if he would only have his hair cut and put on a hat and Pantaloons; but this only convinced Little Crow of Cullen's ignorance of the Dakotas and their religion. Some however adopted Cullen's views and one day dress and work like white men, and the next put on Breech Cloth, leggings and blanket, engage in conjuring over the sick and take part in the sacred feasts and dances. . . .Those who have changed their dress this year have been led to do so chiefly by the hope of assistance . . . besides a good suit of clothes [they] were each furnished with a yoke of oxen,

a cow, and for such as had no house a house was built besides many smaller favors.[153]

In response to this selective acculturation movement, by early 1861 both the Episcopal and Presbyterian Churches had opened mission stations at the Lower Sioux Agency. With the influx of funds earmarked for agriculturalists from the Treaty of 1858, several hundred Lower Dakota men had taken up farming, and the Christians viewed these families as a mission field ripe for spiritual harvest. Thus Gabriel and his relatives were not an anomaly. There were more—possibly many more—Dakota farmers than there were Dakota Christians in 1862.

We can only speculate what went on in the long council at Hazlewood after Gabriel's group moved up on 25 August. Despite their differences the men emerged unified behind a plan to feast the leaders in the Lower Camp and to ask for the civilian hostages, whom the Upper Camp leaders planned to escort to Fort Ridgley. The plan fit a pattern with which they were long familiar. Federal authorities interpreted the trade and intercourse laws to mean the government could withhold its treaty obligations (like annuity payments) to coerce Dakotas into surrendering depredators or freeing captives taken by other Dakota bands, prerogatives the government had repeatedly asserted in the wake of the 1857 Spirit Lake raid by Iŋkpaduta's band.[154] The members of the nascent Peace Coalition were united in their desire to remain settled on their Minnesota homelands and believed the rash actions of several hundred Lower warriors imperiled the survival of the entire nation. At worst, in retribution federal authorities might slaughter the innocent and the guilty alike. At best, the president could declare their treaties annulled by the minority act of war, turn their homelands over to settlers, and force all Dakotas into the arid West, claimed as homelands by other Native peoples. So the peace leaders proactively determined their future interests were linked to the president's interest in the freedom of his captive children. Only a goodwill gesture of that magnitude might compensate for the murder of hundreds of unarmed settlers.[155]

John Renville, who had participated in the 25–26 August council, gave

Gabriel a calf to slaughter to feast the Lower leaders, then undertook a personal mission. His sisters, who had married into the mixed-blood Campbell family at the Lower Sioux Agency, were captive in the Lower Camp.[156] John went down, ascertained that his relatives wanted to move to the Upper Camp, and made a kinship claim for their release. Their captors let them go. But some of Little Crow's soldiers intervened, intercepting the Campbells and driving them back.

While John was away, the Lower Soldiers' Lodge made a raid on Hazlewood. Gabriel recalled, "When all was ready, but before the invitation was sent . . . a large body of horsemen came over from the hostile camp—two hundred or more, and all had their guns, with their faces painted and gorgeously dressed, came up and stopped at our camp." Gabriel told the soldiers he was just about to call them to a feast and invited them to stay and eat. "They got down off their horses," Gabriel recalled, "and forming around our camp said, 'We have come for you, and if you do not move over to our camp immediately we shall have to come again and take you over by force,' and then mounting their horses and firing their guns in the air they departed."[157]

John and the other men returned to Hazlewood, heard what had happened in their absence, and called another council.[158] Likely they had talked about the possibility of forming a Soldiers' Lodge in their previous discussions, because it required almost no time to reach a consensus. Gabriel summarized, "By this time Cloud Man, Mah-zo manne and all those of our people who were about there came in, and were very much angered at what had happened and said: 'The Mdewankantons have many white prisoners, can it be possible they want to make the Wahpetons and Sissetons their captives too? Call together those who are Wahpetons and Sissetons and we will prepare to defend ourselves.'"[159]

Strategically, the Peace Coalition first took the traditional Dakota approach of greatest civility. While preparing a feast, as traditionally held before a public council, they privately sent emissaries like John to appeal to the central Dakota value, kinship. Both avenues failing, and seeing that Little Crow's soldiers were not treating them as Dakotas but as outsiders, the Upper Camp organized a Soldiers' Lodge to oppose the

Lower Soldiers as they would oppose an enemy.[160] "[W]hen about three hundred had arrived," Gabriel recalled,

> we painted our faces and got our guns and mounted our horses, and then went whooping and yelling towards their camp. When we had got near the hostile camp, we commenced firing our guns in to the air until we got within the circle of their encampment, then rode around inside and came out again where we went in and went back.
>
> It was then decided that we would get all our people together and in the future defend ourselves against the hostiles. Acting on this understanding all started to bring in their families for the purpose of forming one general camp of those friendly to the whites and apart from the hostiles.[161]

This time, when as a Soldiers' Lodge the Peace Coalition demanded their relatives, Little Crow's camp surrendered them.

The War (and Peace) in Words (*A Thrilling Narrative*, chapter 4)

Chapter 4 of *A Thrilling Narrative* opens with Mazakutemani leaving for a mission to the Lower camp and closes with a letter he dictated upon his return informing Governor Ramsey about what he learned. Appendix A in this edition places this missive and the other Peace Coalition letters reproduced in *A Thrilling Narrative* into historical context by collecting the extant correspondence between the Dakota camps and white authorities during the war. For the first time, it is possible to listen to the dialogue that transpired as multiple groups negotiated to end the war on their own terms. Privileging these letters as core texts, this section examines the circumstances in which the Peace Coalition negotiated, offering insights into their concerns for the future and laying a broad foundation for considering the grievances of the militant Dakotas in the following section of this introduction.

The scope of the collected letters covers one month, from 2 September to 3 October 1862, spanning the first phase of the war.[162] The Peace Coalition wrote thirteen known letters to Ramsey and Sibley in this period.

On 2 September, the date of the earliest letter, the coalition was still relatively small. John later explained under oath that, although early in the war there were about twenty Dakota families who had banded together at Hazlewood, "there were many more besides those . . . that objected to fighting with the whites and were in favor of making peace with the whites, but were afraid to come out openly on account of the hostiles. It was dangerous to even mention anything of the kind. The enemy were always about listening to catch on to anything of that kind." On cross-examination a lawyer suggested, "The reason that those who were friendly to the whites would not make themselves known was because there was so few that they were afraid that some harm would be done to them, was it not?" John disagreed, clarifying, "No, sir; it was not because there were a few of them, but because the friendlies did not know each other; that is, one friendly would not know another was friendly until afterwards. They had no organization."[163]

Their demonstration as a Soldiers' Lodge around 29 August was the Peace Coalition's opening move. As they began to speak and act in public councils, the Hazlewood men (now strengthened by Gabriel's contingent of agency farmers) refined their objectives for all who listened, drawing out Dakotas who concurred and gradually building the organization historically known as the Peace Party. At the same time they broadcast their determination to free the civilian hostages, which led captives to risk their lives fleeing to the Upper Camp for protection. The defection of both warriors and hostages from the Lower Camp progressively undermined the façade of unity the militant faction had managed to coerce during the first two weeks of the war.

The Peace Coalition also sought to undermine the war effort via clandestine correspondence that supplied white officials with insider information. On the evening of 2 September 1862 Mazakutemani returned from his mission to the Lower Camp and Mary Renville embarked on her impromptu career as an amanuensis. She scribed at least seven of the thirteen Peace Coalition letters—those reproduced in *A Thrilling Narrative*—and possibly many of the six others as well.[164] That day Mary noted that the second letter she copied was composed "after writing the lengthy epistle dictated by Paul."[165] Internal clues in the letters support Mary's claim as scribe. The grammar and composition of the English translations reflect a well-educated writer; during the opening weeks of the war Mary was the only native speaker of English in the Upper Camp.

Mary's acting as amanuensis also explains why, in December 1862, when she sat down at their temporary home in Wisconsin and opened the journal she had kept during the war, the book included copies of letters addressed by others to Ramsey and Sibley. The copies were a byproduct of the three-way translation process. The letters were dictated by native speakers in Dakota, translated from Dakota into English by a bilingual person, and then copied in English for delivery. While a letter might have been directly recorded by the translator, it is reasonable to guess that Mary was not a fluent speaker of Dakota at the time of the war. She may not have had the mastery to understand most of what she heard. Dakota was John's first language, however. John served as the intermediary in a pattern he had learned decades before at Lac qui Parle, listening to his father translate the Bible into Dakota. The likely involvement of two fluent Dakota speakers in the process (the speaker and John B. Renville) lends some confidence that the Renville reproductions of these letters are genuine artifacts of the 1862 negotiations, despite the fact that they were recorded by a white woman. At the same time it must be recognized that Mary was an active participant in the composition process. The letters we have today were in some measure shaped by her sensibilities.[166]

On 2 September, with Little Crow and all but a camp guard of Lower soldiers absent on a foray into the Big Woods, Paul Mazakutemani, Mary, and John concealed themselves in a tent and wrote the first of the extant letters from Dakotas seeking peace.[167] Doing so was well within Mazakutemani's prerogative as speaker for the Upper Camp, and he had over two decades' experience using letters to talk to hearers afar. When Mary had finished transcribing Mazakutemani's dictation, she took up her pen again and wrote a personal note, enclosing a declaration from Simon Anawaŋgmani (president of the Hazlewood Republic) and Lorenzo Lawrence stating that they intended to flee to the whites. Both letters were addressed to Ramsey. As governor, Ramsey was in charge of the volunteer militia, which the writers rightly assumed would form the core of the state's military response.

At this time the Peace Coalition may have been unaware that Ramsey had appointed former fur trader and former governor Henry H. Sibley to head the expedition.[168] Sibley did not send his first letter until after he reached Fort Ridgley and was surprised by the attack on a burial detail of his men at Birch Coulee. On 3 September Sibley left his first message inside a tobacco tin tied to a tall stake on the battlefield at Birch Coulee, establishing his terms for communication: Sibley promised to protect any "half-breed" carrying messages from Little Crow.[169] Besides safeguarding the delivery of letters Sibley's plan called for a bicultural courier, presumed to have dual loyalties that Sibley could (and did) exploit for the federal side.

Both Sibley and the Upper leaders tried to conceal their correspondence from the Lower Camp. Leaders in the latter place were rightly suspicious. Worse than the prospect that the Upper Camp might successfully sue for peace, the Lower Camp suspected the truth: that the Upper Camp was supplying Sibley with information that subverted the war. Within days, yet a third front opened: the peace faction within the Lower Camp, led by Wabaśa, Taopi, and Little Crow's head soldier, Wakiŋyaŋtawa—all of whom had opposed the war from the beginning—initiated their own correspondence with Sibley, also seeking peace.[170]

However, there is clear evidence of gaps in the record. It was not until the twenty-first century that historians began citing the letters published in *A Thrilling Narrative*. While Isaac Heard referred to conversations with Mrs. Mary Renville in his 1864 *History of the Sioux War*—conversations that transpired before Mary left Camp Release in early October—it seems they did not discuss the correspondence for which she had acted as amanuensis. Heard apparently was unaware of those letters, even though he reproduced other missives Sibley collected. In fact, a lingering question remains: which of the Peace Coalition letters did Ramsey and Sibley actually receive? The letters are not extant in holograph form in Ramsey's gubernatorial papers in the state archives at the Minnesota Historical Society, and the letters addressed to Sibley exist only in reproduction, until now scattered in several sources. It seems that Sibley did not receive every letter, and of course, those he did not receive could not have influenced his wartime decisions. Even so, taken together the letters demonstrate that, contrary to the assertions of Sibley's biographer, Nathaniel West, it was Dakota people, not Sibley, who opened negotiations. Whether Sibley received them or not, the letters collected in appendix A of this volume speak pointedly to the motivations of Dakota people on both sides of the war.

"For what reason we have commenced this war I will tell you."
— Taoyateduta [Little Crow] to Sibley, 7 September 1862

On 7 September 1862, in response to Sibley's 3 September promise to protect the bearer of "propositions" from the Lower Camp, Little Crow proposed a then-novel, now-familiar litany of wrongs that led his young men to war:

For what reason we have commenced this war I will tell you. It is on account of Major Galbraith. We made a treaty with the Government, and beg for what we do get, and then cannot get it till our children are dying with hunger. It is with the Traders that commence. Mr. A.J. Myrick told the Indians that they would eat grass or there [*sic*] own dung. Then Mr. Forbes told the Lower Sioux that they were not men. Then Robert he was working with his friends how to defraud us of our money. If the young braves have push the white men, I have done this myself. So I want you to let Governor Ramsey know this.[171]

A holograph of Little Crow's message is not extant.[172] The authenticity of the content, however, is verified by contemporaneous sources. In a letter dated 2 September 1862, quoted in full in appendix A, Paul Mazakutemani reported, "The reason the Chiefs gave me [for starting the war] was that payment was delayed and the traders would not trust them, but told them to leave their stores, and go eat grass like the oxen, that they were a lazy set and would have to starve if they did not. . . . These things he said, made them very angry."[173] Further, Sibley reported to his wife on 8 September, "I received a letter from Little Crow yesterday, by the bearers of a flag of truce. He writes . . . that the reason the war was commenced was because he could not get the provisions and other supplies due the Indians, that the women and children were starving, and he could get no satisfaction from Major Galbraith, the Agent."[174] While in internal councils Little Crow also spoke of the war as a means of reclaiming Dakota homelands, he shrewdly chose not to disclose this objective to Sibley.[175] The concord among these three sources suggests that the immediate grievances made public by the war faction were external pressures like the agent, the treaties, and the traders. The combination, Little Crow alleged, meant Dakota children were "dying with hunger."

The conduct of Sioux agent Thomas J. Galbraith during the summer of 1862 is universally assessed as an immediate contributing cause of the war. Even Mazakutemani, who insisted that Galbraith was "honorable," admitted Galbraith's Civil War recruitment efforts were ill timed and "exasperated the Indians," who were waiting for him to make the 1862 annuity payment.[176] Galbraith, as agent, was the man on the scene tasked with fulfilling the government's treaty obligations to the Dakotas and with enforcing Indian Affairs code, including regulating the traders. Therefore, Little Crow reasoned, if Dakota children were starving it was the agent's fault. If Galbraith had the means to alleviate their suffering and chose not to, he neglected his duty, both as a federal officer and as a human being.[177]

The traders, who a century before had been Dakota allies in the fur trade, by 1862 were frustrated capitalist merchants facing imminent eviction from the Sioux Reservation. The fur trade had become so unprofitable that in 1861, although the incoming Republican administration had the power to oust the Democrats licensed by previous administrations and to replace them with Republicans, only a single newcomer was interested in entering the trade on the Sioux Reservation, the firm of Pratt and Daily. Thus all the old traders retained their permits to trade on the reservation, despite their political leanings.[178] The despised Andrew Myrick's firm was legally bankrupt. While it remained under the management of Andrew's older brother, Nathan Myrick, it was owned by trader Stewart B. Garvie.[179] Garvie, along with the other licensed traders, had heard the rumor that Galbraith would not renew the trading licenses when they expired in the spring of 1863. After taking in the proceeds of an unusually good spring hunt in 1862, the traders cut off credit. With no future treaties on the horizon and their rumored eviction imminent, the annuity payment of 1862 was the traders' last chance to settle debts, and they were unwilling to extend credit beyond what they believed they could collect.[180]

Although it has gone unnoticed by history, trader Louis Robert was doing a booming business on the reservation in the summer of 1862. Dakotas compared Robert's liberality to the prevailing embargo and concluded that Robert was, in Little Crow's words, "working with his friends to defraud us of our moneys."[181] Robert was picking up the business created by the trade boycott: "He (Roberts) trusted promiscuously, no matter who went to his store, no matter whether he was an old customer of ours or not, he trusted him."[182] Apparently promised the sole trade proprietorship on the reservation for 1863, Robert likely felt certain he would be around to collect subsequent annuity payments.[183] David Faribault Sr., operating out of his house just outside the Sioux Reservation, needed no license to trade that summer.[184] Unlike the licensed firms, as a private citizen living off the reservation Faribault was indemnified against potential losses via the private claims channels for Indian Affairs. Faribault's doors were also open to those who wished to trade.[185]

The Lower Soldiers' Lodge was sufficiently alarmed by the apparent collusion of traders to at one point in the summer of 1862, amid rumors that the annuity payment would not be paid at all, bar the licensed traders' stores at gunpoint to prevent other Dakotas from incurring more debt.[186] It was their job as a Soldiers' Lodge to police decisions the lodge had determined were in the best interests of the *oyate* (their people). In the same spirit, in July they reissued an ultimatum forbidding the traders from cutting wood and harvesting reservation hay without paying for it, a right they generally exercised only when they were hungry.[187] "Grass" and "hay" are the same word in Dakota, *peži*, and *peži* was animal fodder. Andrew Myrick's infamous taunt "For all I care, let them eat grass" was a retort to this edict from the Lower Soldiers' Lodge that could be paraphrased, "Fine. You want to keep your hay? Eat it. You won't be getting any food from me." Myrick responded by locking his store for at least two weeks, threatening to penalize any traders who did not join him.[188] Unde-terred by the traders' refusal to reciprocate, in August the Lower Soldiers' Lodge turned to another neighbor, the commander at Fort Ridgley, to enlist his help in preventing the traders from seizing purported debts at the upcoming annuity payment. When two Dakota farmers betrayed this plan to the traders, the Lower Soldiers' Lodge summarily punished the stool pigeons by destroying their possessions.[189] Taken together, stories like these show that Lower Dakota men were not the hapless victims of abuse at the hand of authorities that some secondary sources imply. While clearly oppressed by the federal system, throughout the summer of 1862 some Dakotas continued to purposefully and vigorously resist the coercion to acculturate, including thwarting the machinations of the traders.

Yet Little Crow's claim that Dakota men went to war because their chil-dren were starving implies that some Dakotas found these lesser resistance strategies inadequate. The death of children from preventable means is deplorable under any circumstances. But the truth may be more insidious than historians have recognized. It was not a matter of having nothing to eat (the common meaning of "starvation") on the Dakota Reservation in 1862. Rather, the diet of traditionalists was so nutritionally impoverished that children were dying of diseases that would have been transient in a healthy population. Thus, despite the documented availability of staple carbohydrates like green corn and new potatoes in August 1862, despite the periodic issue of food by the agent, and despite food offered by Robert and Faribault on credit, Dakota children were dying of debility and disease due to the invisible menace of chronic malnutrition.[190]

Primary sources note cyclical periods of famine in Dakota communi-ties dating back at least to the late 1600s, when literate men arrived in the region and began keeping written records.[191] One of these men was missionary doctor Thomas S. Williamson ("The Doctor"), who later described what he found when he arrived at Mde Ia Udan for the first time in 1835. "The extreme poverty of these Sioux strongly impressed my mind at first sight, and further acquaintance did not relieve it. . . . [That spring at Lac qui Parle] the Dakotas, without bread, or grain, or flesh, had subsisted chiefly on roots and wild fruit, with an occasional mess of fish or eggs of wild fowl. . . . it is not strange that many of the men and women and some of the children were shriveled by starvation."[192] Williamson had two decades of experience among the Dakotas by 1856, when he formulated a thesis linking malnutrition to death from disease. In his analysis of the "starving winter" in 1855–56, Williamson noted that among the approximately three hundred Dakotas in his immediate neighborhood, Pejutazizi on the Upper Reservation, fifteen children between the ages of two and twelve had died

> of Mumps and Hooping cough. It brought many of them to a weak and languid state in which they lingered from one to three months and then died apparently from debility rather than disease. Many of them with a better diet and shelter probably would have recovered. Government has neglected to furnish these Dakota with any cattle and their reservation furnishes no large game from which to get even a small supply of meat and last winter they found very few fish. Consequently those who remained on their reservation had to subsist last winter almost entirely on corn and potatoes for five months."[193]

The winter of 1861–62 had been another "starving winter," when deep snow prevented Dakotas from hunting and from digging out cached food reserves until early spring. Dakota farmers almost certainly had food to eat that winter despite weather conditions. They had to go no farther than their farmyards to find livestock (cattle, pigs, and sheep) and poultry. Although many Dakota farmers continued to trap for pelts and furs in the winter months, it was a source of extra income; their livestock provided meat for their families. But traditionalists probably entered the summer of 1862 in nutritionally fragile health. Their families subsisted on crops they grew, foodstuffs they gathered, meat they hunted or trapped, and staple foods bought on credit. When snowbound, traditionalists had very few options for obtaining food.[194] By the summer of 1862 bystanders at the agency could downplay Dakota claims of starvation in the face of obtainable vegetable foodstuffs. However, the availability of ripening carbohydrates in communal fields obscured the underlying nutritional emergency: a critical lack of animal protein.[195] Stephen Riggs captured the paradox in October 1862: "Some of them came to me this morning to say that their families have nothing to eat. I asked if they have not potatoes and corn. 'Oh yes, but they have got nothing else,' was the reply."[196]

This malnutrition thesis is supported by modern research by the World Health Organization (WHO), which finds a direct link between malnutrition and childhood death from disease: "The results from 53 developing countries with nationally representative data . . . indicate that 56% of child deaths were attributable to malnutrition's potentiating effects, and 83% of these were attributable to mild-to-moderate as opposed to severe malnutrition. These results show that malnutrition has a far more powerful impact on child mortality than is generally appreciated."[197] In the Dakota case the statistical magnitude of that impact may be impossible to assess due to the absence of data. Lower Dakota annuity figures, for example, fluctuate significantly from year to year but the census totals for 1851 and 1860 are almost identical, which might indicate little population growth in the Mdewankanton population in the reservation era following the Treaty of 1851.[198] However, birth and death rate figures are missing, as are, most importantly, migration statistics. Federal Sioux Agency reports enumerate horseshoes forged and fence rails split. But the official record is silent on morbidity and mortality.[199]

Scholars have long wrestled to reconcile Dakota claims of starvation with the documented availability of staple foods, assuming that calories from any source were sufficient and that significant starvation would be obvious. But malnutrition is often invisible. Eighty-three percent of children who die unnecessarily from infectious disease suffer from mild to moderate malnutrition, not the degree of "starvation" stereotypical of famine victims.[200] So outsiders like the agent and the traders did little to alleviate the crisis because it was not obvious that the children of Dakota traditionalists were suffering for lack of adequate protein. At the same time, insiders like Little Crow could rightly claim that Dakota children were "dying with hunger," understanding at the very least that Dakotas who refused to participate in the federal acculturation program (and, it seems, who did not have farmer kin to share sufficient food) increasingly had little to eat.[201] Arguably, these were the Dakotas most motivated to go to war and among those most easily recruited to join it.

In light of this, Little Crow's observation that "[w]e made a treaty with the Government and beg for what we do get" is astute. To obtain Dakota homelands for white settlement, federal negotiators promised that signing treaties would place Dakota people "beyond want," which Dakotas probably understood to mean beyond the cyclical periods of famine that had haunted them for generations.[202] Federal negotiators stepped into a landscape fraught with hunger and sought an exchange: land for annuities, leading Dakotas to believe that annuity payments (and promised federal services like medical care) would alleviate their suffering. Yet despite three treaties ratified between 1837 and 1858, Dakota people were begging for food in 1862. Indeed, Little Crow alleged, conditions were still so bad that the most vulnerable of the *oyate*, the children—the future of the Dakota nation—were dying. It was sufficient cause, Little Crow argued, for "commenc[ing] this war."

"We did all we could. We did not go to war. We killed nobody. We helped save the captives." —Peace Coalition petition, 18 December 1862[203]

At a human level Little Crow's logic seems almost irrefutable. As modern Dakota activists ask, how can anyone fault fathers for fighting a war of desperation to throw off the oppressors who were starving their children?[204] More perplexing, the formation of a resistance movement during the war, the Peace Coalition, raises a question: Why would some Dakotas help the enemy defeat their brothers' cause? These continue to be poignant issues for Dakota people, many of whom had ancestors in both pro- and antiwar camps. Modern Dakotas and their future generations will continue to wrestle with answers that resonate with their concerns, which are quite different from the general unconcern of many non-Native Minnesotans who continue to benefit from what Native people lost in 1862.

Having heard Little Crow's representation of the insurgents' position, consider the story from the Peace Coalition's point of view. Their multiple reasons for opposing the war are outlined in the poly-vocal councils held inside the Dakota camps during the war recorded in chapter 10 of Heard's *History of the Sioux War* (published in 1864) and in the letters collected in appendix A of this volume. Heard generically cited captives he had interviewed at Camp Release as his source. Historian Return I. Holcombe asserted that Heard obtained the texts of council speeches from Mrs. John B. Renville, who recorded them during captivity. Holcombe's claim about Mary is not substantiated or refuted in any other source. But it is credible.[205]

However, there is a significant difference between the pro- and antiwar arguments developed in this introduction. While Little Crow's "starvation" plea was constructed explicitly for an outside audience, the record of the intratribal councils reported by Heard largely reflects the concerns that preoccupied Dakota people among themselves. The speakers likely did not expect that their words would become part of the written historical record. Therefore these are difficult texts for non-Dakota scholars to attempt to interpret, and the arguments may be challenging for non-Native readers to appreciate. Yet the likely involvement of John and Mary Renville in the creation and dissemination of the written record makes the subject impossible to ignore.

The Peace Coalition speakers did not directly address Little Crow's public rationale for the war, even though they must have understood how difficult it was for traditionalists to obtain food: they were kin. Instead, Peace Coalition leaders persistently argued that the war was not being conducted in a Dakota way. Paul Mazakutemani, designated speaker for the Peace Coalition, opened the first council on 1 or 2 September in traditional Dakota fashion by appealing to his relatives: "Warriors and young men!—I am an Indian, and you are Indians, and there should be no secrets between us. Why, then, did you not tell us that you were going to kill the whites?"[206] As Mazakutemani explained to Ramsey in a 2 September letter, "Previous to commencing on Monday [18 August], a messenger was despatched [sic] to Yellow Medicine and Red Iron Village, but not one word did the Bands about the Mission know till the slaughter commenced."[207] Later, in council, Mazakutemani elaborated, "I ask you the question again, Why did you not tell us? You make no answer. The reason was, if you had done so, and we had counseled together, you would not have been able to have involved [sic] our young men with you. When we older men heard of it we were so surprised that we knew not what to do. By your involving our young men without consulting us you have done us a great injustice."[208]

There was so little consensus that war was the solution to the Dakotas' problems that had a general council been called the minority who sought war risked being overruled. But Mazakutemani was not smarting just because the traditional consensus process had been short-circuited. The warring faction had done something more flagrantly non-Dakota: they had purposefully disregarded the authority of the elders of *tiošpayes* over their young men.[209] As elders, Mazakutemani and the other peace chiefs were insulted and angry. As Taṭaŋka Nażiŋ (Standing Buffalo), hereditary chief of the Sissetons, told the Lower warriors, "You have brought me into great danger without my knowing it beforehand. By killing the whites it is just as if you had waited for me in ambush and shot me down. . . . I know that neither I nor my people have killed any of the whites, and that yet we have to suffer for the guilty."[210] The majority of the Sisseton bands, including Taṭaŋka Nażiŋ's, had been hunting buffalo in Dakota Territory when the war began. Yet a few Sisseton and more Wahpeton young men who had married into Lower families helped their Lower kin prosecute the war.[211]

The Lower Dakotas did not deny it. As Chief Wabaśa's son-in-law Ḣdainyaŋka, Little Crow's spokesman, observed,

> It was not the intention of the nation to kill any of the whites until after the four men returned from Acton and told what they had done. When they did this, all the young men became excited, and commenced the massacre. The older ones would have prevented it if they could, but since the treaties they have lost all their influence. We may regret what has happened, but the matter has gone too far to be remedied. We have got to die. Let us, then, kill as many of the whites as possible, and let the prisoners die with us.[212]

Wabaśa's consent at first had been avoided; later his opinion was ignored.

On behalf of the people he represented, Mazakutemani also objected to the folly of war against a militarily greatly superior power. In his first speech he warned, "The end of the world is near at hand for the nation of the Dakotas. Every Indian knows we cannot live without the aid of the white man."[213] In a subsequent speech Mazakutemani said, "The Americans have given us money, food, clothing, ploughs, powder, tobacco, guns, knives, and all things by which we might live well; and they have nourished us [farmers] even like a father his children."[214] On another occasion he chided, "I want to know from you Lower Indians whether you were asleep or crazy. In fighting the whites, you are fighting thunder and lightning. You will all be killed off. You might as well try to bail out the Mississippi as to whip them."[215] Elsewhere he repeated, "The Americans are a great people. They have much lead, powder, guns and provisions. . . . No one who fights with white people ever becomes rich, or remains two days in one place, but is always fleeing and starving."[216] Fleeing and starving were the antithesis of remaining settled on their homelands.

Perhaps more significantly the Peace Coalition decried how the war was being conducted as it related to individuals. The modern idea that the massacre of unarmed settlers was justified as the political assassination of oppressors was not raised in intertribal councils in 1862, even by the faction who went to war.[217] To the contrary, Mdewankanton chief Wabaśa framed the killings as "the murder of the poor whites that have been settled in the border."[218] The Peace Coalition concurred, arguing through Mazakutemani that the insurgents' stated ends did not justify the means.

> I am now going to tell you something you don't like. You have gotten our people into this difficulty through your incitements to its rash young soldiers without a council being called and our consent obtained, and I shall use all the means I can to get them out of it without reference to you. I am opposed to their continuing this war, or of committing farther outrages, and I warn them not to do it. I have heard a great many of you say that you were brave men, and could whip the whites. This is a lie. Persons who will cut women and children's throats are squaws and cowards. You say the whites are not brave. You will see. They will not, it is true, kill women and children, as you have done, but they will fight you who have arms in your hands.[219]

Wabaśa concurred, "the poor women ain't the blamed for the fight."[220] Peace-leaning headmen were not alone in this conviction that unarmed civilian women and children were unjust targets, despite the fact that in traditional Dakota warfare enemy women and children were not necessarily spared in raids. Around 19 August Little Crow himself is said to have chided his warriors, "Soldiers and young men, you ought not kill women and children. Your conscience will reproach you for it hereafter, and make you weak in battle. You were too hasty in going into the country. You should have killed only those who have been robbing us so long. Hereafter make war after the manner of the white men."[221]

Modern research on Dakota War deaths verifies that the majority of civilians killed were women and children. In an analysis limited to Marion P. Satterlee's data on Dakota War fatalities, historian Walt Bachman observes, "Including Milford, there were seven sites at which the Dakotas massacred 15 or more helpless civilians away from the scene of any military battle—the majority of whom, at each location, were women and children."[222] My own research on 1862 war deaths in Renville County concurs. At least 70 percent of the civilians killed in Middle Creek, Sacred Heart, and Flora Townships (settlements adjacent to the Lower Reservation, north of the Minnesota River in Renville County) were women and children.[223]

The Peace Coalition also did not sanction the way some of the Lower Dakotas were treating captives. Traditionally, among Santee Dakotas the few captives who were taken in war were adopted into a family and treated as Dakotas, often to replace a child who had died or to become a wife. But around 140 settler women and children were taken captive at the beginning of the 1862 war.[224] Captive-taking on this scale was unprecedented. There was no consensus that civilians should be held hostage and no existing plan for assimilating so many into the community. Waŋbditanka, or Big Eagle, a Mdewankanton who was not a named member of the Peace Coalition, remembered,

> On the morning of the outbreak I went to Wa-pa-sha's house and told him that the Indians were bringing in women and children as prisoners, and that I thought this wrong, and thought they ought to be sent to the fort; he agreed with me, and sent me to speak with Little Crow about it. I told Little Crow that these prisoners had done no wrong and

would be badly off if cared for by the Indians, and that it was our wish to send them to the fort. He desired me not to speak about it; that he had determined to take them with us wherever we went, and that they should suffer with us.[225]

At the onset of the war captive settlers were initially held by the Lower soldiers who had captured them. Over the next few weeks some of these captives were adopted away from their captors into a Dakota family where, with kinship patterns in play, they fared more or less as well as their protectors.[226] However, many of the settler captives were not sheltered in a family and were suffering. Eight days into the war, when the Lower camp relocated to the Upper Agency, Gabriel Renville recalled,

> we came to where the hostiles had formed camp, and as we were passing through it I saw many white prisoners, old women, young women, boys and girls, all bare-headed and bare footed, and it made my heart hot and so I said to Ah-kee-pah, Two Stars, and E-ne-hah, "if these prisoners were men instead of women and children it would not be so bad. It is hard that this terrible suffering should be brought upon women and children, even such of these have been murdered.["] I therefore had in mind to call a council, invite the hostiles and appoint Mah-zo-mane and Cloud Man to say to the hostiles that it was our wish that the prisoners should be sent home.[227]

It was the Dakota way to care for captives as kin, not to hold them as political hostages. Not to starve them. Not to threaten to shoot them. Not to spread terrorizing propaganda to keep them docile and easier to guard. Not to threaten to use them as human shields in battle.[228] Mazakutemani summarized,

> I am ashamed of the way that you have acted toward the captives. Fight the whites if you desire to, but do it like brave men. Give me the captives and I will carry them to Fort Ridgley. I hear one of you say that if I take them there the soldiers will shoot me. I will take that risk. I am not afraid of death, but I am opposed to the way you act toward the prisoners. If any of you have the feelings of men, you will give

them up. You may look as fierce at me as you please, but I shall ask you once, twice, and ten times to deliver these women and children to their friends.[229]

It also was not the Dakota way to hold kin captive. In the words of Taṭaŋka Nażiŋ, "My heart is sad . . . because this day I have seen the destitution of our half-breeds. They are our flesh and blood, and therefore we are anxious for their welfare."[230] Nearly three times as many mixed-blood people as whites were held captive during the war. So were full Dakotas who openly opposed it.[231] Sibley wrote to his wife on 8 September 1862, "The half breed bearers of the flag of truce, both of whom I know, say that the mixed bloods, with their families, are not permitted to leave the camp, and are virtually prisoners, as most of them are believed to sympathize with the whites."[232] Mary Renville, responding to postwar skepticism that anyone of Dakota descent had been captive during the war, wrote in a 13 March 1863 letter to the editor of the *St. Paul Weekly Press*:

About a week before Gen. Sibley arrived at Camp Release, some of the half-breeds formed a plan to escape at midnight and come down to his camp, but so closely were they watched, their plan was discovered, notwithstanding all possible secresy [*sic*]. A guard was placed around the tents in the woods and on the roads; so they were obliged to give up the execution of their design. Many of the half-breeds would have left the Indian country, on first hearing of the outbreak, had they been "free to go where they pleased." I knew many of the Indians, too, would have come below, to escape participation in the robberies, had it been practicable for them to do so.[233]

The fault lines opened by the war were multidimensional, not merely a matter of assimilationist versus traditionalist ideology or of tribal or band affiliation. The war cut through the deference to elders that had for millennia, in the fabric of kin relationships, determined how Dakota people related to one another. It also betrayed how other core values like civility and generosity had been deeply undermined in the years preceding the war.[234] Superficially it may appear that the war shattered traditional culture. But the opposite may be true: decades of cumulative colonial assaults had so undermined the Dakota way of life that the 1862 war was a result, not a cause, of calamitous cultural destabilization.

Razing Hazlewood (*A Thrilling Narrative*, chapter 6)

The growing coalition of Dakotas allied for peace continued to press in councils to end the war and to free the captives. By 3 September, sixteen days into the war, the Lower Camp had had enough and determined to push back. Lower Soldiers, heady with the damage they had inflicted on a detachment of Sibley's soldiers at Birch Coulee, were also now keenly aware that the Peace Coalition leaders would not be swayed. Worse, the Lower Camp knew there were traitors in their midst. A few captives, like Jannette DeCamp and Mrs. Newman, with the help of sympathetic Lower Dakotas, had fled to Hazlewood for refuge. Others, like Helen Carrothers and Charles Blair, had been assisted in escaping toward the settlements.[235]

In the mission boardinghouse at Hazlewood Mary Renville sat down for the last time at a table, opened her journal to the page that would bear the first sentences of chapter 6, and wrote, "Mission Station, Sept. 3. The excitement still increases. Rebels report constant success, and are confident of taking all the smaller towns, and if they could get St. Peter, and Traverse de Sioux, they are going to attack St. Paul in the night."[236] Like most captives, Mary was generally ignorant of the military side of the war, hearing little more than the exploits recounted by soldiers around campfires at night. She did not learn until later the details of the battle at Birch Coulee (reconstructed in chapter 10) and probably did not know that the Dakotas had been repulsed at Fort Ridgley and New Ulm. Nor did she know that Sibley had, that day, openly challenged Little Crow to negotiate.

But Mary knew that the Lower Camp had determined to escalate the internal war. Having left the inhabitants of Hazlewood mostly alone in the week since the raid by the Lower Soldiers' Lodge, the Lower Camp now determined to burn the mission compound. They had already burned the houses of the Dakota Hazlewood leaders—a form of the traditional punishment called "soldier killing"—for their refusal to heed the edicts of the Lower Soldiers' Lodge.[237] Their plan to demolish the Hazlewood station was more strategic. They had already destroyed the agency town at Yellow Medicine and the Williamson mission at Pejutazizi. Razing Hazlewood would erase the last white clapboard home and picket fence from the landscape. It would also deprive any antiwar holdouts of shelter and reduce the "whitewashed Indians" to living in tipis again.[238]

John B. Renville was so acculturated that he and Mary did not own a tipi. As Mary wrote in her journal that day,

> We were much perplexed at first, supposing we should be entirely dependent upon some of the Indians for a tent, but fortunately Mr. R. traded a two-year old colt for one. This is rather a round sum to pay, but cotton is in great demand for building material just now.
>
> The friendly Indians are urging us to leave the house, fearing the rebels will set fire to it at night.[239]

Buying a tipi kept John and Mary from being beholden to his cousin Gabriel (who later claimed to have protected John and Mary throughout the war) and provided a chapel space for the Christian Dakotas who, since the beginning of the war, had met daily for worship and encouragement. Perhaps most significantly, living alone in their "tent," as Mary euphemistically dubbed a tipi, also allowed her to preserve the nuclear family sanctuary that was so equated with home in her culture. It protected Mary's sense of privacy, which was probably more keenly developed than John's. (He had grown up in an extended-family home and did not own his own house until he built one just before he wed Mary.) Practically speaking, with only two children and two adults living in their tipi there was room for Mary's rocking chair, trunk, and case of books. Not having to defer cooking duties to one of Gabriel's wives, Mary was able to keep her stove to make oven-baked bread and to use her frying pan standing upright, not in the fireside posture of a Dakota woman.

Maintaining these incongruous vestiges of home was all the more important because when she moved into the tipi Mary reluctantly exchanged her long, full skirt and fitted basque for a short gown and leggings made two days before by Catherine Tatidutawiŋ, who "thought we were not safe in our [settler] costume." Mary had earlier demurred, hiding her own antipathy for dressing like a Dakota woman under the excuse she offered her readers, that "so many of the company realized we would not be at home in it, [and] persuaded us to lay it aside for the present."[240] Although she was now dressed like a Dakota and living in a tipi, Mary did not immediately lose her sense of otherness as a white woman. In a flash of dry wit that her Dakota relatives must have found endearing in happier times, Mary painted a word picture as incongruous in a captivity narrative as was her favorite seat in the tipi: "We really enjoy the large rocking chair, and could have good times if we were with a company of chosen friends, on a pleasure excursion, instead of being afraid of one's life at every moment. This is something that cannot be described on paper."[241]

Nor did Mary lose her conviction that she had married a man who, despite his blood quantum, was white. In fact, she never told her readers that John was ethnically Dakota, nor did she disclose that he was a fluent speaker of that language. In chapter 6 she publicly claimed the opposite: that John was a white man who needed to disguise himself as an Indian. Because Mary was writing in the wake of the war, we cannot know if the remarkable little scene she penned reflects conscious posing for her white readers or, more simply, her longstanding conviction that "whiteness" was not a fixed feature of biology but rather a matter of culture, which could be cultivated.

> Sept. 4. We are now living for the first time in a tent. This P.M. we went with Mr. R. to take a last look at the Mission buildings . . . two young rebels entered the church, a short distance from us, and made havoc of everything within their reach, until stopped by an older man. . . . By this time the flames were pouring out of Mr. C.'s chamber window. We went a little distance and watched the progress of the fire, keeping our blankets wrapped close about our head, for fear of being known as white persons, for we have all been obliged to lay aside civilized costumes.[242]

Even more remarkable than the literary sleight of hand by which Mary cast her own racial identity like a blanket over the head of her husband is the confession made by one of those young rebels: they were actually captive white boys dressed up and playing "Indian" the night they burned the mission station at Hazlewood. Thus John and Mary were disguised as Dakotas, watching white boys also disguised as Dakotas. Benedict Juni, age ten in 1862, recalled a scene my coeditor has described as "every white boy's dream of burning down the school house and sacking the church":[243]

At Hazelwood there were three buildings still intact when we first formed a camp there, a residence, a workshop and a two story building serving as chapel and school house. It was the best equipped school house I had seen so far. The boys first ransacked the desks, scattered the books and other utensils and rang the large bell that hung in the belfry. When they tired of this the window panes afforded targets for stones and arrows. Next the workshop was visited and some of the rod iron formed into spears and these hurled at fence posts. The day's program was concluded by a monstrous bonfire in the evening. The white frame dwellings of the Riggs and the Williamsons fell prey to the flames. Bear in mind that this was not done by adults but by boys not yet in their teens and elicited no applause from their [Dakota] parents. I well remember the sad look and the depreciating shake of the head when I told my master of the day's work.[244]

While Juni's identification of the buildings was incorrect (the Williamsons lived three miles away), his story stands the "savage Indian" stereotype on its head. As Juni concluded this story, "There were four or five white boys of about my age that now frequently met. . . . If the odds were not too much against us we would accept challenges from parties of Indian boys in which the latter were generally worsted. The applause from the Indians would be unstinted as if their own sons were the victors."[245] Was it really ethnic descent or, as Mary Renville contended, desire and opportunity that determined identity?

"We are all captives." —Paul Mazakutemani to Sibley,
15 September 1862 (*A Thrilling Narrative*, chapters 7–10)

Chapters 7–10 of *A Thrilling Narrative* span two weeks, from 7 to 20 September 1862. In the course of these three chapters readers looking for a war story will founder, as captive to the ennui of captivity as were the subjects of the story. This may be one reason *A Thrilling Narrative* fell into obscurity. The Dakota War was, after all, a war, claimed as such by both Dakota and non-Native military scholars. The historiography of the war is so thoroughly militarized that the story is almost unintelligible in any other form. Without battles to serve as familiar signposts, readers may be as disoriented as the settler women who, after the massacre of their families, spent weeks lost and wandering on the prairie.

Perhaps the militarization of Dakota War historiography has been inevitable. The formative histories of the war were written in the shadow of the Civil War, an era when the whole national story was militarized. The historians themselves had, by and large, served in the Civil War and were ambitious that the Minnesota conflict be viewed on par with national history. Casting the Dakota War as primarily a military engagement also legitimated the state's actions (and reactions) against Native people in 1862–63. In the modern era the claim for war—not massacre or uprising or conflict or any of the other names the cataclysm has worn over time—is also championed by Dakotas seeking to legitimate the actions of Dakota warriors in 1862. Since the authors of *A Thrilling Narrative* were neither participants in nor witnesses to battles, historians to date have found little use for their text.[246] Thus history, too, has been held captive by the limited concerns of the war's early historians.

Readers also feel at sea in this section of the text because it captures the psychological realities of captivity. The war was not yet over. The story had not been digested and packaged for print. The captives did not know they were nearly halfway through their ordeal. They were unaware that they would not be taken to Canada, as had thousands of other settler captives before them in Indian wars on the North American continent. They did not know that they would someday return to a semblance of the life they had known before the war and not spend the rest of their lives, if they lived, as Indians.

In fact, the captives were in renewed peril because Sibley's 8 September edict formalized their status as political pawns, informing Little Crow that the only way to make peace was to surrender the captives. As Sibley hoped, this decree amplified the motivation of the Peace Coalition to obtain and to safeguard the captives and, as the next week would prove, motivated the peace-leaning Lower Dakotas to associate themselves and their captives with the Upper Camp.[247] But Sibley probably did not anticipate that the same order would motivate the pro-war faction to renew threats to kill the captives, which would eliminate a major obstacle to uniting the two camps in war. Without the captives, there would be no peace.

The Lower soldiers who had started the war were not interested in peace. They were intensely frustrated with the accommodations foisted upon them by the elders who had signed the treaties, many of them the same elders who were opposed to war and who favored surrendering the captives. From the pro-war perspective, killing the captives and thus dictating the future of the Dakota nation was no more arbitrary than the treaties that had signed away their birthright for a mess of annuity pottage. Further, another hundred dead settlers would make little difference. As Little Crow observed in council about this time, "Did we ever do the most trifling thing, and the whites not hang us? Now we have been killing them by the hundreds in Dakota, Minnesota, and Iowa, and I know that if they get us into their power they will hang every one of us. . . . Disgrace not yourselves by a surrender to those who will hang you up like dogs, but die, if you must, with arms in your hands, like warriors and braves of the Dakota."[248]

At the midpoint of the war the balance of power was unsettled but still in the Lower Camp's favor. Thus the captives and their story waited—as readers wait on the text—for what would happen next. Chapter 7 opens on Sunday, 7 September 1862, with everyone driven into tipis by Dakotas from the Lower Camp. Only one frame structure remained at Hazlewood—the church, with its steeple pointing the eyes of the Christian captives away from their earthly trials. While the Dakota Christians who had built the church gathered that Sabbath morning at the Renvilles' tent, the Lower Soldiers burned down their house of worship.

That same morning the leaves of another journal changed the course of the war. Lower Soldiers presented Mary with an English diary they had found on the prairie. The daybook, left behind by one of Sibley's soldiers, brought news that Sibley was on the march with a larger army than the Dakotas had imagined Minnesota could muster. It was no coincidence that on Monday, 8 September, the morning after the diary was discovered, the voice of a Lower Camp crier broke the predawn darkness with an edict to strike tents and prepare to march on to Red River, the regional gateway from Minnesota to Canada. The march northwest to Red River not only would put the insurgents closer to freedom and farther from the reach of U.S. troops but also would distance the Peace Coalition from authorities to whom the captives might be surrendered.

It also meant that John and Mary "were completely cut off from any hope of an escape" from captivity.[249] That was, in fact, why that same day Lorenzo Lawrence risked his life to help Jannette DeCamp begin her escape to Fort Ridgley. But Mary could not walk as far as the river, where John had earlier helped Lawrence hide canoes. The Renvilles considered staying at Hazlewood with Simon Anawaŋgmani, who had vowed to die on the mission grounds rather than capitulate to the warring faction. But John's fellow church elders "came on purpose to expostulate with us, saying that if we remained, we would not only cause our own death, but that of all our friends in the camp, for they would not leave us, but remain and die with us."[250]

As they had in the early days in the war, John and Mary ceded their desires to the greater good of their Hazlewood kin and agreed to go north: "The camp had nearly all gone, and soldiers were sent from several standpoints, watching our movements. We were not afraid. The storm had swept over us so bitterly that we were almost paralyzed, or careless as regards this present life. But of necessity we were obliged to take up our line of march. Mr. R. driving the cattle, while we drove the team, and carrying our darling Ella in our arms, clinging closer to her fearing she might be torn from us in any new freak of the enemy."[251]

Their march to Canada was interrupted unexpectedly when, at gunpoint, Sisseton chief Red Iron's soldiers forbade Little Crow from passing west through Sisseton territory. (Red Iron, the leader of an agricultural band, was the brother of Mazamani.) The train of two to three thousand Mdewankanton, Wahpekute, and Wahpeton Dakotas was forced to go into camp outside Red Iron Village. While Mary characteristically omitted political commentary, chapter 7 closes with a scene that illustrates the multiple competing objectives that internally frustrated the Dakota War. Peace-leaning Lower Dakota headmen like Wabaśa, Huśaśa, Wakute, and Little Crow's head soldier, Wakiŋyaŋtawa, took the opportunity to erect their tipis with the Upper Camp for the first time.[252] While Mary watched, fascinated, the Lower Soldiers' Lodge rode into the Upper Camp and began overturning the tipis of those who had defected, punishing their traitor kinsmen with soldier killing.

Within days Mary was acting as amanuensis for Lower chief Wabaśa as well, signaling that by 10 September 1862 he had formally joined the growing Peace Coalition. Yet Wabaśa understood that peace was not simply a matter of pitching his tipi on one side of the camp versus the other. He was caught between the hostility of his young men and the hostility of Sibley's troops. The dilemma had plagued members of the Lower Camp since the beginning of the war. "As Little Crow with his forces left the Lower Agency to ascend the river to Yellow Medicine," Gideon Pond learned from Peace Coalition members interned at Fort Snelling in the winter of 1862–63,

> all the unhostile Indians of the Lower Agency, with their relatives of mixed blood and such white persons as had sought shelter with them, moved along with him. They believed that lives of their friends and their own lives depended on this movement. If they had remained behind, the leader of the hostile party had declared that he would take vengeance on such evidence of alienation from him; and on the other side, the exasperated whites whose friends had already been butchered by the hundred, would avenge their wrongs on the first Indians they should overtake, which, in case they remained, would be themselves.[253]

Chapter 8 closes with the 10 September plea of Wabaśa and two other Lower chiefs to be allowed to return

> to our former homes, at the Lower Agency. . . .
>
>   . . . our fear is now, if we go back without your consent we shall meet your forces in hostility instead of meeting them as friends. Besides, the Lower Agency Bands will probably pursue us and try to destroy us all together.[254]

Time dragged on in the Upper Camp while everyone awaited Sibley's next move. John and Mary's days were filled with the ordinary tasks required to keep their family alive and comfortable. Everyday activities like gathering corn and potatoes, washing clothes, and paying a social call on fellow captives became surreal; John and his relative Solomon Two Star accompanied Mary on domestic excursions as armed guards. The Renvilles were now living much like their Dakota neighbors. Having left her beloved stove behind at Hazlewood, Mary wrote, "We are obliged to remain in a sitting posture in a tent when at work. At first we burned our face and hands by the blazing fire. Once these things would have troubled us, but are hardly worth noticing now."[255] At night in their tipi, after the children were asleep, Mary huddled under a blanket with paper, pen, and a lit candle, reading notes secretly passed from Sibley to the Peace Camp (on 12 and 13 September) and penning replies (dated 10, 12, 14, 15, and 18 September).

The Renvilles were not the only ones endangered by their espionage for the Peace Coalition. Chapter 9 closes with a poignant letter Mary scribed for Mazakutemani on 15 September. Sibley had just directed the peace leaders not to approach his column as Wabaśa requested but to wait for his troops to reach the Upper Camp. Mazakutemani warned Sibley,

> should your troops be delayed we may be destroyed. Little Crow's soldiers are constantly moving us. We would not move where they wished us to-day, and they came near fighting. . . .
>
>   . . . We are all captives because we have adopted the dress of the white man, and renounced the heathen worship, and will not join in

destroying our white friends. Please inform me what time you expect to reach here, and I will get our little band ready and hoist the white flag. Little Crow says the first command he shall give after your troops arrive, is to have every captive put to death.[256]

Sibley would not arrive to relieve the besieged Peace Camp for another eleven days.

Release (*A Thrilling Narrative*, chapters 11–13)

Sibley's army left Fort Ridgley 18–19 September, crossed the Minnesota River, and entered Indian Country. The last federal troops to attempt the river crossing had been decimated by Dakota warriors on 18 August, and for a full month the will of the Lower Soldiers' Lodge ruled on the Sioux Reservation.[257] Now a sixteen-hundred-man militia armed with rifled muskets and artillery reclaimed the land mile after mile in a steady march up the federal wagon road that ran the length of the reservation. Lower scouts kept the Dakota camps apprised of the army's slow but inexorable advance.

The balance of power was beginning to shift, and conditions in the Dakota camps grew more volatile as the system destabilized. The settler captives now had weeks to consider the Upper Camp's offers of asylum. Lower Dakotas also had spent the past four weeks deliberating on their options. Increasingly, they chose to defect to the Upper Camp, taking their captives with them. Other captives fled alone. By 22 September more captives were under the protection of the Peace Coalition than were held hostage in the Lower Camp.[258]

Even at this late date being a member of one camp versus the other was a matter of affiliation, not geography. The tent city of Dakotas encamped outside Red Iron Village extended over several miles. Like any camp, it was constantly shifting for sanitary purposes and to allow livestock to access fresh forage. By this natural process, over the ten days since Little Crow had been stopped by Red Iron's warriors, the entire Dakota camp had migrated several miles north of Red Iron Village. After this removal, defecting to the Upper Camp meant taking advantage of an ordinary relocation to re-erect one's tipi closer to the neighborhood staked out by the Peace Coalition. From the air, however—or to an advancing army—the camp looked like a monolithic tent city. On 22 September Mazakutemani warned Sibley that the Lower Camp planned to exploit that point:

> We have been betrayed about the white flag; have one ready, but our enemies say if we raise it they will hoist one too, and as soon as your troops arrive they will fire into them, making you believe we are all your enemies, and so get us killed in that way. You cannot realize the bitter hatred they manifest towards us for trying to aid the poor captives and not joining in the massacre. We are going to move our camp to-day out on the broad prairie, as you responded in your letter to Wabaxa. Sir, we are exceedingly anxious for the arrival of your troops. We still put our trust in Him who is able to save to the uttermost all that come unto him."[259]

The separation was more challenging than anyone expected, however, for reasons that belied the diversity of the Dakotas who were opposed to the war. The plan began in traditional Dakota fashion: "Deputies were appointed to confer with the different bands in order to determine the place to encamp" to await Sibley, Mary wrote. But

> It soon became apparent that the bands stood in fear of each other. The Yellow Medicine people [Gabriel Renville's and Mazamani's contingent] said if we joined with the lower bands we should excite Little Crow to a battle before the white troops arrived. In this dilemma the Hazlewood Republic, with whom we were, went a short distance from the lower bands that had declared themselves friendly. After a long consultation, the others joined [us]. . . . Before night the friendly Indians all united and all parties, (captive women not excepted,) went to digging entrenchments, or rather sinking pits inside of their tents, to defend themselves from the rebels in case of an attack, expecting one hourly.[260]

The death threats were not directed merely against Mary as a white woman and John as a mixed-blood but even against full-blood Dakotas

78

who opposed the war. One of them, George Crooks, told his granddaughter about his experiences as a six-year-old:

> Some forty or fifty families who were civilized and not willing to fight were forced from our homes by the Hostile Indians. We were taken to Wood Lake to be held captive with the white prisoners. After a few hours there we were taken on to Camp Lee [Release] near Montevideo there to wait with the white captives to be put to death by the warring Indians. . . . My mother at the risk of her own life, brought the white women captives and their children to her tipi and dug a hole under the tent and put the children in to hide them. Myself and the other children stayed in that deep hole to hide from the wrath of the Indians who were holding us prisoners. I personally heard the Indians who were guarding us say that they were going to kill all of us the following day, and then move on.[261]

That same day Sibley's army had crossed from the Lower into the Upper Reservation and was approaching a series of bridges that marked the approach to the Yellow Medicine River crossing. As he retreated west, Little Crow had the foresight to fire the bridges behind him to impede anyone who tried to follow and to erase yet another mark of civilization on the landscape. The bridges, only months old and constructed of fresh oak timbers, did not burn. But some were damaged, so Sibley had to send crews out ahead of his heavy artillery pieces, their limbers, and the ammunition wagons to inspect the bridges and to make any repairs necessary before his army crossed. However, Sibley was hobbled for lack of cavalry. Without a significant number of mounted men he could not send out advance parties to scout or to guard repair work done any farther ahead than his infantry could march to the rescue.

On 22 September 1862 Stephen Riggs wrote to his wife, "Today we had found two bridges on fire—somewhat injured. The one over three mile creek near our camp is, I fear, past repairing. These scamps mean to annoy us and to delay our progress."[262] So that evening Sibley settled his army into an entrenched, defensively secure camp at Lone Tree Lake, expecting another few days' march would bring him within striking distance of the Dakota camp above Red Iron Village.

Sibley had no idea that as his camp slept, a few miles northwest, in the valley of the Yellow Medicine River below the Upper Agency, the Lower Camp was embroiled in a general council to settle strategy for their last stand. Their predawn surprise attack at Birch Coulee had killed so many white soldiers at first fire that the Lower Soldiers' Lodge sought to replicate the strategy on Sibley's camp at Lone Tree Lake.[263] Besides striking fear into the federal army, a decisive victory for Little Crow might persuade the Sissetons to stop resisting and join the rebellion. But Peace Coalition members, secretly trying to create a scenario in which they could warn Sibley of the impending danger, supported a daytime ambush. Some Lower soldiers also favored the idea and a plan was settled to attack Sibley's column as it passed over the agency road the next morning.

For the first time, six weeks into the war, the peace-leaning leaders of the Lower bands who styled themselves in writing as "the three chiefs"—Wabaśa, Wakute, and Huśaśa—joined Akipa and Mazamani (signatories for the Yellow Medicine contingent) and Mazakutemani (for the Hazlewood Republic) in writing a joint letter of warning to Sibley. Their words resounded with the uncertainty of their futures, giving their letter the tone of a last will and testament:

> We, the undersigned, Paul, Akepa, Muzo-mo-my, and the three chiefs, are driven by the rebels to either go down with them to the battle to-day, or engage them in one here. We think it safest for the captives and our own families to go. The rebels say we must take the front of the battle; that we have not borne any burdens of the war, but they will drive us to it. We hope to get one side [*sic*], so as to join you or raise the flag of truce. If not able to do this we hope to return to our families and rescue them. We have tried every possible way of giving you correct information in regard to the war. . . .
>
> Our last prayer is that you will be able to relieve the suffering captives from war, death, and horrible captivity among the rebels, and should we fall in battle, we wish to be numbered among your friends and commend our families to your kind sympathies.[264]

To the end, they were determined to protect their families, even at the cost of sacrificing their own lives and casting their families upon the mercy of the conquering victor. History shows that their fears were not idle. Later that day, after what would become known as the Battle of Wood Lake, Stephen Riggs wrote to his wife, "Simon Washechoontanka was wounded and brought in to die. He says he was forced into the fight—that some of the Mdewankantons stood behind them with guns threatening to shoot them."[265] Mazamani, one of the authors of the letter, was fatally wounded in the same battle.[266]

Defeated at Lone Tree Lake by miscarried luck, most of the Lower soldiers returned to camp around sundown on 23 September and discovered that in their absence the Peace Coalition members who had fallen back from the battle had removed most of the hostages to Camp Lookout. Little Crow surrendered his remaining captives to Antoine Joseph Campbell (a mixed-blood captive who was Little Crow's cousin and wartime amanuensis) and, via Campbell, dictated one last letter to Sibley. Then he instructed Campbell to gather the white captives and take them to Sibley the next morning.[267] That night many Dakotas who had remained loyal to the Lower cause fled with Little Crow northwest toward Canada. Thousands of others who had nothing to do with the war but feared indiscriminate retribution at the hands of whites went away, too.

At Camp Lookout the morning of 24 September "the friendly bands held a council" over Little Crow's last request to deliver the captives to Sibley "and concluded it was not safe to send the captives with so small an escort as they would be able to raise" without endangering their families by leaving the camp with too few men in case the insurgents returned.[268] It was not a hypothetical fear. Little Crow, according to the Renvilles, sent back warriors that same day to overtake and kill the white hostages he believed would be en route to Sibley per his instructions. Instead of Little Crow's letter Campbell delivered one from the Peace Coalition written the morning of 24 September, pleading with Sibley, "Now, dear sir, please come right away without delay, or we may all fall victims, for fight we must soon. The enemy are not large in numbers, but you well know they are cruel savages. . . . All the Indians, with the exception of these, are friendly, and, were we prepared for defending ourselves, we should conquer; and if you don't hasten, our women and all the captives will suffer."[269] Sibley replied,

> My Friends:
>
> I call you so because I have reason to believe that you have had nothing to do with the cruel murders and massacres that have been committed upon the poor white people who had placed confidence in the friendship of the Sioux Indians. I repeat what I have already stated to you, that I have not come to make war upon those who are innocent, but upon the guilty. I have waited here one day . . . because I feared that if I advanced my troops before you could make your arrangements the war party would murder the prisoners.
>
> Now that I learn from Joseph Campbell that most of the captives are in safety in your camp I shall move on tomorrow, so that you may expect to see me very soon.[270]

While Sibley did not specify, it seems the Upper Camp reasonably expected that "tomorrow" meant the next day, 25 September. As historian William Watts Folwell pointed out, Sibley could have reached Camp Lookout on 23 September, the evening of the Battle of Wood Lake; it was only twelve miles from Sibley's camp at Lone Tree Lake.[271] But as military historian Stephen Osman observed, without cavalry Sibley was blindfolded and dependent on intelligence fed to him by the Peace Coalition.[272] Sibley's army was also short on rations and could not sustain a forced march. Further, they may have had to repair the damaged bridge just west of Lone Tree Lake before Sibley could safely move his heavy artillery over it: the cannons that had proved decisive at every engagement with the Dakotas in the war. So Camp Lookout waited for relief all day on 24 and 25 September. On the evening of 25 September the Peace Camp sent out scouts, who reported they had located Sibley camped at Red Iron Village, about five miles downriver.

While Sibley tarried, Camp Lookout was growing. After the exodus of the insurgents on the night of 23 September Camp Lookout consisted of about 100 tipis. By the time Sibley finally arrived on 26 September

Fig. 3. Camp Release, 1862. Courtesy of the Minnesota Historical Society. The only extant photo of Camp Release, possibly taken by Adrian J. Ebell, was taken sometime after Sibley's arrival on 26 September 1862. The tipis were the homes of Dakotas who had sheltered captives awaiting Sibley's arrival and of those who had surrendered or were captured. This photo shows about a quarter of the tipis in the camp.

there were an estimated 150 lodges. The mass exodus divided families, and numerous sources show kinship played a major role in determining who left, who stayed, and who returned. Some Dakotas who stayed, and others who voluntarily came back, may have taken comfort in Sibley's 24 September reassurance that those who "have had nothing to do with the cruel murders and massacres that have been committed upon the poor white people" would be counted as "Friends." As understood by the Dakotas who surrendered, Sibley communicated, in Wabaṡa's words, "Why are you running away from the whites? I do not wish to do you any harm. You know that I am like a father to you, and the Great Spirit has directed me to settle this matter in a friendly manner. Do not be afraid. I will not harm you. Remain in the camp where you are until I come up."[273]

When Sibley finally arrived at Camp Lookout the afternoon of 26

September he found from seven hundred to one thousand people waiting for him.[274] Explicitly following his instructions, the Peace Coalition leadership had worked for weeks to secure the custody of almost all the settler captives, had repeatedly defied the insurgents, had created a separate camp, and had waited for Sibley to reach them.[275] Moreover, they endangered their own and their families' lives by carrying out the espionage that fed Sibley the intelligence he badly needed. Sibley took fifty-six hours to march twelve miles to the relief of the Peace Coalition, subsisted his troops on the products of Dakota farm fields, accepted the safe deliverance of the white and mixed-blood captives they had sheltered, placed everyone who voluntarily surrendered under armed guard, and promptly commemorated his "victory" by redubbing the place "Camp Release."[276]

PART III: AFTERWORDS

Leaves from a Journal

On Christmas Day 1862 readers of the *Berlin (WI) City Courant* found a brand-new serial on the first page of that newspaper, bannered "The Indian Captives: Leaves from a Journal." The first installment carried no introduction beyond a single sentence: "Messrs. Editors: So much has been said about the Indian War that it may not be uninteresting to glean a few leaves from the Journal of one who was a captive during the late trouble."[277] Readers accustomed to the serial fiction that ran on the front page had no reason to guess the story was not fiction, as the first installment's rather melodramatic opening suggested: "This little book, in the providence of God, may fall into other hands, for we are in jeopardy every moment."[278] But a very short item headed "Life among the Indians" in the editorial column on page three informed readers, "On our first page this week, will be found the commencement of a Journal by an intelligent lady who was two months a captive among the Indians during the past season. It will doubtless be full of painful interest to most of our readers."[279] With no further ado, and sans any authorial attribution beyond the anonymous "intelligent lady," the serial debuted that would be reprinted ten months later as *A Thrilling Narrative of Indian Captivity*.

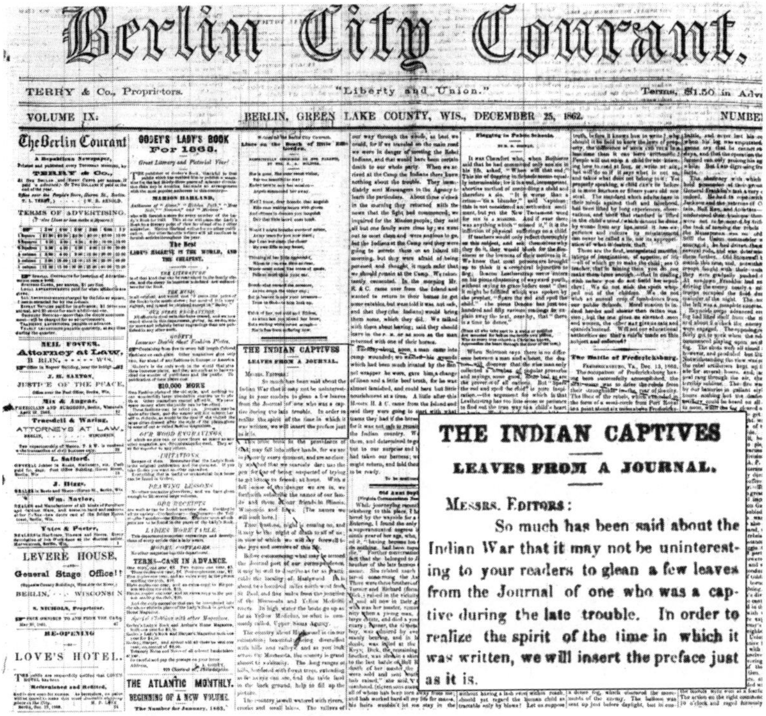

Fig. 4. *Berlin City Courant*, front page, 25 December 1862.

It is not clear that the citizens of Berlin understood that the author lived among them. The surrounding area was the home of several thousand people. At the time the first installment appeared the Renvilles had lived there only a few weeks. Homeless in the wake of the war, John and Mary did not have many options. Mary's parents were dead; there was no childhood home to return to. Her brothers James and Loren and her sister Adelia, with their families, were living in northern Iowa, too close to the frontier for Mary's comfort. John and Mary first went to Beloit, Wisconsin. Discovering their host had relocated, they moved on to Berlin, Wisconsin. Mary's brother Russell Butler lived there, and the Renvilles rented a small house nearby.

Members of John's family, as Dakotas, were given almost no choice about where to live. Although before the war John's brothers Antoine and Michael, like his cousin Gabriel, had been living on homesteads off the reservation, their homes were destroyed in the war. Moreover, their wartime loyalties made them targets for the Dakota insurgents said to be prowling the state's western borders; their old homes on the upper Minnesota River were too exposed. But unlike their settler neighbors who had come to Minnesota from (or via) the eastern United States and could return there, the Renville men were married to Dakota women. Their families had been in Minnesota for generations. There was nowhere else to go; they *were* home. But that home was now occupied as a federal military district where martial law prevailed. Perhaps most significantly, it had become a place where bicultural people like the Renvilles were no longer welcomed as settlers. In the wake of the war they were branded by their physiognomy and language as hated *"Injins,"* Agent Galbraith wrote, quoting and condemning the sentiment prevailing in Minnesota. Even acculturated Dakotas, Galbraith informed his superiors, were unjustly "subjected to all kinds of indignities, even to threats to take their lives."[280]

The earliest known vow to annihilate Dakotas was hatched by soldiers besieged at Fort Ridgley five days into the war.[281] It surfaced again as a plot to shell the camp of surrendered Dakotas while they were still at Camp Release.[282] Later that fall, at Henderson, a mob attacked the convoy of Dakota women, children, and Peace Coalition leaders en route to Fort Snelling, killing a Dakota baby. In a premeditated attack on the convoy of shackled prisoners en route to South Bend, New Ulm citizens killed two Dakota men.[283] At South Bend and Mankato organized attempts were made to storm the prison and lynch the Dakota prisoners.[284] In the volatile atmosphere fueled by land lust and race hatred, anti-Dakota sentiments ran wild with war atrocity stories, some real and many more imagined. By November 1862 most Minnesotans were in no mood to make distinctions among Indians. John's family was given no choice. They were marched under armed guard from the Lower Sioux Agency over the Henderson–Fort Ridgley Road, then up the northern bank of the Minnesota River to their assigned home, an internment camp hastily erected on the river flats below Fort Snelling.[285]

Being mixed-blood people and also being among the fifty Dakota men judged to be above suspicion of participation in hostilities during the war,

John's relatives were privileged among the interned detainees. One of John's sisters was paroled from the camp to live with her married sister at Mendota. John and Mary successfully interceded from outside the camp to liberate four children and to help John's brothers.[286] Because his brothers still retained unredeemed "half-breed scrip," they had financial options their full-Dakota relatives (who had been deprived of their annuities, their farms, and the federal programs that supported their work) did not have.[287]

John Renville, however, even with limited options, was comparatively blessed. It was not because he was a church elder studying for the ministry or because he was a respected schoolteacher and community leader or even because he spoke English. John was privileged because he was married to a white woman. At Camp Release, even though Mary was enumerated with John on the mixed-blood section of the roster of freed captives, they were afforded the privileges of white ones.[288] Like other captives, John and Mary must have been questioned about anything they had seen or heard that might be used in court as evidence against the Dakotas who surrendered. But having spent the entire war in the Upper Camp, John and Mary witnessed no battles or atrocities and could have offered little information beyond, perhaps, transcriptions of the council speeches Heard is said to have obtained from them. For the same reason neither John nor Mary gave testimony in any of the cases brought before the military tribunal.

John, Mary, and Ella probably left Camp Release by the end of the first week of October 1862 with the majority of the settler captives. The Renvilles stopped in St. Anthony to reclaim their adopted daughter, Belle, who was attending school there and had escaped the war. Then they went to the Office of the Superintendent of Indian Affairs in St. Paul and called at the home of Senator Henry Rice, seeking back pay the government owed them as schoolteachers. They also visited (and possibly lived with) John's sister at Mendota before heading east to Wisconsin in November 1862.

The next five months, spent living in Berlin, are chronicled in a series of eight letters that John and Mary wrote to Stephen Riggs, reproduced

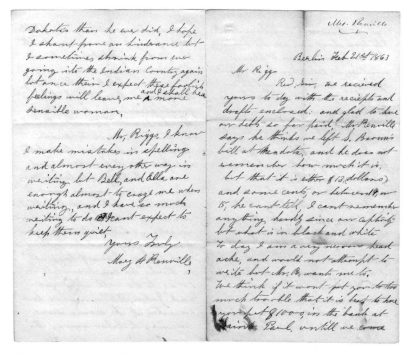

Fig. 5. Mary Butler Renville holograph letter, 21 February 1863. Stephen R. Riggs Papers, Minnesota Historical Society.

in appendix B. The letters are remarkable for the glimpse they offer into the realities of postcaptivity recovery (Mary exhibited what would probably be recognized today as post-traumatic stress disorder) and for the remarkable absence of the idea of "home" as a lost *place*. Instead, both Mary and John mourned the loss of, and sought to be reunited with, the *people* they loved, as a mark of returning home.

The letters also offer insight into the mindsets of the authors at the time they composed the original serial, "The Indian Captives: Leaves from a Journal." In fact, these letters provide a key to one of the remarkable features of the text: that in a day when most people were indiscriminately calling for the extermination or removal of Indigenous people from Minnesota, including the members of the Peace Coalition, a white woman and

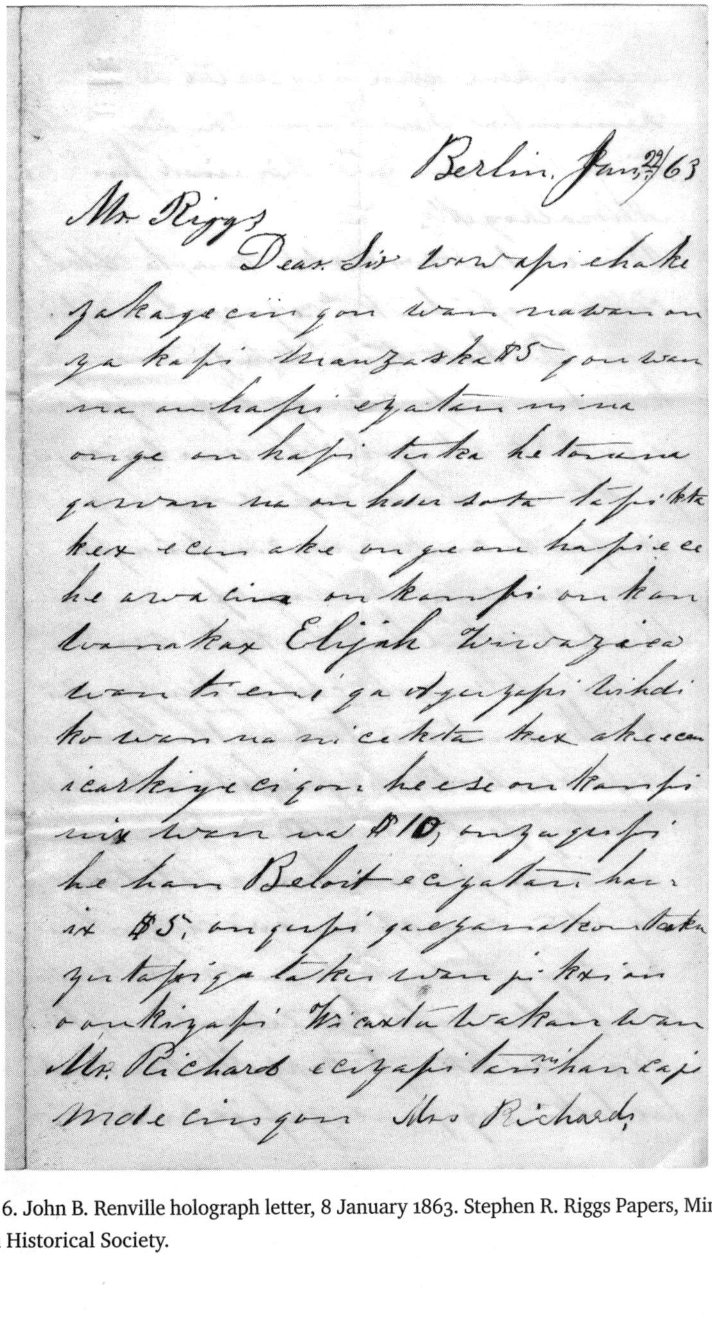

Fig. 6. John B. Renville holograph letter, 8 January 1863. Stephen R. Riggs Papers, Minnesota Historical Society.

her Dakota husband called for "Justice, Morality and Truth" to prevail over race hatred.[289] In the midst of their own trauma and recovery John and Mary understood that public sentiment was shaped by the received story. Their response was to compose and to publicly disseminate the earliest extended narrative of the Dakota War of 1862: the behind-the-scenes story of the Dakota resistance movement that thwarted the efforts of the insurgents. John and Mary together accomplished something that John could not do alone. They used Mary's platform as an "intelligent lady"—pointedly, a white one—to humanize the Dakotas interned at Fort Snelling by telling the Peace Coalition story, first in the *Berlin City Courant* and later in a book for a wider audience.

Was it simply a lapse in editorial oversight or a typesetter's error that led to the first twelve installments appearing in the Berlin newspaper with no byline? The "intelligent lady," who read the paper in which her work appeared, apparently did not call the slip to the editor's attention and ask for credit. Perhaps she and John understood just how slippery their marriage made Mary's grip on the rungs of the racial ladder. Early in the newspaper serial, on 13 January 1863, Mary missed her editor's deadline. Instead of the third installment a short notice appeared in the Local Matters column on page two of the *Courant*, explaining, "The third chapter of the Narrative we are publishing did not reach us until too late for this issue." It was printed the next week, and an installment ran every week thereafter without fail through chapter 12. Again, on 2 April 1863, the expected installment, the last one, did not appear. Readers searched in vain for an explanatory note from the editor. Instead the Local Matters column featured this morsel of editorial spite: "'Lo! The poor Indian,' and several of his dusky friends, may be seen daily traversing the streets of this city. None of them look very savage, or offer menace or insult to citizens, still there are many who, since the revolting butcheries in Minnesota last year, the repetition of which are now seriously threatened, look with suspicion on all red skins, and feel uneasy in the presence of even those who profess the greatest friendship."

The next week, 9 April 1863, the thirteenth and final installment appeared. As readers expected, it finished an ethnographic discussion of warfare begun in chapter 12 and described Sibley's arrival at Camp Release.

Then the text took an unexpected turn. In the first twelve installments the intelligent lady's defense of the "friendly" Dakotas generally took the straightforward approach of storytelling. But the last chapter closed with an extended editorial pleading for the rights of "those who delivered themselves up as prisoners of war, the most of whom are not as guilty in crime [as the insurgents; yet they, too], are condemned. The friends even that protected the suffering ones, are doomed to an exile almost as cruel as that which the captives suffered." The authors indicted the abuses of government and traders and closed with an appeal: "May God guide the people of Minnesota, who have suffered deeply, to act wisely in the present instance, and not drive even the friendly Indians to homeless desperation by driving or sending them among the warlike tribes, to dwell upon their wrongs and talk over the injuries inflicted upon them by those they supposed their friends, until the warriors will not heed the counsel of the older ones, and rise in one mass, with all the tribes, and commence a war more terrible than has yet been recorded in history."[290]

"Homeless desperation" was not hyperbole. As Gabriel Renville wrote of that bitter, trying winter in the internment camp at Fort Snelling, "Amid all this sickness, suffering, and misery we could not help thinking of the future which seemed to us to be most gloomy indeed. With no lands, no homes, no means of support, the outlook was most disheartening. 'How can we get lands and homes again?' was a question which troubled many thinking people, and it was a difficult question to answer."[291]

It was a difficult question for John and Mary Renville, too. Was the editorial suggesting that the "red skins" were not welcome in Berlin directed at John and their three "dusky" daughters? We do not know. But the last installment did not bear the name of its hitherto anonymous author. Instead, the "intelligent lady" came out publicly as "J. B. AND M. A. RENVILLE." Within weeks they left Berlin and returned to Minnesota, at about the same time that the Peace Coalition members, their families, and the families of the imprisoned Dakota men were deported from the state. If Mary had not been a white woman, John, his wife, and their children would have been with them: interned at Fort Snelling and exiled to Crow Creek, Dakota Territory.[292]

"What is be coming of Minnesota?"
—Mary Renville to Stephen Riggs, 10 March 1866

In the spring of 1863, probably using their claims for back pay and war losses as credit, John and Mary purchased a house in St. Anthony, Minnesota, where there was a strong evangelical community and where Stephen Riggs had temporarily resettled his family. There they continued rebuilding their lives one child at a time. Besides Ella, Belle, and Mary Martin, John and Mary took four other Dakota children from the internment camp at Fort Snelling into their family, where the children received a bilingual education while their fathers went out onto the Coteau as scouts.[293]

That summer Mary wrote an article on the war for a missionary paper and read over her collection of clippings of "The Indian Captives: Leaves from a Journal," correcting some typesetting errors, expanding identities for clarity, and cutting a few extraneous sentences.[294] Mary appended an "Addenda" to the *Courant* story and submitted the manuscript to the local printer, the Atlas Company's Book and Job Printing Company, publisher of Minneapolis's only weekly newspaper, the Republican *Minneapolis State Atlas*.[295] Given Mary's family's involvement in the Underground Railroad, it is probably no coincidence that John and Mary chose to patronize the newspaper branded a "bitter abolitionist sheet." Its owner-editor, William S. King, was "a driving, go-a-head, whole-souled business fellow" who advertised for "all kinds of plain and fancy job work in fine style and at as low prices as the same can be had at any office west of New York City."[296] To increase the circulation of his newspaper and his share of the local printing business, King had recently installed a Taylor's Cylinder Press, capable of churning out twelve hundred pages per hour, a rate almost double the platen press competition.[297] *A Thrilling Narrative* was one of the first books King printed on his new machine. In early August 1863, after the booklet's pages were printed and trimmed but apparently before all the copies were bound, the Cunninghams, on their way out to Crow Creek as missionary teachers, belatedly dropped off a manuscript Mary had requested: the story of their 1862 escape in the missionary party. Mary turned over their manuscript to Atlas, which printed and trimmed the story separately, then bound it as unnumbered pages at the back of *A Thrilling Narrative.*[298]

The Renvilles were still living in St. Anthony in November 1864 when John began his career as an itinerant evangelist to Dakotas scattered in the 1862–63 exile. Riggs explained the context of John's postwar work with the members of the Peace Coalition who had been retained as federal scouts:

> When, a year ago, the Indian Camp then at Fort Snelling, was removed to Fort Thompson [Crow Creek] on the Missouri, a portion, including some Half breeds and a few Dakota men who had been loyal during the previous outbreak, were retained with their families and form what is called the Scouts Camp now near the head of the Coteau des Prairies. There are in this camp three Elders of the Hazlewood Church. . . . We count forty-two in regular standing as church members. . . . Within the winter past they have had no instruction but a brief visit from J. P. Williamson—other than religious exercises conducted by themselves. . . . In some respects this portion of the Dakota people have made the most progress in knowledge and ability to sustain among themselves the interests of education and religion. This duty has been pressed upon them, and it is hoped that they will be able to come up to the necessities of the case. . . . [A]t the present time there are more than five times the number of professors of religion and probably five times the number of readers than there were in August 1862. This has created a great demand for books which we have hardly been able to supply. My own work since last December has been preparing a revised edition of the New Testament for the press. This is nearly completed. Besides this Precept Upon Precept has been translated by John B. Renville and is now in press in Boston.[299]

John spent several months on the Coteau at the end of 1864 and also at the end of 1865. Mary's letters to Riggs during this period show that John regularly wrote to her about family matters and about conditions on the Coteau. John also corresponded with Riggs in Dakota and, less frequently, with Thomas S. Williamson in English. Mary continued to educate the children in their family and, for periods, also may have taught at a district school in St. Anthony. The family's support seems to have been Mary's teacher's salary, a stipend from the ABCFM to John for his missionary work, small ABCFM stipends for each of the Dakota children in their family, and a fraction of Mazakutemani's salary that he forwarded to John and Mary for boarding his daughter Nona. With this income, Mary hired out some of the heavy work during John's absences, like paying Riggs's sons to chop firewood for their stoves. John's flock on the Coteau, despite impoverished conditions, faithfully supplied the family with moccasins.

In the wake of the war the Dakota missionaries began ceding to the evidence before them: Dakota men were better able to minister to Dakota people than the missionaries were. Reacting to successes of Dakota lay preachers in the prisons at Mankato and Davenport and to John Renville's reception in the scout camps, retired missionary Gideon Pond mused to Riggs:

Indians know better how to <u>use</u> their own language than any of us ever did or ever shall, only because they know, as we never can know, <u>what an Indian is</u>. If you can only make use of an Indian's tongue to convey the ideas which you may convey to his head, the Lord having tuned his heart, then you'll have a tongue that will make many ears tingle. . . . There is something in the constitution of the Ind. mind & heart that forbids the near approach of a white man. . . . A white man does not know an Indian because he is not an Ind. He may dress like him & eat with him & dance with him, but really he still doesn't <u>know</u> him. What we have done, we have done from the outside. We never got in where they are. There is a shell that covers them from <u>us</u> but does not cover them from one another. . . . If an Ind. can be found who is willing & <u>wishes</u> to be the "medium," I think if you use him, you will find access to the masses, with such results as you've never dreamed of.[300]

John was willing and wished to be such a "medium." In early May 1865 the Dakota Presbytery, meeting at Mankato, Minnesota, formalized John's relationship with his Dakota flock by licensing him to preach, the first step toward ordination.[301] "The occasion had a dramatic interest about it," Stephen Riggs wrote. "For while we the Presbytery were licensing one man, who was part Dakota, to preach the gospel of peace and good will to his fellow men, the people of Mankato were, in plain view of the church, summarily trying and executing another part Dakota for participation in the murder of a white family."[302] In a reprise of their frustrated attempts to lynch the Dakota prisoners in Mankato in 1862, a mob broke into the county jail and hung John Campbell (John Renville's in-law via his sisters' marriages) from a tree in the courthouse yard. Next, taken with the idea that missionary Thomas S. Williamson, engaged nearby in the licensure of a Native pastor, had "brought the Indians with him from Dakota" to their fair city, the mob headed up the street to the Presbyterian Church. Williamson, forewarned, fled rather than face the manic crowd.[303]

This was the atmosphere in Minnesota a full two years after Dakota and Hochunk people were banished from the state. A year later, with John now fully ordained as a minister of the Gospel, Mary proudly made a tongue-in-cheek comment to Riggs about an honor John had been given in church the past Sunday: "Mr. Smith [the pastor] made Mr. Renville walk up in to the pulpit with him and sit through all the sermon don't you suppose some of the people fainted. What is be coming [sic] of Minnesota."[304]

The decade after the war was an unsettled period for the Renvilles because it was an unsettled period for the Dakotas. In the spring of 1863 Governor Ramsey fulfilled his vow to exterminate or otherwise remove the Dakotas from Minnesota. Just before the Fort Snelling internees were removed to Crow Creek and the scouts banished to the Coteau, the men imprisoned at Mankato were moved by steamboat to a prison at Camp McClellan, near Davenport, Iowa. In 1866 the remaining Dakota prisoners (some had been paroled earlier) were freed and sent to the new Sioux Reservation at Santee, Nebraska, where they were reunited with the members of their families who had survived the hellish intervening years at Crow Creek.[305]

In the summer of 1866 John was among thirty-five Dakotas recognized as a "Friendly Indian" for having assisted the federal side in the Dakota

War.[306] John and Mary sold their house in St. Anthony for $600 and moved west to Beaver Creek, Renville County, where they were living by November 1866, apparently on the same claim Mary had purchased in 1861. Although their letters show that conditions in rural Minnesota made it more difficult for Mary to support the children during John's absences, their homestead created a western home base for his itinerant pastorate to Dakota congregations from 1866 to 1870.

The Peace Coalition, functionally reinvented as scouts, did not have it easy on the Coteau despite their loyalty in 1862 and meager government handouts. The scouts' job was to defend forts in Dakota Territory, and the Minnesota frontier as well, from attacks by Dakotas still hostile to federal authority. The position required them to kill fellow Dakotas if necessary, even relatives. If a scout refused, he would be executed as a hostile and his family left to fend for themselves, without support.[307]

The factions among the pro-government Dakotas evidenced before the war and temporarily suppressed during it re-emerged in the late 1860s. The Christian scouts were concentrated in a few scout camps, while many scouts remained religious traditionalists. The difference between the two groups was highlighted in 1867 when, despite John's hope to attend a council in Washington DC to negotiate the future boundaries of Sisseton and Wahpeton land on the Coteau, he and other Christians were passed over.[308] When the treaty delegation returned, the Christians learned that the president had made Gabriel Renville the chief of the new reservation. Gabriel envisioned a Dakota future populated by occupationally "civilized" yet religiously traditional Dakotas like himself and his friends, who believed being Dakota was about maintaining right relationships with people and other spiritual beings in the world, not about mode of subsistence.

In contrast, Dakota Christians like John believed that mere conversion to agriculture was dangerously superficial. As Mary wrote in *A Thrilling Narrative*, let those who doubt the necessity of Christian conversion "spend six long weeks in captivity . . . and by the aid of the friendly bands, get to the mission Indians, they will find a great difference between a civilized and Christian Indian, and one that merely adopts the white man's costume

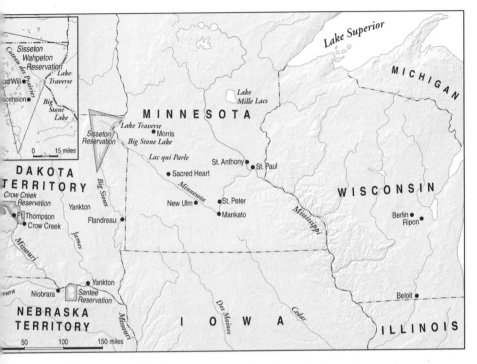

Map 4. Minnesota and Dakota, 1871. Courtesy Pond Dakota Heritage Society.

and firmly adheres to his own idolatrous religion."[309] Paraphrasing one of John's sermons, the editor of *Iapi Oaye* wrote:

> Much progress might be made in such things [agriculture and "domestication"], and the people remain Indians still. Their old Indian thoughts remain unchanged. . . . Indeed according to Mr. Renville's experience and observation, an Indian needed a new heart just as much as a white man. And nothing could give that but the Holy Spirit through the Gospel of Jesus Christ. And no civilization, in his mind, was worth much, if it did not make a new man of Indians. Therefore he concluded that the only effective way to *civilize Indians* was to lead them to Jesus. To which all of us say, *Amen*.[310]

The differences between the Christian and non-Christian farmers were exacerbated in 1871, when the U.S. government adopted its Peace Policy

97

that assigned oversight of reservations to religious denominations. Due to the Presbyterian missionaries' decades of work among the Sissetons and Wahpetons, that reservation was assigned to the Presbyterian Church, pitting the secular tribal government headed by Gabriel Renville against early agents who were sympathetic to the church. John, a Christian Renville, was in the middle of the fray.

"Are not this people my people and has not God called me to be one of
their Shepherds[?]" —John B. Renville to the ABCFM, 10 August 1869

A decade after she first saw the new reservation on the Coteau, Mary Renville described her first extended encounter since the Dakota War with the people among whom she would spend the rest of her life. At Sisseton, as the Lake Traverse Reservation was familiarly known, the Renvilles found that their friends and neighbors from Minnesota, through no fault of their own and despite the substantial aid they had given the federal government during the war, had fallen on hard times compared to their lives in the brick and clapboard homes of Hazlewood, with their plastered walls, bread ovens, pantry shelves, and kitchen gardens. "In the summer of 1869 I accompanied Mr. Renville in his preaching to the Sisseton Reservation," Mary wrote.

Ascension was our next stopping place. Here were friends glad to see us, and eager to hear the preached word, as day after day they assembled for that purpose. None sought excuse for staying away. Poor in spirit as well as in temporal things, they, with one accord, gathered for prayer and praise. They were almost entirely without horses, but having a few old horses, and two broken plows, they were trying to till the soil. . . . The Indians were living mostly on roots. Government had hardly got to work on the Reservation. The children were crying for food. Certainly we must not eat before them. We tried to eat in our wagon, but the children flocked around us. Giving Madeline and Ella something to put in their pockets, with the caution not to let the poor children see them eat, we waited for our opportunity to divide with the sick. That was better than to enjoy it ourselves.[311]

Shortly after their return to Minnesota from their two-month sojourn at Sisseton, John told Selah B. Treat of the ABCFM that they had no illusions about what life on the reservation would be like. But he and Mary were determined to return permanently:

We often meet with discouragements indeed with very many trying to human nature but we do not have to depend on human aid or we should faint by the way. . . . I intend Providence permitting to go to my people again soon and in fact see a great necessity of my living constantly among them and my wife's health is so far recovered as to make her very anxious to move too this fall but Sir we can't do this unless we sell our place but no purchaser stands ready and soon the season will be too late. You can perhaps imagine the danger to my health and even life in crossing our Prairies [to Sisseton] in the severe Minnesota winters, and Mrs. Renville still being subject to very dangerous attacks I cannot feel safe to leave home for any great length of time.[312]

John then urged the ABCFM to see to the Dakotas' material wants for food and for buildings to accommodate churches and schools, closing with the rhetorical question "I speak with great boldness for are not this people my people and has not God called me to be one of their Shepherds[?]"[313] Mary's brother Russell Butler purchased their farm in Renville County, moving his family from Berlin, Wisconsin, to Beaver Creek, Minnesota.[314] But Mary suffered a relapse in her physical health, so John moved to Ascension, on the Lake Traverse Reservation, by himself in 1870. He wrote,

for this people I came up here last spring after securing board for my wife and daughter at St. Peter where Mrs. Renville, (who has been very much out of health for 3 years past) could be under good medical treatment Bad roads and sickness prevented me from getting here till the Indians had got through with most of their planting but having a variety of early seeds I put them into the ground with strong faith that the Lord would send the increase with what help I could hire I cut split and fenced ten acres, plowed and planted seven, which I broke the year before myself in June Here I may mention that in the four weeks I preached 27 times besides breaking my land. Tired as I was, the more so not being used to oxen or breaking new land Government officers seemed anxious and said I ought to set an example to the Indians of Industry and encouraged me in so doing. I was fearful I should not make my family comfortable for the winter but succeeded in putting up a comfortable log house 20 x 18 drawing most of the needed lumber 1.5 miles.[315]

Mary recovered sufficiently that she and Ella moved to Sisseton in 1871. A pair of messages they received at Ascension captured the ambiguities still attached to John and Mary's marriage. That spring a letter arrived from E. S. Parker, commissioner of Indian affairs, as John wrote,

cutting me off from all Treaty stipulations. . . . The ground for my being cut off is that I am an American Citizen and as such have availed myself of the preemption act At the present time I am at the mercy of the Indians were they so disposed they could drive me off the Reserve at any time, I don't even anticipate they will. . . . I don't say it is wrong my being cut off but the Treaty makes no such provision as I can see Now I am anxious to learn how and what I am to do how can I stand my ground cut off from the Dakotah tribes entirely.[316]

John also learned that, as a Dakota, he was cut off from being made a missionary of the ABCFM. As Treat explained,

Before receiving your letter I did not know that you were a citizen of the U.S. & what effect of this will be on your _tribal_ rights, I am not accurately informed. It seems not improbable that Comr. Parker is right. . . . When you speak of becoming a member of the Am. Board I presume you mean, "Become a missy of the Am. Board," like Mr. Riggs. We do not appoint any _missionaries_ from the people among whom they labor. Persons in Turkey India, &c. who preach, are made pastors, &c,

Fig. 7. Ripon College, ca. 1880. Ripon College Archives, Ripon, Wisconsin.

are never made Missionaries by us; but they work <u>in connection with</u> <u>the missionaries,</u> on such terms as shall be agreed upon.[317]

The difference between a missionary and a pastor in terms agreed upon was substantial. In 1867 the ABCFM paid Thomas S. Williamson $700 and Riggs $800 annually as missionaries, but they paid John B. Renville only $300 as a pastor. As a mixed-blood person John may have felt, in terms of the classic scholarly analysis, "at home in both worlds." But according to the gatekeepers in both realms, he was fully welcome in neither. At this juncture, as at many others, John and Mary could have given up but did not. They adapted their expectations and chose to walk the path open to them: John remained a pastor, supported by his devoted but impoverished congregation at Ascension. Mary accepted a position as a government schoolteacher there.

Their daughter, Ella, was sixteen in the autumn of 1877 when she boarded the train at the nearest station, Morris, Minnesota, and headed east on her way to her first year of school in Ripon, Wisconsin.[318] John and Mary escorted her, stopping in St. Paul for the annual meeting of their synod. There they encountered Mrs. Mary E. D. Ainslie, a retired missionary to the Cherokees, who was a correspondent for Presbyterian publications. A few months later the *Missionary Herald at Home and Abroad* published an open letter from Ainslie to "Aunt Jenny" under the headline "The Dakota Mission—A Plea for Help."[319] The article gives a fascinating glimpse into the Renvilles' life at Ascension as related by Mary herself.[320]

Dear Aunt Jenny,

. . . [Y]ou wish me to tell you something of the Dakota Indian Mission. . . . [T]heir Indian churches are as poor as the pastors, most of them live as did Paul,—working with their own hands. That of course leaves them far less time for preaching than they should have. One of them, Rev. John B. Renville, has a white wife. I met her last fall, at St. Paul, and from her I learned things that you don't read in the *Herald*. She had with her a daughter, sixteen years old, on her way to Wisconsin, to enter school. Inquiring of Mrs. Renville if Ella was her only child, she replied, "Yes, and No. Since my marriage to Mr. Renville I have brought up and educated sixteen Dakota children. So you may say I have others beside my daughter."[321]

Remembering that you good Eastern people often send boxes of clothing to our home missionaries, I asked, "Is there not some way in which we can aid you in your work?" thinking, of course, that she would understand that I meant by means of a box of clothing. How do you think the woman took me? She said, "Yes; the wild Dakotas beyond us are asking for preaching. We have an Indian minister ready to go to them. We have organized Dakota Women's Mission Societies at all the stations, and are trying to earn money, by sewing and the sale of bead-work, to send a preacher far out on the plains. The work sells well, but we are troubled for material. If any one would send us bits of velvet, upholsterers' rep, and bright scraps of delaine and silk, it would help us much. Last year these Dakota women raised in this way $80 for mission work." "Indian women?" "Yes, converted Indian women, not so very long out of heathenism and blankets."

"Is there nothing else you need?" I asked, still thinking of the box. "Yes. I am much among the sick. When an Indian is converted he throws his medicine-man or conjurer overboard, and comes to the missionary for care and medicine. The most useful thing ever sent me was a bundle of soft linen and bandages—fourteen pounds of them. I laughed at the amount, but in time I used them all among the sick."

"Do you need nothing for yourself?" I said at last, finding that she had no thought save for the work among her husband's people. Then she opened her heart to me, and told me that, while it was all right that these Indian churches should be taught to maintain their pastors, and that while she and her husband tried to be very patient in the teaching of the lesson, yet their inadequate support so hampered them that she felt obliged to turn aside from the true mission work, which she saw lying all about her and which she longed to do, to teach a government school for means to piece out their living, and to educate their one child. It has long been her wish to be adopted by the Woman's Board, that set free by the support which they give their protégé's, from this continually recurring question, "How shall we live?" she may give her time and strength entirely to direct mission work. Application has once been made on her behalf to the Woman's Board of the Northwest. The reply is, "We do not adopt married ladies, as they cannot give all their time to the work." Well, perhaps that is all right, and yet it might be in order to ask just how many single ladies have gone into this work, and after a few years' labor have gone out of it, while she is abiding in it still?

We may not judge rightly, but we here think that her marriage to Mr. Renville binds her to the work, as no single lady can be bound to it. Is the steady, ceaseless work of all the past eighteen years or more to be ignored because she is married to an Indian pastor, and goes into this work with him, heart and hand, as a single lady cannot go? I trow not.[322]

"Be in haste to be at home with Jesus." —Mary Renville, October 1881

The effects of Ainslie's appeal were more far-reaching than anyone guessed. The material gains were obvious. The *Herald* received eighty-five offers of textiles and bandages for the Sisseton Reservation.[323] Donors also pledged sufficient financial support to allow Mary to quit her government teaching job and join John in more active ministry there. But a devastating loss was shrouded inside a request Ainslie made near the end of her letter: "[Ella's] parents wish to fit her for usefulness among her people; but, unaided, they cannot support themselves and send her into the States to school. Is there not some home of wealth from which a beloved daughter has gone to the higher school of heaven, Jesus and the angels being now her teachers, that would receive to its tender care this daughter of the prairies, giving her the advantages that shall qualify her to do hereafter a good work for her people?"[324]

Offers to fund Ella's education came in from Massachusetts, New York, and California. Mary and John chose to continue sending Ella to the college preparatory school in Ripon, Wisconsin, where she boarded, coming home on summer breaks. But in her fourth year at school John and Mary received a frightening "letter brought by the iron lightning," a telegram that read, "Your daughter is sick. Come get her."[325] John and Mary hurried east to bring Ella home to Ascension. Like too many other Dakota children sent out from their homes for education in the States, at school Ella contracted a fatal disease, probably tuberculosis. At Ascension, in the white clapboard house on the hill above the church, Ella lingered for eighteen months as the disease waxed and waned. Finally, on Valentine's Day 1882, Ella was "invited by the call of the sacred."[326] She was almost twenty-two years old.

In her obituary, John wrote,

"He has come for me," Ella said.

"Who has come, my child?" I asked.

"Jesus has come for me. Goodbye, Papa. Goodbye."[327]

Mary was out of the room and Ella spoke to her father in Dakota in words reminiscent of a story that John, blending Dakota storytelling with Christian imagery from the Twenty-Third Psalm, often told grieving parents. Tragically, the death rate among Dakota children was so high that Ella probably had heard the story many times: "There was a shepherd who wanted to take his sheep over the river. But the mother sheep was unwilling. But the good shepherd took up two lambs in his arms and carried them over the stream. When the mother saw this, she went over, and on the other side he took them into green grass and by the side of good water. So Jesus would take us—although sometimes unwilling—there he will gather us all into Life."[328] Ella's faith led her to believe the Good Shepherd would carry her over the river of death. Her last earthly act was to assure her parents that Jesus had kept his word. As her mother had written just a few months before, "May we all, like them, be ready when the summons comes, and be in haste to be at home with Jesus."[329]

Ella, who had not married, was buried in a white gown, in a casket crafted by her parents' Dakota friends, blanketed with white flowers. After her death her parents found she had marked a song for her funeral in her hymnbook; friends gathered at Ascension sang Ella's conviction that Jesus was "Mine by Choice." After the service friends placed her casket on a wagon and walked with Mary and John up the steep road to the hilltop cemetery.[330]

Ella's death produced one of Mary's most affecting compositions, "Trying to Overcome."[331] In it Mary struggled with the human realities of losing a beloved only child, her heart's "Darling," and with spiritual truths she held equally dear about God's sovereignty and the hope of heaven. Mary also laid bare the outlook on life that helped her overcome so much more than Ella's death. As she wrote in A Thrilling Narrative at one of the bleakest points in their captivity, when they were being driven to Canada, "It being contrary to our nature to remain long on the hill of difficulty, or in the Slough of Despond, we whipped up the horses, and looked around to see what nature offered to assist us in raising our thoughts to the Creator, who wisely orders all things."[332]

After Ella's death, Mary freely admitted, she went through a period where "[p]ray—I could not—only bow down. Tears did not come. Clouds and darkness seemed to be around about us." Yet it was soon true that while "[i]t may [do] for some to darken the windows, but I felt we needed all the sunshine we could have. . . .When the flowers came, I placed them on the table as she was wont to do."[333] Twenty years earlier, during the Dakota War, Ella had been one of "[t]he little children, unconscious of danger, [who] have filled the air with their merry laughter, gathering flowers for us, nicely arranging them in glasses. By their fragrance and beauty we are led to adore the Creator in his wisdom and love to fallen man; and as these frail beauties fade and fall we are reminded that life and death are written on every page of the universe."[334]

In her grief, Mary found a tonic in immersing herself in God's world, in his work, and in his word. "Again, I find it necessary to take much exercise, not only in doors, but out, doing what little I can for the people—thinking of more I would like to do—committing a verse daily from Daily Food, which Ella, dear, used till the very day Jesus called for her. God's own words have been my greatest comfort."[335] For Mary, Christianity was not simply a traditional cultural form. It was a spiritual reality that served as her moral compass in public, guiding her opposition to the Dakota War and her commitment to speaking out for the unjustly oppressed Dakotas, and in private, going without food herself to feed the sick and starving. It also gave her a resilient hope that allowed her to embrace choices bound with adversity, like marrying a man others considered an Indian and spending the last decades of her life in "a large outdoor poor house" (an Indian reservation) serving outcasts that many in her generation wanted to exterminate.[336]

Mary's Reformed (Calvinist) worldview informed her authorial voice in ways that may startle modern readers. The Reformed tradition viewed the world as polarized between spiritual forces: those allied with God and those allied with Satan. There was no neutral, uncommitted middle ground. The Renvilles and many of their contemporary Christian readers were convinced that the Dakota War was not simply a conflict between oppressed people and their oppressors. Rather, Dakota traditional lifeways, language, and spirituality were so intimately intertwined that the 1862 war was viewed as a contest between spiritual powers. It followed that some of Mary's harshest language was spiritually loaded ("Satan's emissaries," "fiends in human form," "wicked ones") and that it was specifically applied to the minority of the Dakota people who murdered unarmed settlers. However, readers will note that Mary applied similarly condemning language to the German women of New Ulm, assumed (too broadly) to be atheists, who attacked the manacled, defenseless Dakota men as they passed outside that city en route to Mankato in November 1862. Thus the characterizations Mary made in writing, while clearly ethnocentric, are not inherently racist; rather, they are spiritual distinctions.

After Ella's death John and Mary continued their ministry at Ascension. Thirteen years later, Mary died in December 1895. John laid his wife to rest in a grave at his daughter's side. On a clear day, they said, from the cemetery above Ascension, John could see east to their old home in Minnesota where he and Mary had been wed thirty-six years before. On weary days when he felt his advancing age, John may have heard her familiar voice in memory: marveling over the birth of their daughter at Hazlewood; cautioning him that the dark blanket would better hide the light of the candle by which she wrote in their tipi during the war; overcoming her fears to stand by his side in ministry to his people at Ascension; at all times urging others to cast their spiritual eyes upward from present circumstance to their eternal hope in God.

Three decades earlier, comforting the Riggses upon their daughter, Isabella Riggs Williams's, departure for China as a missionary, Mary composed an appropriate epitaph for herself:

It must be sad for you to part with [her] but . . . it will not be long before China and all the distant lands will be as though they had never been and all the families of the earth that are redeemed shall meet in Heaven no more to part and it seems to me that those who have given their

Fig. 8. John B. Renville, ca. 1890.
Courtesy of the Southern Minnesota
Historical Center at Minnesota State
University, Mankato.

lives for the service of their Master among the poor will be received with joy unspeakable. . . . But as one star is different from another star in glory, so I expect if ever I reach heaven to see among the brightest stars of Heaven hang a Missionary, (others of course) but me thinks I shall recognize them first, then the redeemed they were the humble instruments of pointing to the Savior.[337]

Two years after Mary's death, in September 1897, John married Josephine (Jessie) Faribault, a Christian woman of French-Dakota descent whom he had known since the childhood days when his father, Joseph Renville, and her father, Oliver Faribault, were engaged in the fur trade in Minnesota.[338] John retired from preaching at Ascension in 1900 after a pastorate of thirty years. By the time he died in December 1903 the fact that he and Mary had ever composed their insiders' view of the Dakota War was forgotten, eclipsed by his later ministry. John was not remembered as a core member of the 1862 coalition of Dakota men who sought to negotiate a peaceful end to a horrific war. Rather, he was remembered as the "Prince of Indian Preachers":

> Without disparaging any of his brethren in the ministry, this title can properly be applied to the Rev. John Baptiste Renville, of Iyakaptapte, (Ascension) South Dakota, who recently passed on to join the saved Sioux in glory.
>
> Timid as a little child, yet bold as a lion, when aroused; shy of conversation in private, yet eloquent in the pulpit and in the council-chamber; yielding yet firm as a rock, when duty demanded it; a loving husband, a kind father, a loyal citizen, a faithful presbyter—a pungent preacher of the gospel, a soul-winner—a courteous, cultured Christian gentleman; such was this Indian son of a Sioux mother, herself the first fullblood Sioux convert to the Christian faith. . . .
>
> He was the first Sioux to enter the ministry . . . [at a time when] the Sioux Indians were in a very unsettled state, and his labors were very much scattered. . . . In 1870 he became the pastor of Iyakaptapte a little church in what subsequently became the Sisseton reservation. Both physically and in mental and spiritual qualities, he was best adapted to a settled pastorate. His quiet and unobtrusive character required long intercourse to be appreciated. However, in the pulpit, his earnestness and apt presentation of the truth ever commanded the attention even of strangers. . . . No one among the Christian Indians was more widely known and loved than Mr. Renville. In the councils of the church, though there were seventeen other ministers in the presbytery before his death, he was ever given the first place for both counsel and honor.[339]

The boy who witnessed the first words of the New Testament translated from French into Dakota at Lac qui Parle lived to see the entire Bible translated into the language of his people.[340] John was buried at Ascension in the old graveyard on top of the hill, next to Mary and Ella. Decades later the cemetery was abandoned in favor of a more accessible site near the church. Today encroaching woods vie with fading memory to reclaim the unmarked graves on the windswept brow of the Coteau. The story of the 1862 Peace Coalition has been equally obscured over time in a thicket of competing interests. This volume pulls back the historical brush to reveal fallen headstones: several lost chapters in the story of the U.S.-Dakota War of 1862 as seen by John and Mary Renville.

EPILOGUE: CONTESTED CREDIT

Careful consumers of the history of the Dakota War—written and oral—are aware that the contest to settle the question of who turned the captives over to Sibley in 1862 has never been settled. The written record, including literal volumes of oral testimony recorded in Dakota claims cases at the turn of the twentieth century, makes clear that in the wake of the war the possession of the captives upon release was a focal measure of who was "friendly" in 1862.[341]

The Sissetons generally did not need to prove themselves. Their semi-permanent homes were on Lake Traverse and Big Stone Lake in Minnesota near the border with Dakota Territory, and they freely ranged onto the Coteau and beyond. They had camped near the Yellow Medicine Agency in early August 1862, where they vigorously protested the tardy payment of their annuities. But after the agent enumerated them (created the annuity roll, the first step in making the annuity payment) they went back out on their seasonal rounds, leaving the corn ripening in their fields while they hunted buffalo in Dakota Territory. On 18 August 1862 most of the Sisseton men were hundreds of miles away from the scene of war. Taṭaŋka Nażiŋ, Waanataŋ, and Scarlet Plume returned to the Upper Reservation briefly around 16 September. For three days they counseled with Upper and Lower leaders while Sisseton women and children harvested and cached corn at Lake Traverse and Big Stone Lake, safely west of the ongoing hostilities. On 19 September these Sisseton chiefs wrote a letter to Sibley declaring their loyalties, then gathered their families and returned west.[342] They were in Dakota Territory on 26 September, when Sibley arrived at Camp Release.

The Wahpeton case was not as clear cut.[343] Many had made permanent homes on the Sioux Reservation and had intermarried with Mdewankanton people. Some Wahpeton young men chose to fight alongside their Lower relatives—these were the young men Mazakutemani derided the Lower Soldiers for recruiting while hiding war plans from Upper headmen. The Wahpeton leaders, like the Lower peace chiefs, had a mess on their hands: some of their young men were embroiled in hostilities the headmen did not sanction but were powerless to stop. It must have been deeply troubling for Wahpetons to feel forced to choose between kinship loyalty to their young men and the future of the *oyate* on their homelands, perhaps even the physical survival of their people. Like the Sissetons, the Wahpetons lost their homes, their homelands, and their treaties. But in addition, the Wahpetons suffered for decades under the allegation that they were "mixed up" in the battles with the hostile Dakotas in 1862. It can be no coincidence that Wahpeton leaders are among the most visible, public opponents of the war in the Renvilles' story; that they went to such lengths to obtain, shelter, and free the captives; that Wahpetons formed the majority of the fifty men who were deemed above suspicion and not subject to postwar trial; that after the war they maintained their prominence as scouts and later as leaders on the Lake Traverse Reservation. They may have felt that traditional Dakota courage in the face of opposition was their only hope to redeem their people's future.

If the Wahpeton leaders who opposed the war had a lot to lose, the Mdewankanton peace chiefs had more. To date white historians have generally weighed in on the side of Lower leaders like Wabaśa and Taopi as those who turned the captives over to Sibley at Camp Release. It has been easy to credit the claims those men made for themselves because when Sibley arrived the majority of the Dakotas he found waiting there were Mdewankanton.

The Lower warriors who surrendered may have done so at the urging of Lower chiefs like Wabaśa, who believed Sibley had promised to treat them fairly. At the time they surrendered, Dakotas could not have predicted the outcome of the postwar tribunal convened to assess their guilt: every man who admitted firing a weapon in battle—an ordinary activity for a soldier in war—was sentenced to death. Later, when President Lincoln had the trial records reassessed to identify only those Dakotas convicted of actual war crimes (the murder of unarmed civilians and rape), Mdewankanton soldiers were still in the majority of those whose executions Lincoln authorized. The proximity of Mdewankanton villages to the focal point of the war on 18 August, the agency town at Lower Sioux, meant Mdewankanton men were more easily caught in the maelstrom of fury that immediately spread into the settlements surrounding the Lower Reservation. Thus, in the wake of the war, Mdewankanton peace leaders were motivated to highlight their own influence in freeing the survivors of massacres committed by Mdewankanton young men. These settler-survivors were the majority of the "white" captives turned over to Sibley at Camp Release.[344]

A Thrilling Narrative of Indian Captivity unsettles this Mdewankanton-centric master narrative of the peace process. The first seven installments of the Renvilles' story appeared in serial form before Congress backed out of the Sioux treaties in February 1863. So while John and Mary's perspective on the war was limited to their purview inside the Wahpeton camp, the restoration of millions of dollars in annuities, with interest, was not riding on their story of who was (or was not) "friendly" in 1862, as it was in 1901 in the Sisseton and Wahpeton claims case. And because John, Mary, and Ella were the only people in Berlin, Wisconsin, who had experienced the Dakota War firsthand, their story is also free of the burden of outside consensus. By contrast, in 1901 Mdewankanton witnesses (who disputed the idea that any Sisseton or Wahpeton people were to be credited with freeing captives in 1862) volunteered under oath that their testimonies agreed in so many particulars because Mdewankantons had been discussing the war for thirty-nine years and had arrived at a mutual understanding of who was responsible and for what.[345]

The present volume does not settle the question of who released the captives to Sibley on 26 September 1862. Instead, it significantly complicates the story. As all good stories do, *A Thrilling Narrative* raises more questions than it answers, questions descendants and scholars will wrestle with for generations. In the process, it clearly exhibits the power of stories in history: what is at stake in telling them and what is at stake when they go untold.

LITERARY PERSPECTIVES ON
A THRILLING NARRATIVE
OF INDIAN CAPTIVITY

Kathryn Zabelle Derounian-Stodola

In 2009 I posted a message on the Association for the Study of American Indian Literatures discussion list requesting information on Native theories of "home." I received many responses that helped me draft this introduction, including the following poem by the great Acoma Pueblo writer Simon J. Ortiz:

> What is home anymore?
> Is the "Indian reservation" home?
> Is Acoma home?
> Is Cherokee home?
> Is Pine Ridge home?
> Is Chinle home?
> Is the land under your feet and where you work and
>   have lived for three years home?
> Is San Francisco, New York City, Seattle, or Chicago
>   home?
> Where is home anymore?[1]

Though brief, this poem interrogates the complications and contradictions of linking identity to home, homelands, homelessness, and homecoming. Such issues are poignant and pressing for Native Americans today. But they originated centuries ago when Natives were first driven from their traditional land base and, as displaced people, were forced to grapple with "geographies of belonging."[2] Ironically, European American colonizers

A THRILLING NARRATIVE

OF

INDIAN CAPTIVITY.

BY

MRS. MARY BUTLER RENVILLE.

MINNEAPOLIS, MINN.:
ATLAS COMPANY'S BOOK AND JOB PRINTING OFFICE.
1863.

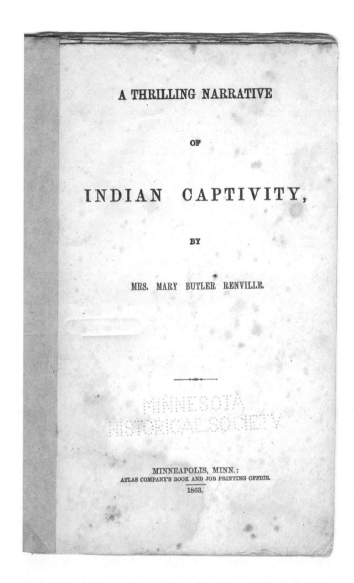

A THRILLING NARRATIVE

OF

INDIAN CAPTIVITY,

BY

MRS. MARY BUTLER RENVILLE.

MINNEAPOLIS, MINN.:
ATLAS COMPANY'S BOOK AND JOB PRINTING OFFICE.
1863.

Figs. 9 (*left*) and 10 (*above*). *A Thrilling Narrative*, cover and title page, 1863. Held in the Reserve Collection, Minnesota Historical Society. The title, *A Thrilling Narrative of Indian Captivity*, appeared on both the cover (fig. 9) and the title page (fig. 10) of the 1863 edition. The booklet measures 8¼ by 5½ inches. The original binding was sewn, with the golden-yellow wrap cover glued on. The staples visible on the cover are not original.

also had to reassess their identity and allegiance when faced with cross-cultural contact in their new locale. In these ways both groups confronted issues of definition ("What is home?") and space ("Where is home?").

The U.S.-Dakota War of 1862 literally caused Dakotas and non-Dakotas to leave the place both claimed as home. For in the wake of war most Dakotas were forcibly exiled from their homelands, while most whites relocated but always had the option to return. Diane Wilson points out that there is an "immense difference between losing one's homeland, as the Dakota did, and losing a homestead on land that was obtained through coercive treaties."[3] Nevertheless, one could say that all parties in the U.S.-Dakota War fought over "home rights" as well as land rights. Establishing a joint sense of home and belonging proved particularly challenging for John and Mary Renville, since their backgrounds and upbringings had been so very different before they married. Their captivity narrative locates them at a liminal point in that search as they confronted what and where their physical, cultural, emotional, and spiritual home might be. Focusing on "home" therefore provides a useful thematic entrée into this text.

Initially titled "The Indian Captives: Leaves from a Journal," the narrative appeared in thirteen installments, mostly a week but sometimes up to two weeks apart, in a small-town Wisconsin newspaper called the *Berlin City Courant.* The first installment came out on 25 December 1862, the day before the mass hangings at Mankato, and the last on 9 April 1863. First exiled *to* Berlin from the home base they had established at Hazlewood, the Renvilles were essentially exiled *from* Berlin when John's Dakota background became public.

Later in 1863 the Atlas Company of Minneapolis published a slightly changed book version with the more inflammatory and salable title *A Thrilling Narrative of Indian Captivity.* The thirteen chapters in the book corresponded to the serialized newspaper articles. Mary copyrighted the volume under her name, and its title page stated "By Mrs. Mary Butler Renville," but its last chapter still carried the joint signature "J. B. AND M. A. RENVILLE," which had appeared at the end of the final *Courant* installment.[4] Significantly, John's initials appeared before Mary's to claim that the text belonged to him as much as to her and that both took respon-

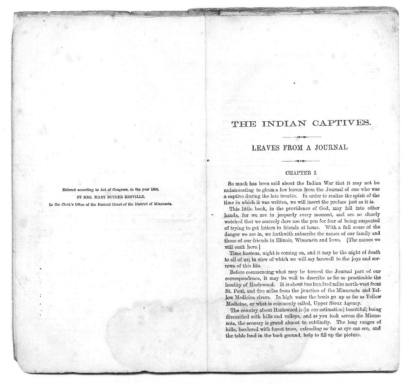

Fig. 11. *A Thrilling Narrative*, copyright statement and page 1, 1863. Held in the Reserve Collection, Minnesota Historical Society. *A Thrilling Narrative* was entered for copyright in July 1863 by the Clerk of the District Court for the District of Minnesota by Mrs. Mary Butler Renville. The first page bore the title that appeared at the head of the first newspaper installment, "The Indian Captives. Leaves from a Journal."

sibility for it. Two addenda rounded out the book: the first giving information about the providential rescue of missionaries during the war and the second bolstering *A Thrilling Narrative*'s credibility with a statement by one of those evangelists, H. D. Cunningham. The Renvilles' narrative has not been published since 1863.

It is not known who decided to change the title of the newspaper version, with its sense of immediacy and reportage ("captives," "leaves," "journal"), to that of the book version, with its emotionalism and affectation ("thrilling narrative"). Both versions of the title retain the key concept

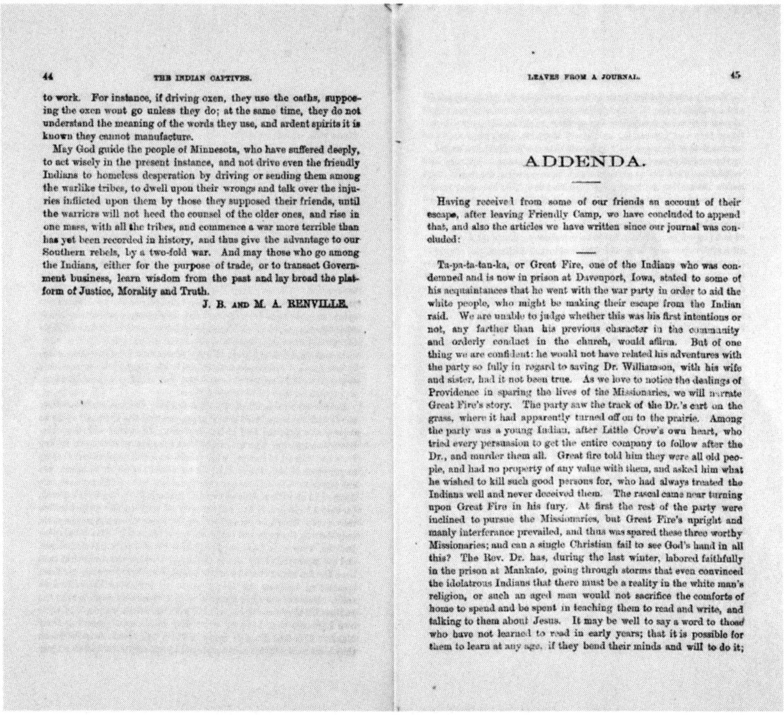

44 THE INDIAN CAPTIVES.

to work. For instance, if driving oxen, they use the oaths, supposing the oxen wont go unless they do; at the same time, they do not understand the meaning of the words they use, and ardent spirits it is known they cannot manufacture.

May God guide the people of Minnesota, who have suffered deeply, to act wisely in the present instance, and not drive even the friendly Indians to homeless desperation by driving or sending them among the warlike tribes, to dwell upon their wrongs and talk over the injuries inflicted upon them by those they supposed their friends, until the warriors will not heed the counsel of the older ones, and rise in one mass, with all the tribes, and commence a war more terrible than has yet been recorded in history, and thus give the advantage to our Southern rebels, by a two-fold war. And may those who go among the Indians, either for the purpose of trade, or to transact Government business, learn wisdom from the past and lay broad the platform of Justice, Morality and Truth.

J. B. AND M. A. BENVILLE.

LEAVES FROM A JOURNAL. 45

ADDENDA.

Having received from some of our friends an account of their escape, after leaving Friendly Camp, we have concluded to append that, and also the articles we have written since our journal was concluded:

Ta-pa-ta-tan-ka, or Great Fire, one of the Indians who was condemned and is now in prison at Davenport, Iowa, stated to some of his acquaintances that he went with the war party in order to aid the white people, who might be making their escape from the Indian raid. We are unable to judge whether this was his first intentions or not, any farther than his previous character in the community and orderly conduct in the church, would affirm. But of one thing we are confident: he would not have related his adventures with the party so fully in regard to saving Dr. Williamson, with his wife and sister, had it not been true. As we love to notice the dealings of Providence in sparing the lives of the Missionaries, we will narrate Great Fire's story. The party saw the track of the Dr.'s cart on the grass, where it had apparently turned off on to the prairie. Among the party was a young Indian, after Little Crow's own heart, who tried every persuasion to get the entire company to follow after the Dr., and murder them all. Great fire told him they were all old people, and had no property of any value with them, and asked him what he wished to kill such good persons for, who had always treated the Indians well and never deceived them. The rascal came near turning upon Great Fire in his fury. At first the rest of the party were inclined to pursue the Missionaries, but Great Fire's upright and manly interferance prevailed, and thus was spared these three worthy Missionaries; and can a single Christian fail to see God's hand in all this? The Rev. Dr. has, during the last winter, labored faithfully in the prison at Mankato, going through storms that even convinced the idolatrous Indians that there must be a reality in the white man's religion, or such an aged man would not sacrifice the comforts of home to spend and be spent in teaching them to read and write, and talking to them about Jesus. It may be well to say a word to those who have not learned to read in early years; that it is possible for them to learn at any age, if they bend their minds and will to do it;

Fig. 12. *A Thrilling Narrative*, signatures and addenda, 1863. Held in the Reserve Collection, Minnesota Historical Society. The booklet bore the original title, "The Indian Captives. Leaves from a Journal" as the running head throughout. The last page of chapter 13 bore the same dual signature that had appeared at the end of installment thirteen in the *Berlin City Courant*. The addenda was new to the 1863 edition.

of capture: but while the *Courant* title focuses on the people (*captives*), the book title focuses on the experience (*captivity*). Curiously, on the first page of the narrative proper and present in the book as a running head thereafter, the *Courant*'s title appears. This discrepancy may be accidental, or it may signify that despite the supposed single author shown on the book cover and title page the original newspaper title better indicated the two captive-authors. Additionally, the presence of both titles emphasizes the importance of the people involved as well as the experiences they underwent.

In penning the newspaper and book accounts, the Renvilles drew on a popular genre that had been part of the American literary landscape from earliest times: the Indian captivity narrative. Traditionally the term "Indian captivity narrative" refers to stories of non-Natives captured by Natives during wars or other hostilities. But this classification has widened in the past few decades so that it now accommodates stories of Native Americans themselves being captured or confined: at boarding schools, in prison, and by other Natives, for example.[5] As a corollary to the generic shift, modern Indian writers engage with the form's new as well as old definitions through intertextuality and irony.[6] A *Thrilling Narrative*'s input from an Anglo woman and a Dakota man provides a particularly interesting perspective on captivity narratives in general and the Dakota War in particular.

The narrative is significant in other ways too: it is the earliest Dakota War captivity narrative to be published as a separate book, it is the first book to be copyrighted in Minnesota by a woman living in the state, and it is a work whose authors were the only captives to spend the entire war in the Upper Dakota camp. Alongside their own personal story, the Renvilles provide an in-depth assessment of the Dakota Peace Coalition and also manage to include information about other key players, both Dakota and non-Dakota. These three elements—autobiography, political commentary, and biography—are woven into the generic fabric of *A Thrilling Narrative*.

Applying the following characteristics to this text reveals how it simultaneously exploits and undermines expectations about nineteenth-century Indian captivity narratives: authorship and mediation (exploring the evidence for joint authorship and for ways in which Mary and John Renville both contributed to the narrative), narrative perspective (showing how the authors' distinctive approaches to and underlying beliefs about the war and the people involved in it affected their narration), rhetorical uses of sentiment (indicating the methods the authors used to appeal to their readers' emotions), didactic intent (uncovering the social, political, and religious morality that underlay aspects of the narrative), and readership and circulation (considering who might have read the work when it first appeared as well as how it was produced and marketed).

A Thrilling Narrative is not unusual in the captivity narrative literature for raising questions about multiple authorship and textual mediation. Historically, even when accounts were written in the first person,
evidence of editorial intervention exists for stories concerning male as well
as female hostages. Because captives tended to be ordinary people with
few literary skills, it might be necessary for amanuenses, ghostwriters, or
editors to shape material so that it transcended basic reportage and made
money, demonized enemies, preached morality, or set the record straight.
For example, Lorrayne Carroll's *Rhetorical Drag: Gender Impersonation,
Captivity, and the Writing of History* traces the gender politics of a series
of powerful men who strategically assumed women's voices and identities in seventeenth- to eighteenth-century Indian captivity narratives.[7]
The male authors she discusses used the experiences of female subjects
to create politically charged if not outright propagandist works.

Editorial mediation occurs in many of the individual captivity narratives
within the three earliest book-length histories of the Dakota War: Isaac
Heard's *History of the Sioux War and Massacres of 1862 and 1863* (1864),
Harriet Bishop McConkey's *Dakota War Whoop* (1863), and Charles Bryant
and Abel Murch's *History of the Great Massacre by the Sioux Indians in
Minnesota* (1864).[8] But unlike the captivity narratives subsumed within
these contemporaneously published works, *A Thrilling Narrative* was not
subject to outside editorialization.[9] Rather, in a significant gender reversal
of the norm, Mary retained more authorial control than John, though she
consistently employed the first-person plural and though each of them
contributed to the text. Composing this narrative therefore empowered
two minority figures in mainstream culture: Mary as a woman and John
as a Native.

As with countless other collaboratively written captivity narratives, it
is tricky and sometimes impossible to tease out who contributed what.
In *A Thrilling Narrative*, Mary was the scribe who took basic personal and
political information from her recollections and from the wartime journal
she kept, which is no longer extant. She also seems to have provided the
dominant textual voice. John, however, was the resource for discussion,
translation, and reconstruction of events and motives, especially politi-

cal negotiations and Peace Coalition meetings that may have excluded Mary. Also, it seems reasonable to assume that John may have supplied or corrected the ethnographic information on Dakota customs within chapter 9 of the account. In the nineteenth century other marriages between Anglo women and Native men that involved various kinds of collaborative writing also raised significant issues about composing and editing.[10] In such cases modern scholars believe it is vital to recognize the contributions of both parties, no matter how compromised or muted some of their material may be.

Mary's correspondence with Stephen Riggs reproduced in appendix B of this edition sheds light on the composition of *A Thrilling Narrative*. For example, in her letter dated 13 February 1863, she says, "I am writing a story every week for the Berlin City Current [*sic*]. I kept a kind of journal during the troublous times while I was a captive. I have written 7 stories, and for the sake of my friends and little Ella, I think of having it published in the form of a pamphlet."[11] Here Mary states that during the war she logged entries which formed the narrative's basis and that her rationale for book publication was private (for her friends and family) not public (for her own gratification). Similar but sometimes spurious statements within the captivity narrative literature, especially when written by women, reinforced a narrator's credibility and altruistic publication motives. Paradoxically, as long as ex-captives said they did not want to exploit their misfortune, it was more acceptable for their story to be circulated for donations or sold. Protestations of humility also concealed a narrative's covert propagandist potential by making its author appear naïve.

In the opening of chapter 1 Mary refers to "the Journal of one who was a captive during the late trouble."[12] While there is no reason to doubt that she really did record events during her six-week confinement, she later admits needing memory prompts as well as additional data. For instance, in her letter to Stephen Riggs dated 13 February, she asks if his daughter Isabella "has any facts she is willing to *part with* that would serve me", and in her letter dated 21 February she confesses, "I cant remember anything hardly since our captivity but what is in black and white."[13] Surely Mary's husband helped her with material that she forgot to write down or could not readily recall. Indeed, from testimony that John Renville gave in 1901 when the Sisseton and Wahpeton bands sued the U.S. government, we know that for safety's sake the family refused to be separated during the war and that they shared similar experiences: "My wife was a white woman, and I stayed right with her," he said under oath.[14]

Also, *A Thrilling Narrative* contains speeches and correspondence that augmented the original wartime journal but must have been added later.[15] For instance, both John and Mary transcribed strategic letters that were reprinted in the narrative from pro-government Dakotas like Lorenzo Lawrence, Paul Mazakutemani, and Simon Anawaŋgmani (fellow members of the Hazlewood Republic) to Governor Ramsey and General Sibley. The narrative describes the Renvilles' writing process, which applies not only to the letters but probably to the journal too:

> We have already given one letter dictated by Paul. We now copy one from some other chiefs. Before doing so, we will state that we endangered our lives by writing, and had to be very cautious so as not to be discovered. If in the day time, we usually secreted ourselves in the tent some way; but generally the Indians wished us to write in the night. Sometimes we have waited until we thought every one ought to be asleep, and then put out the fire, Mr. R. [i.e., John] would hold a blanket over us and the candle, so as to keep the light from shining through the tent; besides this caution, a guard was placed outside the tent to report any intruder who might be approaching.[16]

Thus *A Thrilling Narrative* is a composite text: the joint production of a captive couple who expanded their own contributions with material by others. And claiming this narrative for Mary and John recognizes not only joint production but joint agency. The above quotation clearly indicates that both were vitally important in the peace process and that both felt so strongly about their roles that they risked their lives by essentially acting as spies.

As I have written elsewhere, one notable feature of *A Thrilling Narrative* concerns its intrusive but ambiguous use of the first-person plural.[17] The effect is like a series of textual gears to signal shifts in perspective and inclusion. Thus "we/our/us" might refer to Mary alone, to Mary and John, to the Renville family, to the Peace Coalition, to whites, to fellow missionaries, to sympathetic readers, or to a mixture of subjectivities. And even parsing the referents of "we" does not guarantee consistency from these separate entities. One reason for so many definitions of "we" may go back to the wartime journal's impressionistic entries that were not changed for publication. But another reason may involve complex layers of authorial identity and collusion that caused, and probably will always cause, confusion.

For example, consider this extract from chapter 5:

> When Mrs. DeCamp came we were scarcely able to walk, and could not bestow as much attention on her and the little children as we desired. We had an attack of the pleurisy, and suffered extremely for several days. . . . We sent for Paul and Lorenzo and held a council of five, as to what was best for Mrs. D. to do, it not being safe for her to remain long with us. . . . Some evil person, we supposed, had listened to the council, though all had been spoken in a whisper. We think they must have placed a chair under the safe of the stove pipe, as we found one there when we went into our room.[18]

The first three uses of "we" refer to Mary, whose health was poor. But did the Renvilles as a couple send for Paul Mazakutemani and Lorenzo Lawrence (which seems unlikely), or does "we" here indicate John and other leading men in the Peace Coalition? And if it was not safe for Jannette DeCamp to stay "with us," does "us" here mean the Renvilles specifically or everyone in what the narrative calls "Friendly Camp"?[19] Finally, the authors fail to clarify who supposed that an "evil person" over-heard plans for the DeCamp family's escape and tried to thwart it. In this instance "we" seems to be Mary and John. However, to fully explore the postwar meaning of "we," and to understand how it affects other issues like representations of "home," it is necessary to go further back than its rhetorical presence in *A Thrilling Narrative*.

Within his influential essay "Indigenous Language Consciousness: Being, Place, and Sovereignty," Simon J. Ortiz explains that many Natives claim "'home' to be the social-cultural context that's clearly Indigenous with regard to Indigenous family ties, cultural customs, spiritual traditions, community gatherings, and so forth. And the social-cultural Indigenous context is 'home' as an identity."[20] In other words, "we" for Natives is not just tied to but is actually synonymous with "belonging" and "home." As a Dakota, John knew that despite his acculturation to white ways his primary cultural identity lay in his kinship ties, famously described by the Sioux anthropologist Ella Deloria:

> By kinship all Dakota people were held together in a great relationship that was theoretically all-inclusive and co-extensive with the Dakota domain. Everyone who was born a Dakota belonged in it. . . .[T]he ultimate aim of Dakota life, stripped of accessories, was quite simple: One must obey kinship rules; one must be a good relative. . . . In the last analysis every other consideration was secondary—property, personal ambition, glory, good times, life itself. Without that aim and the constant struggle to attain it, the people would no longer be Dakotas in truth. They would no longer even be human.[21]

Living in Hazlewood before the hostilities allowed John and Mary to adapt elements of Native culture (his by birth, hers by marriage) and white culture (hers by birth, his by marriage) to their own needs as a couple. He saw himself, and his wife saw him, as someone who partook of both cultures. And she, in turn, adapted to such elements of Dakota culture as kinship obligations. But when they were forced to flee from their home and community, they became physically and psychologically displaced for seven years, until they settled at the Sisseton Agency. The war and its aftermath forced them to confront anew what Adrienne Rich calls "a politics of location."[22] Or maybe I should say "a politics of relocation," for as a bicultural couple, especially during and immediately after the racially charged war, they were constantly dealing with identity issues depending on where and among whom they lived. Who were they? Where did they belong? How did they situate themselves in the world?

These questions were easier for John to answer than for Mary because his solution to various displacements was returning to his people to consolidate his identity as a Dakota and to shape theirs as Christians. While the Renvilles still lived in Wisconsin, we have evidence from their 1863 letters to Stephen Riggs that John strongly desired to rejoin the Dakotas. For instance, in her 23 January 1863 letter Mary admitted, "I know he often wishes he could spend his life among the Dakotas, and when their is any opening I will try to not hinder him from doing good." Her letter a week later clarified her concerns, "Please excuse my nervous writing," she apologized to Riggs, "the least noise makes me jump[.] I don't get over being a captive yet, or rather the effects of it."[23]

In a joint letter dated 13 February—part written by John and part by Mary—she acknowledged her fears once again, "Mr. Renville laughs at me, but I can't forget the late Massacre." And on 21 February she explained further, "[H]e seems more anxious to labor among the Dakotas than he ever did. I hope I shant prove an hindrance[,] but I sometimes shrink from ever going into the Indian Country again[.] [B]ut once their I expect these foolish feelings will leave me and I shall be a more sensible woman." Finally sense did indeed prevail over sensibility, and she realized that if John's earthly home was with the Dakotas, then her earthly home was with them too.[24]

Despite Mary's postwar doubts, for decades afterward she and her husband exemplified both Christian and Dakota kinship ideals in their missionary work: John was ordained in 1865 as the first Dakota pastor in the Presbyterian Church, and Mary continued as his helpmeet and supporter. Once again Ella Deloria and other Native scholars indicate that these culturally different principles went hand in hand. For example, Deloria says of a hymn written by a Dakota priest, "It identifies Christian brotherhood with the old Dakota kinship system and its laws of interpersonal responsibility and loving kindness."[25] The Renvilles were known to be hospitable toward travelers, generous toward the poor, and parental toward the children of John's relatives whom they took in as their own.[26] When Mary was interviewed around 1876 and asked if Ella was her only child, she responded, "Yes, and No. Since my marriage to Mr. Renville I have brought up and educated sixteen Dakota children. So you may say I have others beside my daughter."[27]

Their faith was sorely tested when Ella died in 1882, age twenty-one. A free translation of John's obituary for Ella written in Dakota recalls her last moments and her heavenly homecoming, "'Jesus has come for me. Goodbye, Papa. Goodbye.' She was gone. She was well. God had taken her home. She was no longer with us but had entered, white-robed, into heaven."[28] Several months later in the same newspaper—*Iapi Oaye*, the Dakota language version of the *Word Carrier*—Mary published a personal response to her loss titled "Trying to Overcome." Although she was still grief-stricken, she found solace in caring for John and their adopted son and in reaffirming her Christian beliefs. Here is her final paragraph, filled with conviction that the family will be reunited in heaven: "The grave is always in sight. Together the parents often visit it; and though we cannot understand all the mysteries of the Resurrection, or the glories of Heaven, we are satisfied that the Lord of Heaven and Earth doeth all things well, and will help us to *overcome* and OVERCOME, till we are prepared to hear the summons: 'Welcome to the Father's Home above.'"[29]

As parents the Renvilles may have wished to keep their grief private, but as missionaries they may have decided to make their memorials public. I do not mean that their sorrow was superficial or that they consciously wrote about Ella's death in order to convert others. But by recording her last moments, they allowed a biographical reality to morph into a moral exemplum. Their words would also have reminded readers of a common nineteenth-century trope: the premature death of a pious child or young woman (like Ella) whose spiritual strength transformed doubters into believers.[30] Writing *A Thrilling Narrative* twenty years earlier, the Renvilles had also combined sentimentality and sensationalism to enhance their basic account and to promote their political and religious agendas.

The use of sentimentality in Indian captivity narratives, particularly those by, about, and for women, has already attracted scholarly attention.[31] But in *A Thrilling Narrative* the references to "home" provide an emotional shorthand that rapidly elicits sympathy regardless of the reader's gender. Critic Rosemary Marangoly George attempts to define the complex theoretical parameters of "home" in *The Politics of Home*:

One distinguishing feature of places called home is that they are built on select inclusions. The inclusions are grounded in a learned (or taught) sense of a kinship that is extended to those who are perceived as sharing the same blood, race, class, gender, or religion. Membership is maintained by bonds of love, fear, power, desire and control. Homes are manifest on geographical, psychological and material levels. They are recognized as such by those within and those without. . . . Home is the desired place that is fought for and established as the exclusive domain of a few. It is not a neutral place. It is community.[32]

The Renvilles' literal and symbolic references to "home" within their narrative allowed their original audience the vicarious experience of its dispossession and loss. For example, when members of the Peace Coalition decided to hide in the plundered mission buildings, *A Thrilling Narrative* states, "It is impossible to describe the desolation, confusion and destruction that had been made at these houses, and the feelings that took possession of us when we thought of the many families that had thus been driven from their homes."[33] Significantly, these empty homes would have belonged to Dakota as well as non-Dakota families. Still in the same location some days later, the authors remark, "The desolate appearance of the once happy home of a christian family, the howling of the wind through the broken casements, all tended to fill the mind with gloom."[34]

But it was not only desecrated Christian homes that elicited such powerful responses. Although the Renvilles were politically and morally opposed to white Minnesotans avenging themselves on Dakota people, they seemed to understand the newcomers' deep attachment to their damaged property: "We cannot blame them for feeling injured," the authors admit, "for their homes have been made desolate."[35] Despite acknowledging the cost of war for both sides, the narrative ends by privileging the *Dakota* losses and warning European Americans to "act wisely in the present instance, and not drive even the friendly Indians to homeless desperation."[36] For homelessness meant hopelessness, and hopelessness might foster further resistance, the Renvilles implied.

The narrative employs emotional resonances other than "home" to draw in its readers. For example, the titular use of "thrilling" is echoed later in a key incident where captive Jannette DeCamp reports that several women (Mary Schwandt, Mattie Williams, and Mary Anderson) were abused by Dakota men. "The most thrilling incident related by this reliable woman," the narrative states, "was the suffering of three young ladies brought to camp in the evening—six young drunken Indians (or Satan's emissaries) taking these helpless girls."[37] The modern meaning of "thrilling" as "exciting" seems inappropriate here, and in the title, too, for that matter. But the Oxford English Dictionary specifies that in the nineteenth century the word also meant "piercing the feelings," which makes far more sense.

From earliest times captivity narratives had appealed to readers' sympathy and hatred through the figure of the violated female. So when the Renvilles referred to the three vulnerable women, they relied on a familiar symbol in their attempt to define Christianized (and therefore "civilized") Indians against what they called "Satan's emissaries," "superstitious savages," and "Satan's destroying demons."[38] And that is why these tag phrases state that the abusive Dakotas were not just violent but demonic or pagan.

Going even further back than the famous Puritan captivities, like Mary Rowlandson's, the genre had tended to brand all Native Americans as savage and uncivilized. Even the so-called Praying Indians in Puritan accounts were viewed as potentially if not actually treacherous. But Mary and John Renville saw the world less in terms of Dakota and non-Dakota and more in terms of Christian and non-Christian. A Thrilling Narrative thus differs from the traditional captivity literature in its generally positive stereotyping of converted Dakotas and its negative stereotyping only of unconverted Dakotas. Making this key distinction helped reinforce the text's religious and social politics.

Because the Renvilles believed so strongly in Christianity's moral power, they sometimes strategically present information in their narrative that is historically skewed. In particular, their text suggests that the entire Dakota Peace Coalition was either Christian or somehow positively influenced by Christianity. It served the Renvilles' reformist purposes and perhaps helped to protect the entire group of "peace seekers" (to use Elden Lawrence's term).[39] The truth was that many, but by no means all, members of the Peace Coalition were Christian converts. But blurring the truth was important since *A Thrilling Narrative* was apparently written with a view to raising money for missionary work.

For example, in chapter 3 the account overtly addresses its readers: "Had it not been for the gospel which had been planted by these true worthies [early missionaries], the massacre would have been more terrible and awful than it was. . . . Dear reader, please bear this in mind when you are contributing to the Mission cause, for you know not what the fruits of your labor may be."[40] A little later, the narrative says this of a mother and her three children who found their way to the Peace Camp: "How glad the captives are to get among the friendly Indians! The praise is all due to that gospel which makes the savage heart become humane, and man respect the rights of his fellow man."[41] Here and elsewhere the text plays on readers' responses to the vulnerable female as mother (not as virgin, which the earlier reference to the three young women invoked).

Yet like some other mainstream missionaries and historians of the time, the Renvilles target the Turner community of New Ulm for what they consider to be its dangerous radicalism. The American Turner communes were experiments in utopian and socialist living that German immigrants brought with them from the old country. But because the Turners were clannish and insular, they became useful scapegoats for Anglo culture. Although *A Thrilling Narrative* blames European Americans in general for distributing alcohol to Native Americans, it cannot resist singling out New Ulm: "Oh, that another drop, not even for medicine, may ever be carried in the Indian country again; New Ulm, we are confident, furnished its share heretofore." The narrative even goes so far as to state that "God may have visited New Ulm in offended wrath."[42]

Finally, where the narrative voice is Mary's, the text contains an interesting aspect of gender and class politics by referring to John as "Mr. R." or "Mr. Renville." As critic Marcy Tanter indicates, when wives called their husbands "Mr." (and husbands called their wives "Mrs.," as John did), they employed "a convention that was used among all the classes,

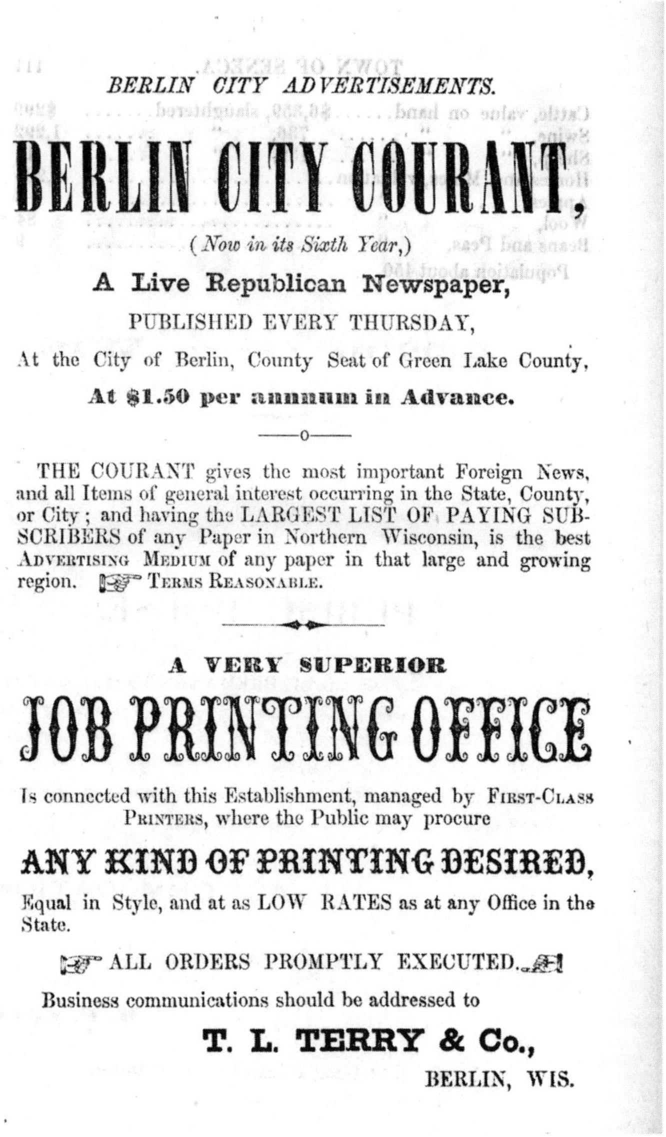

BERLIN CITY ADVERTISEMENTS.

BERLIN CITY COURANT,

(*Now in its Sixth Year,*)

A Live Republican Newspaper,

PUBLISHED EVERY THURSDAY,

At the City of Berlin, County Seat of Green Lake County,

At $1.50 per annum in Advance.

———o———

THE COURANT gives the most important Foreign News, and all Items of general interest occurring in the State, County, or City ; and having the LARGEST LIST OF PAYING SUBSCRIBERS of any Paper in Northern Wisconsin, is the best ADVERTISING MEDIUM of any paper in that large and growing region. ☞ TERMS REASONABLE.

——◆——

A VERY SUPERIOR

JOB PRINTING OFFICE

Is connected with this Establishment, managed by FIRST-CLASS PRINTERS, where the Public may procure

ANY KIND OF PRINTING DESIRED,

Equal in Style, and at as LOW RATES as at any Office in the State.

☞ ALL ORDERS PROMPTLY EXECUTED. ☜

Business communications should be addressed to

T. L. TERRY & Co.,

BERLIN, WIS.

Fig. 13. *Berlin City Courant* advertisement, 1860. Held in the Minnesota Historical Society. The advertisement appeared in Gillespy's *History of Green Lake County [Wisconsin]*, printed by the Berlin City Courant Press, 1860.

but more prevalently among the middle and upper classes." Outside the family circle, using Mr./Mrs. was a class-based formality and a mark of respectability. So Mary's consistent referencing of John in this way accords him "the proper respect he is due as a man of a certain class," reinforces her reformist and egalitarian zeal, and invites readers to treat him in the same way.[43] Mary also refers to John as "Mr." in the letters included in appendix B of this edition, indicating that this was a term she favored in both public and semiprivate contexts.

What readership might the Renvilles have had in mind when they wrote their account, why did they choose the Atlas Company as their publisher, and how widely did their book circulate? Scholars ask similar questions about other Indian captivity narratives, but unfortunately, answers are not always forthcoming because these publications were so often ephemeral. We know that *A Thrilling Narrative* reached several strata of readers. Initially, as Mary indicates, she kept the journal to record a traumatic time in her family's life and intended it for family and friends. By December 1862, however, she had published the first chapter of what was then called "The Indian Captives: Leaves from a Journal" in the *Berlin City Courant*. Evidently this local Republican newspaper found the story and its twelve succeeding installments appealing enough to place them on the front page, but there is no record of whether the Renvilles were paid for the material. Also, as with small town newspapers elsewhere, there was so little local news to report that the *Courant* published national news taken from various sources and cities.[44]

The book version seems to have been aimed at a variety of groups, including missionaries, Minnesotans, young people, philanthropists, and general readers outside the state. The evolution of a narrative from diary, journal, or letter to newspaper account to separately published pamphlet or book is common within the Indian captivity narrative genre (and in contemporary memoir), as the story moves from private to public consumption. Usually, too, a newspaper's readership was regional and therefore limited; whereas a book could circulate to a much larger group. Further, author-participants manipulated these media so that when their story lost currency in one outlet it could be republished in another to reach fresh readers.

The U.S.-Dakota War was such a sensational event that many captives wanted to capitalize on their experiences as soon as they could. Looking back on this tumultuous time, Mary Riggs wrote to her son Alfred on 30 March 1864, "I think we have never sent you Mrs. Renville's narrative. I will send one soon. Mrs. Doct. Wakefield also published a pamphlet 'Six Weeks in the Sioux Teepees' was the title. Besides one or two other pamphlets, there have been three books of considerable size published—one by I. V. Heard, Esq. of Saint Paul and second, The Dakota War Whoop by Mrs. Harriet Bishop McConkey & a third by Mr. Bryant of St. Peter."[45]

It is interesting that Mary Riggs mentions *A Thrilling Narrative of Indian Captivity* in the same breath as Sarah Wakefield's *Six Weeks in the Sioux Tepees*, since both booklets were published by the Atlas Company of Minneapolis in 1863. These books were also advertised in the *State Atlas*, printed by the same company: the Renville text on 30 September 1863 and the Wakefield one on 14 October 1863. Little is known about the Atlas Company; indeed, there is a dearth of information about similar small, nineteenth-century presses that published cheap copies of Indian captivity narratives. In 1863 the press was named Atlas Company's Book and Job Printing Office to indicate that it printed books and also undertook other, more short-term jobs. But by 1864, when it published another captivity narrative about the U.S.-Dakota War, Lavinia Eastlick's *Thrilling Incidents of the Indian War of 1862: Being a Personal Narrative of the Outrages and Horrors Witnessed by Mrs. L. Eastlick in Minnesota*, it was called Atlas Steam Press Printing Company.

Two years later, in 1866, the same press published a thirteen-page poem by Otis A. E. Miller, "Luther Lee; an Episode of the Indian Massacre in Minnesota in 1862."[46] Even though this poem actually has little to do with the U.S.-Dakota War, the addition of "the Indian Massacre in Minnesota in 1862" within the title may have been a sales ploy to spice up readers' expectations of an otherwise bland work. Thus four years after the war the topic had been subsumed within a poem, not a first-person captivity narrative.

We do know that the Atlas Company was not one of the five major firms responsible for two-thirds of the job printing in the Twin Cities between 1866 and 1876. However, an overview of early printing in Minneapolis and Saint Paul shows that it was still in business as late as 1876 and that it published twelve imprints during this same decade.[47] The three longer books Mary Riggs mentions (by Isaac Heard, Harriet Bishop McConkey, and Charles Bryant and Abel Murch) came out from more prestigious presses, two of which were outside Minnesota: Heard's publisher was in New York and Bryant and Murch's was in Cincinnati. Very likely, authors who published with the Atlas Company could expect a booklet to be printed cheaply and quickly so that they (or book distributors) could turn around and sell it reasonably. While the sales price of *A Thrilling Narrative of Indian Captivity* is not known, the first edition of Sarah Wakefield's narrative cost twenty-five cents.[48]

Apart from Mary Riggs's mention of *A Thrilling Narrative of Indian Captivity*, there is one other clue about who else may have read it. The copy of the narrative at the Minnesota Historical Society was accessed as a donation from the family of Janet Pond, whose relatives Gideon and Samuel Pond were in the same missionary circle as the Riggs family. Thus, not surprisingly, the printed version of the story seems to have interested some of the missionaries among whom John and Mary Renville moved. We do not know what the narrative's original press run was, but we do know that only five copies have survived: they are at the Minnesota Historical Society, as previously mentioned, and at the Wisconsin Historical Society, the Newberry Library (Chicago), Oberlin College, and Yale University.

In 1915 ex-captive Mary Schwandt Schmidt commented that the country was flooded with U.S.-Dakota War stories as soon as the hostilities ended.[49] Therefore, the Renvilles were competing with a lot of other material for readers' attention. Some of the separately published booklets, like Sarah Wakefield's, may have captured the public interest for particular reasons. In Wakefield's case, her captivity narrative became infamous because she tried to defend her Dakota protector, Chaska (Wicaŋhpi Waśtedaŋpi or, as sometimes spelled, We-chank-wash-ta-don-pee), who had been hanged at

Fig. 14. The Coteau des Prairies, 1885. Courtesy of the Minnesota Historical Society. This 1885 view of the Good Will Mission gives a glimpse of the topography of the Coteau on the Lake Traverse Sisseton and Wahpeton Reservation. Good Will was the mission station closest to the Renvilles' home at Ascension.

Mankato, allegedly by mistake, and because she chastised the government for its slow response in rescuing captives.

Mary Riggs's oblique statement to her son, "I think we have never sent you Mrs. Renville's narrative," has a comfortable intimacy to it. But she does not indicate whether *A Thrilling Narrative* was popular or widely read. Presumably not, since unlike Sarah Wakefield's *Six Weeks in the Sioux Tepees*, which was republished by a different press in 1864 in an enlarged edition, *A Thrilling Narrative* was not reprinted and remained unknown after 1863 until recovery today as a "resurrected text," to use the words of Florestine Kiyukanpi Renville, the great-granddaughter of John's cousin Gabriel Renville.[50]

In the opening pages of her haunting memoir *Out of Africa*, Isak Dinesen describes the intense sense of belonging she felt toward her adopted home, which became her real home even though she was not born there:

"In the highlands you woke up in the morning and thought: Here I am, where I ought to be."[51] Her use of "ought" means not duty but desire, not "should be" but "want to be." After the war the Sisseton Agency gave the Renvilles a home base from which to work and forge a coupled identity. When they met, they may have assumed that they could straddle cultures and choose their social identities. The U.S.-Dakota War shattered that belief and forced them to confront the implications of their marriage: that John's assimilation *to* white culture did not mean assimilation *by* white culture.

The term "a culture of belonging" is explored by African American critic bell hooks in *Belonging: A Culture of Place*.[52] For decades John and Mary Renville strove to convert exile from homelands into a culture of belonging for themselves and those they served. They may also have derived some comfort from the fact that Sisseton was, as Gwen Westerman points out, in "close proximity to Lac qui Parle and the seasonal migration of Dakota people from the Red River Valley to Big Stone Lake along the Minnesota River and beyond."[53] Dakota people had no choice in being expelled from Minnesota, although they did have a choice in whether they could accept a site like Sisseton as their home and final resting place.

But perhaps the last word on home as a mesh of people and place belongs to contemporary Ojibwe writer Linda LeGarde Grover, who teaches at the University of Minnesota–Duluth. Here is how she ends a story in her recent collection, *The Dance Boots*, through an Ojibwe character named Rose: "See, for me, what I have learned is that we have a place where we belong, no matter where we are, that is as invisible as the air and more real than the ground we walk on. It's where we live, here or aandakii." An earlier story in the book had explained that "aandakii" is "the Ojibwe word for 'somewhere else.'" Unable to live in the traditional homelands after the war, John and Mary Renville had to privilege place through people, not people through place. Yearning for the homelands would never go away, but it might be assuaged by staying among the Dakotas. As the character Rose concludes, "Any of us by ourselves, we're just one little piece of the big picture, and that picture is home. We love it, we think we hate it sometimes, but that doesn't change anything. We are part of it; we are in the picture. It's home."[54]

A THRILLING NARRATIVE

OF

INDIAN CAPTIVITY

BY

MRS. MARY BUTLER RENVILLE

MINNEAPOLIS, MINN:

ATLAS COMPANY'S BOOK AND JOB PRINTING OFFICE

1863

ENTERED ACCORDING TO ACT OF
CONGRESS, IN THE YEAR 1863,
BY MRS. MARY BUTLER RENVILLE,
IN THE CLERK'S OFFICE OF THE DISTRICT
COURT OF THE DISTRICT OF MINNESOTA.

PREFACE

In the year 1859, we left Galesburg, Ill., for Minnesota, where we have been in the employ of Government, as Teachers among the Indians, as our readers will learn, without any further preface, from the narrative before them.

At the time of the outbreak, we were living only a few rods from the Mission at Hazlewood, five miles above Yellow Medicine.

THE INDIAN CAPTIVES

Leaves from a Journal[1]

///

CHAPTER ONE[2]

So much has been said about the Indian War that it may not be uninteresting to glean a few leaves from the Journal of one who was a captive during the late trouble. In order to realize the spirit of the time in which it was written, we will insert the preface just as it is.

This little book, in the providence of God, may fall into other hands, for we are in jeopardy every moment, and are so closely watched that we scarcely dare use the pen for fear of being suspected of trying to get letters to friends at home. With a full sense of the danger we are in, we forthwith subscribe the names of our family and those of our friends in Illinois, Wisconsin and Iowa. (The names we will omit here.)[3]

Time hastens, night is coming on, and it may be the night of death to all of us; in view of which we will say farewell to the joys and sorrows of this life.

Before commencing what may be termed the Journal part of our correspondence, it may be well to describe as far as practicable the locality of Hazlewood.[4] It is about two hundred miles north-west from St. Paul, and five miles from the junction of the Minnesota and Yellow Medicine rivers. In high water the boats go up as far as Yellow Medicine, or what is commonly called, Upper Sioux Agency.

The country about Hazlewood is (in our estimation) beautiful; being diversified with hills and valleys, and as you look across the Minnesota, the scenery is grand almost to sublimity. The long ranges of hills, bordered with forest trees, extending as far as eye can see, and the table land in the back ground, help fill up the picture.[5]

The country is well watered with rivers, creeks and small lakes. The valleys of the rivers are covered with heavy timber, while the lesser streams are skirted with wood land.

At some future time we may speak more at length of Hazlewood Republic and why it was formed.[6]

HAZLEWOOD REPUBLIC, AUGUST 21ST, 1862.[7]

This is the first opportunity we have had to note down anything since the terrible massacre commenced, which was August, Monday 18th inst. The first intimation we had of what the Indians were doing, was about 6 o'clock Monday evening. We had just arisen from the table when two men came in, and with the most intense feelings expressed in their countenances, begged us to hasten for our lives, in the meantime giving a brief account of the massacre.[8] People become so accustomed to Indian stories that they are not willing to believe any reports, no matter how they come; so it was with us; we did not even go to our nearest neighbors to tell what he had heard, but remained quiet; we were soon aroused by our friends calling again, and with authoritative tones told us to hasten away or we would certainly be massacred. While the horses were being harnessed we gathered up some articles of clothing and a little provisions and, threw them, pell-mell, into the wagon, ready to make good our escape.

By this time, some of the Friends from the Mission Boarding School, called, to see if we believed the reports. It was now nine o'clock in the evening; the excitement growing more intense every moment. As we passed the church some Indians, (strangers) with their guns, were busy talking; when asked what they were doing, they replied in a sullen way, "stop your noise." The Indians were already trying to steal Mr. Cunningham's horse, and, as we afterwards learned, went to our stables but found them minus of their prey.[9] They, however, succeeded in getting Mr. Rigg's horses.[10] He managed to save one horse which had been left in his care by a volunteer, by sending a man on it to the Agency, to see if the disturbance had commenced there.[11]

As we passed the Mission house, some of them inquired where we were going; we told them, and hurried on to a camp of friendly Indians, for protection.[12] Cutting our way through the woods as best we could, for if we traveled on the main road we were in danger of meeting the Rebel Indians, and that would have been certain death to our whole party. When we arrived at the Camp the Indians there knew nothing about the trouble. They immediately sent messengers to the Agency to learn the particulars. About three o'clock in the morning they returned with the news that the fight had commenced; we inquired for the Mission people; they said all but one family were close by; we went out to meet them and were anxious to go, *but* the Indians at the Camp said they were going to secrete them on an island till morning, but they were afraid of being pursued and thought it much safer that we should remain at the Camp.[13] We reluctantly consented. In the morning Messrs. R. and C. came over from the island and wanted to return to their homes to get some eatables, but were told it was not safe, and that they (the Indians) would bring them some which they did.[14] We talked with them about leaving; said they should leave in the P.M., or as soon as the man returned with one of their horses.

Tuesday, about noon, a man came into camp wounded; we washed his wounds which had been much irritated by the flannel wrapper he wore; gave him a change of linen and a little beef broth, for he was almost famished, and could bear but little nourishment at a time.[15] A little after this, Messrs. R. and C. came from the island and said they were going to start with what teams they had if the horses did not come, for it was not safe to remain any longer in the Indian country. We agreed with them, and determined to go at the same time, but to our surprise and horror some one had taken our harness; we still hoped it might return, and told them we would try and be ready.

///

CHAPTER TWO[16]

We made all needful preparations to leave the camp, but were disappointed.[17] Immediately after our friends left us, there came up a most terrific thunder storm, seeming literally as if the whole heavens were on fire; and the whole earth was to be shaken from its foundation. One could but think that the superstitious savages would have quailed before their Gods, and felt that they were exceedingly angry with them, and were about to render a quick retribution for the terrible tragedy they had but just commenced. The rain descended in torrents, the lightning came flash after flash, the thunder kept pace; and indeed language fails to describe the scene. It seemed as if the whole artillery of Heaven was about to burst. The storm continued till about sunset, when as if to compete with the horror before, the sun came out in glorious splendor, clearing away every cloud, and giving a life picture to every tree and shrub. During the storm we were in an unfinished house without doors or windows; we kept partially dry by placing a hide over a small space where the chamber floor ought to have been.[18] Here we were seated on the few goods we had saved from *home*, wishing, nay praying, that some way would be opened for our escape from such a miserable life. Place yourselves for a moment in imagination, in such a situation, not knowing but some enemy had crept into camp ready at the first opportunity to end your existence.

Enos came from the island; the Missionaries had left.[19] While he was returning, or when in sight of the camp, he met a Rebel Indian who questioned him minutely as to where he had been. He waived the answer, by telling him he had been looking for some cattle, at the same time showing his coat, how wet he had got it in the rain. It was the general opinion that the blood-thirsty savage was searching for the Missionaries. Having come from the Lower Agency, where he had doubtless "washed his hands in innocent blood," two of our company thinking they might find our friends, believing they had secreted themselves somewhere else, they started in pursuit, creeping through bushes and grass some of the way, fearing they might be seen by some hidden foe. They were absent some time, and we were very anxious for their safety. It was now dark, and we were told that should we attempt to leave camp that night, the doom of death to some, and the misery of a long captivity to the rest, would be the consequences. Terrible accounts are constantly coming from the massacre, but we dare not vouch for the truth of them till the excitement subsides a little and our own nerves become stronger.

But let us return to our Missionaries again, for too many pleasing associations of the past and anxiety for their present safety, will not permit us to be silent, and the Department people at Yellow Medicine; what has become of them? God only knows. We may hear from them.[20]

While our friends, fourteen in number, men, women and children, had remained on the island, they were without any shelter from the scorching sun, but the surrounding trees; not daring to build a fire, to cook a little food, or raise a smoke to keep off the mosquitoes, which in times of peace are almost intolerable, and would have been thought foe enough to contend with, and one a great hero that gained a victory over them by the aide of smoke, mosquito bars, &c. But in this instance they were merely "accidents attending greater evils;" had they made fire they might have called around them the savage warriors, thus ending all hopes of escape; the men being killed and worse than death to most of their families, for the young Braves had made their boast, they would have *those beautiful girls for their captives.*[21] But they left during the storm, and were exposed to the descending rain, in addition to the fatigue incident to camping on the island. Here we leave our early pioneers and christians [*sic*], carrying their lives in their hands, for in all probability they will be overtaken by the band of warriors that have gone (or reported to have gone) to the Big Woods.[22] "They know in whom they have trusted," and He who has so wisely guarded them through so many perils of a Missionaries life of twenty-five years, will we hope take them through in safety.[23]

Can we keep a journal through such times as these? For the sake of our friends we will try to do so.

Here comes a messenger with the sad tidings of Mr. Gleason's death, the young man who was taking Mrs. Dr. W——d from the Upper to the

Lower Agency, a distance of thirty miles, to aid her on her journey, as she had started on a visit to her friends.[24] This was on Monday A.M., the 18th, they had almost reached the place they intended taking dinner, when two Indians sprang up out of the grass; Mr. G., with his usual calmness and pleasing manners, inquired where they were going, not knowing the massacre had commenced at the Lower Agency. The Indians waited till they had passed them a little way, then one fired his gun, the ball striking him [Mr. G], he fell back a little, the horse being frightened commenced running, when the ball from the other Indian's gun reached him, causing him to fall, exclaiming, "Oh! My God! My God!" the last words he was able to utter. These fiends in human form took the Dr.'s wife and two children captives; taking away her trunk which had about $500 worth of clothing for herself and children.[25]

We may have occasion to refer to her again, for we saw her during her captivity. In the meantime let us nerve ourselves for what may be before us, for we know not what a day may bring forth, but God has promised as our day is so shall our strength be. If our readers can endure to hear the account (we were obliged to hear) and many exaggerated ones we don't record.

There was a trading post at Yellow Medicine, licensed by Government; this was attacked before the Department buildings. Forbes' store was conducted mostly by Mr. Quin, who was then absent at St. Paul.[26] On Monday evening the Indians informed the Clerk of the intended plot, telling him to make his escape as quick as possible, or his life would be forfeited. The Clerk broke the news to Mrs. Quin; the plan devised was to get a team (theirs being gone) and take Mrs. Quin to a place of safety. He started, and had gone but a short distance, when he saw Indians coming; he hastily returned, advised Mrs. Quin to take her children and flee; the Clerk went with them to some of the farmer Indians, (Muzomony) who tried to secrete the Clerk, but having reason to fear he might be found, he told him to run for his life; he hesitated, not willing to leave Mrs. Quin and her helpless family; but Muzomony said we had no team, it would be fruitless for her to start with the children on foot.[27] This prevailed. The

Clerk took to his feet, crossed the Minnesota River, called at a house, two men starting with him. One of them had a dog he prized highly, and was not willing to shoot him; the other man says we must part, for the dog will bark and betray us; he left them, and as we never heard of his death, we hope he made his escape. Not so with the Clerk and the other man, their bodies were found by the road near the Lower Agency. The most of those who travel on the main road are met and destroyed by Satan's destroying demons.[28]

There were four trading houses destroyed; report says the Clerks of two of them got away.[29] Not so with Mr. Garvie, one of the firm; he defended himself most all night, vigorously firing the guns he had in his possession.[30] The Indians fearing to enter while he kept up such a brisk firing, called to him to desist; but true to his *nature*, he determined to protect his property; at last the Indians concluded to fire into the window, hoping to hit him, which they succeeded in doing.[31]

CHAPTER THREE[32]

We are still at Friendly Camp, and are more closely watched than ever. Scouts are on the constant lookout. Garvie made out to reach the warehouse on the hill, a distance of about half a mile from his store. The Department people had all gathered there for self-defence, as well as to try to protect the Government property.[33] Mr. Garvie appearing among them so badly wounded, aroused them to a full sense of their danger and the necessity of escaping at once. They accordingly, with the efficient aid rendered them by Otherday and their own speedy movements, soon had teams ready at the door for the reception of their families—leaving their well-furnished homes without taking even the most movable and valuable articles, and glad to escape with their lives.[34] We have since learned that they were obliged to leave Mr. G. at a friends, where he was well cared for during his last illness, caused by the wounds he had received. The Department people passed the Indians, and were not molested. Probably the Indians were so engaged in plundering the stores that they cared for nothing else.

Wednesday, Aug. 20.—Rev. Dr. Williamson came to camp last night; we rejoiced to meet him once more.[35] It seemed as if an age had passed, for time flies swift in such conflicts as we are passing through, though hours seem long. The Dr. was unwilling to leave his house, but his true and faithful friends among the Dakotas said he must leave, for they could not bear to have him murdered in his own house without trying to escape. Robert Hopkins, who is now in prison, told them if they chose to remain with his family, he and others would protect them as long as their own lives were spared.[36] The Dr. appeared unwilling to leave the Mission ground. For this the spirit of the world may censure him, but those who have the spirit of Him who said, "go preach the gospel to every creature," certainly must admire the self-sacrificing man, willing rather to die if needs be, if he could only say to the little flock, *be firm*, and go not among those who are hastening on to certain destruction.[37] They had labored thirty years in this benighted land, and expected to end their days here. We might speak at length of their abundant labors, in connection with their co-workers, the fruits of which we have witnessed during our captivity. Had it not been for the gospel which had been planted by these true worthies, the massacre would have been more terrible and awful than it was, and the suffering captives have found no relief from their hated capture, as some of them did during the last few days of their captivity. Dear reader, please bear this in mind when you are contributing to the Mission cause, for you know not what the fruits of your labor may be.[38]

The Indians held a council with the Dr. as to what he had better do; and he wisely concluded to leave as soon as all could be got ready.[39] As for himself he said he had no fears, and manifested it by returning to his house about three miles distant, and getting some valuable books.[40] We feared for his safety, but God protected him. After he returned he went to a small pond a little distance from camp to water his horse. The Indian women gave a despairing moan, and raising their hands pointed to an Indian that had sprung up out of the grass and was following the Dr. with his gun. Paul and Simon hastily threw their powder horns over their shoulders and went in pursuit.[41] Overtaking the Indian they pertinently asked him what he wanted, and where he was going. He replied that he was looking for cattle. They told him in short metre to go where the cattle were. He soon made for the woods. They waited for the Dr., afraid to have him walk back alone to camp, fearing the Indian might return with a stronger party, and succeed in his cruel design, which they supposed was to kill the Dr. and take his horse.

While the Mission Indian women who had learned the art of cooking were preparing some refreshments, we saw an Indian talking to a small boy who pointed at our company. The rebel was raising his gun when we observed him, and quicker than thought, almost, we had our friends secreted in one corner of the unfinished house.

One of our friends, Miss Jane Williamson, remarked, "well, if they kill me my home is in heaven; let us try to keep heaven in view."[42] As soon as we could get ready we determined to leave camp with our friends. When it became known we were told that should we attempt to leave we would certainly be pursued, and thus endanger the lives of our whole party. This, it was said, was on account of the knowledge some of us had of the country, and the assistance we might render to the white settlements should we ever reach them. These were only reports, and we were not inclined to notice them; but reports had proved true in the first instance. We told them we had rather die than remain. They insisted that if we started we would share the fate of many others, a part being killed, the remainder being captives perhaps for life. We were almost deranged with excitement, and not being willing to depart with our dearest friend, we bade farewell to the Dr.'s family, or rather those he had with him, having sent the younger members away with his son-in-law.[43]

This was a sad parting. Not a tear moistened the eye but the heart felt; and even now we can't dwell on the scene. The friendly Indians said that they thought the rebels would all leave in a few days, and then as many of them as could leave their families would go to protect us and be certain of our safety. This fond delusion was never realized.

Paul advised us to remain in his tent, for so many were stealthily watching us, there was danger of our being shot.[44] It was finally thought best to move to where they could defend themselves better. On Wednesday P.M. we started, some of us fearing that every rustle of the leaves as we went through the woods, was some savage about to spring upon us. It was decided to occupy the Mission buildings, as they, being larger, would accommodate more, and thus render the chances for self-protection better. Besides, the fields were near, so that we would not endanger our lives by going after vegetables. Our numbers were small then, though many joined us afterwards.[45]

It is impossible to describe the desolation, confusion and destruction that had been made at these houses, and the feelings that took possession of us when we thought of the many families that had thus been driven from their homes. It needs a panorama to represent one-half of what was seen.[46]

We had our choice of a room at what had been the boarding-school house, and chose the most retired one, where we would not be as liable to be seen by passing Indians. The stoves were all standing, and most of the tables and chairs remained. Dry goods boxes and trunks were rifled of their contents, and lay in fragments about the house and yard. We immediately went about searching for any writings the Missionaries had left in their flight, and found some of value. Whiledoing [*sic*] this we partially forgot our own danger, so true it is that the mind occupied about others forgets its own troubles.

When the supper hour came we seated ourselves at the long table, which we had so often seen filled with happy children and loving teachers. We could hardly refrain from weeping while the blessing was being asked, and as soon as we could be excused we went to our rooms, where, for the first time, we permitted our tears to flow, somewhat to the relief of our aching hearts.

It would not do to indulge in sadness, for if we remained among this people it was necessary to wear an air of cheerfulness. After tea we all assembled for worship in the family sitting room, where Mr. C. had so often led the children in prayer and praise to God.

///

CHAPTER FOUR[47]

Paul and some others have gone to the Lower Agency, to learn if possible, what plan the Indians have in view, and to see if there is any possibility of getting word to the white people.

We had quite a gathering for prayer the other evening; most of those at Mr. R.'s house came; a chapter was read, a hymn sung and a word of exhortation given to the faithful few. It reminded us of early times, when it was not safe to go to the house of God without weapons of defense.[48]

The Northerners are expected daily, and much danger is apprehended from them. A few have been lurking about for several days, and during the night stole five horses.[49] There is no rest for the weary. While at worship Mr. R. was called out to see to his horses, as some one was trying to untie them from the wagon. The thief soon left for safe quarters, being afraid of a gun in the dark. Dogs are quite a help these times; almost every Indian keeps from three to six, and some even a greater number for hunting, and in case of famine, use their flesh for food. The wild shouts of the Indians, and the constant barking of the dogs, were we in a forest, would be intolerable. As for sleep we get a little, and very little it is.

Katherine came in the evening; the first we had seen of her since the trouble.[50] She threw her arms about us and wept like a child, partly in sympathy for us, and for the loss the church had sustained and the sufferings of the white people. Katherine thought we were not safe in our costume; and immediately devised means of getting a Dakota one, which, with a little help, was soon ready for wear, but so many of the company realized we would not be at home in it, persuaded us to lay it aside for the present.

Reports are constantly coming that the Indians are committing great depredations. They are confident of taking New Ulm and Fort Ridgely. May *the All Wise* keep them from it, is our earnest petition. God may have visited New Ulm in offended wrath, for we have reason to believe they burned the Saviour in effigy only last Sabbath, (Aug. 17th;) and their laws are strictly against selling lots to any person who will aid in supporting the gospel.[51]

We have busied ourselves to-day in making preparations for an escape, should one offer, and we may have to secrete ourselves in the woods a long time; then we shall value our sack of biscuit. While we were making them, two gaily dressed Indian girls called at the door exclaiming, this is the last time we shall ever see a white woman. They were entire strangers, and startled us a little. Some of our party gave them a little cool advice, which they deemed prudent not to stay and consider. We have had to secrete ourselves several times during the day, for strangers are passing to and fro all the time, and the sight of a white person may cause them to yield to *the wicked one* and devour us.[52]

It is quite evident that the white people have not taken any of the fire-water, as the Indians call it, from the country or towns.[53] Oh, that another drop, not even for medicine, may ever be carried in the Indian country again; New Ulm, we are confident, furnished its share heretofore.

Miss Laframboi called here on her way from Lacquiparle.[54] Her brother went after her. She did not have time to give a full account of Mr. Huggins' cruel death; but having learned the particulars since, we will give them in this part of our journal. This sad event was on Tuesday P.M.[55] Mr. H. had been out tending to some hay and did not return until after the thunder storm. While he was absent two young Indians called and inquired when Mr. H. would be at home. After being told they seated themselves and commenced making observations about the sewing machine, intent on examining its rapid movements, and making cheerful remarks in regard to it. They seemed rather anxious for Mr. H. to return. When Mr. H. came into the house, his wife, addressing him, he replied in his kind endearing way, passed out and went to his oxen. The Indians followed, not awakening any suspicion. The ladies in the house heard the report of the gun, but thought they were only firing at ducks. Soon the Indians tried to enter the school-room; the door being fastened they endeavored to break it open with their guns. Even then, Mrs. H. supposed they were frightened by seeing Chippeways, and were fleeing from them. They entered the house, knocking over the children and telling Mrs. H. and Miss L. (the assistant teacher) "go, go, we wont kill you, but don't stop to take anything with you."[56] Driven from her home, Mrs. H. soon saw the corpse of her beloved husband; the only sign of life was a little pulsation above the eyes, his body smoking from the moisture of his dripping clothes; she spread over him a lounge cover she fortunately held in her hand, and was hurried away from this last kind act by the ruthless murderers. Miss L. led this widowed mother and two fatherless children to a Chiefs house for protection, where she remained the most of the time during her long captivity; for bear in mind, that Lacquiparle is thirty miles above the Mission Station.[57] The Indians of that place said their teacher should not have been killed if they had known of the massacre. This was their first intimation of it. The murderers belonged to another band.[58] Though we mourn the loss of our dear friend, we rejoice that his daily walk and conversation and earnest labors among the benighted people by whom he was surrounded, leave no doubt of his happy entrance into the mansions above.

Paul has returned and related his interview with the Rebel Chiefs. The substance of which is contained in a letter dictated by him shortly after, and as our readers may be interested in its contents, we give a copy herewith.[59]

Hazelwood, September 2d, 1862[60]

Gov. Ramsey:

Your Excellency has probably heard ere this of the terrible massacre committed by the Indians Aug. 18th, and continuing up to this date.

As it is difficult to give correct information from a distance, I will give you a statement of all the facts I have been able to glean from the Chiefs concerned. Little Crow has been one of the most active and cruel. The others wished to put off the work of death till payment and see how matters stood with government [*sic*], but Little Crow, to use his own language, held several councils long before the 18th in order to hurry the other bands.[61] On the 17th, four men of Shakopee band went to the Big Woods, killed some white men, and stole some horses. The next A.M., they went to Little Crow and told their crimes. Now, says he, you have commenced, let us strike the fatal blow, and rid the country of the whites, taking possession of all goods, cattle, and provisions, and become the rightful owners of our lands again. And as far as I am able to learn they have fulfilled their purpose in the most outrageous manner. Previous to commencing on Monday, a messenger was despatched [*sic*] to Yellow Medicine and Red Iron Village, but not one word did the Bands about the Mission know till the slaughter commenced. We tried to aid the Missionaries in their escape.

Lacquiparle people kept quiet for some days, then went to Big Stone Lake, and joined with the few in killing the small number of defence-less whites there. The most of the Indians were away on a hunt.[62] The reason the Chiefs gave me was that payment was delayed and the traders would not trust them, but told them to leave their stores, and go eat grass like the oxen, that they were a lazy set and would have to starve if they did not. (Little Crow is a wicked, crafty deceiver.) These things he said, made them very angry, and after they had killed the trader named, they stamped his head in the dust till it was as fine as powder.[63]

He farther [*sic*] stated that the trader told them they could not fight, and that he could chew them all up as fine as dust.[64] I do not think that many blamed our Hon. Agent, only his volunteering about that time caused them to believe he did not intend making any payment, and rather exasperated them. He is, we believe, an honest man, and has always given us good advice; encouraging us to labor, and assisting us in all possible ways, so we think.[65]

We fear our Great Father at Washington has not realized the danger of leaving his people exposed to our savage tribes, and so has failed to furnish sufficient troops to protect them, or the civilized Christian Indians; for I think there is quite a difference between a Christian Indian and one that merely changes his costume and customs a little without changing his motives of moral action.[66]

I have held two councils, and tried by all the persuasions in my power to have the Rebels liberate the captives, willing to lose my own life, if by so doing I could send these poor suffering captives safe to St. Paul. I have succeeded in getting one family and shall persevere until the end.[67] But, my Father, we are all captives; a small band of Christians surrounded by our persecuting neighbors, and whither, oh whither, shall we flee? Our trust is in God, and we hope He will put it into your heart, our Father, to tell us what we shall do. Think of it, our Father, and don't let our wives and our little ones starve, or, what is worse, move on to Red River with our savage foes and perish for lack of food for both soul and body.

I am a friend to the whites, to civilization, and christianity [*sic*].

Yours Respectfully,
Paul, or Muza Ka-te-ma-ne.

Gov. Ramsey:

Dear Sir—If you will allow us to address you thus familiarly, for the name of a white man is even dear to those who though not an eye witness, yet as one hearing of the awful tragedies almost daily committed by the lower bands; we will not detain you with our family sufferings, after writing the lengthy epistle dictated by Paul; but at the earnest request of Lorenzo and Simon, state that they, with their families, are very anxious to escape to the white settlements, and will the first opportunity; our lives are threatened if we attempt to leave; we have but little provision on hand.[68] If in the all wise Providence, we are not permitted to go among our white friends, we have resolved to die on Mission ground, rather than go among the idolatrous and wicked Indians. Please publish this at the request of

Simon and Lorenzo.[69]

///

CHAPTER FIVE[70]

About the 25th of August Gabriel removed from Yellow Medicine, where he had been staying with his own and his sister's family a short time.[71] Mrs. Brown was warned of the intended massacre in time to have escaped; but with others did not credit the report. She started to go with her family, to the Fort, accompanied by her son and wife and son-in-law and his family. They were stopped by the Indians, and would all have been killed or taken captive, had not Mrs. B. satisfied them in regard to her mother's family. Happily the relationship saved them.[72] They let the son-in-law go. He barely escaped with his life, his health poor, having been under the care of physicians for a long time, and taking only five small crackers with him, and being obliged to lie hid in a marsh for a long time, surrounded by Indians who were searching for him. You can easily imagine in what an emaciated state he reached his destination.[73] Mrs. Brown remained at the Lower Agency till her brother went after her.[74] The Indians dressed them up in the poorest kind of Dakota clothes, and then laughed at them, saying, "these are the people who used to dress in silks so rich and fine," little realizing that one cared not for fine dress in such perilous times as these.

The day before this family moved from Yellow Medicine Mrs. A. B. had a little son. She was a delicate lady, and was preparing to go and make her mother a long visit before they were taken captive.[75] They all suffered much during captivity, but not as much as those who were entire strangers; the most of them having lived in the Indian country a long time, and being familiar with the language.[76] The 26th the Lower Bands moved up to Yellow Medicine, seeming disappointed that Gabriel had moved away with their captives. A day or two after they sent a company of thirty soldiers to Hazlewood with the intention of making them move back, which they positively refused to do. Chagrined at their failure, they went back. Big Amos told them they had no business at Hazlewood, and that they had made themselves work enough below and had better remain there.[77] It is strange how impudent these Indians are to each other, and still live in constant fear of the same ones. They frightened us very much, passing through the house, singing their war songs and threatening to burn all the buildings that P.M. Some of us kept hid; the rest went to packing up their things. Our readers will have to allow their imagination full scope to realize all that we suffered; there being none but women in the house at this time. The men, with one exception, had gone to attend a council.

Mr. R. had gone to the Lower Bands to see his sisters, and their families, who were taken captives by Little Crow's band.[78] They wanted to come and stay with us, and started to do so, and were driven back on to the prairie away from wood or water, and their children were crying for food. Mr. R. returned, called a council, which formed themselves into soldiers; this took some time, as they all came out on dress parade.[79] We prepared the uniform for one of the principal officers, and became so interested in it as to almost forget we were captives, and enjoyed a real hearty laugh at its fantastic appearance.[80] They all mounted their fiery steeds which seemed to have breathed the spirit of war, and at a given signal formed the line of march, firing their guns into the air, and giving one simultaneous shout. They were joined by some other bands on the way.[81] Confident of success they surrounded Little Crow's camp and demanded the captives mentioned above. We expected they would have a serious time, but this wicked cowardly set hid their cattle and horses and remained perfectly quiet in camp.[82]

Sept. 3d. Mrs. DeCamp came this A.M. with her three children, the eldest nine years of age, the youngest not two, her own health very delicate.[83] She gave vent to her feelings by weeping, but we restrained her as well as ourselves for fear of those who are on the watch to see if our sympathies are not all enlisted towards the whites.[84] This was the second time we had seen a white woman, and could we have wept freely it would have relieved our aching head.[85] At the time the trouble commenced her husband was absent from home, and a chief who had always been befriended by their hospitality, came and told her of the imminent danger, saying "get into the wagon and I will protect you as long as I can, till you can obtain a better place."[86] She had suffered much, walking twenty-five miles, carrying her babe, and leading another little son, wading streams, being told by the wicked ones if any of the children were troublesome they would dispatch them.[87] She had always been spared any hardships by indulgent parents and a more indulgent husband. The chief treated her as well as the economy of a large family would allow. She lived in a tent, sleeping on the ground, laying her sick children on an over-coat she had obtained from the Indians that had plundered her house. The food was not eatable. One day she made up her mind for some nice fresh beef, when she saw the woman put it over for boiling; but was soon disappointed by her throwing the entrails into the same kettle. Had she understood them she might have prepared her own food. The chief had Mrs. D. write a message to her husband, and endeavored to take it to him, but was wounded on the way and obliged to return. The most thrilling incident related by this reliable woman, was the suffering of three young ladies brought to camp in the evening—six young drunken Indians (or Satan's emissaries) taking these helpless girls.[88] They clung to Mrs. D. crying, "save, oh, save us!" She could only listen to their heart-rending moans.

One of them had been seriously wounded in the morning trying to make her escape, and died the next day.[89] These fiends in human form, not satisfied with their crimes, took them to a tent where there was another drunken rabble, and afterwards returned them to the first camp. The chief seemed very sad about the whole affair, and said had he been at home he could have prevented it. Satan tempted them. But who left the liquor in the country for them? The captives doubtless suffered much worse than they would have done had it not been for this fire-brand left by the white people, and which has caused so many crimes by all nations.

When Mrs. DeCamp came we were scarcely able to walk, and could not bestow as much attention on her and the little children as we desired.[90] We had an attack of the pleurisy, and suffered extremely for several days. We gave Mrs. D. an upper room, which was the best circumstances afforded, but was almost unendurable from the heat of an August sun, and served to highten [sic] the disease which had fastened itself on the little ones. We sent for Paul and Lorenzo and held a council of five, as to what was best for Mrs. D. to do, it not being safe for her to remain long with us. It was decided to get a canoe, as she felt confident she could manage it by the help of her boy, and follow a French family Paul was going to send that evening with a dispatch to Gov. Ramsey.[91] Accordingly Mr. Renville and Lorenzo went four miles, found a large canoe, and labored hard to paddle it back over the rapids. But on their return to the house some one told them that the plan was known, and they must not send away the captives; if they did a plot was laid to kill them all. Some evil person, we supposed, had listened to the council, though all had spoken in a whisper.

We think they must have placed a chair under the safe of the stove pipe, as we found one there when we went into our room. This was trying indeed, and grieved us to inform Mrs. D. of the result. But she had wrestled in prayer all afternoon, and was ready for any way Providence seemed to open.

///

CHAPTER SIX[92]

MISSION STATION, SEPT. 3.

The excitement still increases. Rebels report constant success, and are confident of taking all the smaller towns, and if they could get St. Peter, and Traverse de Sioux, they are going to attack St. Paul in the night. We are quite sure they will find some men in the country yet, though the prevailing opinion is, that they have all gone South, and none but old people and little children are left at home. This was circulated by Little Crow about a year since, when he says he went to Shakopee to spy out the land; and when Government called for men at Yellow Medicine it seemed to confirm them in this opinion.[93]

The Mission Bands are much more quiet, seeming to have a little hope that God will yet appear and deliver them. Chande, an old wicked heathen woman, said to Catherine, "Where is your God? why don't he come and help you? You see now that our gods are strong and mighty, and have driven away all your teachers. You had better renounce your worship, and serve our Idols." We have had meeting every Sabbath so far, one of the Elders reading and explaining a portion of scripture. White people, in times like these, might omit praising God for fear of calling around them the enemy, and so scatter the assembly. Every evening almost as many convene as on the Sabbath, and the same course is pursued in giving instruction. It may be providential that some have been detained as captives for the encouragement and example they are able to give this people.[94]

We have been to Rev. Mr. Riggs' house to see what prospect there is of saving a part of his valuable library. The Dakota books will be distributed, and the others buried, if men enough can be found to do it; but the most of them think it is of no use, for the enemy are ever on the watch, and would dig them up and destroy them.[95] The sewing machine, the first time we saw it, was injured but a trifle; the clock stands in its place keeping time and constantly pointing to the fleeting hours as they pass, the same as the owner had done many years to the Dakotas, pointing them to a crucified and risen Savior. The garden, trees, shrubbery and flowers, are nearly all destroyed. The last have rendered us daily pleasure. The little children, unconscious of danger, have filled the air with their merry laughter, gathering flowers for us, nicely arranging them in glasses. By their fragrance and beauty we are led to adore the Creator in his wisdom and love to fallen man; and as these frail beauties fade and fall we are reminded that life and death are written on every page of the universe.

Mr. Renville, Simon and Lorenzo, have succeeded in burying the church bell, so that if the house is burned we shall be spared the sad scene witnessed at the Dr.'s church—young men ringing the bell and choosing one of their number to stand in the pulpit ridiculing the reverend man who had so lately been driven from its courts.[96] Being afraid that we cannot get the books buried securely, we have selected a few, and boxed them up, and shall keep them as long as we have any hope. In our search we found a large ledger belonging to Government, in the dining room closet, looking as though it had come through mud and water and was stained with blood. It has probably been brought here by some of the Indians.[97] It is a kind Providence in our not getting our salaries for teaching, for the present Administration may allow our claims, and if we had received it when due, it would have all been destroyed in this massacre, and if we ever reach a place where property is of any value, we shall need something to purchase the bare necessaries of life, for every article but what can be packed in one trunk has been taken from us.[98] We have kept the cattle so far; furnished one of the small ones towards a feast Paul held last week. We were almost wicked enough to wish it had choked Little Crow and all the crowers in the rebellion, but we were quite official in searching for pans, bowls and spoons, or anything else less than a small wash-tub, for this feast, hoping that it might result in the liberation of the captives. Paul is said to be very eloquent, but neither his feast nor eloquence prevailed.

Mrs. DeCamp is still with us; we should not consent to have her leave us could we protect her from the Lower Bands, and have concluded that it is best for her to live in Lorenzo's family when we leave this house; and we will take care of her oldest boy.

The people have all left Mr. R.'s. An Indian has been breaking windows, blinds, and everything else his strength was able to accomplish, preparatory to setting fire to the building; some of our friends made him desist, and promise to wait until we were all removed.[99]

They have not taken the Fort yet. Little Crow says he has been a great warrior, and fought many battles, but this is the best sport he ever had, and as for those little cannon at the Fort they only make him laugh to see the balls roll around and not harm any one.[100] Killing white people, he says, is like shooting ducks.

All are busy making preparations for living in tents; we were much perplexed at first, supposing we should be entirely dependent upon some of the Indians for a tent, but fortunately Mr. R. traded a two-year-old colt for one. This is rather a round sum to pay, but cotton is in great demand for building material just now.[101]

The friendly Indians are urging us to leave the house, fearing the rebels will set fire to it at night.

Sept. 4. We are now living for the first time in a tent. This P.M. we went with Mr. R. to take a last look at the Mission buildings.[102] He went with the intention of getting some boards, for making a shed over our cooking stove near the tent, determined to keep this vestige of civilization as long as possible. We really enjoy the large rocking chair, and could have good times if we were with a company of chosen friends, on a pleasure excursion, instead of being afraid of one's life every moment. This is something that cannot be described on paper. Before we had time to get many boards, two young rebels entered the church, a short distance from us, and made havoc of everything within their reach, until stopped by an older man.[103] They came then to where we were, went into Mr. C.'s house, singing and appearing to be very joyful, going through the house, making sport of the Dakota hymn book they had found, and continuing this till they reached Mr. Riggs' house. By this time the flames were pouring out of Mr. C.'s chamber window. We went a little distance and watched the progress of the fire, keeping our blankets wrapped close about our head, for fear of being known as white persons, for we have all been obliged to lay aside civilized costumes. After Mr. C.'s house had become completely enveloped in flames, the smoke and fire were seen issuing from the lower part of Mr. Riggs' house. They had set fire to a small house used for the Mission school, and where we had both been employed as teachers by government some years before—government renting the house of the Mission here. Again our thoughts were concentrated on the past, as we called to mind the men, women and children we used to meet daily, often thirty in number. We had a few trials then, which were made as smooth as possible by our experienced friends, the Missionaries; but they are not here now, and we must look to a higher source for aid and comfort in these greater trials.

Frank Bascom, a blind boy who has been a member of our family and school for a long time, and dear little Lillie, who had become accustomed to our ways of living, are now wanderers we know not where.[104]

Lillie has been with us ever since she was three years old, and is now seven, her father promising to pay for her board; and being a white man employed by government several years, acquired a sufficient sum to afford to hire her board.[105]

When her grand father, Bad Track, came for her, it was almost like letting our own darling go into captivity. Dear Lillie was so sad, and begged us not to let her go. We could not persuade the old man, and to have refused would only have irritated him. Poor Lillie does not understand their language or customs.

We can certainly realize in a measure, how those mothers, who have had their dear children torn from them and taken captives by others, must mourn.[106]

It has led us to forget ourselves, thinking of these dear children. At some future time we will try to give a short history of Frank Bascom's life for the benefit of our young readers. At present we shall have time only to introduce Mrs. Newman and her three children, captives, taken by the Lower Bands and who have succeeded in getting to Simon's for protection since the rebels moved up.[107]

We called to see her on our way from the fire; we found in her another example that in trials, deep trials, Jesus is the only real comforter and soother in our afflictions. Friends may try to alleviate sufferings, but it is sometimes beyond human agency to relieve the anguish of the heart. She seems a meek and loving disciple of her Lord and Master.

How glad the captives are to get among the friendly Indians! The praise is all due to that gospel which makes the savage heart become humane, and man respect the rights of his fellow man.

CHAPTER SEVEN[108]

CAMP NEAR RUSH BROOK.

The rebels are camped on the opposite side of us. We have only six tents in our company. A part have gone about half a mile above; we came here with the intention of deceiving the enemy, thinking that if we showed no signs of fear or desire of escaping, they might remove their diligent watch. We are confident that by leaving the tent and team standing we could make our escape if we were only able to walk the distance necessary to take a canoe, though we have been a little intimidated by one woman being shot, or reported to have been, for trying to get away. That would be our fate or similar should we be discovered.[109]

Sabbath Sept. 7th. —Lorenzo addressed the people, about forty in number. The tents being all small, seats were made of the boards we had saved from the Mission and placed in front of our tent. Mrs. Decamp and Mrs. Newman, with their families, came. Quite an excitement arose during the exercises by the rebel soldiers suddenly appearing, about one hundred in all, mounted, and firing off their guns into the air, and singing triumphant songs. Only a few came into our camp, but not a Dakota left their seats. The white captives were not so quiet. Some of them having more reason for fear than we had, tried to secrete themselves in the tent.[110] The cause of this sudden move was the return of a war party from Forest City, bringing more captives.

The day has been truly a sad one; rebels, as if to show how much disregard as possible to all sacred rights of christians, burned the church in the forenoon. Paul tried to prevent this by calling a council the day previous, and endeavoring to persuade them to desist, and to spare the church; that it was no use for them to think they could escape the penalty of justice, and that they had done terrible deeds, and continuing, would only add vengeance to justice in their final retribution; pleading with them and even demanding the captives, telling them the white people would pursue them though they might secrete themselves in the forests, or flee to the mountains, and the husbands and brothers of the captives, if not restrained by a Higher Power, would literally destroy them root and branch.[111]

We learned afterwards that the superstitious savages were almost afraid to commit to flame the house dedicated to the Most High, especially on the Sabbath. Undoubtedly had some ghastly figure been represented on the wall it would have prevailed more than all the combined force of Paul's argument.[112]

Early Sabbath forenoon, one of Little Crow's head warriors came to our camp with a small day-book which had been found by some of his war parties. It was a brief sketch of the times, at that place. The object, he said, in bringing it to us was to see if we interpreted it the same as the others who had read it. He eyed us closely while it was read. At any other time we might have quailed beneath his stern gaze, but we were so elated at the good news contained in the little book that we could scarcely keep from expressing by our countenance what we felt in our hearts. It stated that General Sibley was marching forward with a large force.[113]

About three o'clock Monday forenoon Mrs. De Camp sent Catherine for her boy.[114] We awoke him, asking no questions, fearing that some traitor might be lurking around the camp. Soon the whole camp was aroused, guns answered to guns, loud speeches were made, which were answered in the same vehement manner. The order was given to take down tents, load the wagons and march forward. We found we were completely cut off from any hope of an escape, for the distance Mrs. DeCamp and Lorenzo's family would have to walk to get to their canoes, was too far for us to make an attempt, as we would be overtaken in our slow march. Mrs. DeCamp lay hid all day in a swamp.

We had almost resolved to remain when some of our friends from the upper camp came on purpose to expostulate with us, saying that if we remained, we would not only cause our own death, but that of all our friends in the camp, for they would not leave us, but remain and die with us.[115] We told them we were entirely opposed to starting to Red River. Cold weather would come and our provision be gone, and the horses famished for want of grain before we could reach there with the Indian camp.

Nepansi came in and said if you remain, don't cry for mercy, for none will be shown you. The rebels will surely put you to a cruel death, as they have declared they will do if they find any deserting or remaining.[116] To all this we replied, the rebels in the confusion and hurry of moving, would forget us, or think we only tarried awhile; but says he, soldiers are to be left to watch the movements of all the bands, and especially the captives, and they are now in pursuit of Lorenzo. We laid down upon our couch in a kind of exhaustive despair. Worn out with excitement, fatigue, and exposure, we laid in a kind of stupor till nearly daylight, then we arose and went calmly to work, making preparations for moving.

Mr. R. went to see Simon, for the good old man was fully determined to never move on towards Red River, with the idolatrous Indians. Simon came back with him. The same emphatic words were said to Simon that had been to us; he was decided; said he could only die if he remained on Mission ground, and that was our certain doom, if we went to Red River.[117] It was a sad parting; he shook hands with all, wiping the tears from his eyes, which he could not keep from falling. We had already tarried. The camp had nearly all gone, and soldiers were sent from several standpoints, watching our movements. We were not afraid. The storm had swept over us so bitterly that we were almost paralyzed, or careless as regards this present life. But of necessity we were obliged to take up our line of march. Mr. R. driving the cattle, while we drove the team, and carrying our darling Ella in our arms, clinging closer to her fearing she might be torn from us in any new freak of the enemy. To realize in the least what our feelings were, place yourselves in imagination in the same condition, leaving the last vestige of civilization, not even daring to wear a bonnet or hat to protect your eyes from the blazing sun as you rode across the broad prairie.[118] It being contrary to our nature to remain long on the hill of difficulty, or in the Slough of Despond, we whipped up the horses, and looked around to see what nature offered to assist us in raising our thoughts to the Creator, who wisely orders all things.[119]

By this time Mr. R. joined us, having found a young man to drive the cattle. We were really happy to have his company again. This, with the renovating atmosphere, had almost a happy effect.[120]

We went slow or fast, just as we pleased. There were three or four wagons in company. At one of the Indian camps we found a nice wagon seat, which proved a valuable article as we had to travel over two hundred miles, in an open wagon, before we left Minnesota, and this good spring seat added much to our comfort. At the several camps we saw trunks, boxes, tubs, barrels, oyster cans, and various other articles, scattered in helpless confusion. Mr. R. loaded his wagon with strings of corn the Indians had left; many of them having no teams were forced to leave all that would prove a hindrance in their march. The rebels have decided, if the upper bands will allow, to march direct to Red River.[121]

Nothing of importance transpired on our way to Red Iron village. We met scouts who eyed us keenly then passed to where there had been a camp the night previous, and went about preparing a feast for themselves and comrades. We could easily judge what was to be the chief dish at the feast, for a young Indian went by carrying a good sized dog they had just shot. We were detained some time by one of our company breaking his wagon, so as to render it necessary to place his load on the other wagons.

We reached Red Iron village about the middle of the afternoon. We had a fine view of the rebel camp; small flags were flying in every direction to direct the occupants to their various lodges, for there is as much danger of getting lost here as in a city.

First in order was Little Crow's camp. Second, all the lower bands connected with him in crime. Third, those forced to join his camp, not daring to separate themselves for fear of bringing on a civil war. Fourth, the Hazlewood band. Fifth and last, Red Iron band, which had stopped Little Crow in making any farther advance into the country. We rode about some time searching for a suitable place to camp, all the desirable ones near water having been selected before we arrived.

The point determined, we waited patiently for some one to assist in putting up the tent. Soon Red Feather's wife put up the tent, making it secure against the winds, for the winds in Minnesota are very searching at this season of the year.[122] She then brought a few brands and made a blazing fire in the center of the tent, and then, like a thoughtful mother, brought a pail of water, Mr. R. being busy taking care of his horses and cattle.

We were thankful to Mrs. Red Feather, and in return gave her a small brass kettle we had saved to barter with. We had scarcely arranged our buffalo robe, and other useful articles in a tent, before summoned to the door by the war songs of the soldiers, who always go upon their horses, firing their guns into the air. These savage demonstrations always frighten us more or less. Their business seemed to be turning over tents, and as though we did not know but our tent might be the next, it being the nearest to them, still we could not suppress a silent laugh at the apparent unconcern of the occupants, as they sat in the form of circles around the fire, some inclining on their elbows listening or talking, while others were smoking their kinnekinnick, the women busy making or preparing moccasins, not seeming to hear or see what the soldiers had done.[123]

Others went to taking down their own tents, in preference to having the soldiers do it for them, and packed up their effects. There were some of the lower bands entirely innocent of the massacre, and who were anxious to separate from Little Crow and all his followers. This was the occasion of their joining our band. The soldiers succeeded in driving them all back, for resistance only makes them more furious, and their numbers are the largest. How long we shall have a respite from their unearthly songs and firing of guns, we know not.

///

CHAPTER EIGHT[124]

RED IRON VILLAGE.

Everything moves on in about the same way. War parties returning. Councils held. Criers go about the camp making known the commands of the rebels. Occasionally one returns from battle wounded, and a death in any of the camps produces great lamentation. The female relatives go about with their hair disheveled, and tattered garments, making the most heart-rending moanings that can be imagined, varying from a boisterous cry to a low, deep sound; then again we can think of nothing but an old deserted building, whose walls creak and groan with the burden of years as the wind howls through the frail tenement; inhabited only by the dim spectres of haunted imaginations. Who has not listened to the low murmuring whistle among the trees in the Autumn? Add to this the tremulous appearance of the popple leaf, supposing it to be sound instead of motion, and you have in partial effect a description of the mourning for the dead, which is like most of the heathen nations, and not much unlike the weeping of Israel. The time chosen for these scenes is usually just as day is departing, or at midnight, or before the day dawns.[125]

The friendly Indians will doubtless get killed or make themselves trouble in the future, by trying to get horses from deserted settlements. The Indian's reason that the owners cannot return after them, and that the rebels will take them, if they don't, and as they still expect to be driven on to Red River, and have no teams of their own; it seems to us they act much the same as white people would in the same circumstances. Their love for the aged ones, and helpless children is very strong, and to plunder for these objects of their care, they do not believe to be wrong; for, say they, we are driven to it by the rebels, who threaten our aged parents and helpless children with death, if they cannot keep pace on a march with the able-bodied men. It would be better if they would put their trust entirely in their Heavenly Father,—but that is what men are often slow to do.

The Indians are using up the powder and shot very fast. It being a season for ducks, a constant firing is kept up morning and evening; this adds to the wild excitement, for the running to and fro in haste to procure guns, left momentarily in their tents; and to one not initiated in all the strategems [sic] of Indian warfare, it is hard judging what these movements mean, until you hear the guns explode, one after another, into the air. This wasting of powder is a matter of rejoicing, for it gives us reason to believe they cannot carry on the war much longer.

Wednesday.—We called on Maj. B.'s family to while away a few tedious moments; they have a large and commodious tent, but many to occupy it with them. Nellie's walking habit looked very becoming with her rich broadcloth skirt and fashionable shawl, thrown gracefully over her shoulders. The shawl and habit she had when taken captive, and had been allowed to keep them by getting to the friendly Indians for protection.[126]

We throw in this to give a ray of cheerfulness to the narrative. But while we were there, none of us dared to speak above a whisper in English, and if we forgot ourselves, some friend outside would warn us of our danger. Mr. R. came for us with a buggy he had borrowed; this was a rare treat, and we accepted with a cheerful heart.

Thursday.—Mary went with us to Mr. Pettijohn's house, to do some washing, for we are too poor to hire a Dakota woman now, although we have been forbidden by friends and medical advisers to attempt such labor when we were living in civilized life.[127] We had to go about four miles,—found the stove standing,—the feathers flying, the bureau rifled of its contents. The front door was locked. The teachers were at the Missions on the eve of the outbreak, and made their escape with the Missionaries. We took one tub with us and found another at the house. Mr. R. carried the things to the spring. We met two soldiers that had been acting as scouts; one of them had on a table spread belonging to Mrs. Riggs. They watered their horses, inquired what we were going to do, and appearing satisfied, went their way.[128] We are saving our beef for the last extremity. The Indians have plenty, but probably think we are selfish, in not killing ours, and so do not give us but a very little. Washing in cold, hard water, is not very pleasant, but we have plenty of soft soap we borrowed from some of our company, or rather begged, for we can make no return here, except kind words. We have a little hard soap for colored clothes we saved from our own dear home. When about half through Ella cried so much we carried her up the long hill, hoping to find her father there. The desolate appearance of the once happy home of a christian family, the howling of the wind through the broken casements, all tended to fill the mind with gloom. We were looking for Mr. R., when we saw several Indians coming with their teams after corn. Frightened almost out of our senses we took Ella in our arms and started down the hill as fast as possible. They called to us, asking what we wanted or who we were looking for; we told them. They probably knew us, though we did not them.

Mr. R. came back just as we were through washing. He had to go much farther than he expected after corn. Our clothes did not look very white, but were cleaner.

We had gone about a mile towards home when Mr. R. found that he'd left his axe at the house.[129] He ran back after it, while we held the horses. They were very uneasy, and kept backing all the time. Two Indian women came along with their hatchets in their hands, flourishing them about and looking "daggers" at us, inquiring of Mary what white woman that was, and what business we had off on the prairie. Mary told them very pleasantly. The muscles of their faces relaxed. We have always felt they intended doing us harm, but finding out who we were, discouraged them. Some of the women, it is said, can fight as well as the men. Whether they can equal the German women at New Ulm or not, is a question; for they were much more courageous it is said than their husbands during the seige [*sic*] of that place.[130]

We have already given one letter dictated by Paul. We now copy one from some other chiefs. Before doing so, we will state that we endangered our lives by writing, and had to be very cautious so as not to be discovered. If in the day time, we usually secreted ourselves in the tent some way; but generally the Indians wished us to write in the night. Sometimes we have waited until we thought every one ought to be asleep, and then put out the fire, Mr. R. would hold a blanket over us and the candle, so as to keep the light from shining through the tent; besides this caution, a guard was placed outside the tent to report any intruder who might be approaching:

Red Iron Village, Sept. 10th, 1862.[131]

Gen. Sibley:

Our much esteemed friend—We (that is) Wabaxa Hoxaxa and Wakata, have carefully considered our positions, as Chiefs of three Bands, and being desirous of returning to our former homes, at the Lower Agency; we consult your wish in regard to doing so.[132]

Our bands did not commence the trouble, but contrary to our wishes some of our young men joined in with the guilty ones; we were driven to act, and our fear is now, if we go back without your consent we shall meet your forces in hostility instead of meeting them as friends.[133] Besides, the Lower Agency Bands will probably pursue us and try to destroy us all together. Now, dear Sir, we, with all our bands, are anxious to move back. Please write immediately and let us know what you think we had better do. We shall not move from here if we can help it, until we receive an answer to this letter. Direct yours to Wabaxa.

Yours, very truly,
Wabaxa
and the above named Chiefs.

CHAPTER NINE[134]

RED IRON VILLAGE.

The Rebels are becoming more and more excited since they have found out that Gen. Sibley has command of a large force instead of a few companies, as they at first supposed. Little Crow would like to make terms of peace, but seems to infer, from the last message he received from Gen. Sibley, that there is no peace for him. He says the Gen. demanded all the captives, and when they were delivered, he would talk to him like a man.[135] A little while ago he could laugh at cannon balls; but he is not willing to place himself in front of its mouth, or end his existence on the scaffold. He is now threatened by his own soldiers for his cowardice. He is a cunning warrior, and lays many plans to defeat his enemies. He set fire to the numerous bridges, so as to detain Gen. Sibley in his march. The lumber being green they were not destroyed so but what the white soldiers soon repaired them.[136] Though sometimes obliged to hide himself for the night from the fury of his soldiers, the next morning he will call an open council, and every man is ready to do his bidding. He has what is called a council house, or home for the soldiers, consisting of a large tent near the center of the camp. From its top waves our stars and stripes, they plundered from the department.[137] In this council home they are provided with the best provisions the camp affords, carried voluntarily by any who have a good supply, or variety of eatables.

When a messenger returns from battle, he goes at once to the council home, and delivers his message. Then a public crier, usually an aged man, is sent to call the members of the house. From this home they send out small companies of soldiers to watch the movements of the white people, and to return to camp, or punish any captives they may find trying to escape. As we intended giving some customs of the Indians, we will say more about this council home, which has been a long established custom, not only in war but in the chase.[138] When there is to be a buffalo hunt, the hunters all assemble at the council home, where a bounteous feast is prepared, in which all join. After this the best of tobacco and kinnekinnick is passed around, and when they have talked and smoked long enough, they send two or three of the most active men on foot to look for the buffalo. When they return they satisfy the whole party of the relative position of the buffalo, the distance from the camp, &c. All hands prepare as quickly as possible, saddling the fleetest horses.

If the dogs bark, their mouths must be tied, for fear of alarming the buffalo. When ready, all start; if any get ahead, they are whipped into line. As soon as near enough they separate, so as to surround the buffalo, narrowing the circle, till the signal is given for the chase to commence. If the buffalo do not scent their pursuers the hunt is a successful one; but if the wind is to their advantage, and they scent the approach of the hunters, they rush in one body through the ring. Then none are successful but those on the very fleetest of horses. Mr. R. knows of one instance where a strong athletic man sent an arrow clear through the buffalo, and left it standing in the ground.

This is a rare feat, and only done when the arrow passes between the ribs. If the hunt has been a joyful one, as it always is, if they get plenty of meat, they return to their homes with glad hearts; and those that were too poor to have horses are met by their wives five or six miles from home, relieving them of their heavy burdens by placing it on two poles, fastened each side of a dog, the ends dragging on the ground. A kind of rack or frame of bark or strips of buffalo hide or deer skin. On this they carry their heavy loads, sometimes their little ones besides.

One law in relation to these hunts is severe, and always put in practice if violated. If two or three men go independent of the whole and frighten the buffalo, their property, whatever it may be, is destroyed; and if disposed to resent it, their lives are forfeited.[139] The flesh of the buffalo is much like our common beef, only coarser grained, and in our estimation much sweeter. The buffalo came very near Hazlewood this summer, and we procured a quantity of beef, and came very near to going on to the prairie in search of them, in company with the Mission School and some young ladies and others, to have a grand time.[140] News came that the buffalo had left. It was very providential, for we should doubtless have been off on the desert wilds of the prairie when the massacre commenced, subject to the fury of the savages.

We have just returned from a ride, and though we had cause to fear some if not all of us might be killed, we find ourselves in better spirits than when we started. Mr. R. and Two Star were going after wood, and being nearly out of potatoes, we resolved to accompany them, with Mrs. Lucy T., a captive that had been staying with us sometime.[141]

Two Star took his gun with him. We wrapped our blankets about us so as to appear as much like the Dakotas as possible. The Indian women smiled at the way we put the blanket over our heads, for we have not quite learned the art of arranging our new costume. We had to go about three miles to where the potatoes were buried. The men opened the ground, and found a tin boiler, coffee pot, tea kettle, and some soup spoons made from the ribs of an animal.[142] Mr. R. hesitated about leaving us while they went for wood, but to expedite matters we felt it necessary to remain. Lucy said she would pick up the potatoes while we watched outside. We stood awhile, resting from the tent posture, but fearing we might be seen we hid in the grass. Lucy had the sack partly filled when we discovered an Indian walking stealthily some distance south of us. We could not secrete ourselves in the potato hole, it being too small, so we carefully watched his movements till he entered a ravine leading to the woods where the men had gone.

Lucy said we must run across to the woods, or he might shoot the men before they would see him.

We started, but having to carry Ella we could not go fast. Lucy said she would run, and we could watch. We consented, determined in our own minds not to be left. We tried carrying Ella on our back like the Indian women, but could not keep her from falling off or raise ourselves up so as to walk. The next plan was to carry her under our arms. We kept pace with Lucy who was not a swift runner; we met Mr. R. coming up the hill with the load of wood, but Two Star was still in the woods. Mr. R. went back for him, and we were soon on our way back to camp, leaving the Indian searching in vain for us, if that was his object.

Red Iron Village, Sept. 15, 1862.[143]

Brig. Gen. Sibley:[144]

Hon. Sir—I have just read a letter you sent to Wabaxa and the other two Chiefs, who intend doing as you advised, as soon as practicable.[145] We shall join them, but should your troops be delayed we may be destroyed. Little Crow's soldiers are constantly moving us. We would not move where they wished us to to-day, and they came near fighting.

The Cin-ci-ti-wans came down to-day; they have just returned from a scouting expedition, and have had nothing to do in the rebellion.[146]

They appeared sorry about the trouble at first. Little Crow made them a great feast, and tried to buy them by presenting them a quantity or powder and shot. I hope they will not join, but can't tell.

I am still laboring for the captives. Eight have come to me for protection. Little Crow allows them to remain. We are all captives because we have adopted the dress of the white man, and renounced the heathen worship, and will not join in destroying our white friends. Please inform me what time you expect to reach here, and I will get our little band ready and hoist the white flag. Little Crow says the first command he shall give after your troops arrive, is to have every captive put to death. We trust that our Heavenly Father will send you soon, to deliver us from this bondage and then we will try to show how much we honor our great Father at Washington.[147]

Paul, or Mu-za-ka-te-mane.

CHAPTER TEN[148]

RED IRON VILLAGE.

Our readers will review, in memory, the leaves we have already given them. They will recall what we said about Simon remaining at his house. We learned afterwards, from his family, that he took Mrs. Newman and children and went to the Fort.[149] Lorenzo also reached the Fort in safety, with his own and Mrs. DeCamp's family, and another family he overtook trying to make their escape.[150] Mrs. DeCamp started with the bright hope of meeting her husband at the Fort, but her cup of sorrow was not yet full. Her dear companion had received a mortal wound at the battle of Birch Coolie, and his body had been consigned to the grave before she could reach the Fort. The soldiers sympathized deeply with her, and a lent a helping hand by raising one hundred dollars to aid her on her journey.[151]

Gen. Sibley had sent a party to bury the dead that had fallen victims in the massacre. They had completed their mournful task, and encamped for the night at Birch Coolie, feeling comparatively secure, believing the Indians far distant from them. Just before day they were aroused by the savage war whoop, and found they were surrounded by Indians. They had taken the precaution to construct a rude fort by placing the wagons and mules so as to form a circle. We can readily imagine what a terrible confusion it must have made among the animals, as they were shot down one after another. It would seem as if they would rend the heavens in twain by their hoarse braying in their dying agonies. The men fought bravely. They dug entrenchments with the few spades, shovels, and axes they had taken to bury the dead. Some of the party ran away at the commencement of the battle and gave the information at headquarters.[152] Gen. Sibley sent troops immediately to their assistance. The Indians saw them coming and divided their forces, leaving one party to fight the almost defenseless camp, while others were detached to keep back the re-enforcing [sic] party. How long they fought in this way we do not certainly know, but believe it was nearly all day. Rev. Mr. Riggs said the sight was beyond description. Men half dead lay buried beneath the carcasses of the mules, and the moans of the dying and wounded were heart-rending. It seemed but one great mass of corruption as they separated the dead from the heap of dirt and fallen bodies of the animals. The few that were saved for further action were suffering from their protracted labor and fasting. How appropriate the passage: "Prepare to meet thy God."[153] The golden bowl is broken. Mourners go about the streets. The windows are darkened. Let us wail and lament over our once happy country.[154]

This eventful battle occurred while we were at the Mission Station; but not learning the particulars until long afterwards, we failed to give the details in that part of our journal. We will take the liberty to go back a few weeks in our history. Mrs. DeCamp was then with us. None slept or tried to that night, hoping the white soldiers would conquer and come to our rescue; but alas! our cherished hopes were dashed to the ground by the Indians reporting that every gun was silenced, and every voice hushed within that temporary fort!

We regret not being able to keep dates better. The almanac we found at the Mission Station and carried so long with us, is lost. We should not have been able to keep the proper day for the Sabbath had it not been for that valuable little book; for there was nothing to mark the days of the week. The same routine of moving tents so as to have forage for cattle, and the same busy life of cooking; for it is more laborious doing work in a tent than in a well furnished kitchen. Besides, we have been rather more liberal lately, for we are expecting Gen. Sibley up soon. We have cooked several days in succession all day, and in the morning had nothing remaining.[155] Being completely tired out, we were obliged to stop this and let others cook for themselves.

Mr. R. has watched the horses every night for about six weeks. He ties them in front of the tent door, and takes his gun and blanket and lies down near the door so that he can easily see any intruder that may venture to come near. If he could only sleep in the day time; but there is no rest for the weary here. We prevailed on him to let us take his place at the door towards morning. We did this until we took a severe cold, and were obliged to surrender to Mr. R.'s request, which we should have done long before had we not feared he would fail entirely; for he was becoming weaker every day, and losing flesh until he was almost a skeleton.

Tent life is not very agreeable. Sometimes the wind blows the smoke, ashes and dust all about. We try to clear up the tent, but cannot make it look like home. Ella cries every day to go home, saying, "Mamma, I want to go home." She is getting more contented, having learned a little of the language; and the girls carry her on their backs, and the women fetch her all the *goodies* they can. She is a great favorite, and should we punish her we should have half a dozen women to see what is the matter with Ella. She has learned this, and will not be washed or combed without screaming like the Dakota children, and we dare not punish her.[156]

But we want to tell a little more about living in a tent. Those that are able have a straw mat to eat on. When we have none but our own family we use the wash-tub for a table; but of late we have had from ten to fifteen to eat with us, for provisions are getting scarce; and by persevering and getting potatoes we have made ours last longer than many of our neighbors. The frying pan we brought from home was the most useful article we saved. We use it for both baking and frying. We baked apple pies in it which were very good. The apples were given us by Mrs. Williamson.[157]

While our faithful old cow gave plenty of milk, we had plenty of good bread; but she has had too hard fare to afford to give us milk, as all the cattle have to be tied to stakes or they will be shot for beef. The Dakota Indians make quite good bread with soda and water and a little butter and lard, without any acid.[158]

We are obliged to remain in a sitting posture in a tent when at work. At first we burned our face and hands by the blazing fire. Once these things would have troubled us, but are hardly worth noticing now. We spend but little time in arranging our toilet. When our broad cloth skirt gets dusty we shake it and brush it with moistened hands. No better costume could be adopted for tent life.

It has been reported about camp that a white boy has been shot. The woman who had taken him was always at variance with him, and the boy, being very resolute, would not obey her. She became enraged, and tried to kill him, but did not succeed. When her husband came in she told him about the boy. He led him very coolly out of the tent and shot him. He said that he had compassion on the poor boy; that his father and mother were both dead, and his wife was always quarreling with him; but now he had gone to the spirit world. (If we had time we would give the Indian views of Spiritualism.)

Since we moved to Red Iron we have had no quiet night or day. Such horrible yells—it is beyond all description. It comes the nearest to the punishment of the wicked, as described by Holy Writ, to anything we ever witnessed before.

One evening, when Mr. Renville was at worship, several of these barbarians marched around the tent, howling, and struck Mr. Renville three times on the head through the tent. We often wish our tent was longer, so as to accommodate all who love to attend worship morning and evening. Amidst all our trials we can truly rejoice that there are so many that love to praise God.

///

CHAPTER ELEVEN[159]

CAMP HOPE, SEPT. 21, 1862.

We are now about five miles above Red Iron village. We do not know of any name being given to this camp by the Indians, but for convenience we will call it Camp Hope; for we have a faint hope that Gen. Sibley will reach here soon, probably this week. In the meantime we will give a brief history of some of the captives.

Mrs. Crothers we never saw, but learned a little about her.[160] She had two little children, both too young to walk any distance. Her life being threatened, she was told that she had better try to escape. She weighed the matter, and concluded that between two evils she would choose the less, and start for the Fort. We do not know how far she had to walk; but if she fled from camp at Yellow Medicine she must have walked over forty miles. She had little or no food, depending upon what she could pick up. At one time she was obliged to secrete herself in a cellar, and being afraid her little child would cry, she gave it the last pin she had to play with. This kept the child quiet until the Indians, who were right above her, left. Had they found out that she was in the cellar, we can imagine what cruelty, and perhaps death, awaited her. She tore strips of cloth off from her broadcloth skirt, which was an old one, to tie one of her children on her back, carrying the other in her arms. When she became too exhausted to carry both, she put one down, went on a short distance, and then went after her other child. In this way, she finally succeeded in getting to the Fort. When the officers saw her coming one of them carried her a blanket, we are told, that she might appear more comfortably clothed. Her husband was more than overjoyed to see his dear companion and darling children once more, and spoke to others of her prudence and untiring energy in a way that showed he felt she deserved much praise, especially from him.

Mrs. White told us they had been in Minnesota only about six months when she was taken captive with her daughter Julia, and a little girl of about ten summers, and an infant she carried in her arms.[161] Mrs. White always maintained a cheerful, quiet spirit, at least to observers; said she thought it the best way. The first time we met her she could scarcely refrain from weeping; but soon assumed a cheerful look. Many other captives we became partially acquainted with, but not knowing much of their sufferings we leave them for the present at least. One day Paul was in our tent, and hearing a white woman talking in another tent; told Mr. R. he had better invite her to call in, as it might be a pleasure for his wife to talk with her. We were always glad to see any of the captives. When she came in she threw her arms about our neck and wept bitterly. She was about twenty years of age. Though we never saw a murder committed, yet they were brought before us so vividly by the captives it seemed as if we were living in the scenes. Mrs. Adams, on the morning she was taken, had just returned with her husband and little one to their home, having been absent some time on account of the Indian raid.[162] Thinking it safe for them to remain at their house long enough to do some washing and pack up some clothing, they did so, not waiting for the clothes to dry. They started for Hutchinson, and had got within a few miles of the place, when some Indians, three, I believe, in number, ran after them. Having an ox team, they took to their feet. Mr. Adams took the baby in his arms and ran for life. His wife seeing that the Indians were gaining on him called for him to put the child down. He ran to where there were some more white men, but could not return in time to save his wife and child.

Mrs. Adams took up her child and hid while the Indians were pursuing her husband, but they soon found her, and caught hold of the child's feet and dashed it to the ground. They then shot him through the body. Mrs. Adams said she believed the child was dead before it reached the ground, for they jerked it so she thought the breath left its body, but was not sorry they shot it for then she knew positively it was dead. She said a little way from her they shot a mother, leaving her helpless infant alive by her side in the road. The Indians seemed in a great hurry, and did not stop to plunder or burn any of the buildings. We learned afterwards that Mr. Adams found his child's body and buried it. Mrs. A. said she knew her husband would seek revenge on the Indians as long as his life was spared, and that she joined heartily with him.[163] This is the feeling that pervades the minds of the majority of the people of Minnesota. We cannot blame them for feeling injured, for their homes have been made desolate. But the policy they wish to pursue will bring on them or their children a greater woe than has yet gone forth from the wilds of the border States. We would like to speak more at length on this subject, after we get through our journal.

Night after night Paul has held councils at our tent, devising plans and means to separate from the rebels. The fire is smothered in the ashes, and all talk in a whisper, keeping a guard outside. Paul's life is in jeopardy; the rebels say they will poison him if they do not kill him some other way. They are constantly threatening the half breed captives, and we are afraid they will put their threats into execution, for they made an attempt to kill one of them whom they had employed to carry letters to Gen. Sibley, mistrusting his loyalty to the rebels.[164] The friends and relatives of the half-breeds keep a strong guard about the tents whenever the sky looks dark in regard to them. One day just at night Mr. R. came in, took his gun and said "make haste and get your dishes washed." "Why?" we asked. "Oh, nothing," he replied, "only they say that the half-breeds are going to be killed very soon now." We told him if that was the case we should not stop to wash the dishes. He continued, "it may be only a story. You may as well finish your work." No doubt they would have killed them long before this had they not feared a war among themselves. They have been around numbering all the captives.

Some of the wicked chiefs called on Paul and demanded of him if he was fully determined to join the white people when they came, trying to intimidate him, by saying that some of the lower chiefs had said *they* would, but had given it up. They alluded to Wabaxa and the others we have mentioned in other parts of our journal. Paul plainly told them he should ever befriend the whites. They called him a coward, saying, if you were a brave man you would help us destroy them all. Paul replied, I am not brave to commit such horrible deeds as you have,—but I am brave to do right, and if I lose my life I wish my relatives to live with the Missionaries. Paul had to have his son, a boy about fifteen, tied up to keep him from trying to kill Little Crow. He and some other boys did finally succeed in destroying most of his property while Crow was away.

Our readers may think it strange that Paul should tie up his son, but prudence demanded it; for had the boy succeeded he would have endangered the lives of all the friendly Indians.

CAMP HOPE, Sept. 22, 1862.

Gen. Sibley:

Hon. Sir—The Lower Bands are holding a council this forenoon, and are desirous to have us join them; but knowing them to be false-hearted we prefer holding our own councils and sending our own letters. We have more captives with us now than the rebels, for they keep coming to us for protection, and we are in danger of having a battle in consequence. We have been betrayed about the white flag; have one ready, but our enemies say if we raise it they will hoist one too, and as soon as your troops arrive they will fire into them, making you believe we are all your enemies, and so get us killed in that way. You cannot realize the bitter hatred they manifest towards us for trying to aid the poor captives and not joining in the massacre. We are going to move our camp to-day out on the broad prairie, as you responded in your letter to Wabaxa. Sir, we are exceedingly anxious for the arrival of your troops. We still put our trust in Him who is able to save to the uttermost all that come unto him.

Yours, respectfully,
Paul.

CHAPTER TWELVE[165]

CAMP LOOKOUT, SEPT. 22, 1862.

We are now on the lookout for Gen. Sibley, having heard the joyful news that he has started from Fort Ridgley. The rebels keep a constant watch of the troops. Some of them have reported around camp that Gen. Sibley is marching forward with a small army, composed chiefly of old men and little boys, and say they are anxious for him to come on; that it will be fine play; and they can get plenty of powder and shot, besides a quantity of flour. The more truthful state that there must be over a regiment.[166] The rebels are preparing to meet Gen. Sibley. As we cannot hasten the General's march by being idle, we will make an attempt to tell what has been going on among the friendly bands.

You recollect Paul was going to move on to the prairie.[167] Deputies were appointed to confer with the different bands in order to determine the place to encamp. It soon became apparent that the bands stood in fear of each other. The Yellow Medicine people said if we joined with the lower bands we should excite Little Crow to a battle before the white troops arrived. In this dilemma the Hazlewood Republic, with whom we were, went a short distance from the lower bands that had declared themselves friendly. After a long consultation, the others joined Wa-ke-an-no-pa, or Two Thunder, a civilized Indian who acted an honest and wise part, we believe, during the massacre, his very countenance showing his innocence. He is an influential man, and with Paul, Muzo-mo-my, Akepa, and others, took an active part in trying to make peace and to restore to their homes those captives that had not been bereft of friends and homes, and the others to the white people to be provided for.[168] Before night the friendly Indians all united and all parties, (captive women not excepted,) went to digging entrenchments, or rather sinking pits inside of their tents, to defend themselves from the rebels in case of an attack, expecting one hourly.

Camp Lookout, Sept. 23, 1862.

Gen. Sibley:

Dear Sir—We, the undersigned, Paul, Akepa, Muzo-mo-my, and the three chiefs, are driven by the rebels to either go down with them to the battle to-day, or engage them in one here.[169] We think it safest for the captives and our own families to go. The rebels say we must take the front of the battle; that we have not borne any burdens of the war, but they will drive us to it.[170] We hope to get one side [*sic*], so as to join you or raise the flag of truce. If not able to do this we hope to return to our families and rescue them. We have tried every possible way of giving you correct information in regard to the war.

Joseph Campbell has a letter from us and one from Standing Buffalo, who says he will persuade, if possible, his people and all the Northern Indians, to meet you in peace, and destroy the wicked ones that have caused all this great sorrow upon our land.[171] We don't want to fight, and shall fire into the air, if we can stand the bullets; but if they come too thick and fast we are afraid some of our men will take good aim.

The rebels say they shall search our camp to see if every man has gone to the battle, and if any remains they will punish them. This threat they have partially fulfilled, riding about camp, singing as usual their frightful war songs. We trembled, for several remained. General, we wish you to inform us what to do at the earliest opportunity. Rest assured we are not your enemies. They have threatened the captives with instant death, but are going to see what a battle will result in.

Our last prayer is that you will be able to relieve the suffering captives from war, death, and horrible captivity among the rebels, and should we fall in battle, we wish to be numbered among your friends and commend our families to your kind sympathies.

Yours, respectfully,
Paul or Muza-ka-te-ma-ne,
Akepa,
Muzo-mo-my
and the three Chiefs

[Camp Wood Lake, Sept. 24, 1862][172]

Mr. and Mrs. Renville:

My Dear Friends—I am glad to hear that you are all alive. I think God will preserve and deliver you. I have just seen the letters you and others have sent to Col. Sibley. We shall move up to your assistance very soon, to-morrow, I think. The fight yesterday was a rather a serious one to the Dakotas. We have buried fifteen of them, and four of our soldiers. I wrote to you to send up by Simon, but he did not go. I have written twice to your friends in Illinois, telling them you were still alive.

May God still keep you all. I hope to see you soon and to rejoice with you in God's deliverance of you all.

Tell all who are in captivity that my prayers and efforts are still for them.

Yours truly,
S. R. Riggs

The day the men all went to the battle the Indian women and captives busied themselves making preparations for coming events; baking, cooking, and washing.[173] It was Little Crow's intention to fall upon Gen. Sibley's camp during the night and butcher with their knives, and kill with the tomahawk, all they could; but so many objected to this, especially the friendly bands, that he was constrained to wait till morning. The battle commenced, we believe about ten o'clock, and lasted about an hour. The morning of the 24th, messengers arrived stating that the battle had commenced. The Indians began to chant their songs of praise, as is always customary at such times; calling the names of their brothers and husbands, saying the people took you with them, because you are brave men, to protect them and to be a shield to their faces. This is the substance of their song. Another custom is for the braves or soldiers to make a sacrifice to their God.

//

CHAPTER THIRTEEN[174]

CAMP LOOKOUT, SEPT. 25, 1862.

We alluded, in our last chapter, to some of the customs of the Indians before going to battle, and of sacrificing to their God.[175] This consists sometimes of killing a puppy, and painting it either red or several bright colors, and presenting it as an offering to a large stone, which is decorated with paint, ribbons, and fine feathers, such as the softest down, colored red and scattered over the stone. To this god they pray and plead that he will accompany them in their battles, and help them to conquer.[176] We were quite interested in a similar account, given by one of the friendly Indians, though not a Christian, who said he saw a brave fall in battle just after getting off from his horse to worship his god, while some of the Christian Indians went to and from Gen. Sibley's camp when the bullets were falling like hail, and not a hair of their head was hurt. This he considered a great miracle.

When the friendly Indians returned from the battle they were very happy; said they had shaken hands with their white friends, and had even seen Mr. Riggs.[177] Towards night, on the day of the battle, the rebels were moving in every direction; women were weeping because their friends had fallen on the battle field. During the night the rebels nearly all fled. After the battle Little Crow delivered up all the white captives, (or pretended to, for he took some fifteen with him,) and gave Joseph Campbell a letter to Gen. Sibley, telling him to take down the captives and deliver the letter, and then afterwards sent a company of his soldiers to overtake them, and put Mr. C. and the captives to death.[178] He was thwarted in his plan. The friendly bands held a council and concluded it was not safe to send the captives with so small an escort as they would be able to raise. Rusty, and some others went with Mr. Campbell, and by keeping a by-path reached the Fort in safety.[179]

On the night of the 25th, some messengers were sent to see if they could hear anything from Gen. Sibley. They found he had encamped at Red Iron Village, some five miles below. Oh, how every heart bounded at the glad news, and then came the anxiety till morning to see their friends. But little sleeping was done that night, and as soon as the morning dawned all were on the move, exchanging smiles and kind words. The morning was a beautiful one, long to be remembered on account of its associations; and though we had been too feeble to walk about for several days, we could not be kept from using all the strength we had to call on the captives. It seemed as if heart beat against heart; and the air vibrated with the emotions of the camp. A change had been wrought in the appearance of all. The Indians that used to dress in white man's costume donned it with pride, and divided their spoils with the women and children, trying to make them look as happy as possible. White flags were flying in every direction; the largest and most conspicuous was raised by Paul. Little children were running to and fro with their miniature flags; captive women and children were seated in wagons anxiously waiting the arrival of their long absent friends, who were equally as anxious to meet their dear companions and friends in exile. At last the troops came in sight. Deputies were sent out to meet them. When they came near some of the soldiers left their ranks to come to our camp, so eager were they to see if their friends were still alive. They forgot for the moment all discipline and were soon reminded by their officers ordering them back to wait until a proper time.

At two o'clock P.M., Gen. Sibley, accompanied by his staff, came to our camp. Paul and some others made brief speeches, and the captives were formerly [*sic*] delivered up by those who had taken them, and by others who had protected them.

Let me say in conclusion that the friendly Indians, and especially the Christians manifested much happiness that the time had come to deliver the captives and themselves from the cruel war waged by Satan's emissaries, who are, or at least the most wicked ones, fleeing from the pursuit of justice, while those who delivered themselves up as prisoners of war, the most of whom are not as guilty in crime, are condemned. The friends even that protected the suffering ones, are doomed to an exile almost as cruel as that which the captives suffered, for they had long had the opportunity of hearing the gospel before they were taken captives; and if they were christians the rebels could only destroy the body but could not harm the soul.[180] But these poor Indians, who have but just learned of Christ, have but little light, and are surrounded by dense darkness, besides the evils that have been thrown about them by white people who have been among them transacting business for Government, or enriching themselves in trade. Some of our most flagrant vices were never known among the Indians till they became acquainted with the white people. In their own language they have no word they can use in profaning their Maker. The first English many of them can speak, is oaths which they have learned from men employed by Government to teach them to work. For instance, if driving oxen, they use the oaths, supposing the oxen won't go unless they do; at the same time, they do not understand the meaning of the words they use, and ardent spirits it is known they cannot manufacture.

May God guide the people of Minnesota, who have suffered deeply, to act wisely in the present instance, and not drive even the friendly Indians to homeless desperation by driving or sending them among the warlike tribes, to dwell upon their wrongs and talk over the injuries inflicted upon them by those they supposed their friends, until the warriors will not heed the counsel of the older ones, and rise in one mass, with all the tribes, and commence a war more terrible than has yet been recorded in history, and thus give the advantage to our Southern rebels, by a two-fold war. And may those who go among the Indians, either for the purpose of trade, or to transact Government business, learn wisdom from the past and lay broad the platform of Justice, Morality and Truth.

J. B. AND M. A. RENVILLE.

//

ADDENDA[181]

Having received from some of our friends an account of their escape, after leaving Friendly Camp, we have concluded to append that, and also the articles we have written since our journal was concluded:[182]

Ta-pa-ta-tan-ka, or Great Fire, one of the Indians who was condemned and is now in prison at Davenport, Iowa, stated to some of his acquaintances that he went with the war party in order to aid the white people, who might be making their escape from the Indian raid.[183] We are unable to judge whether this was his first intentions or not, any farther than his previous character in the community and orderly conduct in the church, would affirm. But of one thing we are confident: he would not have related his adventures with the party so fully in regard to saving Dr. Williamson, with his wife and sister, had it not been true. As we love to notice the dealings of Providence in sparing the lives of the Missionaries, we will narrate Great Fire's story. The party saw the track of the Dr.'s cart on the grass, where it had apparently turned off on to the prairie. Among the party was a young Indian, after Little Crow's own heart, who tried every persuasion to get the entire company to follow after the Dr., and murder them all. Great Fire told him they were all old people, and had no property of any value with them, and asked him what he wished to kill such good persons for, who had always treated the Indians well and never deceived them. The rascal came near turning up on Great Fire in his fury. At first the rest of the party were inclined to pursue the Missionaries, but Great Fire's upright and manly interference prevailed, and thus was spared these three worthy Missionaries; and can a single Christian fail to see God's hand in all this? The Rev. Dr. has, during the last winter, labored faithfully in the prison at Mankato, going through storms that even convinced the idolatrous Indians that there must be a reality in the white man's religion, or such an aged man would not sacrifice the comforts of home to spend and be spent in teaching them to read and write, and talking to them about Jesus. It may be well to say a word to those who have not learned to read in early years; that it is possible for them to learn at any age, if they bend their minds and will to do it; for these poor degraded Indians have surprised many an educated and intelligent man, by their application and final success in learning to read and write intelligibly—some even at advanced ages. Here Great Fire and Chas-ca-da, or Robert Hopkins, have been used as instruments of great good—if we admit that Indians have souls—by their faithfulness in teaching their fellow prisoners. We may as well declare that the Anglo-Saxon race have no souls; for, trace this nation back a few centuries, and you find them just emerging from barbarism; and still farther back and not a glimmer of civilization existed. We might come down to our own times and look at the poorer class among the Southern rebeldom, or the recent barbarous acts of some in our own State. We have reference to the digging up of the graves of helpless infants and aged Indians, and scattering their bones to the wind.[184] We are glad for the credit of the State that the proper authorities interfered and stopped such barbarous deeds. Hunt the Indians who are now and have troubled the frontier; shoot them if necessary; condemn them to prison or the gallows if justice demands it, but let the graves of the long-since dead lie in peace until God himself shall bring them to judgment.

How true it is that God's ways are not our ways, and His thoughts our thoughts. His ways of disseminating the Gospel are often not visible to mortals until long after. It is a fact well known in many places, though not it all, that New Ulm suffered deeply from the terrible massacre, and as we have before mentioned, may it not have been a visitation of Divine wrath, for burning the image of the Incarnate Son just the Sabbath before? The army stationed at New Ulm has been the means of the Gospel being preached to them. We have not heard of a house being dedicated to God before the massacre, but have reasons, from good authorities, that none existed in the place before.[185]

It is acknowledged that the truths of the Gospel are effectual in civilized communities, but hardly admitted that the same great Agent is carrying forward the work among the heathen. Missionaries have no time to be idle. Those who had always turned a deaf ear to them before, are now anxious to lisp the name of Jesus. Books are needed to instruct them in the first elements of truth. Laborers are called to go, like the Apostles, and carry the Gospel to every creature. And for the encouragement of those who aid in sustaining the mission cause, we will say, those you have sent into Minnesota are not idle; they are each and all engaged in some good work; not as formerly, in their commodious homes or churches, instructing in one form or other, from daylight till sunset, the benighted people around them; and do any say their labors have all been in vain? Let them spend six long weeks in captivity, and if they can, as many captives did, and by the aid of the friendly bands, get to the mission Indians, they will find a great difference between a civilized and Christian Indian, and one that merely adopts the white man's costume and firmly adheres to his own idolatrous religion.

The labors of the Missionaries are truly arduous. One of them is still laboring in prison for the salvation of its inmates with untiring zeal. We have had occasions often to refer to his abundant labors during a life of thirty years among the Dakotas. His years will soon be numbered, and he is ready to receive honors greater than mere mortals are capable of bestowing.[186]

Another takes fast hold on justice, determined not to let her go; whether it is for the afflicted and torn and bleeding hearts of the bereaved Minnesoteans [sic], or pursuing the wild demons of Satan's empire through the dry and thirsty land, or for the wronged Indians, for such they are, gaining much popularity by some, and stripes from others, (if not of many cords, of many words.)[187]

May the Author of all good use him as an instrument in bringing about the right state of mind among the intelligent classes of our much beloved country.

The youngest though not the least zealous for the advancement of his Master's kingdom, has bid farewell to the parental home and Christian society of civilized life to endure privations incident to the removal of the different tribes on our borders; and like the ancient Law-Giver, is striving to lead the people in that straight and narrow path that leads to the heavenly Canaan, and not much unlike the Ancient One are his trials; and how many Aarons are there staying up his hands by fervent faithful prayer for the salvation of the heathen.[188]

Since the above went to press, Mr. and Mrs. Cunningham, who have labored so faithfully for years past in the boarding school at Hazlewood, have called to bid us farewell, and are now in company with the Mr. Pond [sic] on their way to the Sioux Agency, in Missouri, to aid Rev. Mr. Williamson in his arduous duties as a Missionary in that field. May God protect them all, and should there ever be another outbreak, make a way for their escape, as He did in an almost miraculous manner but one short year ago.[189]

H. D. CUNNINGHAM'S STATEMENT.

On the afternoon and evening of the 18th of August, 1862, the community around the Mission stations, among the Dakota Indians, was thrown into an intense excitement by reports that the Indians on the lower reservation were murdering and driving off the whites at the Lower Agency, and of the settlements on the opposite side of the river, and that it was extending up the Minnesota River, as well as to all the adjoining settlements. Many of the Indians came and warned us to flee for our lives, and among others were those who had always been the most calm in times of excitement, and in whom we had the most confidence. The parents of the children of the boarding school soon relieved us of the responsibility of them, at the same time urging us to get to a place of safety.[190] The first thing that convinced the more unbelieving ones of us of the reality of our danger, was the stealing of Mr. Rigg's [sic] horses and wagon from Mr. Petijohn [sic], some two miles from our place, who was moving his family to Saint Peter.[191] During the evening and fore part of the night the excitement seemed to increase. The Christian and Friendly Indians gathered about our houses and offered to protect us all they could, but said they were but a few when compared to the others. We felt as though we didn't like to expose them, to protect us when the odds seemed so much against us. They all gave one voice, and that was to get to a place of safety. We had, during the night, seen some of those who had come in, of the baser sort, trying to get the horses out of my stable, while they had taken several in the neighborhood. It was evident about midnight that the best thing we could do was to put ourselves under their care, follow their advice, and the sooner the better. About one o'clock A.M., we left our homes, never to return. When we started we had but one two-horse team and a single buggy to carry twenty-two persons, mostly women and children. Some of our company thought we had best not try to take my horses, as they would probably be taken from us. But we thought that we would only have to walk if they did, and we should start with them anyhow. Some of the Indians went with us as guides and guards. We followed them through the timber about three miles, to an Indian village, where we found some of our neighbors who had started before us. After a long council it was decided that we had better conceal ourselves on an island two miles from the village, and wait till the next night before we went any further. This was not at all agreeable to our feelings, but we submitted. Two men went with and ferried us across to the island in a canoe that would only carry about two persons beside the one who paddled it, at a time. We were all over in safety about daylight. When we got to our place of concealment we felt as though the flesh was weak indeed, and that it was necessary to rest if we could, which was a very difficult matter among the swarms of mosquitoes that infested the place. After an hour spent in our vain endeavors to court sleep, we gave it up; we arose and read a portion of scripture and committed ourselves to the keeping of Him who alone could grant us deliverance in such a time of distress. After so doing we partook of some refreshments, which consisted of about three small crackers, as our desire for food seemed to have left the most of us. The supply for the whole party was about three or four quarts of said crackers; but the Lord who fed the five thousand with but little more bread than we had, could feed us also. Soon after we had thus refreshed ourselves, an Indian woman came with some forty or fifty pound of provisions sister E—— had prepared, and we had forgotten to take with us in our haste to be gone.[192]

Mr. Riggs and myself visited the village early in the morning where we learned that the work of destruction had commenced at the Agency, five miles from our homes, and that our houses had been rifled also. We soon returned [to] our hiding place, where we spent the forenoon in great anxiety, drenched with the rain and tormented by the mosquitoes.

About one o'clock P.M., Mr. Riggs returned the second time from the village, with the painful news that the man he had left his horse with had refused to give him up, having heard that the owner had been killed, as he said, and he thought he had as much claim to him as any one else. We immediately began to prepare for our departure. While the rest of the company were moving from the island to the other side of the river, Mr. Pettijohn and myself made another visit to the village to get my horses, and secured one of them. There we found Mr. Orr, who had been wounded by the Indians some fifteen miles above. We started together. The other two soon joined the company and seemed surprised that I was still behind, as I had a horse and they were on foot. I was detained by having to go some distance around to get across the river. The company, soon after they crossed the river from the island, joined a part of Dr. Williamson's family and son-in-law, and two other families who had been in the employ of the Department. About the time they were fairly under way they were overtaken by a violent rain storm. I did not come up with them till late in the evening. Owing to the rain and wind I was unable to follow their trail. The Indian who had the care of my team came with me some distance, as a guide. They had begun to fear for the worst long before I came up with them. We travelled till dark, and stopped for the night on the open prairie. After refreshing ourselves with a little food, and thanking out Heavenly

Father for his protection thus far, and a continuance of it sought for the night, we retired and slept as best we could under the circumstances. Early in the morning we were on our way again. The day passed without anything of special interest until late in the afternoon, when three Germans joined us, who had left Other-day's party that morning. Just before night we crossed two Indian trails. About dark we camped again for the night. After partaking of the last bit of cooked food we had, and again committing ourselves to the keeping of Him who never sleeps, we retired for the night. Our company now numbers forty-two. The night passed slowly away to many of us. It rained during the whole night, and until ten o'clock A.M. We started again, after committing ourselves to the guidance of Him who alone could guide in the path of safety. Cold, wet and hungry, we traveled until noon to get to a grove some ten miles from us, and then had to stop two miles from it. Dead Wood island is surrounded with a marsh and some lake.[193] Six others and myself went forward, I leading the way through grass higher than our heads, and water to our knees a good portion of the way. By the time we returned, some of the others had butchered a calf, and many of the juveniles were soon roasting or warming meat on a stick and eating it. We passed the afternoon at this place, and started the next morning, somewhat refreshed. At noon we stopped at Birch Cooley, about five miles from the Lower Agency, where we were joined by Dr. Williamson, wife and sister. We then learned that we were in the midst of danger. When the first part of the Dr.'s family started, he was determined to stay and see it out. Said he was willing to die then if it was the Lord's will. Some time the next night he started, accompanied by several of the Indians who had stayed by him the whole time guarding him and his property as best they could. After a short rest and consultation, it was decided to reach Fort Ridgley that night, which was some fifteen miles distant—at that time surrounded by the hostile Indians. This was somewhat of an undertaking, with worn-out ox teams. Some distance above the Fort evidences of the work of destruction which had been done and was still going on, began to increase. About five miles above the Fort we passed the remains of a dead man.

When some distance from the Fort, Mr. Hunter went forward, and after crawling some distance on his hands and knees, got to see the commanding officer, who advised not to come into the Fort at all, but drive to Henderson that night if possible. He then returned to his buggy, where he had left his wife and children, hid in the grass, and soon met the rest of the party, about one mile and a half from the Fort. The hostile Indians were then camped not more than one mile from us, as we subsequently learned, who had just withdrawn from a most desperate attack on that place, and were expected to renew it as soon as it was light in the morning. We all felt very much disappointed, and were somewhat divided in what was the best course to pursue. Some said go to the Fort, and some were for leaving the road again. We had reason to fear the Indians were following us, as some had been seen not far from the Lower Agency. We felt that delay was dangerous. About ten o'clock we left the road, and started across the prairie, passing almost under the enemy's guns. On we went, guided by the stars, until two o'clock A.M. when we stopped to wait the morning light, in sight of burning buildings at the Fort. Some who were the most fatigued and the least afraid, slept. As soon as we could see we were on the move again. After we had gone about five miles, the three Germans and another man left us to go to New Ulm. They have not been heard of since. About nine in the morning we stopped for breakfast, and to rest our worn out teams. At one o'clock P.M. we stopped at the first house we came to, where we spent several hours refreshing ourselves. We traveled that night until eleven. As we had been during the day, we were still in sight of the burning buildings. The next morning being the Sabbath we were a little later in starting than usual. We had now reached the settlements, but the settlers had all fled. We traveled that afternoon only about six miles, when we reached a place where there were a number of settlers collected to protect themselves. We stopped near them, having heard that reinforcements had past [*sic*], on their way to Fort Ridgley. In the afternoon we had religious services, and O, what a precious season that was. We felt that we had been under the special care of Providence, that we had put our trust in Him, and had been so far delivered.

The next morning, after having spent a week together in the most trying circumstances, we separated, never to meet again in this world, some of us going to St. Peter, and others going to Henderson, St. Paul, and further on, we going with the former party. We reached our place of destination sometime after dark, weary and worn, without anything of this worlds goods but what we had worn away.

Then and not until then did we realize the danger to which we had been exposed, and what a signal deliverance the Lord had granted us while so many others had met with a worse fate.

H. D. Cunningham.

APPENDIX A

Correspondence between the Dakota Camps and
Authorities, September–October 1862

Paul Mazakutemani to Alexander Ramsey, 2 September 1862[1]

Hazelwood, September 2d, 1862.

Gov. Ramsey:

Your Excellency has probably heard ere this of the terrible massacre committed by the Indians Aug. 18th, and continuing up to this date.

As it is difficult to give correct information from a distance, I will give you a statement of all the facts I have been able to glean from the Chiefs concerned. Little Crow has been one of the most active and cruel. The others wished to put off the work of death till payment and see how matters stood with government [*sic*], but Little Crow, to use his own language, held several councils long before the 18th in order to hurry the other bands. On the 17th, four men of Shakopee band went to the Big Woods, killed some white men, and stole some horses. The next A.M., they went to Little Crow and told their crimes. Now, says he, you have commenced, let us strike the fatal blow, and rid the country of the whites, taking possession of all goods, cattle, and provisions, and become the rightful owners of our lands again. And as far as I am able to learn they have fulfilled their purpose in the most outrageous manner. Previous to commencing on Monday, a messenger was despatched [*sic*] to Yellow Medicine and Red Iron Village, but not one word did the Bands about the Mission know till the slaughter commenced. We tried to aid the Missionaries in their escape.

Lacquiparle people kept quiet for some days, then went to Big Stone Lake, and joined with the few in killing the small number of defence-less whites there. The most of the Indians were away on a hunt. The reason the Chiefs gave me was that payment was delayed and the traders would not trust them, but told them to leave their stores, and go eat grass like the oxen, that they were a lazy set and would have to starve if they did not. (Little Crow is a wicked, crafty deceiver.) These things he said, made them very angry, and after they had killed the trader named, they stamped his head in the dust till it was as fine as powder.

He farther [*sic*] stated that the trader told them they could not fight, and that he could chew them all up as fine as dust. I do not think that many blamed our Hon. Agent, only his volunteering about that time caused them to believe he did not intend making any payment, and rather exasperated them. He is, we believe, an honest man, and has always given us good advice; encouraging us to labor, and assisting us in all possible ways, so we think.

We fear our Great Father at Washington has not realized the danger of leaving his people exposed to our savage tribes, and so has failed to furnish sufficient troops to protect them, or the civilized Christian Indians; for I think there is quite a difference between a Christian Indian and one that merely changes his costume and customs a little without changing his motives of moral action.

I have held two councils, and tried by all the persuasions in my power to have the Rebels liberate the captives, willing to lose my own life, if by so doing I could send these poor suffering captives safe to St. Paul. I have succeeded in getting one family and shall persevere until the end. But, my Father, we are all captives; a small band of Christians surrounded by our persecuting neighbors, and whither, oh whither, shall we flee? Our trust is in God, and we hope He will put it into your heart, our Father, to tell us what we shall do. Think of it, our Father, and don't let our wives and our little ones starve, or, what is worse, move on to Red River with our savage foes and perish for lack of food for both soul and body.

I am a friend to the whites, to civilization, and christianity [*sic*].

Yours Respectfully,
Paul, or Muza-Ka-te-ma-ne.

Simon [Anawaŋgmani] and Lorenzo [Lawrence] to Alexander Ramsey, ca. 2 September 1862[2]

Gov. Ramsey:

Dear Sir—If you will allow us to address you thus familiarly, for the name of a white man is even dear to those who though not an eye witness, yet as one hearing of the awful tragedies almost daily committed by the lower bands; we will not detain you with our family sufferings, after writing the lengthy epistle dictated by Paul; but at the earnest request of Lorenzo and Simon, state that they, with their families, are very anxious to escape to the white settlements, and will the first opportunity; our lives are threatened if we attempt to leave; we have but little provision on hand. If in the all wise Providence, we are not permitted to go among our white friends, we have resolved to die on Mission ground, rather than go among the idolatrous and wicked Indians. Please publish this at the request of

Simon and Lorenzo.

Henry Sibley to Little Crow, ca. 3 September 1862[3]

If Little Crow has any propositions to make, let him send a half-breed to me, and he shall be protected in and out of my camp.

H. H. Sibley, Col. Com'g Mil. Ex'n.

Little Crow to Henry Sibley, 7 September 1862[4]

Yellow Medicine, September 7th, 1862

Dear Sir—

For what reason we have commenced this war I will tell you. It is on account of Major Galbraith. We made a treaty with the Government, and beg for what little we do get, and then cannot get it till our children are dying with hunger.[5] It is with the Traders that commence. Mr. A. J. Myrick told the Indians that they would eat grass or there [*sic*] own dung. Then Mr. Forbes told the Lower Sioux that they were not men. Then Robert he was working with his friends how to defraud us of our money. If the young braves have push the white men, I have done this myself. So I want you to let Governor Ramsey know this.[6] I have great many prisoners, women & children. It ain't all our fault the Winnebagoes was in the engagement, two of them was killed.[7] I want you to give me answer by the bearer. All at present.

Your truly friend,
his
Friend Little X Crow
Mark

Henry Sibley to Little Crow, 8 September 1862[8]

Little Crow
Sioux Chief
Yellow Medicine,

You have killed many of our people without any sufficient cause. Give me the Prisoners and send them to my camp under a flag of Truce, and I will talk with you then like a man. I have sent a copy of your letter to Gov. Ramsey.

H. H. Sibley, Col. Com'g Mil. Exp'n.

When you send a half breed to my camp with a flag of truce he will be protected and safely conducted in and out of the camp. Don't send any one in Indian dress.

Wabaśa, Huśaśa, and Wakute to Henry Sibley, 10 September 1862[9]

Red Iron Village Sept. 10th, 1862.

Gen. Sibley:

Our much esteemed friend—We (this is) Wabaxa Hoxaxa and Wakata, have carefully considered our positions, as Chiefs of three Bands, and being desirous of returning to our former homes, at the Lower Agency; we consult your wish in regard to doing so.

Our bands did not commence the trouble, but contrary to our wishes some of our young men joined in with the guilty ones; we were driven to act, and our fear is now, if we go back without your consent we shall meet your forces in hostility instead of meeting them as friends. Besides, the Lower Agency Bands will probably pursue us and try to destroy us all together. Now, dear Sir, we, with all our bands, are anxious to move back. Please write immediately and let us know what you think we had better do. We shall not move from here if we can help it, until we receive an answer to this letter. Direct yours to Wabaxa.

Yours, very truly,
Wabaxa
and the above named Chiefs.

Wabaśa and Taopi to Henry Sibley, 10 September 1862[10]

Mayawakan, Sept. 10th, 1862.

Col. H. H. Sibley, Fort Ridgley:

Dear Sir,—You know that Little Crow has been opposed to me in everything that our people have had to do with the whites. He has been opposed to everything in the form of civilization or Christianity. I have always been in favor of, and of late years have done every thing of the kind that has been offered to us by the government and other good white people—he has now got himself into trouble that we know he can never get himself out of, and he is trying to involve those few of us that are still the friend of the American in the murder of the poor whites that have been settled in the border, but I have been kept back with threats that I should be killed if I did any thing to help the whites; but if you will now appoint some place for me to meet you, myself and the few friends that I have will get all the prisoners we can, and with our family go to whatever place you will appoint for us to meet. I would say further that the mouth of the Red-Wood, Candiohi, on the north side of the Minnesota, or the head of the Cotton-wood River—one of these places, I think, would be a good place to meet. Return the messenger as quick as possible. We have not much time to spare.

Your true friends,
Wabashaw[11]
Taopi

Little Crow to Henry Sibley, ca. 10 September 1862[12]

Red Iron Village, or May awakan.

To Hon. H. H. Sibley:
    we have in mawakanton band One Hundred and fifty five presoners—not I the Sisiton and warpeton presoners, then we are waiting for the Sisiton what we are going to do whit the prisoners they are coming doun. they are at Lake quiparle now. The words that il to the govrment il want to here from him also, and I want to know from you as a friend what way that il can make peace for my people—in regard to presoners they fair with our children or our self jist as well as us

Your truly friend
Little Crow
per A. J. Campbell

Henry Sibley to Little Crow, 12 September 1862[13]

Headquarters Military Expedition, September 12, 1862.

To Little Crow, Sioux Chief:

I have received your letter of to day. You have not done as I wished in giving up to me the prisoners taken by your people. It would be better for you to do so. I told you I had sent your former letter to Gov. Ramsey, but I have not yet had time to receive a reply. You have allowed your young men to commit more murders since you wrote your first letter. This is not the way for you to make peace.

H. H. Sibley, Colonel Commanding
Military Expedition

Henry Sibley to Wabasa, Taopi, and
Maz zatro Jan Jan, 12 September 1862[14]

Headquarters Military Expedition September 12, 1862

To Wabashaw and Taopee and Maz zatro Jan Jan:[15]

I have received your private message. I have come up here with a large force to punish the murderers of my people. It is not my purpose to injure any innocent person. If you and others who have not been concerned in the murders and depredations will gather yourselves together, with all the prisoners on the prairie in full sight of my troops, & when a white flag is displayed by you a white flag will be hoisted in my camp, and then you can come forward and place yourself under my protection. My troops will be all assembled in two days time, and in three days from this day I expect to march. There must be no attempt to approach my column or my camp except in open day, and with a flag of truce conspicuously displayed. I shall be glad to receive all true friends of whites, with as many prisoners as they can bring, and I am powerful enough to crush all who attempt to oppose my march, and to punish those who have washed their hands in innocent blood. I sign myself the friend of all who are friends of your great American Father.

H. H. Sibley
Colonel Commanding Expedition.

Henry Sibley to "those of the Half-Breeds and Sioux Indians," 13 September 1862[16]

Headquarters in Camp, September 13, 1862.

To those of the Half-Breeds and Sioux Indians who have not been Concerned in the Murders and Outrages upon the White Settlers:

I write a few lines by Simon to say to you that I have not come into this upper country to injure any innocent person, but to punish those who have committed cruel murders upon innocent men, women, and children.[17] If, therefore, you wish to withdraw from these guilty people you must, when you see my troops approaching, take up a separate position and hoist a flag of truce and send a small party to me when I hoist a flag of truce in answer, and I will take you under my protection.

Given under my hand in camp the day and year above written.

H. H. Sibley
Colonel, Commanding Military Expedition

Wabaśa to Henry Sibley, 14 September 1862[18]

Maya-wakan, September 14, 1862.

Dear Sir,—The first time that the young braves that brought the prisoners in camp I was opposed to it, but Crow opposed it and other things. I am afraid to come back on my reserve, but you will decide this for me. You told us that you wanted the prisoners, so we quit fighting. Some of the prisoners have run away from our camp.[19] There is three parties out, but when they come back we will quit the war for good. In regard to half-breeds, if you say that I should give them, I will do so. My friend, you know Wabashaw—that I am not a bad man. I am a kind-hearted man. I know myself that the poor women ain't the blamed for the fight. I am always in for good. If you want to make peace with the Friendly Indians, we want to hear from you in regard to it. I am trying to do what is right. I hope that you will do so, and deal honestly with us. I want you to write me a good letter.

Yours truly,
Wabashaw
his X mark.

Paul Mazakutemani to Henry Sibley, 15 September 1862 [Letter 1][20]

Red Iron's Village, September 15th, 1862.

Ex. Governor Sibley:

Hon. Sir,—I have just seen your letter to Wabaxa and the other two chiefs. They intend to raise the white flag. It is our intention to join these bands; but if your troops do not reach here till the last of the week, it may be too late for our rescue.[21] The Red Iron and the lower bands have held two councils already about killing off the captives, which includes the whites, half-breeds, and all those that have dressed like the whites. I have tried all that I could to get the captives free; have held two councils with the lower bands, but Little Crow won't give them up. Eight have come to me for protection till they can get better from their own people. I keep them in my family. I have tried to send a letter to you several times, but am watched very close. This letter, or rather a copy of it, was sent one day by a young man, but he could not get away from the other Indians in safety, so he returned. The half-breeds, and all the white captives, are in the greatest danger, for they declare they will put them to death as soon as your troops appear. We shall do as you requested as soon as practicable (that is, to raise the flag). Now, dear sir, please let me know what time we may expect you, for our lives are hazarded if we move before we can receive aid.[22] I am glad you are powerful and strong, for, if God helps, you will conquer.

As Christians, we are looking to him, and trust he will send you to free us. We have held meetings every Sabbath since the missionaries left. Oh! deliver us, if possible, from our savage foes, and we shall try to show you how much we honor our great American Father.

Very respectfully, Ma-za-ku-ta-ma-ne, or Paul.

Paul Mazakutemani to Henry Sibley, 15 September 1862 [Letter 2][23]

Red Iron Village, Sept. 15, 1862.

Brig. Gen. Sibley:

Hon. Sir—I have just read a letter you sent to Wabaxa and the other two Chiefs, who intend doing as you advised, as soon as practicable. We shall join them, but should your troops be delayed we may be destroyed. Little Crow's soldiers are constantly moving us. We would not move where they wished us to to-day, and they came near fighting. The Cin-ci-ti-wans came down to-day; they have just returned from a scouting expedition, and have had nothing to do in the rebellion.

They appeared sorry about the trouble at first. Little Crow made them a great feast, and tried to buy them by presenting them a quantity of powder and shot. I hope they will not join, but can't tell.

I am still laboring for the captives. Eight have come to me for protection. Little Crow allows them to remain. We are all captives because we have adopted the dress of the white man, and renounced the heathen worship, and will not join in destroying our white friends. Please inform me what time you expect to reach here, and I will get our little band ready and hoist a white flag. Little Crow says the first command he shall give after your troops arrive, is to have every captive put to death. We trust that our Heavenly Father will send you soon, to deliver us from this bondage and then we will try to show how much we honor our great Father at Washington.

Paul, or Mu-za-ka-te-mane.

M. A. Butler [Mary A. Renville] to Henry Sibley, 18 September 1862[24]

September 18th.

Hon. Sir,—We think it just to witness our hands to the above, and also to state that this is the fourth letter we have written for him to send to you, but, as he said, he could not send it. Paul held a council with some of the lower chiefs, and talked very bravely to them.[25] They wished to know if he was going to join the whites, telling him, at the same time, that chiefs had given themselves up and been killed (we didn't believe it). He told them plainly he should join them. They said he was no brave; says Paul, "I am not brave to murder, and do such wicked acts as your people do, but you shall see I am brave to do right." His life is in danger every moment from his speech. Paul requests us again to urge you to write immediately when he may expect you, so he can get his band ready, if possible, before the slaughter commences among the captives. We dare not give our names in full, but Rev. Mr. Riggs will know, for he married John and—

M. A. Butler[26]

"Lower Friendly Indians" to Henry Sibley, 18 September 1862[27]

September 18th.

The Lower Friendly Indians to Hon. Governor Sibley:

Dear Sir,—We are in trouble about putting up the white flag. Some of the young men say they will go along with us, and, when near enough, will commence firing at your troops, so you see we are betrayed. Do let us know what we shall do; we are in jeopardy every moment. Great excitement last night about killing the captives, but nothing done. Please understand about the flag, and a part of the soldiers making you believe we are the enemies; so do write what we shall do. We hope you will hasten on, and spare the lives of the innocent.

(No signature.)

Tataŋka Nażiŋ to Henry Sibley, 19 September 1862[28]

Red Iron's Village, September 19th, 1862.

Colonel H. H. Sibley:

I would like to see you in person this day, but I am in a hurry and can not come, so I send you a letter, which will answer the purpose. My brother, I talk to you on this paper to let you know that I have not forgotten that you are my friend. I still remember it was with the white man's provision that I have lived through the severe winter; for that reason, my friendship to you is unshaken. Although I have known of one bad thing this day, it was none of my fault. I had nothing whatever to do with it. I came down here to this place to find out who disturbed the peace between us, and for what reason. I have now found out, and am in a hurry to return. The nation is about to sacrifice itself for the sake of a few foolish young men. As for me, my great Father wished me to live, therefore he gave me provisions and money; and now it seems as though they had suddenly taken it from me, and thrown it into the water. My heart is sad, not only because I have not seen my goods, but because this day I have seen the destitution of our half-breeds. They are our flesh and blood, and therefore we are anxious for their welfare. My heart is still made more sad at the sight of the many captives; but they are not my captives, and, were my band strong enough, they should be released. My brother, I want to say something which I hope you will regard. I heard of this trouble while I was away from home, but did not believe it, and so I came down to see for myself; and now that I have seen and heard, I am in a hurry to get back, and tell my relatives the straight of it. Although they have tried to shake our friendship, yet I am anxious to renew it, and let it be stronger than ever. You are anxious to punish the offenders; but I ask a favor—that is, to wait on me until I have gathered my people and relatives together, for they are many and scattered. I ask this favor because I am fearful lest your hurry should fail my intentions.[29]

Tatanka Najin (Standing Buffalo), Chief of the Sissetons.

Paul Mazkutemani to Henry Sibley, 22 September 1862[30]

Camp Hope, Sept. 22, 1862.

Gen. Sibley:

Hon. Sir—The Lower Bands are holding a council this forenoon, and are desirous to have us join them; but knowing them to be false-hearted we prefer holding our own councils and sending our own letters. We have more captives with us now than the rebels, for they keep coming to us for protection, and we are in danger of having a battle in consequence. We have been betrayed about the white flag; have one ready, but our enemies say if we raise it they will hoist one too, and as soon as your troops arrive they will fire into them, making you believe we are all your enemies, and so get us killed in that way. You cannot realize the bitter hatred they manifest towards us for trying to aid the poor captives and not joining in the massacre. We are going to move our camp to-day out on the broad prairie, as you responded in your letter to Wabaxa. Sir, we are exceedingly anxious for the arrival of your troops. We still put our trust in Him who is able to save to the uttermost all that come unto him.

Yours, respectfully,
Paul.

Paul Mazakutemani, Akipa, Mazamani, and the
Three Chiefs to Henry Sibley, 23 September 1862[31]

Camp Lookout, Sept. 23, 1862.

Gen. Sibley:

Dear Sir—We, the undersigned, Paul, Akepa, Muzo-mo-my, and the three chiefs, are driven by the rebels to either go down with them to the battle to-day, or engage them in one here. We think it safest for the captives and our own families to go. The rebels say we must take the front of the battle; that we have not borne any burdens of the war, but they will drive us to it. We hope to get one side [*sic*], so as to join you or raise the flag of truce. If not able to do this we hope to return to our families and rescue them. We have tried every possible way of giving you correct information in regard to the war.

Joseph Campbell has a letter from us and one from Standing Buffalo, who says he will persuade, if possible, his people and all the Northern Indians, to meet you in peace, and destroy the wicked ones that have caused all this great sorrow upon our land. We don't want to fight, and shall fire into the air, if we can stand the bullets; but if they come too thick and fast we are afraid some of our men will take good aim.

The rebels say they shall search our camp to see if every man has gone to the battle, and if any remains they will punish them. This threat they have partially fulfilled, riding about camp, singing as usual their frightful war songs. We trembled, for several remained. General, we wish you to inform us what to do at the earliest opportunity. Rest assured we are not your enemies. They have threatened the captives with instant death, but are going to see what a battle will result in.

Our last prayer is that you will be able to relieve the suffering captives from war, death, and horrible captivity among the rebels, and should we fall in battle, we wish to be numbered among your friends and commend our families to your kind sympathies.

Yours, respectfully,
Paul or Muza-ka-te-ma-ne,
Akepa,
Muzo-mo-my
and the three Chiefs

H. H. Sibley to [no addressee], September 23, 1862[32]

Wood Lake, September 23, 1862

When you bring up the prisoners and deliver them to me under the flag of truce I will be ready to talk of peace. The bodies of the Indians that have been killed will be buried like white people and the wounded will be attended to as our own; but none will be given until the prisoners are brought in. I will wait here a reasonable time for the delivery of the prisoners, if you send me word they will be given up. A flag of truce in the day-time will always be protected in and out of camp if one or two come with it.

H. H. Sibley
Colonel, Commanding

Paul Mazakutemani, Taopi, and [Wikinyantawa?]
to Henry Sibley, 24 September 1862[33]

Red Iron's Village, September 24th.

Ex. Gov. Sibley: Hon. Sir:

I have written some three or four letters to you, but never could send them. From the first I was anxious to extend and renew our friendship, and that of all the whites, and also are my friends, the Lower chiefs, that wish for peace. I held two councils as soon as the enemies came to our peaceful republic, in order to get the captives free, willing to hazard my own life could I obtain the liberty of the poor captives. The enemy are holding a council this morning, and wanted us to join them. They are rebels. We prefer our own councils and writing our own letters. The captives have been coming to us for safety until we have the greatest number, and so we are in danger of a battle from them immediately. Now, dear sir, please come right away without delay, or we may all fall victims, for fight we must soon. The enemy are not large in numbers, but you well know they are cruel savages (and the women, in the writer's opinion, can fight as well as the men).[34] All the Indians, with the exception of these, are friendly, and, were we prepared for defending ourselves, we should conquer; and if you don't hasten, our women and all the captives will suffer.

Yours respectfully,
Ma-za-ku-ta-ma-ne,
Taopee, and
Wake-wan-wa

§

Hon. Ex. Gov. Sibley, Col. Commanding.

This letter [above] is at the request of all our people. Maza-moni and Akipa are desirous of having their names put down with the Friendly Indians, feeling that they have had trouble enough, and are desirous of peace. All in great haste.

Henry Sibley to Paul Mazakutemani, Taopi, and [Wikinyantawa?], 24 September 1862[35]

Headquarters Wood Lake Camp, September 24, 1862.

Ma-za-ka-tame, Taopee, and Wa-ke-nan-nan-te,
At Red Iron's Village

My Friends:

I call you so because I have reason to believe that you have had nothing to do with the cruel murders and massacres that have been committed upon the poor white people who had placed confidence in the friendship of the Sioux Indians. I repeat what I have already stated to you, that I have not come to make war upon those who are innocent, but upon the guilty. I have waited here one day, and intend to wait still another day to hear from the friendly half-breeds and Indians, because I feared that if I advanced my troops before you could make your arrangements the war party would murder the prisoners.

Now that I learn from Joseph Campbell that most of the captives are in safety in your camp I shall move on tomorrow, so that you may expect to see me very soon.[36] Have white flag displayed so that my men may not fire upon you.

Your friend,
H. H. Sibley
Colonel, Commanding

Henry Sibley to Taṭaŋka Nażiŋ et al., 24 September 1862[37]

Headquarters Wood Lake Camp, September 24, 1862.

Ta-tanka-nazin,
Chief of the Sisseton-wans and Tah-ton ka-na-ken-yan
Soldiers of Wa-na-tans Band, Red Iron Village

If you are the friends of your Great American Father you are my friends also. I have not come up to make war upon any bands who have not been concerned in the horrible murders upon white people, who depended upon the good faith of the Indians. You would do well, therefore, to advise your bands not to mix yourselves together with the bands that have been guilty of these outrages, for I do not wish to injure any innocent person; but I intend to pursue the wicked murderers with fire and sword until I overtake them. Another large body of troops will meet these bad men if they attempt to escape either to the Red River or to the Missouri. Such of the Indians as have not had anything to do with the murders of the whites will not be injured by my troops; but, on the contrary, they will be protected by me when I arrive, which will be very soon. Those who are our friends must raise a white flag when they see me approaching, that I may be able to know my friends from my enemies. Take these words to your bands, that they may know that they are in safety as long as they remain friends of your Great Father. Your friend,

H. H. Sibley
Colonel, Commanding Military Expedition

Henry Sibley to Wanaatan et al., 3 October 1862[38]

Headquarters Camp Release, Oct. 3, 1862.

Wa-na-ta, Standing Buffalo, Tah-ton-ka-Nagee,
and Wa-ma-de-on-pe-dut-ta,
Chiefs of the Sioux,

My Friends:

I am sorry to hear that you allowed Little Crow and the bad men to escape into your country. After I had beaten them and killed many of their number you should have stopped him until I could have overtaken him and his band and have destroyed them. Now he must be pursued by my troops into your country, but you will not be injured nor any of your men who have not been engaged in the murders perpetrated by the bad Indians. I learn that you intend to come down and see me with some of your bands. I do not wish you to do so, because I have a great many men who are very angry because so many of their white relatives have been killed and they might not be able to distinguish you from the guilty bands and fire upon you. I do not wish you to suffer from any such mistake; therefore I desire you to remain at your own villages until I can have time to go and talk to you in council. Keep your bands separate from the wicked men who have broken peace with their Great Father. There are many other troops going in search of those bad men besides those I have with me, and they will be caught and punished.

Your friend,
H. H. Sibley
Colonel, Commanding

APPENDIX B

*Selected Correspondence of John B. Renville
and Mary A. Renville, 1862–1888*

John B. Renville to Stephen R. Riggs, 8 December 1862[1]

BERLIN, WISCONSIN

Dec 8th 62

My Dear Friend,
    Heciya taŋhaŋ uhiyupi
ehaŋtaŋ tuktedaŋ uŋ waŋjidaŋ uŋkupi
śni. Ohiŋni icimani uŋyakuŋpi.
Mitawiŋ taku wicaye kiŋ owasiŋ
waŋ wicabdake owasiŋ taŋyaŋ
uŋpi. Waŋji Beloit uŋti waŋdake
çikoŋ he kici waniyetu kiŋ de
uŋyakuŋpi kte uŋkicipi uŋkan uŋhdaka
iyaye Chicago. Heci oti ekta uŋkipi
hen kiciuŋkaŋpi kiŋ tka tipi waŋ
cistiŋna oti hecen en aŋpetu wakaŋ
waŋji uŋyakuŋpi k'a naka ha otuŋwe
kiŋ den uŋhipi. Tibdo waŋji
nakuŋ den uŋhe kici uŋyakoŋpi tka
cica ota k'a tipi iś eya cistiŋ oti hecen
nakaha tipi waŋ uŋkodotapi k'a
uŋki śnana nakaha uŋtipi. Tahaŋ
waye kiŋ Wicaśta waŋji kci ob uŋkiŋ
hena taku yutapi uŋ ouŋkiyapi. Aġuyapi
koka waŋ uŋkupi nakuŋ taku waniyetu
kiŋ de wowinyuŋ uŋyuŋpi kte ciŋ.
Hena uŋkoḳupi. Tipi owadote kiŋ heceyedaŋ
wakajuju tka nakuŋ teḣi śni yaŋ micaġapi.
Wicaśta wakaŋ waŋ otuŋwe kiŋ den ti
hetaŋyaŋ sdoniyakiye. Mr. Richard
eciyapi. He wicaśta kiŋ sdoniyakiya
uŋkaŋ he uŋkici sdouŋkiciyapi se ca.

My Dear Friend,
　　Ever since we left from over there
we have never settled down.
We are always moving around.
We saw all my wife's relatives.
They are all doing well.
We thought we were going to stay this
winter with the one who lives in Beloit
that you know but then he packed up and
went to Chicago. We went there to live
but the house was small
so we stayed one week and
we arrived in this town recently.
My wife's older brother also
is here but has too many children
and has a small house so
we rented a house and
now we live alone. We are helping
my brother-in-law and another man
with food. We gave them
a bread box to get ready for
the coming winter.
We help them. I pay for the house
I rented but this makes it harder for me.
A minister in town here
says he knows you. Mr. Richard
is his name. The only reason I know
him is he knows you.

Mitawiŋ miciŋca ob taŋyaŋ wauŋ
tka Mazaska e waŋna manice kta
Taŋnihaŋ mazaska zi tonana bduha. Uŋkan
imnijaska kiŋ en wowapi tokiyepiwaye ca
uŋge saŋpa wakamna. Okiŋni wetu uŋkupi
kta hehan uŋnicapi kte. Imnijaska en wicaṡta
waŋ Gilfillan eciyapi. He mazaska mitawa
kiŋ ecuŋ waṡi tka nahanhin tukten uŋ kiŋ
nauŋhuŋpi ṡni.
Niṡ wowapi mayakaga uŋkanṡ epca owasiŋ
enana kiŋ ya uŋko mdecahaŋpi k'a toki kiya
uŋpi. Wiyoepca taku wicawaya owasiŋ toki
uŋpi nakuŋ Dakota taku wicawaya kiŋ hena
k'a mdoketu kiŋhan tukten uŋpi kta. Niṡ ake
owasiŋ tukteya uŋpi kta. Hena ohiŋni heci
ahi waciŋ wauŋ.
Iye Wakaŋ tanka wouŋṡida hci ҫikoŋ
uŋṡi uŋkidapi k'a ake makoce waŋji en
uŋyuwitayapi kta uŋkidapi. Nuwe.

Yours Truly
John B. Renville

My wife, my children and I are well
but I am running low on money.
I had a few gold coins and traded for
paper in St. Paul and made some
more money. Maybe we will come in
spring, until then we will have nothing. In
St. Paul there is a man named Gilfillan.
I told him to get my money but
we haven't heard from him.[2]
You, when you wrote me a letter, I realized
our people are scattered and they are all over
the place. All I can think of is my relatives
wherever they are. And in the summer
where will my Dakota relatives go.[3]
And where will all of you be. I always
think about all of those things.
God, himself, forgives, forgives us
and we ask him to gather us in one
place. Amen.

Yours Truly
John B. Renville

Mary A. Renville to Stephen R. Riggs, 10 January 1863[4]

Berlin, Jan. 10/63

My Dear Friend,

Mr Renville is anxious I should answer the letter we have just received with our acknowledgments of the $5.00 enclosed, which came very unexpectedly; and you may be certain is truly appreciated. We have asked ourselves what we can render to our Heavenly Father, for his goodness to us, in raising up friends in time of such adversity. It seems impossible almost to get employment. I have been into taylor shops & shoe shops for work, but did not succeed[.] Mr Renville has engaged a few days of chopping. We have been blessed with general good health. Ella has been quite sick but we did not call a Physician, fearing strong medicine more than disease. Belle is happy and a great favorite with all. My dear little Lillie; I wonder if her father will ever try to get her[.][5]

Mr Renville is glad he is not in Minnesota this winter thinks he should be tried in his feelings about the Indians, that [are] in the camp at fort Snelling.[6]

We believe that you will act wisely in regard to all matters concerning the Dakotas, for it needs one of great prudence in times of such trials and excitements[.] We were pleased as well as my Brother with your correspondence in the St. Paul paper. The people of Minnesota need not fear for their beloved land for many good farmers are talking of going their in the spring thinking the people of Minnesota are so frightened, that they will be able to get farms for a trifle.

Mr Renville wishes me to say when their is any opening for him that you will be so kind as to write. [H]e wants to return in the spring but I am afraid of the *Germans*, they are so furious.[7]

If you have not already seen Mr Gilfillan[,] Mr Renville would like very much to have you see him. [W]e sent our affidavits to him regarding two claims (vis) loss of property, by the burning of the M.L. School house, and the goods we were obliged to purchase at our own expense.[8] The Bills of the articles accompanying the affidavits[,] we felt that all just claims might be settled now. Mr Gilfillan can tell you about the whole better than I can write. We could never get a settlement with Maj Brown for his books were not ready; but we had kept an account, and did not lose them.[9]

Please give my love to your family[.] How I should like to visit them which I should have done when at Mendota[,] but was obliged to ride to St. Paul so many times over the rocks, I felt wearied out and though urged by Mr Renville to visit St Anthony, I had not the ambition after my siege during captivity.

Which I have not entirely recovered from yet. Last Sabbath was communion here. I could not go on the account of Ella's being sick but Mr. R. went. [T]he last time I communed was with your church at Hazlewood. I find I am writing as I used too to my Dear Father for, forgetting or rather believing that you have the same care for us that he used to.

Yours, Truly,
M. A. Renville

John B. Renville to Stephen R. Riggs, 22 January 1863[10]

Berlin, Jan 22 / 63

Mr. Riggs
Dear Sir wowapi ehake
yakage çikoŋ waŋna wauŋyaŋkapi.
Mazaska $5 kiŋ waŋna
uŋhapi iyotaŋ nina
uŋġe uŋhapi tka he tonana
k'a waŋna uŋhdusotatapi kta.
Keṡ eciŋ ake uŋge uŋhapi e ce.
He awaciŋ uŋkanpi. Uŋkan
wanakaṡ Elijah Wiwazica
waŋ ti en i k'a aġuyapi wihdi
ko waŋna nice kta. Keṡ ake ecuŋ
icaḣkiye çikoŋ he e se uŋkanpi.
Niṡ, waŋna $10 uŋyak'upi.
Hehan Beloit eciyataŋhaŋ
iṡ $5 uŋk'upi k'a eya nakuŋ taku
yutapi k'a taku waŋji kci uŋ
ouŋkiyapi. Wicaṡta Wakaŋ waŋ
Mr. Richard eciyapi taŋnihaŋ caje
bde çikoŋ Mrs. Richard
called here and requested us to
remember her to you. She says the
time she saw you they lived in
Massachusetts.[11]
Minesota wicaṡta caŋte uŋkicaŋnicapi
tka ake deciya eke heceuŋpi
ṡni. Dakota tona taŋyaŋ ecuŋpi
kiŋ hena hanke iyutapi opawinge
k'a $50, ota iyohi hecen wicak'upi
kta naceca keyapi. Waŋna
numpa hecen nauŋḣuŋpi niṡ
taŋyaŋ nayahun na ce.

Mr. Riggs
Dear Sir, Now we have all seen
the last letter you wrote.
We have the $5 now.
We have some more
but that is a small amount
and just as we are about
to use it up, we always get some more.
We have been thinking about that. And
long ago Elijah went
to a widow's house and bread and lard
were getting low. Then again
we were raised like that.[12]
You, you have given us $10 now.
Then from Beloit
they gave us $5 and also some
food and they helped us with one
other thing. A minister,
Mr. Richard is his name, long ago
mentioned Mrs. Richard
called here and requested us to
remember her to you. She says the
time she saw you they lived in
Massachusetts.[13]
Minnesota people don't like us
but over here it is not like that.
All of those Dakota who did
good will be given much, a half-section
of land and $150
maybe, they said.
Twice now we heard that, you
probably heard more about it.[14]

Mendota etaŋhaŋ wowapi micagapi.
Uŋkan Michel k'a Wanyagupi
Zitkadaŋtawa tohan taŋkan
yapi e ca witkopi k'a ake wicakaśkapi
ce e keyapi. He nawahuŋ kiŋ uŋ
nina iyomakiśice. Ito tuwe
he itaŋcaŋ awanwicayaka
he kiŋhaŋ tohan mini wakaŋ
tipi ekta yapi kta ca anawicapta
iyececa kta. Tka iye Wakaŋ taŋka
he tokiŋ iyope içiyapi k'a
uŋśiwicakida k'a wicakicicajujuŋ.
Iye tawa uŋśida taŋka kiŋ
uŋ dehaŋ ake piya uŋkiyuśkiŋpi
k'a uŋ yataŋ iyececa.
Taku śica ehna uŋyakuŋpi
tka taŋyaŋ uŋhiyupi kiŋ uŋ.
Antoin k'a taku wicawaya
owasiŋ wowapi waŋ wica
weca k'a waŋyakapi k'a iś
toketu he kiŋhaŋ
iś ya deci Hokśiyopi nina
tapi k'a nina wawica
yazaŋke. Maŋka cage kiŋ
tokeca ohiŋni Maǵajuju
sa k'a opśija ya waŋka k'a
nakaha Aŋpetu tonana
wa tka nakuŋ ota śni.
Nakaś caŋpahmi henana
eceyedaŋ uŋpi.
Tiyohnaka owasiŋ taŋyaŋ
uŋyakuŋpi.

Yours Truly
John B. Renville

I got a letter from Mendota.
They say that when Michel and Wanyagupi
Zitakadaŋtawa go outside the
community they get drunk and get
jailed. I heard that and am
very sad. Well, it seems that whoever
is looking after them when
they go to that place where there is
liquor should stop them.
But God himself
desires that they would repent and
cherishes them and paid for their sins.
As his forgiveness is great
now we are again renewed
and drawn to Him.
We are among bad things
but we came out of it well.
I wrote a letter to Antoin
and all of my relatives
and they read it and I don't know
how things are over there
but here many babies
are dying and there is much
sickness.[15] This season
why is it always raining
and muddy everywhere and
a few days it snowed
but not much.
In spite of all that they
only use wagons.
All the household is
doing well.

Yours Truly
John B. Renville

Mary A. Renville to Stephen R. Riggs, 23 January 1863[16]

Berlin Jan. 23/63

Mr. Riggs
Rev. Sir,

   We received your letter four days from its date[.] [W]e were somewhat prepared to receive the sad news of Agnes death, having had
the letter from you and two or three others from Mendota. [W]e are
alarmed: what can be done, what Physicians do they employ, is he an
honest man, do Mr Renville's family keep well, and are they drinking
as we heard[?] Mr Renville says ask Mr. Riggs if my Brothers and their
families cant move from that Camp[.] They have Scrip and they have
some horses have they not.[17] We both feel as if we must not let them
die. [I]f they cannot support themselves any way, we are willing to pay
the rent of a house[.] Will you not, Mr. Riggs, see what can be done[?]
[D]ont let them stay in that camp till they all die, for if God gives us our
claims against government we both [are] ready to help them all you
think their situation demands[.] [W]e don't know anything about them,
but I am afraid for *one* to have them move to Mendota and cant you[,]
Mr. Riggs[,] advise with Gov. Sibley and save my husband's Brothers
from that foul camp without their being exposed to drinking[?] What
can we do[?] [T]ell us and we will try to act wisely, if we get anything
to do with.

   I cannot sleep well nights thinking of my Dear Mary, is she still
well[?] I think she may have had the measles[.][18] If her Mother would
only consent to her coming here I could do well, should we get the
means. I cant rest until I try every means of trying to get her. Mary told
Mr Cunningham she wants to come to me.[19] I wish you would write
what you think, and perhaps I shall feel easier[.] I took Mary for my
own child and she has taken a deep root in my affections[.] [D]oes she
think of Jesus, or is she still thoughtless[?] Ella makes the tears start
every day almost, asking Mama where is Mamie & Lillie[.] Dear little
Lillie, I wonder if her Father can give her up[?] I cant[.] [I]f ever I go
back and can get her I shall.

We feel sad to hear of Agnes death, but feel better about it than we should if you had given consent for her to go to the camp. Poor Angelique will take it hard. I do hope[,] Mr Riggs[,] you wont let Angelique go back over to her Mother, if you can help it. I saw so much of her during our captivity that I cant have much confidence in her. Madeline wrote she had married The [O]ther [D]ay.[20] Madeline scolded Mr R and myself very badly, but we have tried to pray for every one in camp[,] especially our friends[.] May their and their children [*sic*] be blest with the Holy Spirit that is hovering over that camp[.]

Mr R studies the [B]ible with Barnes notes a good deal but sometimes gets discouraged[.] I try to aid him all I can I know he often wishes he could spend his life among the Dakotas, and when their is any opening I will try to not hinder him from doing good[,] [i]f I cant do but little.[21] The most of the people here feel that the Minnesotians are besides themselves acting and carrying out such a spirit of revenge[.]

[In margin] I see I have made many mistakes[.] Bell & Ella are noisy and you know I am nervous.

We are truly glad to hear the prospect of getting money soon[.] As regards the vouchers[,] Mr Gilfillan has them or rather sent them for us to sign sometime since we were advised to place all our claims in his hands for collection. The amount will be a good deal less than $1800, for Brown had so many orders charged on his books we feel afraid of being cheated but have acted according to our best ability. Un. Sol. Brown said when he gave us a copy of the things lost by fire[,] ["K]eep this it may be a great help to you. [Y]ou ought to have your pay for your goods.["] I hope we shall get enough to pay him. I guess if he had lived a captive two months with his family he would not feel so bitter.[22]

Mr. N. Myrick has persevered on getting an order on Gilfillan. [W]e suppose it is all right but are afraid of so many orders.[23] Mr. Gilfillan was not to share our 5 per cent unless he employed some other person, then he said it should not exceed ten per cent and said we might get information from any source we choose[.] If it will or can be in your way to find out please do so[.] It is hard doing business by writing.

Yours Truly
Mary A. Renville

[D]o please write all about Mary when you see her I wrote her and Anna, but am afraid of Madeline[.][24]

John B. and Mary A. Renville to Stephen R. Riggs, 30 January 1863[25]

Berlin, Jan. 30, 1863

Mr. Riggs,

Rev. Sir, you will doubtless before you get this receive a letter from each of us. We are glad of the encouragement given us by the lines from you and Gen. Sibley.[26] Their is probably an acknowledgment due to Gen. Sibley which we should have rendered to him, had we received his articles sooner. [B]ut as they went to Beloit they came in the same mail as yours.

Please speak to him about it when you see him and it will save us one letter. In the letter I wrote to you I mentioned our having given or rather sent vouchers to Gilfillan. In this we will only say we shall be glad to get the money, *not forgetting our debts.* When we were at Saint Paul we called on Supt Thompson, and he advised us to see Senator Rice, and gave us a letter to present to him, but at that time he was very ill and his Physicians forbid his seeing any company, he sent word to us by his sister to the door that he would do what he could but she said one needed to employ a claim Agent. We went again to Mr. Thompson and he said he did not like to advise what claims Agent we had better employ, but as we were strangers he would mention that Gilfillan was getting many claims, and probably we would get our claims sooner by placing it in his hands [with Gilfillan].

We hope it is all right in our giving an order on Gilfillan for Mr. N

Myrick[.] [T]hey wrote from Saint Paul, that it would be filed in Gilfillan's office, and when the draft came, they would have it cashed. Now you know[,] Mr Riggs[,] that our acquaintance with such business is limited, and sometimes for want of proper knowledge we feel quite uneasy about doing so much business by writing. And if at any time you can give us information we shall be thankful and hope you will be frank and free to do so[.]

Mr. Renville says tell Mr. Riggs he had rather get the money without Gilfillan getting percent on it and that he would write to Gen. Sibley, but feels afraid to tell him every thing[.] [B]ut he is not afraid to write what he wants to to you[.] [H]e hopes he will not have to pay any percent and if you can tell him anything what is best for him to do next spring please to do. Please excuse my nervous writing[.] I have worked hard for me and the least noise makes me jump[.] I dont get over being a captive yet, or rather the effects of it.

Mr. Riggs[,] I cant give up Mary very well, without doing all I think I ought to[.] [I]f you hear anything from her please let me know.

Yours Truly
J. B. & M. A. Renville

John B. and Mary A. Renville to Stephen R. Riggs, 13 February 1863[27]

Berlin, Feb. 13th 1863

Mr. Riggs,

Rev. Sir[:] We have before us a letter from Gen. Sibley, stating that our drafts were at Saint Paul, and that he detained them until we wrote to you[.]

Now we are owing[:]

1st to Mr & Mrs Riggs and Isabella. Please make out your bills and take your pay from the draft.

2nd to Mrs Huggins for potatoes bo't of Mr Huggins[.] [T]en barrels I bo't in the fall. Mr. H. said I could have them for $1.00 a bar. I think he wanted to accommodate me and I am willing to pay his widow what you think the potatoes were worth in the fall. Four (4) barrels I bo't in the spring[.] [P]lease pay her what those were worth and much oblige.

John B Renville.

3d, we are owing Mr & Mrs Cunningham. [P]lease have them present their bills, and pay them.
4th Please pay to Joseph R. Brown the sum of ($299 76/100) two hundred ninety nine dollars and seventy six cents.
5th I owe Mr. Forbes I think about $20. Mr. Quin will know. [P]lease settle the account.
6th Uncle Sol. must have his pay. I should like to have him get his pay of his brother Nathaniel as he owes us almost $50 on Lillie's board when we first took her. Please pay Uncle Sol if you think it best. I am anxious to be free from debt.

J. B. Renville

NB [T]he amount you probably, know, or have[.][28]

Mr Riggs please take the whole amount of these several bills from my draft[,] that is from Mrs Mary Renville's draft. Mr Renville thinks it best on the account of your sending the lesser draft to us. We wish to put $1000 in the *Bank* drawing interest. Mr Renville says tell Mr Riggs to put it in the Saint Paul Bank. The balance send to us that is after the debts are deducted from the drafts.

Mr. Riggs, I mentioned to Mr. Renville that it might be best to put the money in the Chicago Bank. I am sure I dont know. [B]ut you will please advise us, what you think is best[.] [I]f you think it best to put it in the Saint Paul retain the $1,000, till you write to us. I am a little suspicious of the safety of the State of Minnesota. We hear so many accounts that the Indian are agoing to rise very strong. [T]he last report is that, a man, who intended to move to Minnesota soon with his family, has received a letter from a friend living at New Ulm, advising him by all means not to move, for the Indians were all agoing to rise, or that 30,000, were preparing for battle, in the spring. Mr. Renville laughs at me, but I can't forget the late Massacre. I don't believe the reports, but I am still afraid a portion of them may be true.

We are owing some here, we meet with gains and losses. Jack was or has been hurt badly and the man sold him for $50. But in all God be praised. He has given us life and prosperity more than we have deserved.

We looked for Mr Cunningham and family last week and shall look this week. I hope Mary will come[.] [I]f they don't start till this reaches you and Mary can come, please do have her comfortably clothed for a journey, and as respectable as you think I would wish my own daughter to be. We can purchase things here cheaper than in Saint Paul, so that a good travelling suit may be about all necessary to buy for Mary. Mrs Riggs will know or Mrs Cunningham. My Mary[,] can it be I shall ever have her with me again. The Lords will be done and not mine. You will understand about Mary's expenses, that we will willingly bear them.

Mr. Riggs I am writing a story every week for the Berlin City Current [sic]. I kept a kind of journal during the troublous times while I was a captive. I have written 7 stories, and for the sake of my friends and little Ella, I think of having it published in the form of a pamphlet. [A]nd if Isabella has any facts she is willing to *part with* that would serve me, and will be so kind as to send them to me[,] I shall be much obliged[.] I am almost sorry I have written this, for you may all be surprised[,] as well as sorry[,] I should make such an attempt.[29]

Mr Richard bid us all[,] or rather the church[,] farewell yesterday, very unexpectedly, to the most of the church and to himself. [H]e has been slandered. I think the true cause is he is to much of a Union man for some of his permanent members. They have been true friends to us and it makes us feel sad. The Presbytery meets here this week commencing this evening.

When you write tell us if you think their is any possibility of our going back to Minnesota or what you think we had better do. Please remember us to your family.

Mary B. Renville

We mentioned to Gen. Sibley about Isabella['s] scrip[.]

Mary A. Renville to Stephen R. Riggs, 21 February 1863[30]

Berlin Feb 21st, 1863

Mr Riggs

Rev. Sir, We received yours to day with the receipts and drafts enclosed, and [are] glad to have our debts so far paid. Mr. Renville says he thinks we left S. Brown's bill at Mendota, and he does not remember how much it is, but that it is either $13 (dollars) and some cents, or between 14, or 15, he cant tell. I cant remember anything hardly since our captivity but what is in black and white[.] [T]o day I am a very nervous head ache, and would not attempt to write but Mr. R. wants me to. We think if it wont put you to too much trouble that it is best to have you put $1000, in the bank at Saint Paul till we go to Minnesota and have time to look about and see the building lots or farms, so as to please ourselves in selecting. The remainder you may send in a draft to us[.] We have promised to let one of my Brothers have some money, for which he will give land security and it will save his farm. We think we can spare the $1000, long enough in the bank to earn a little money. Mr. Renville is anxious to return to Minnesota in the spring[.] [H]e is busy all the time since you wrote to see about teaching. I wish in your next you would please tell wheare we would have to live if he was engaged in teaching[,] for I must have a little quiet from Indian callers until my nerves are somewhat stronger. I shall try and not hinder Mr Renville from laboring among his people and if ever I recover my health [i]t will be my desire to aid him in any way I can.

Mr. R. is translating Precept upon Precept, and takes great pleasure in doing it. [H]e thinks it will interest the Dakotas very much. He wants to know what part has been translated and if it has all been destroyed[.][31]

Mr. Riggs, I hope you can speak an encouraging word to Mr. R. even if it can't be published in a long time, for it aids him in getting a little better command of our language and the task of plying himself diligently[.] [H]e thinks he can translate it so as to do well after you and John Williamson have corrected it[.] [H]e seems more anxious to labor among the Dakotas than he ever did. I hope I shant prove an hindrance[,] but I sometimes shrink from ever going into the Indian Country again[.] [B]ut once their I expect these foolish feelings will leave me and I shall be a more sensible woman.

Mr. Riggs, I know I make mistakes in spelling and almost every other way in writing but Bell, and Ella are enough almost to craze me when writing, and I have so much writing to do I can't expect to keep them quiet.

Yours Truly[,]
Mary A Renville

John B. Renville to Stephen R. Riggs, 24 February 1863[32]

Berlin Feb 24th 1863

Mr. Riggs Dear Friend
Wowapi ahake
yakaġe çikoŋ wanna waŋuŋyakapi.
Eya tohaŋ waŋji uŋġe
kaġapi eca hena owasiŋ
uŋkiyuśkiŋpi ece.
Dowaŋpi wowapi uŋ mazaska
mnayaŋpi. Caje date kiŋ he eya
uŋkiś ecuŋkuŋpi kte. Dehaŋ uŋkiyaciŋpi
uŋkan mazaska wikcemna
$10, mitawiŋ miciŋca ob
hena dehaŋ uŋkicuŋpi kte k'a
tona ciŋpi kiŋ iye na mnayaŋpi
śni kiŋhaŋ ake tohaŋ heci
uŋkipi kiŋhaŋ ake uŋġe uŋkic'uŋ
kte uŋkokihipi kiŋhaŋ.
Hehaŋ Michel k'a TiWakaŋ k'a nakuŋ
waŋji kci ob Pehijutazizi
ekta yapi kta kehe ciŋ tokecauŋ
heciyapi kte kiŋ taŋyaŋ
nawahuŋ keś epca tawicu ob yapi kte
ciŋ heuŋ heciya uŋpi kte ca
iś ake ecadaŋ hdipi kta. Toketu
hwo epca.
Hehaŋ wowapi waŋ Dakota ia
owakaġe tka wani haŋtaŋhaŋ
ecamuŋ uŋkanś waŋna ota
bduśtaŋ kta tka aśkatudaŋ
ecamuŋ hecen nahaŋhiŋ tona
owakaġe he aokahniħ waśte
wake ca uŋ etaŋhaŋ owakaġa

Mr. Riggs Dear Friend
We now saw
the last letter you wrote.
Whenever you make us one
we are always
delighted.
They are saving money for
song books. We are going to
use the ones you named.
We think they have
about $10, my wife and children
will deliver this and I don't know how
much they want but if it is not enough
then whenever we come over there
again we will give some more
if we can.[33]
Remember you said Michel and
Tiwakaŋ and another one
are going to Pehijutazizi even though I
didn't hear fully why they are going over
there, I think they are going with their wives,
or if they are staying over there
or are they coming back soon.
How is that, I am thinking.
I have been writing in Dakota
since last winter but
I should have finished more.
But lately
the ones I wrote are easier
to understand.
I wrote from my thoughts.

he uŋśpaśpa waŋna Dakota ia
okaġapi tka weksuye śni
hecen niś omayakiya ka
waciŋ k'aiś ake ocowasiŋ
okaġapi kta iyececa. Heciŋhaŋ
he nina ecamuŋ tka uŋ nakaha
iśta maŋyazaŋ kte sece.
hecen ehaŋtaŋhaŋ ecamuŋ
śni tka uŋkupi śni itokab
tona owakihi ecamuŋ kte.
Ake wowapi yakaġe ciŋhaŋ
taku num caje mda kiŋ
he omaŋyakiyaka waciŋ
oyakihi kiŋhaŋ.
Wakaŋ taŋka tawa uŋśida
eceyedaŋ tuŋ kuŋ iye uŋśi
uŋkidapi k'a niyepi owasiŋ
k'a uŋkiyepi uŋketaŋhaŋpi
ko ota iyohi awanuŋhdakapi.
Nuwe.

Yours truly,
J. B. Renville

Those pieces are now written in Dakota
but I don't remember,
so I want you to help me
or perhaps we can all
write together.[34] If
I do more, then it seems
my eyes are going to be sore.
So I haven't done anything
since then but before we come
I will do as much as I can.
Before you write me again
I want you to tell me two things
that I mentioned
if you can.
Through God's mercy
only we are
forgiven. All of you,
and all of us are His and
each and every one of us is taken care of.
Amen.

Yours truly,
J. B. Renville

Mary A. Renville to the editors of the
St. Paul Weekly Press, 5 March 1863[35]

"Did the Indians Hold the Half-Breeds as Prisoners:
a female captive vs. Mr. Frenier"

Editors of the Press:

Permit one who was a captive among the Indians for seven weeks, to state a few facts which fell under her own observation.

Mr. Antoine Frenier in an article recently published in your columns says:

"There was no guard around the Indian camp at any time during the Indian outbreak. Indians and Half-breeds were alike free to leave the camp when they pleased" and that it had been agreed the half-breeds "should be allowed to go where they pleased." Being obliged to flee from my home on that dreadful morning of August 18th, and finding the road to Fort Ridgley closely watched by the Indians, I hid in some woods on the edge of a bluff. From my hiding place, I could, when standing, see the road for a considerable distance. I could distinctly see Indian sentinels reclining on a mound at a short distance from the road. Several times during the twenty four hours I remained hid there, I saw wagons filled with Indian women and children, passing down the road. When they approached this mound the sentinels would come to them, and after a halt and conference the wagon would return. I was not near enough to hear anything that was said, but I could see that whenever a wagon came there, it was turned back again. When the Indians moved up to Yellow Medicine, some of the half-breeds wished to remain in their houses, but they were not allowed to do so. About a week before Gen. Sibley arrived at Camp Release, some of the half-breeds formed a plan of escape at midnight and come down to his camp, but so closely were they watched, their plan was discovered, notwithstanding all possible secresy [sic]. A guard was placed around the tents in the woods and on the roads; so they were obliged to give up the execution of their design. Many of the half-breeds would have left the Indian country, on first hearing of the outbreak, had they been "free to go where they pleased."[36] I knew many of the Indians, too, would have come below, to escape participation in the robberies, had it been practicable for them to do so. But without stating all the obstacles which prevented the friendly Indians from coming below, I will say that we who were captives have much reason to feel grateful to them. It was they who protected us to a great extent from insult, and who, when they had time to rally and unite, protected us from Little Crow and his murderous bands and restored us to our friends. Mr. Frenier says he knew but two half-breeds who were entirely innocent. Of the others, he says, "they preferred to remain with those who were committing the murders and robbing the people of their property." Surely Mr. Frenier does not mean to include in this latter clause, his own nephew, Mr. Angus Brown. I never heard him charged with the least participation in the outbreak. I can assure Mr. Frenier, for his gratification, of my full belief that the reason Mr. Brown with his wife and father's family, remained among the Indians until the arrival of Gen. Sibley at Camp Release, was that they in common with the half-breeds were as really prisoners as the white captives. I saw a large amount of plunder hid, but most of it was secreted by the Indians who fled with Little Crow. The Indians who remained were mostly those who had so small a share of the plunder that they felt that if they fled and left their crops, they would be in danger of starvation.

M. A. R.

Mary A. Renville to the editors of *Iapi Oaye*, October 1882[37]

"Trying to Overcome"

BLESSED PROMISES are contained in the Bible for all WHO OVER-COME. How can we overcome grief, when we part with our loved ones? When Jesus came for our Darling, taking her gently away in His loving arms, many sympathetic friends did all that was possible to aid us in our great sorrow. Thus they fulfilled the injunction, "Bear ye one another's burdens." But there are afflictions which none but the Heavenly Father can help us bear. So it seemed when Darling went away to the brighter world and left us parents to wait till ready for our summons.

Pray—I could not—only bow down. Tears did not come. Clouds and darkness seemed to be around about us. Truly, one must walk by faith in times like this, or sink. One thing we knew: "Darling's Savior was our Savior too;" and that he makes no mistakes, but doeth all things well. The loving kiss and happy "good-night," given by daughter so many years, we can never forget. Can it be we shall hear it no more; only the sad, mournful good-night from the boy who is trying to fill a son's place in our hearts, and the pleading, agonizing prayer of my dear husband, that the Lord would help us through this hour—this day—for tomorrow may never come—so uncertain is life!

In this extremity, the question would arise, how can I overcome all this loneliness, so as to cheer up our home? How I have wished to be a noble Christian woman, able to endure all things for the sake of the loved ones left. Friends at home! Friends abroad! Friends everywhere! And for aught we know, friends long since gone to the Heavenly Home; these last saying to Darling: "See, are you not glad that your parents have so many friends on earth?["] I can imagine the answer Darling would give: "Oh, how kind [of] them, but the dearest friend they have is Jesus, for my Savior is their Savior, too."

It may [do] for some to darken the windows, but I felt we needed all the sunshine we could have. I remember a mother who had lost her only child, say, that for four years her piano had been silent. But the organ, which our Darling loved to play, for our enjoyment no less than her own, I opened for the adopted brother, that he might not lose the instruction she had given him. The rooms she arranged I have left the same. When the flowers came, I placed them on the table as she was wont to do. I hope she sees how hard I try to overcome.

Again, I find it necessary to take much exercise, not only in doors, but out, doing what little I can for the people—thinking of more I would like to do—committing a verse daily from Daily Food, which Ella, dear, used till the very day Jesus called for her. God's own words have been my greatest comfort. Hours, days, weeks, and months have passed, and when my dear husband and son are at work, the mother-heart has so yearned the darling daughter—alone, no not alone, for Jesus is with me.

The grave is always in sight. Together, the parents often visit it; and though we cannot understand all the mysteries of the Resurrection, or the glories of Heaven, we are satisfied that the Lord of Heaven and Earth doeth all things well, and will help us to *overcome* and OVERCOME, till we are prepared to hear the summons: "Welcome to the Father's Home above."

NOTES

ABBREVIATIONS

ABCFM	American Board of Commissioners for Foreign Missions	NARA	National Archives and Records Administration, Washington DC
CWS	Oahe Mission Collection, Riggs Family Papers, Center for Western Studies at Augustana College, Sioux Falls, South Dakota	NMM, MHS	Northwest Missions Manuscripts Collection, Minnesota Historical Society
MHS	Minnesota Historical Society, St. Paul, Minnesota		

HISTORICAL INTRODUCTION

1. Taylor, *Tell Me a Story*, 6. Taylor's "tremor half a world and two millennia away" may reference the birth and death of Jesus Christ, making it doubly appropriate for this story.

2. This section is a fictional story woven from historical facts. The thoughts and dream of young Jean (who would grow up to be John Baptiste Renville) are imagined from a Dakota perspective based on his later recollections in the Presbyterian publication the *Home Missions Monitor*, July 1897, p. 206, Presbyterian Historical Society, Philadelphia. Details of the interior of Joseph Renville's house are gleaned from period and archeological records and sleeping arrangements from Ella Deloria's *Dakota Way of Life*, vol. 1. The "Doctor" was missionary Thomas S. Williamson, whose rusty continental French was his earliest form of conversation with Renville, who spoke Canadian French. The literate clerk was Roman Catholic. In the Catholic tradition Bible study was the province of priests, not common people, and Williamson recalled that the clerk disliked reading from the Protestant Bible that Joseph Renville Sr. had

obtained by mail order from Geneva around the time he settled at Lac qui Parle. "Ikće Wićaśta," which means "the common people," is the name Dakota people use for themselves. "Winter" is used in the Dakota sense of "year." "Weak womenfolk" was the Dakota conclusion drawn from observing the missionaries sheltering their wives from strenuous work. The stories Joseph Renville told Jean are among Ella Deloria's translations of Dakota tales in the Franz Boas Papers at the American Philosophical Society, Philadelphia, and among the notes Doane Robinson made of conversations with John Baptiste Renville in Robinson's papers in the South Dakota State Archives at Pierre. Robinson said that John was "especially well versed in the lore of the Sioux." Robinson, "Sioux Indian View," 307.

3. While John's mother's name has historically been written as "Tokanne," the sound is not close to any Dakota word used as a personal name. Dakota place-names in this volume are taken from Durand, *Where the Waters Gather*. Durand's work is based on Dakota place-names reported to cartographer Joseph Nicollet in the late 1830s.

4. The standard biography of Taoyateduta (Little Crow IV) is Gary Clayton Anderson's *Little Crow*. Both Anderson and more recent biographer Mark Diedrich, in *Little Crow*, give detailed genealogies of the Little Crow family. I have chosen not to include a Renville–Little Crow family tree in this volume so as not to perpetuate historical errors. An updated genealogy composed in consultation with descendants of both families is needed.

5. Tokanne's unnamed sister was the mother of Joseph Napeśniduta, another of Little Crow's principal men and an early and staunch ally of acculturation. On Chatka and Napeśniduta see Stephen R. Riggs and Gideon H. Pond to David Greene, 10 September 1846, NMM, MHS.

6. In June 1944, when Dakota Renville soldiers stormed Normandy on D-Day, they fought their way ashore on the beaches of Calvados, their French ancestral homeland.

7. I am indebted to Steve Misener, who shared Arthur Rainville's genealogical collection; to Ed Merk, whose "Ancestors of Margaret Jane Jerome," privately published in 2009, confirms the Arthur Rainville data; and to Lois Glewwe for compiling both, along with her own data, into "Joseph Renville Family Overview," in my project files for this book. The Arthur Rainville collection is now at the Chippewa County (Minnesota) Historical Society. Merk's data, available online at http://edmerck.tripod.com/merckfamily/jerome/jeromeancestors.pdf (accessed 27 September 2011), document the descent lines of François Joseph Renville.

8. The American branch of the Rainville family began spelling their surname "Renville" in Joseph Renville Sr.'s generation. However, given that French explorer Joseph Nicollet spelled the name "Rainville" in his diary, it is quite possible that as late as John Baptiste's generation the name retained the French pronunciation, despite the change in spelling.

9. In *Little Crow*, Gary Clayton Anderson draws on the Dakota custom of exogamous marriage to argue that Miniyuhe may have been born into the Wabaśa clan of the Mississippi. That band's location in that era is compatible with the story of Miniyuhe's white grandmother.

10. Miniyuhe's father is given as "probably" either Centaŋwakaŋmani (Tokanne's grandfather) or his brother, Ishtamaza (Estamuzza). See G. Anderson, *Little Crow*, 188. But culturally that relationship seems too close to be likely. I thank Dakota scholar and Little Crow family descendent Gwen Westerman for insights like this one, offered on an early draft of this manuscript, in my project files for this book.

11. Wanmdi Okiya to Wokchan awakan koda [Joseph Nicollet], n.d., translated by Raymond J. DeMallie in Bray and Bray, *Joseph Nicollet on the Plains and Prairies*, 279–80. Wambdiokiya was the brother of (Paul) Mazakutemani. This means that unless historians have misunderstood their parentage, Mazakutemani, the speaker for the Peace Coalition, prominent throughout *A Thrilling Narrative*, was also descended from the mysterious white woman. Neither Wambdiokiya nor Mazakutemani identified themselves as mixed-bloods. Nor were they ever cast as such by others, including Dakotas who were opposed to this family's early and enduring support for acculturation.

12. S. Riggs, *Dakota-English Dictionary*, 536.

13. Grace Lee Nute's 1932 study, "Pioneer Women of Minnesota," concluded that the earliest known white woman in the region was an unnamed Orkney girl disguised as a boy working for Pembina trader Alexander Henry in 1807. The first French Canadian woman Nute found was Madame Marie-Anne Lagimoniere, the wife of a voyageur, around 1810. The establishment of the Selkirk Colony from 1812 to 1821 brought an influx of women born in Scotland, Ireland, Switzerland, and Canada to the region. Grace Lee Nute Papers, MHS; Silver, *Introduction to Canadian History*.

14. Thomas S. Williamson, "Obituary of Joseph Renville," in Thomas S. Williamson to David Greene, 15 May 1846, NMM, MHS. The obituary was abridged in *Missionary Herald*, vol. 42, 313–16. The standard modern biography of Joseph Renville Sr. is G. Anderson, "Joseph Renville." Most biographies of Joseph Renville Sr. are derived from the work of early Minnesota historian Edward Duffield Neill. Neill's "A Sketch of Joseph Renville," published in the inaugural volume of the *Collections of the Minnesota Historical Society* in 1850, was reprinted in *Dakota Tawaxitku Kin—The Dakota Friend* in August 1852.

15. We don't know how old John was when his father named him Koda Mitawa, although it was certainly before Joseph's death in 1846, when John was fourteen. Traditionally Dakota ordinal names ended at the fifth child. While the language was robust enough to improvise "ninth child, if a boy," other children are known to have carried a non-ordinal name from birth, like Charles Eastman, whose birth name,

commemorating his mother's death in childbirth, was Hakadah, or "The Pitiful Last." Thus John Baptiste Renville may have borne the name "My Friend" from an early age.

16. Durand, *Where the Waters Gather*, 51. The Durand spelling, taken from Nicollet, is used here.

17. Thomas S. Williamson, "Obituary of Joseph Renville," in Thomas S. Williamson to David Greene, 15 May 1846, NMM, MHS.

18. The American Board of Commissioners for Foreign Missions (ABCFM) was a nondenominational evangelical missionary society founded in 1810. In the words of its mission statement at the time the Dakota Mission was founded, "The Board is, pre-eminently, a society for preaching the gospel. This is its primary and leading design—the grand object for which it exists. All its plans have an ultimate reference to the preaching of the gospel. The heathen are educated, and books are translated, printed, and distributed among them, that they may become attentive, thoughtful, intelligent hearers of the gospel." Benjamin B. Wisner, Rufus Anderson, and David Greene, "The General Objects of the Board Stated," *Twenty-Fourth Annual Report of the American Board of Commissioners for Foreign Missions*, 1833, 139, quoted in Charles A. Maxfield, "The Formation and Early History of the American Board of Commissioners for Foreign Missions," 2001, accessed 22 December 2010, http://www.maxfieldbooks .com/ABCFM.html.

19. Thomas S. Williamson, "Obituary of Joseph Renville," in Thomas S. Williamson to David Greene, 15 May 1846, NMM, MHS.

20. "No. 3. Extracts from a deposition of Rev. Stephen R. Riggs October 13, 1863," in U.S. House of Representatives, *Executive Document No. 58*, 11.

21. Renville's soldiers were clearly traditionalists despite Renville's acculturation. For example, in October 1835, just a few months before Thomas S. Williamson began teaching them to read, Agent Lawrence Taliaferro registered complaints about their raids on Ojibwe bands and the scalp dances they held outside Fort Renville. By the time he visited them in 1838, Nicollet reported they had acquired a "secret title," "Wowapi wakan okondakitchie, the company of the holy book (the Bible)," despite the fact that most members were not Christians. Quoted in Bray and Bray, *Joseph Nicollet on the Plains and Prairies*, 277. Twenty-seven years later, members of Renville's Soldiers' Lodge formed the core of the Dakota Peace Party, which opposed the 1862 war. I have chosen to rechristen this group the "Peace Coalition" to recognize its diversity, a subject that will be developed later in this introduction.

22. Thomas S. Williamson, "Reminiscences: The First School for Teaching to Read and Write Dakota," *Iapi Oaye*, March 1876, 12.

23. Thomas S. Williamson, "Reminiscences: The First School for Teaching to Read and Write Dakota," *Iapi Oaye*, March 1876, 12.

24. Quotation is from the Bible, Romans 1:16.

25. See Wambdiokiya to 'His Iron has a Good Sound,' Letter "4a" [ca. winter 1838], in Ella Deloria, Letters and Misc. Materials from the Minnesota Manuscripts, Franz Boas Papers, American Philosophical Society, Philadelphia. Thus the hundreds of letters written between imprisoned and interned Dakotas separated in the wake of the 1862 war were not an innovation but rather an amplification of a culturally relevant practice that was already several decades old.

26. Wambdiokiya to Huggins et al., "9th letter Wozupi-wi, Omaka 1838," in Deloria, Letters and Misc. Materials from the Minnesota Manuscripts, Franz Boas Papers, American Philosophical Society, Philadelphia. Deloria worked from copies in the Samuel and Gideon Pond Papers at MHS. While Wambdiokiya's name is given in the Dakota missionary literature as "Eagle Help," Deloria, who did not know him as a historical personage, translated the name literally as "Leagued with the Eagle-spirit." His mother was Old Eve, one of the first Dakota converts to Christianity. This classic Dakota kinship exchange illuminates a cultural practice that outsiders often interpreted as begging. Here Wambdiokiya's appeal for the missionaries to "be kind to me" is actually an appeal to help his mother.

27. On Mary Tokanne Renville, see Stephen R. Riggs, "Mrs. Renville," *Minnesota Free Press*, 30 June 1858. Monica L. Siems, in "How Do You Say 'God' in Dakota?," rightly observes that the missionaries' inability to accurately grasp the worldview embodied in the Dakota language is reflected in their Dakota translations. Therefore, Siems argues, "the missionaries may have concluded that they had effected conversions among the Dakotas when they had only scratched the surface of Dakota religiosity." In the Reformed worldview, however, "effectual" (genuine, enduring) conversion was the work of the Holy Spirit, which Thomas S. Williamson explicitly credited in the conversions of Joseph and Mary Tokanne Renville. Williamson was observing that God was not limited by human shortcomings but worked his will in spite of them. While the missionaries consistently expressed the hope that their converts were effectually saved, they were not certain of that fact because professing Dakota Christians regularly relapsed (as the missionaries viewed it) into traditional Dakota ways.

28. See Thomas S. Williamson, "The Polygamy Question," 15 June 184[6], NMM, MHS. Williamson was the sole Dakota missionary to believe polygamy ought to be tolerated in the Dakota church, in part because the injunction to divorce a wife was unbiblical. Parts of Williamson's article were reprinted in the *New York Evangelist* and the *Boston Recorder* circa October 1846.

29. Stephen R. Riggs to Selah B. Treat, 12 September 1850, NMM, MHS.

30. Unless otherwise noted, the stories alluded to in this section are drawn from the period correspondence collected in the NMM, MHS.

31. Lawrence Taliaferro journal, 19 October 1835. I thank Taliaferro scholar Tom Shaw for his transcription of this passage, corresponding to pages 172–73 in the typed

edition of Taliaferro's journals at MHS. On the disputed Dakota-Ojibwe territory north of Lac qui Parle, see the map facing page 87 in Wingerd, *North Country*.

32. Monogenism held that human beings, regardless of race, were descended from common ancestors and were therefore genetically compatible, an idea rooted in the Biblical story of the creation of a single man and a single woman. However, as this introduction will show, monogenists were not necessarily more accepting of interracial marriage.

33. Taliaferro wrote that Renville's "pride is great—his dignity equally so—& his discernment of the conduct, or deportment of others in reference to himself is quick—his inferences strong and his conclusions not unapt—very jealous of attentions even to a weakness. so that flattery is the very unction of his soul." Lawrence Taliaferro journal, 19 October 1835, MHS, Shaw transcription.

34. Thomas S. Williamson to David Greene, 19 December 1843, NMM, MHS.

35. Stephen R. Riggs, "Toteedutawin, Her Scarlet House," *Minnesota Free Press*, 16 June 1858. Riggs wrote that among the boys' mothers Catherine Tatidutawiŋ, Lorenzo's mother, alone "manifested more of the self-sacrificing spirit in giving up her own children to be educated."

36. Gideon Pond to Samuel Pond, 26 June 1842, Pond Papers, MHS.

37. Stephen R. Riggs to Gideon Pond, 8 August 1842, Pond Papers, MHS.

38. Stephen R. Riggs to David Greene, 24 July 1843, NMM, MHS. The identities of the slain Dakotas are not known beyond Pond's explanation that "[a] young man whom we assisted to build a house at Lac qui Parle last spring, was killed together with another Indian in the latter part of June by a war party of Chippeways within five miles of Lac qui Parle." Samuel Pond to David Greene, August 1843, NMM, MHS.

39. Henok Maḣpiyahdinape, who had been received into the church in Ohio on profession of his faith, apostatized four months after his return to Lac qui Parle, running away with another man's wife. Thomas S. Williamson to David Greene and Thomas S. Williamson to Gideon Pond, both 16 November 1843, NMM, MHS. Lorenzo Towaŋiteton Lawrence held out a little longer, remaining a church member for three years, until he took his brother's wife in 1846. Thomas S. Williamson to Samuel Pond, 27 January and 11 February 1846, and Jonas Pettijohn to Samuel Pond, 16 May, 1846, NMM, MHS. Maḣpiyahdinape and Lawrence later returned to the church. On Maḣpiyahdinape, see "Historical Introduction," note 56.

40. "Story of Mrs. Helen Furber," in Easton, *History of the St. Croix Valley*, 1:144.

41. "Old Wakaya-ska is very much scandalized by the fact that so many, whose fathers were nothing, have come to be kings. But I begin to think more and more that this is the way which Dakota Society will be broken up to its elements and that when a man becomes a man they will be ready for better constitution of society." Stephen R. Riggs to Alfred Riggs, 23 January 1862, Oahe Mission Collection, CWS.

42. Douglas A. Hedin's extended foreword discusses the legal and historical contexts of Stephen R. Riggs's translation, "The Minnesota Constitution in the Dakota Language, 1858," accessed 21 December 2010, www.MinnesotaLegalHistoryProject.org.

43. Thomas L. Riggs, untitled manuscript, Riggs Family Papers, South Dakota State Archives. Thomas Riggs collapsed the original seven articles into five.

44. Stephen R. Riggs to Selah B. Treat, 31 July 1856, NMM, MHS. Thomas L. Riggs recalled seventeen signers. Paul Mazakutemani remembered forty (eventual?) members.

45. Stephen R. Riggs to Selah B. Treat, 31 July 1856, NMM, MHS.

46. Statement of Paul Mazakutemani et al., 29 July 1856, in Diedrich, *Little Paul*, 55–56. Cherokee scholars interpret the Indian Removal Act of 1830 as a direct, if bureaucratically delayed, response to the land claims made in their Constitution of 1827. See "Origin of the Cherokee Nation West," accessed 6 February 2010, http:// victorian.fortunecity.com/rothko/420/aniyuntikwalaski/old_settlers.html.

47. Although the requirements varied and were often difficult to meet, this generally meant granting a Native American a legal patent to the land he had improved. The practice would be institutionalized in the Office of Indian Affairs as the Dawes Act of 1887.

48. Stephen R. Riggs explained his rationale for supporting individual landownership:

The permanency of [Indian] reservations is another question. If they were on the moon, and there was no way of getting there even by balloons, they might be permanent. My own conviction is that no Indians, any where in North America, can long hold arable land in common. When the land is wanted the faith of treaties will not prove stronger than a tow thread. The tribal title to land must be abolished. If Indians hold lands they must hold them as individuals. . . . But they can have no security of their long possessing that country unless they become citizens of the U. S. and hold their lands as individuals under the laws and regulations of government. (Stephen R. Riggs to David Greene, 29 April 1846, NMM, MHS)

49. Henry B. Whipple diary, vol. 4, 5 July 1862, Protestant Episcopal Church Diocese of Minnesota Papers, MHS. The founders of the Hazlewood Republic were prescient. On the verge of the Dakota War, they believed their plea to be legally granted a piece of Mni Sota Makoçe was about to come to pass. In Wabaśa's words at the end of the speech quoted here, "I have heard of your wise words to our Great Father and that he will now give the Indians who live like white men deeds for their land, and my heart is glad."

50. This was a pattern in the implementation of the Indian Removal Act among eastern tribes. In some cases Natives who had become farmers and tradesmen and had integrated themselves into the frontier community via marriage and/or citizenship

were given land grants to stay, even when their traditionalist kin were removed to Indian Territory. The Nishnabecs (Potawatomis) of Indiana are one example, discussed briefly later in this introduction.

51. Statement of Paul Mazakutemani et al., 29 July 1856, in Diedrich, *Little Paul*, 55–56.

52. On Dakota identity in the pre-1862 era, see C. Anderson, "Dakota Identity," chaps. 1–2.

53. The list of men named as founders of the Hazlewood Republic is a reconstruction based on extant sources. Because most of the documents were created retrospectively, this list is neither definitive nor complete. Isaac and Daniel Renville, Peter Tapetataŋka (Big Fire, Great Fire), and Amos Ecetukiya, among others, may also have been founding members.

54. Figures on membership in the Hazlewood Republic are drawn from the recollection of Paul Mazakutemani and federal Sioux Agency annuity records for 1861.

55. The Yanktonais, who were not party to the Treaties of 1851 and 1858, contended that some of the land designated as the Upper Reservation in 1851 belonged to them, not to the Sissetons and Wahpetons. The Yanktonais were scheduled to make a treaty with the government in 1863, but the war aborted the effort.

56. Stephen R. Riggs to Alfred Riggs, 20 February and 1 June 1860, Riggs Family Papers, cws. Henok Maḣpiyahdinape, one of the four Dakota young men who spent a year in Ohio and the first secretary of the Hazlewood Republic, was implicated as an accomplice in one of the murders. He fled. The men of Hazlewood, nearly all relatives of Maḣpiyahdinape, temporarily left, fearing retribution at the hands of the dead man's kin. Maḣpiyahdinape returned to Hazlewood after the incident blew over and was a member of the Peace Coalition in 1862.

57. The question is open. Present-tense references to the Hazlewood Republic and to its officers appear in federal and ABCFM records through 1862. Historians who framed the Hazlewood story as a failed experiment may have missed these later references because they believed there would be none.

58. Lydia Weaver Butler (ca. 1788–ca. 1832) was born in Somerset, Bristol County, Massachusetts, the daughter of Hannah Law (1759–1831) and Thomas Weaver (1756–1832). The Weavers were Quakers. Lydia married James Butler around 1810. I thank family historian Marcia Loudon for sharing several hundred pages of documentation on this family, including her "James Butler Family Sheet," in my project files for this book. Mary Renville's obituary gives her birth date as 17 October 1832. However, census data consistently date her birth to 1830.

59. Potential evidence of remarriage is the presence of a woman who was between the ages of sixty and seventy in James Butler's household in the U.S. Federal Census,

1840, Lake County IN. Descendants surmise she may have been his wife. If so, she was five to fifteen years his senior and probably died before 1850.

60. Marvin B. Butler, "History of the Benjamin Butler Family of North Hero, Vermont," 3, Butler Family Collection, Carnegie Public Library of Steuben County, Angola, Indiana. Mary's father, James Butler, and John's father, Joseph Renville, fought on opposite sides in the War of 1812, although never in the same theater of action.

61. Benjamin Butler III, son of Lydia and James Butler, was born around 1811 in Peru, Clinton County, New York. He married Hannah Parsons before 1840 and died 3 December 1882 in Chicago, Cook County, Illinois.

62. Dorothy L. Wilson, "The Butlers and Bodelys of Steuben County," privately published, 1977, Carnegie Public Library of Steuben County, Angola, Indiana.

63. Marvin B. Butler, "History of the Benjamin Butler Family of North Hero, Vermont," 3, Butler Family Collection, Carnegie Public Library of Steuben County, Angola, Indiana.

64. U.S. Federal Census, 1840, DuPage County IL; U.S. Federal Census, 1850, Kane County IL.

65. The historic designation "Potawatomi" is derived from Anishinabe for "keepers of the fire"—the council fire that is said to have once united the Anishinabes, Potawatomis, and Ottawas in a single tribe. Modern Potawatomis call themselves "Nishnabec," which means "True People."

66. On the Potawatomis who persisted in Indiana, see "Hiding in Plain View: Persistence on the Indiana Frontier," chap. 7 in Sleeper-Smith, *Indian Woman and French Men*.

67. For an ethnohistorical approach to the Nishnabec story, see Clifton, *Prairie People*. R. David Edmunds provides a readable scholarly history in *The Potawatomis*.

68. The Hochunks ceded their lands east of the Mississippi in 1837. Fred L. Holmes, "Mascoutin Indian Tribe Left State, All Traces Gone: White Man Had Hard Task to Oust Aborigines from Wisconsin," *Milwaukee Sentinel*, 30 April 1922, Wisconsin Historical Society.

69. David Parsons entry, U.S. Federal Census, 1850, Dundee, Kane County IL. Adeline began using the name Mary in the 1850s. Dundee is on a known route of the Underground Railroad in Illinois, although there is no direct reference to David and Adelia Butler Parsons's involvement. See Turner, *Underground Railroad in Illinois*.

70. Fergus M. Bordewich provides an accessible, engaging overview of the Underground Railroad in *Bound for Canaan*. For the Butler family's involvement, see Butler, *My Story*; and "Historical Introduction," note 73.

71. Coffin is one of the best-known conductors in Indiana, in part due to his literary ambitions. See Hendrick and Hendrick, *Fleeing for Freedom*. The truth about the Underground Railroad is that the men historically recognized as leaders, like Coffin

and Butler, are the same men who published stories about their involvement. The genuine scope of the movement remains untold, existing in unpublished stories that may not have survived the men and women who lived them.

72. Quotation from the Bible, Matthew 25:40.

73. Marvin B. Butler, "History of the Benjamin Butler Family of North Hero, Vermont," 3, Butler Family Collection, Carnegie Public Library of Steuben County, Angola, Indiana. Was Adeline's cousin writing hagiography or history? While modern articles cite Marvin's 1914 book *My Story of the Civil War and the Underground Railroad* as evidence of the Underground Railroad in northeastern Indiana, documentation predating the book is thin. However, corollary sources support Butler family stories that trace their abolitionist roots back to North Hero, Vermont. A map of the Underground Railroad in Siebert, *Vermont's Anti-Slavery and Underground Railroad Record,* shows the inland lines from St. Albans, Vermont, converging on the maritime Lake Champlain line, then crossing Lake Champlain at North Hero on the way to Rouses Point, New York, a few miles from the Canadian border. Although Adeline's grandfather Benjamin Butler died four years before the organization of the Vermont Chapter of the American Anti-Slavery Society in 1835, Siebert states that slaves had been helped to freedom via Vermont as early as the 1820s. On the New York side of Lake Champlain a men's chapter of the New York Anti-Slavery Society was organized in Peru, Clinton County (the township where Adeline and her siblings were born), in 1837, the year before James Butler's brothers left New York for the Midwest. In Indiana the town of Orland, Steuben County, with well-documented Underground Railroad connections, was only one night's journey north of the Butler brothers' homes in Salem Township. While the evidence rests heavily on family history, given the extended Butler family's participation in the Underground Railroad in Illinois and Kansas as well, Marvin Butler's stories are credible.

74. Linda K. Kerber explores the relationship between the abolition and the Indian Reform movements in "Abolitionist Perception"; quotation on p. 288.

75. Marvin B. Butler, "History of the Benjamin Butler Family of North Hero, Vermont," 3, Butler Family Collection, Carnegie Public Library of Steuben County, Angola, Indiana. James Butler "Wild Bill" Hickok was the son of Adeline's father's cousin, Polly Butler Hickok. See Rosa, *Wild Bill Hickok.*

76. In the wake of the U.S.-Dakota War a soldier found a copy of a book inscribed to Mary Butler, whom he presumed had been killed in the war. See Thomas Watts, "Sight of Women and Children Rescued from Indians Fired Soldiers with a Scheme for Revenge," *Minneapolis Tribune,* 15 July 1923. The story Eli Huggins told William Watts Folwell (see "Historical Introduction," note 98) places John in Galesburg in 1855.

77. For example, R. J. Creswell wrote, "He was rather delicate, which hindered his being sent east to school as much as he otherwise would have been. However, he

spent several years in excellent white schools, and he acquired a fair knowledge of the elementary branches of the English language. The last year he spent at Knox College, Galesburg, Illinois, where he wooed and won Miss Mary Butler, an educated Christian white woman, whom he married and who became his great helper in his educational and evangelistic work." Creswell, "Prince of Indian Preachers."

78. Elizabeth I. Dorris, Knox College, to the author, 16 April 2007; and Mary McAndrew, Knox College, to the author, 3 December 2010. Copies in author's files.

79. Thomas S. Williamson, probably at Joseph Renville's request, acted as guardian for the children after his death. Williamson's letters show he routinely received direct donations from mission supporters who were unwilling to support the ABCFM due to its toleration of slavery among Native church members in the South. The ABCFM left to the discretion of its missionaries the expenditure of privately donated funds. Hence the ABCFM papers do not fully reflect the missionaries' financial activities.

80. Mary was actually twenty-eight, not twenty-five, years old. Since census data consistently place Mary's birth in 1830, she may have been about a year older than John. Perhaps concerned that being an "older woman" might be socially awkward, it seems Mary consciously adjusted her birth year to 1832 sometime before they announced their engagement. She could not completely evade the truth about her age, however, which persisted in rumor.

81. In 1903–4 John P. Williamson's son John married Dakota Annie Antelope. While John P. welcomed Annie and the couple's children, the family historian, Winifred Williamson Barton, omitted Annie from the official family story. Eli Huggins to William W. Folwell, 4 November 1914 and 30 May 1918, William Watts Folwell Papers, MHS. Annie was not restored to the family record until the late twentieth century.

82. On white men marrying Native women, see Smits, "'Squaw men,' 'Half-breeds,' and Amalgamators."

83. The best known of these may be Eunice (Kanenstenhawi) Williams (1697–1785), the subject of Demos, *Unredeemed Captive*. The classic work on Mary (Dehewamis) Jemison (ca. 1743–1833) is Seaver, *Narrative*. On Cynthia Ann (Naduah) Parker (ca. 1827–1870) see Hacker, *Cynthia Ann Parker*.

84. The classic work on Slocum is Meginness, *Frances Slocum*.

85. The marriage of Miniyuhe's grandmother might have been arranged by her fur trader father to create kinship ties for economic reasons. Another possibility is posed by Fred Pearsall's story of Waśiçuŋ, a white child found abandoned who was adopted and raised by Dakotas. Waśiçuŋ was one of the two men mistakenly executed on 26 December 1862. See Pearsall, *Short Stories*, 13–17 (in the MHS collections).

86. Thomas Jefferson to Benjamin Hawkins, 1803, quoted in Bieder, "Scientific Attitudes," 19. Jefferson was a monogenist. See "Historical Introduction, note 32.

87. See Bieder, "Scientific Attitudes."

88. Kenschaft, *Lydia Maria Child*, 21–23.

89. *North American Review* 19 (1824): 282–63. Harvard professor of literature George Ticknor, who liked the book, arranged for a second, more positive review. As Ticknor's protégée, Child's career was assured—until 1830 (the same year Mary Butler was born), when Child embraced the abolition cause and again was socially and professionally marginalized for her forward-thinking views on racial equality. See Kenschaft, *Lydia Maria Child*, chaps. 2, 3.

90. Boudinot and Ridge both signed the 1836 Treaty of New Echota, which ceded Cherokee homelands in Georgia. Harriett Gold Boudinot died the same year. The treaty led to the 1838 forced removal known as the Trail of Tears. In June 1839 John Ridge and Elias Boudinot were assassinated by Cherokees in Oklahoma—Ridge in front of his wife.

91. Gaul, *To Marry an Indian*, 1–2.

92. Ruoff, *Life, Letters and Speeches*, 29.

93. See Theresa Strouth Gaul's helpful discussion of this controversial pattern in "The Northrup-Ridge Marriage," *To Marry an Indian*, 8–13.

94. Atkins, *Creating Minnesota*, 50. Dalton (Dolton) was born 14 February 1828 in "Shawnee town Indiana" Cecelia Campbell Stay to Grace Lee Nute, 6 July 1925, Minnesota Historical Society Institutional Archives, MHS.

95. Rosanne and John Otherday were married at Hazlewood in March 1859. After the war, when Rosanne left him, Otherday married Therese Renville, the widow of John's brother Joseph Renville III. See Mary Adeline Renville to Stephen R. Riggs, 23 January 1863, appendix B. I thank Stephen Osman for his collaboration reconstructing Otherday's marital history.

96. Atkins, *Creating Minnesota*, 51.

97. On 21 March 1858 Stephen R. Riggs wrote to S. B. Treat,

This day I married a couple—a white woman and a Dakota man. The woman is from Washington City—a bad character I presume and quite ignorant. They have been living together ever since last summer without being married. . . . Their getting married is I think an omen for good although some white people shake their heads at it. . . . He reads Dakota. He wished to know what he should do to be saved. I directed him to the Word of God. I feel much interested in him. In regard to the woman also, it is certainly quite as possible that God has brought her out here and associated her with an Indian, to bring her to the knowledge of the truth as it is in Jesus, as that he permits Africans to be brought to America and sold as slaves, that he might make Christians of them. But in neither case would the end justify the means. (NMM, MHS)

98. Eli Huggins to William Watts Folwell, 4 November 1918, Folwell Papers, MHS. Coming from Eli Huggins, John's peer, the son of missionary Alexander Huggins, we

might expect a kinder story—if not, perhaps, for the fact that Huggins was hiding (from his family and from the state's preeminent historian) the fact that he had fathered a child in an interracial relationship with an Inuit woman. I thank Walt Bachman for sharing this discovery from the Huggins Papers in the Bancroft Library at the University of California at Berkeley. It is not true that John and Mary's union was sterile. The Riggs letters capture both Mary's pregnancy and Ella's birth. Ella's death, which did in fact leave the Renvilles without biological descendants, is discussed in part 3 of this introduction.

99. See "Configuring Race in the American West," chap. 3 in Pascoe, *What Comes Naturally*; and "Intermarriage Laws become Public Issues, 1831–1865," chap. 3 in Fowler, *Northern Attitudes toward Interracial Marriage*. See also Woods, "Wicked and Mischievous Connection."

100. See Wingerd, *North Country*; and Green, *Peculiar Imbalance*.

101. Fowler, *Northern Attitudes toward Interracial Marriage*, 380, citing *Bailey v. Fiske*, 34 Maine 77, 18. The case apparently concerned whether the part-Native defendant was "white" for purposes of prosecution under the state's white-black miscegenation law.

102. Fowler, *Northern Attitudes toward Interracial Marriage*, 405, citing North Carolina Revised Code, 1854.

103. Performing the ceremony was "a misdemeanor: 1 to 3 years in prison." Fowler, *Northern Attitudes toward Interracial Marriage*, 400, quoting Nevada laws for 1861. The Nevada statute evenhandedly applied these same penalties to whites who married "Negros, mulattos, Indians, or Chinese."

104. Fowler, *Northern Attitudes toward Interracial Marriage*, 436, citing Washington State Acts, 1854–55.

105. Curiously, Elaine Goodale, whose decision to marry Dakota Charles Eastman in 1890 was based in part on her observations of Mary and John's marriage, expressed a similar idea in milder terms: "The gift of myself to a Sioux . . . will seem to some readers unnatural. Others will find it entirely human and understandable. In reality, it followed almost inevitably upon my passionate preoccupation with the welfare of those whom I already looked upon as my adopted people." Graber, *Sister to the Sioux*, 169. Eastman was speaking specifically of the context of their engagement: the massacre at Wounded Knee. See also Jacobs, "The Eastmans and the Luhans."

106. "A Trip to the Upper Country," *St. Peter (MN) Statesman*, 25 May 1860.

107. Martha Riggs to Lucy Drake, 15 February 1859, Stephen R. Riggs and Family Papers, MHS.

108. An informant told William Watts Folwell that after the 1862 war Joe Campbell deserted Mary Anne Dalton Campbell "and took up with another woman. Mrs. C. made her way to Mendota where she lived for some years in abject poverty. I saw her and

the girls there in the fall of 1865." Eli Huggins to Folwell, 20 February 1910, Folwell Papers, MHS.

109. Unfortunately, due to the obscure provenance of the only known copy of his photo, it cannot be reproduced in this volume.

110. Mary Riggs was reluctant to leave their station at Traverse des Sioux in part because she cherished the picket fence around the garden, which was "a means of keeping our children from constant contact with the Indians." Stephen R. Riggs to David Greene, 3 October 1846, NMM, MHS. Linda Clemmons has written extensively about the Dakota Mission, including "Our Children Are in Danger of Becoming Little Indians."

111. On the Riggs family see S. Riggs, *Mary and I*; and the front matter in M. Riggs, *Small Bit of Bread and Butter*. For biographical data on Stephen and Mary Riggs, see *A Thrilling Narrative*, note 10.

112. Complementing the letters written to Alfred Riggs during this period are his sister Martha Riggs's correspondence from Hazlewood to her friend Lucy Spooner Drake and his father, Stephen Return Riggs's, correspondence with the ABCFM. Alfred Riggs's papers are in the Oahe Mission Collection at the CWS. Copies of Martha Riggs's correspondence with Lucy Spooner Drake are in the Riggs Papers, MHS. Between 1925 and 1935 MHS employed typists who transcribed an estimated three thousand items from ABCFM originals dating from 1766 to 1926 pertaining to the history of missions in the region that became Minnesota. The typescripts make up the ABCFM Papers and form the spine of a more comprehensive collection, the Northwest Missions Manuscripts Collection (NMM, MHS), both at MHS. ABCFM material cited in this edition was culled from the NMM collection. See Grace Lee Nute, "The Mission Publication Project of the Minnesota Historical Society," ca. 1933, and related items in the Grace Lee Nute Papers, MHS.

113. Lois Glewwe, "Soul Sisters: Jane Williamson and the Women of the Dakota Mission," paper presented at the Pond Dakota Heritage Society, 17 August 2009. I thank Glewwe for a copy of her presentation.

114. See Martha Riggs's letters to Lucy Spooner Drake in the Riggs Papers, MHS.

115. Martha Riggs to Alfred Riggs, 11 September 1860, CWS.

116. Nathaniel Brown was married to two Sisseton women (sisters) simultaneously. He had four children: Lydia, born February 1854 (mother Winona); M'Dazizi (mother Winona); Ellen, born November 1857 (mother Tunkangiiceyewin); and Mary, born December 1860 (mother Tunkangiiceyewin). See Record Group 75 E 529, Late-Filed Lake Pepin Scrip Affidavits 1860, NARA. The author thanks Walt Bachman for sharing this source. Mary Renville's 1863 letters call the Brown daughter they boarded "Lillie."

117. Martha Riggs to Alfred Riggs, 11 January 1860, CWS.

118. Mary Riggs to Alfred Riggs, 25 March 1860, CWS. "She seems to feel very kindly

just now" may refer to gratitude that Mary and Ella had survived the pregnancy, during which Mary had been incapacitated by her first bout with malaria.

119. Stephen R. Riggs to Alfred Riggs, 21 April 1860, CWS.

120. "A Trip to the Upper Country," *St. Peter (MN) Statesman*, 25 May 1860.

121. "A Trip to the Upper Country," *St. Peter (MN) Statesman*, 25 May 1860.

122. Anna Riggs to Alfred Riggs, 1 November 1859, CWS.

123. Mary's property was Township 113, Range 25, Section 12. Land Office records cited in Curtiss-Wedge, *History of Renville County*, 1:101. John P. Williamson was stationed at the Lower Agency and did itinerant preaching in the surrounding settlements. See John P. Williamson diary, Williamson Papers, Dakotah Prairie Museum, Aberdeen, South Dakota.

124. Anna Jane Riggs to Alfred Riggs, 3 June 1862, CWS. Although John could and did write in English, he never grew so fluent as to feel at home expressing himself in that language. He chose to speak and write in Dakota whenever his audience permitted it.

125. See the warning given by Gabriel Renville to Thomas S. Williamson in G. Renville, "Narrative Account," 6. Big Eagle recalled, "soon the cry was 'Kill the whites and kill all those cut-hairs who will not join us.'" Big Eagle, "Sioux Story of the War," 389.

126. *A Thrilling Narrative*, Cunningham's Statement.

127. *A Thrilling Narrative*, chap. 1.

128. For Thomas S. Williamson the events of the unfolding war must have borne an eerie resemblance to the 1847 massacre at the Whitman Mission in Oregon, from which his Lane Seminary friend and fellow Presbyterian missionary Henry H. Spalding narrowly escaped with his life. Williamson determined to stay at his station, Mary Renville wrote, to encourage the Christian Dakotas to stand "*firm*, and go not among those who are hastening on to certain destruction." See *A Thrilling Narrative*, chap. 3.

129. *A Thrilling Narrative*, chap. 3.

130. G. Renville, "Narrative Account," 6.

131. Dakota oral history holds that Lorenzo Lawrence hid the Williamsons under buffalo robes in the back of a Red River ox cart. Lawrence then returned to the reservation. The author thanks Elden Lawrence for sharing this story. On Friday, 22 August, the Williamsons caught up with their children, who had earlier overtaken the Riggs party. The Williamsons spent the rest of the war in St. Peter, Minnesota.

132. In early 1863 missionary Gideon H. Pond, after interviewing Dakota men interned at Fort Snelling, wrote,

At the time of the Indian outbreak in Minnesota, last August, there was a number of Dakota men living on the Reservation, at Lower Agency, Yellow Medicine, and other points, with their families, which exceeded the whole number of those who finally fell into the hands of the Colonel in command of the Expedition against Hostile Indians, and who knew nothing of the matter, nor had any suspicions that such an event was about to transpire. They did not know about it until considerable advance had been made in the work of destruction, but were, at the time, about their ordinary affairs, and as much surprised to find what was transpiring as were their white neighbors. These families were seized with a panic much like that which was experienced by our fellow citizens near the Reserve, only that in their case there was no place to which they could "flee and be safe." (Gideon H. Pond to Messrs. Editors, 16 February 1863, published as G. Pond, "True History")

133. See figure 2, a photograph of Hazlewood. The school boardinghouse is the two-story clapboard building framed by the two tipis on the left side of the picture. Situated on a rise, the school boardinghouse had a vantage point that from the upperstory windows gave a view of several miles of surrounding prairie.

134. *A Thrilling Narrative*, chap. 3.

135. *A Thrilling Narrative*, chap. 1.

136. The stories of the Browns, DeCamp, and Wakefield are examined at length in Derounian-Stodola, *War in Words*.

137. Captive Samuel J. Brown's stories also comment at some length on the formation and activities of the Peace Coalition, and I refer interested readers to those texts. While Brown was of Dakota descent and in his old age became the darling Dakota source for a generation of historians, including William Watts Folwell, Thomas Hughes, and Doane Robinson, the Brown family's lifestyle had, arguably, moved beyond "bicultural" to become "settler" or "white" before the war, as reflected in Brown's perspective on events in 1862. With inadequate space to explore the ambiguities here, I have privileged sources whose Dakota identities are less contested. The irony, of course, is that as a descendant of Miniyuhe's "white" grandmother, Mazakutemani was technically of mixed blood as well as being bicultural. Yet Brown's and Mazakutemani's stories both show that before the war lifestyle had much more to do with determining identity than blood quantum. After the war the dominant society found blood quantum definitions more expedient. With the loss of the family's fortune and the death of his white father, J. R. Brown, Samuel Brown was socially demoted to being Dakota enough for European American historians to privilege as a source. See "Captivity of the Family of Joseph R. Brown," in Heard, *History of the Sioux War*, 202–7; and Brown, *In Captivity*.

138. *A Thrilling Narrative*, chap. 5.

139. The first page or two of Gabriel Renville's manuscript is missing. The extant story opens abruptly with his arrival at the Yellow Medicine Agency on 19 August. Gabriel's son Victor, who turned the manuscript over to Samuel J. Brown and Thomas

A. Robertson for translation, told Brown the manuscript was written "soon after the outbreak of 1862." The last events reported in the manuscript date to 1863. See Brown's certification and memorandum reproduced at the head of G. Renville, "Narrative Account," 4–5.

140. 1857 Territorial Census of Minnesota.

141. Only Gabriel's first wife, Mary, is listed in his household on the 1860 census. Gabriel may have filed half-breed scrip to lay claim to the land he farmed, which until the Treaty of 1858 had been part of the Sioux Reservation.

142. On 7 July 1865 Thomas S. Williamson wrote to Selah B. Treat, "Mr. Gabriel Renville Captain of all the Indian Scouts on the Coteau was formerly a member of our church but has apostatized having become a polygamist" (NMM, MHS.) Later Gabriel was appointed chief on the Lake Traverse Sisseton and Wahpeton Reservation. See the eight-part biography by Sisseton historian Ed Red Owl, "Traditional Man."

143. Susan Frenier Brown (1819–1904) was the daughter of Narcisse Frenier and Winona (Mazardewin, Madeline/Abigail Crawford). When Susan was very young, Winona married Victor Renville, brother of Gabriel Renville. After Victor's death, Winona married Akipa (see "Historical Introduction," note 146), the brother of Maza Ša (Mazaxa, Red Iron) and Mazamani. See Goodman and Goodman, *Joseph R. Brown*, 290–92.

144. Gabriel named them: "Mah-zo-manee, Basswood, Shu-pay-he-yu, Clothed-in-Fire . . . Ah-kee-pah, Charles Crawford, Thomas Crawford, Han-yo-ke-yah . . . myself, Two Stars, and Eh-ne-hah . . . Koda and Wing." G. Renville, "Narrative Account," 7.

145. The death figure of more than five hundred settlers is conservative, based on a decade-long collaboration of scholars to corroborate the deaths reported by amateur historian Marion P. Satterlee and to update his work using primary sources that were not available to him. This estimate includes only named dead and is limited to those killed in the first phase of the war, through 26 September 1862. The number of captives is taken from my database of settlers and bicultural Dakotas reported in period sources as having been held captive. More Dakota families self-identified as captives in 1862 than were recorded by white observers.

146. Akipa (Coming Together; Meeting) or Ta-chan-du-hupa-hotanka (His Big Sounding Pipe), Wahpeton, ca. 1800–91, was a half brother of Gabriel Renville.

147. Stephen E. Osman provides a detailed discussion of the war from the perspective of the state and federal military in "Sibley's Army in November 1862."

148. G. Renville, "Narrative Account," 8. Razing the Upper Agency was a strategic necessity. The agency had fortified, winter-tight brick buildings, some of them loop-holed for defense. Left standing, it might have been an ideal western base camp for Sibley's army.

149. On the legislation, see Henry B. Whipple diary, vol. 4, 5 July 1862, Protestant Episcopal Church Diocese of Minnesota Papers, MHS.

150. Perusing decades of Indian Rights literature, including *Iapi Oaye* (the Dakota-English newspaper published in South Dakota by the Dakota Mission between 1871 and 1939), shows that Governor Alexander Ramsey's calls for the extermination of Dakota people in 1862 was not mere political hyperbole spouted in the heat of war but rather a deeply entrenched, long-standing proposition for solving "the Indian problem," which social reformers like the Renvilles and the editors of *Iapi Oaye* sought to obviate by helping Native people acculturate. Ironically, ideas like acculturation that today are characterized as cultural genocide were, in the nineteenth century, promoted as enlightened social reform. Linda K. Kerber helpfully compares the Indian Reform and abolition movements in "Abolitionist Perception." Some abolitionists, pointing to the success of the campaign to end slavery in the United States, "refused to accept extinction either as *fait accompli* or as a possible goal" for Native Americans (286). Kerber places this within the larger context of race theory in nineteenth-century America, reporting that abolitionists drawn to the Indian Reform movement believed that

> [i]f blacks should be integrated into American society [as reformers hoped], so should the Indians. The Indian should be recognized as people in a less advanced state of civilization who, properly encouraged, might be absorbed into American society. The Indian should be treated with the respect due to his individuality, his humanity. But not, it should be emphasized, the respect due his culture. . . . There was no room in the abolitionists' perception for the recognition of tribal identity, no angle from which tribal identity might be seen as a value to be preserved. . . . In part this is because abolitionists were not cultural relativists and did not try to be. (288)

Kerber concludes, "the tribe appeared to be yet another institutional artifact standing between the individual and his moral and religious freedom as slavery had once done" (290). This inability to posit cultural relativism is, essentially, the ethnocentrism that characterized the majority of reformers whose consciences were sensitized to social justice issues in the Great Awakening, including Mary Renville's family of origin. While their known writings do not explicitly show that John and Mary viewed Indian Reform in Kerber's terms, their appeal at the end of chapter 13 in *A Thrilling Narrative* hints at it. Supporting evidence is found in *Iapi Oaye*, whose editors explicitly maintained these ideas in print. John Renville was a frequent contributor (in Dakota) to *Iapi Oaye*, as was Mary, less often (in English).

151. For a full-length biography of Mazakutemani, see Diedrich, *Little Paul*.

152. Stephen R. Riggs to Selah B. Treat, 11 July 1856, NMM, MHS. See also Thomas S. Williamson to Selah B. Treat, 3 January 1856, NMM, MHS. "[T]he use of the rod" alludes to the nineteenth-century child-rearing axiom about corporal punishment, "spare the rod and spoil the child."

153. Thomas S. Williamson to S. B. Treat, 18 November 1859, NMM, MHS.

154. "Revised Regulations No. IV Concerning Trade and Intercourse with Indian Tribes," part 5, "Depredations of Indians on the Property of White Persons," points 34–35, stated, "Whenever directed by him [the president], a demand will be made by the superintendent, agent, or sub-agent, upon the nation or tribe to which the Indian or Indians committing the injury belonged for satisfaction. If within that time, the Indian nation or tribe shall refuse or neglect to make satisfaction, the superintendent, agent, or sub-agent will make a return of his doings to the War Department . . . that such further steps may be taken as shall be proper, in the opinion of the President, to obtain satisfaction for the injury." The sorry state of the federal administration of the Office of Indian Affairs is reflected in the fact that this act, dated 17 June 1837, was still on the books as enforceable at the time of the Dakota War. See the 1861 imprint of *Office Copy of the Laws, Regulations Etc. of the Indian Bureau, 1850*, Records of the U.S. Congress, House of Representatives, Session 37A, NARA.

155. In 1901 Peace Coalition member Amos Ecetukiya testified, "In order to bring about this good, the peacemaker [*sic*], we consulted together with some of the Mdewankantons. . . .We were looking ahead when we were doing this. We intended to work with the Government, and expected that in the end that the Government would assist us in getting what we considered our dues." *Sisseton and Wahpeton Claims*, pt. 1, 128.

156. John's sister Rosalie Iron Hair Renville (b. 1826) had married Baptiste Campbell. Rosalie died in January 1860, leaving two children, Daniel (b. 1855) and Mathias (b. 1857). Baptiste Campbell had remarried by 1862 and was tried for participation in the war. He testified, "Crow told us, 'if you don't help to kill some white men you shall be killed.'" Bachman, trials transcription, trial no. 138, copy in author's files. I am indebted to historian Walt Bachman for the use of his transcription of the original trial records. The records of the 1862 Military Tribunal, in many cases, are abridged notes rather than being a full transcript of the trail. They are available at the National Archives, Record Group 46, and on microfilm (variously titled) at a handful of research libraries, including the library at Minnesota State University, Mankato. Baptiste admitted he had fired at a white man "a long distance off," was convicted, and was executed at Mankato, Minnesota, on 26 December 1862. John's sister Marguerite Renville (b. 1828) married Alexander Duncan Campbell in 1849. They had at least one child, Scott Campbell, living in 1862.

157. G. Renville, "Narrative Account," 8.

158. *A Thrilling Narrative*, chap. 5. All three of the key accounts (by Mary and John Renville, Gabriel Renville, and Samuel J. Brown) agree on the major points of this story, varying only on who is credited as the key leader and on the date. While other scholars have ventured to assign dates to these councils, I have resorted to approximations because I found much of the data conflicting.

159. G. Renville, "Narrative Account," 8–9.

160. Samuel J. Brown explained, "The Soldiers' lodge is put up for the purpose of being the headquarters for any government for behavior while hunting or in warfare against their enemies. The young men of the tribe would go there to decide upon what course to pursue, and a general agreement was had before they left the camp. The decision of the lodge was regarded as an order from a commanding officer to soldiers; they must obey whatever is decided upon in the lodge." *Sisseton and Wahpeton Claims*, pt. 1, 28.

161. G. Renville, "Narrative Account," 8–9. Translators supplied terms like "hostiles" and "friendlies," which have become ubiquitous in the language of the war. The period words that Dakotas used to refer to the factions within their nation in 1862 are not known. The fact that these men were able to so quickly exchange their pants and shirts for breechcloth and paint also speaks to their selective acculturation. Their personal elements of traditional dress were ready at hand; they had not been discarded when the men became farmers and clerks.

162. Communications written by Dakotas to federal authorities exist after this period as well, collected in the War Department records of Sibley's expedition at the National Archives.

163. *Sisseton and Wahpeton Claims*, pt. 1, 132–33. John testified in Dakota. In 1863, after speaking with Peace Coalition members interned at Fort Snelling, Gideon Pond summarized, "There was such a state of feverish excitement from the first, which was increased by succeeding events, that deliberation and free speaking on the part of anyone friendly to the whites was out of the question." G. Pond, "True History."

164. The historical record notes only one other amanuensis for the Upper Camp, Julia La Framboise. When the Upper Camp received letters in English from Sibley to Taṭaŋka Nażiŋ, Julia translated them into Dakota before they were forwarded.

165. Lorenzo [Lawrence] and Simon [Anawaŋgmani] to Ramsey, ca. 2 September 1862, appendix A.

166. In some places Mary's voice is readily apparent, as in the 2 September letter that opens in her voice and ends in the declaration of Simon Anawaŋgmani and Lorenzo Lawrence. In other places the reader must wonder, as with the parenthetical "(Little Crow is a wicked, crafty deceiver)" in the 2 September 1862 letter from Mazakutemani to Ramsey (appendix A).

167. Early historian Isaac V. Heard credited Little Crow with attempting to open a dialogue with authorities the day before, on 1 September 1862: "Joseph Campbell told the writer that at his (Crow's) dictation on their way to the Big Woods, on the 1st day of September, he wrote letters to Governor Ramsey and Colonel Sibley, requesting a cessation of hostilities and a treaty of settlement, and that these letters Crow exhibited to his braves, and they would not allow them to be sent." Heard, *History of the Sioux*

War, 144. Joseph (Antoine Joseph, A. J.) Campbell was Little Crow's amanuensis during the war. See letters of 10 and 25 September 1862, appendix A. Campbell's wife, Mary Anne Dalton Campbell, was white. His brother Baptiste Campbell, who had married John B. Renville's sister Rosalie (Iron Hair), was executed for participation in the war. A. J. and Mary Anne were the parents of Cecelia Campbell Stay, age fourteen in 1862, whose recollections of the opening days of the war at the Lower Agency are among the most detailed on that subject. Two of Cecelia's stories are excerpted in Anderson and Woolworth, *Through Dakota Eyes*. A. J. Campbell testified for the claimants in *Sisseton and Wahpeton Claims*, pt. 1, 255–65.

168. Sibley, however, understood as early as 30 August that Little Crow was the leader of the warring Dakotas. See Sibley's 30 August 1862 letter to his wife in the Henry H. Sibley Papers, MHS.

169. G. Renville, "Narrative Account," 10; Sibley to Little Crow, 3 September 1862, appendix A.

170. In 1901 David Weston, a member of Mdewankanton Travelling Hail's band in 1862, testified about the emergence of the Lower peace faction early in the war, "'[Oyeicasna, or Jingling Footprint] stopped at my home, and told father that he came from Wabaśa and that Wabaśa sent word that all the Indians on the lower side of the reservation should remain quiet, and the young man then started for another man by the name of Hu-sha-sha—meaning Red Legs—to tell him of this message. Then the word was sent around that they would camp at one place; move away from their villages and camp—all of these people—at one place. . . . Right next to Little Crow's camp." A lawyer asked, "Did you hear anything about any peace movement that was started among the Lower Indians at that time?" Weston answered, "Yes, sir. . . . I first heard it through Wa-kin-yan-ta-wa—meaning His Thunder—who said that Wabasha, Taopi, and himself and others had talked of it quietly." *Sisseton and Wahpeton Claims*, pt. 2, 305.

171. Little Crow to Sibley, 7 September 1862, appendix A.

172. The reproductions available today vary in grammar and punctuation, evidence of editorial intrusion. Compare, for example, the versions of Little Crow's letter to Sibley, 7 September 1862, printed in Heard, *History of the Sioux War*, 147–48, and in West, *Ancestry, Life and Times*, 263, with the Order Book copy reproduced here (from vol. 103, Sibley Papers, MHS). In the absence of holographs, the editors have privileged the earliest known copy of each letter.

173. Mazakutemani to Ramsey, 2 September 1862, appendix A.

174. Sibley, extract of letter to his wife, 10 September 1862, Sibley Papers, MHS.

175. See Mazakutemani's report on the council in his letter of 2 September 1862, appendix A. This is also a strong thread in Dakota oral (and now, written) history of the war. For example, in the 1975 Sisseton-Wahpeton tribal history *Ehanna Woyakapi*

Elijah Black Thunder called the war "a last stand to regain their lands." Black Thunder et al., *Ehanna Woyakapi*, 9.

176. Mazakutemani to Ramsey, 2 September 1862, appendix A. The week before the war began Galbraith recruited a small company of former agency employees dubbed the "Renville Rangers" and led them off the reservation toward Fort Snelling, where they intended to enlist as soldiers in the Civil War.

177. Unfortunately, a critical analysis of Galbraith's actions in 1862 is both lacking in the literature on the Dakota War and beyond the scope of this introduction. Mark Diedrich offers an impassioned indictment of Galbraith in *Little Crow*, chaps. 8–10. However, Diedrich did not consult the voluminous unfilmed agency records at the National Archives and neglected to investigate the biases of Galbraith's early detractors. Diedrich's analysis, colored by his opinion of Little Crow, is incomplete.

178. See testimony of Clark Thompson, 1885, Office of Indian Affairs, Special File 274, NARA.

179. Testimony of A. J. Campbell and Nathan Myrick, 1885, Office of Indian Affairs, Special File 274, NARA.

180. In 1868 U.S. commissioners asked Mdewankanton chief Wabaśa if the Lower Dakotas were indebted to the traders in August 1862. Wabaśa answered,

> Our credits with the traders had amounted to little or nothing. We received each year twenty dollars in gold per head as an annuity, so that a family of five received one hundred dollars. We paid our credits with this every year; besides this we brought in large quantities of furs, and paid our credits with these; and if an Indian had nothing the traders took his horse; so that it was impossible we could owe them much. The traders were always eager to take credit to the amount of our annuities, but past this they would not trust us at all. (Wabaśa to the Indian Peace Commission, 15 June 1868, *Papers Relating to Talks and Councils*, 93)

181. On 26 July 1862 trader Andrew Myrick reported to his brother the rumor that

> the agent will do away with the annuity system or confine the [?] to one trader and he a copartner. In their [Lower Dakota] secret council there were some intimations that the present traders were to be driven off and some one new to have exclusive control of the trade. Now whether the agent had anything to do with it we can't find out but it looks very much as if that was the programme. . . . If there should be anything in their [*sic*] being but one trader why should we not make a bid for it. We could afford to give 12 prct. to 15 prct. on the gross cash business of the year which would net the officers from 7 to 10,000 per year and leave us an equal amount of nett [*sic*] profits providing they will adopt the order system which would be better than to be driven out of the country at a loss of from 5 to

10 thousand because of credits even if we should be allowed to stay and collect at the pay table. Some one at present in the trade for the above reason can pay more for the exclusive privilege than an outsider. You had better consider this matter thoroughly as I am satisfied it is to be brought about before long. (Office of Indian Affairs, Special File 274, NARA)

In the same source William Quinn was questioned by a lawyer: "But it was your understanding there, and the understanding of the other traders at the time, that Robert had formed sort of a combination with the agent to get the advantage of the other traders in this trade, and that is why you curtailed your credits and Robert extended his?" Quinn affirmed, "That was my belief; that is why I done so; that is why I was so careful in not trusting the Indians that summer, because I was afraid I would have some difficulty in collecting my debts."

182. 1885 testimony of three individuals—William Quinn (quoted), Noah Sinks, and Robert's clerk, Moses Mireau—in Office of Indian Affairs, Special File 274, NARA. Parentheses in original.

183. Deposition at Large of Thomas J. Galbraith, 1863, Office of Indian Affairs, Special File 274, NARA; and financial records of the Northern Superintendency, MHS and NARA. With the collapse of the meaningful kin relationships between traders and Dakotas (witnessed by the fact that traders were colluding to manipulate the trade by the 1860s), which had, in earlier years, helped moderate competition between traders, the Office of Indian Affairs projected returning the Sioux Reservation to a sole trade proprietorship under federal regulation. With the purchasing power created by contracts large enough to supply almost seven thousand Dakotas, a single proprietor would be able to buy at low prices and make a profit despite government controls capping selling prices. On the erosion of kin relationships, see Gary Clayton Anderson's seminal work *Kinsmen of Another Kind.*

184. Nancy (Winona) McClure Faribault Huggan, "Statement of Nancy Huggins [sic] Wa-pa-la [Wapaha] (Hat)," Fort Ridgely State Park and Historical Association Papers, MHS.

185. Nancy (Winona) McClure Faribault Huggan, "Statement of Nancy Huggins [sic], Wa-pa-la [Wapaha](Hat)," Fort Ridgley State Park and Historical Association Papers, MHS. Huggan was, in 1862, David Faribault Sr.'s wife.

186. See testimony of A. J. Campbell, Office of Indian Affairs, Special File 274, NARA; testimony of Johnson Red Owl, *Sisseton and Wahpeton Claims*, pt. 2, 359; and July 1862 conversations between Lower Dakotas and Henry B. Whipple, recalled in Whipple, *Lights and Shadows*, 106.

187. A. J. Myrick to Dear Brothers, 26 July 1862, Office of Indian Affairs, Special File 274, NARA; and Thomas A. Robertson to George A. Allanson, 28 November 1922,

and George A. Allanson to William W. Folwell, 7 December 1922, Folwell Papers, MHS. Riggs wrote, "It did not matter that we had . . . worked for them day in and day out almost the whole spring —we were white men and could afford to do it. . . . [I]t did not in the estimation of these lords of the soil free us from the obligation to pay for the wood we burned and the grass our cattle plucked. When the time of want came, as it did, often more than once a year, the old men with their pipes and the young men with their guns came to demand or take the tribute. Sometimes it was in the power of the mission to give them something; and then it was generally done because they were in need." S. Riggs, "Sermon June 1860," NMM, MHS, 5.

188. In the earliest known version, copied into Sibley's campaign Order Book (vol. 103, Sibley Papers, MHS), Myrick's taunt ends, "let them eat grass or their own dung." In a 26 July 1862 letter to his brother Nathan, Andrew Myrick explicitly connected the Soldiers' Lodge injunction with his infamous insult, quoting the speaker for the lodge as having told him, "'You have said you have closed your stores for 2 Sundays and that we should have to eat grass. We warn you not to cut another stick of wood or to cut our grass,' feeling themselves probably much relieved departed." Office of Indian Affairs, Special File 274, NARA. Bruce M. White explores the symbolic significance of Myrick's insult in "Mouthful of Grass." The story of Myrick's death and his Dakota wife's escape was carried by granddaughter Mary Myrick Hinman LaCroix, preserved in an oral history at South Dakota Oral History Center, University of South Dakota at Vermillion.

189. See Andrew Myrick to Nathan Myrick, 26 July 1862, Office of Indian Affairs, Special File 274, NARA; and William W. Folwell to Samuel J. Brown, 21 October 1921, and Samuel J. Brown to William W. Folwell, 26 October 1921, Folwell Papers, MHS.

190. I develop the thesis that Dakota children probably were suffering from a syndrome called protein energy undernutrition (the most common source of vitamin A deficiency among children in developing nations) in "'Our Children Are Dying with Hunger': Malnutrition, Morbidity and Mortality on the Sioux Reservation in 1862" (presentation, Gideon Pond House, Bloomington MN, 21 August 2011); a transcript is available in the archives of the Pond Dakota Heritage Society, Bloomington MN.

191. Written documentation of seasonal hunger and episodic starvation among Dakota people commenced with the arrival of literate men like Louis Hennepin in 1680. The establishment of Fort Snelling in 1819, followed by the arrival of missionaries in 1834, brought other literate observers. See, for example, the 8 August 1842 letter from Stephen R. Riggs quoted earlier in this introduction in which Riggs said he thought the cattle killing at Lac qui Parle was due to the fact that "the Indians there are starving very badly." Stephen R. Riggs to Gideon Pond, 8 August 1842, Pond Papers, MHS.

192. T. S. Williamson, "The Dakotas of Lac qui Parle in 1835," *Iapi Oaye*, November 1875.

193. Thomas S. Williamson to Selah B. Treat, 8 May 1856, NMM, MHS. In a letter written two months before, Williamson reported, "Even those who have corn enough complain and say (doubtless with truth) that it does not satisfy. . . . They are compelled to subsist on vegetable food all winter except as they can get fish or musk rats which are becoming scarce about here and without salt or grease are at best but poor food. Living on such a poor diet is not only uncomfortable but injurious to health causing schrophula [sic] in many of the children and some of the women and men." Thomas S. Williamson to Selah B. Treat, 6 March 1856, NMM, MHS. Scrofula, a bacterial infection of the lymph nodes related to tuberculosis, and "sore eyes" (trachoma), are indicator diseases for vitamin A deficiency, which is most often caused by protein energy undernutrition. Anecdotal primary sources show both diseases were endemic to the Sioux Reservation in Minnesota. Dakota informants told Ella Deloria, "Scrofula was an abhorrent scourge that although not new, became alarmingly common at the beginning of the reservation period." Deloria, *Dakota Way of Life*, 127. While effective treatment for trachoma was still decades in the future, the causes of and remedy for scrofula were known in the medical community by the time Dakotas were relocated to the Upper and Lower Reservations and assigned treaty-funded physicians. "When children are fed . . . on vegetables, with little or no admixture of animal food, they die in great numbers of scrofulous afflictions. In the families of the poor, who cannot command better aliment, this is one principal cause of mortality." William Lamb, *Water and Vegetable Diet in Consumption, Scrofula, Cancer, Asthma, and Other Chronic Diseases* (Boston: Fowlers and Wells, 1854), 189, accessed August 23, 2010, at www.archive.org. "The means to be employed in the radical cure of scrofula, are those which produce the greatest benefit in states of debility generally. Pure air, and exercise, with warm clothing, (in winter,) are essential. . . . The diet should be generous; and animal food should be taken twice a day," a London physician advised in 1845. "There is, indeed, no form of disease which is not aggravated when it occurs in a child who is of a scrofulous habit of body; and a child of unhealthy constitution, when attacked by any infantile malady, is also less able to contend against it, in consequence of the inroads which previous disease has gradually made in its system." P. Hood, *Practical Observations on the Diseases Most Fatal to Children* (London: John Churchill, 1845), 207–19, accessed August 23, 2010, books.google.com.

194. On the effects of the winter of 1861–62 on the Upper Reservation, see *A Thrilling Narrative*, note 97.

195. This may shed new light on the incident that triggered the Dakota War—the murder of four settlers at Acton on 17 August by Dakota hunters who, it is said, were returning home empty-handed from hunting for game in the Big Woods and squabbled over protein (eggs). As Ella Deloria poignantly observed, when little Dakota girls "played at camping, with their dolls . . . to her babies she promised, 'Don't you cry

now . . . [s]oon your father will be coming home with meat.'" Deloria, *Dakota Way of Life*, 140. Commanders at Fort Ridgley also made gifts of protein to Dakotas—albeit barrels of pork designated unfit for consumption by the U.S. Army. See Fort Ridgley Post Administration Records, microfilm, MHS.

196. Stephen R. Riggs to Mary Riggs, 13 October 1862, MHS. The vast majority of the Dakotas who surrendered had been disarmed on 11 October, including most of the members of the Peace Coalition. Without guns and as captives of the army, the men had no way to hunt. All were subsisting on what produce they could gather from the Dakota farmers' fields surrounding the agency. The Renvilles also understood that corn alone was not sufficient for subsistence, explaining in chapter 8 of *A Thrilling Narrative* that while some thought Mary and John were stingy for not slaughtering more cattle in captivity, they were "saving our beef for the last extremity"—as a hedge against starvation during the expected long winter ahead in captivity on the northern plains.

197. D. L. Pelletier, E. A. Frongillo Jr., D. G. Schroeder, and J. P. Habicht, "The Effects of Malnutrition on Child Mortality in Developing Countries," *Bulletin of the World Health Organization* 73, no. 4 (1995): 443–48. Modern research also offers commentary on a seeming anomaly in the anecdotal sources: traditionalists were not the only Lower Dakotas whose children were dying from disease and debility. Wakiŋyaŋwaste and Snana (Andrew Goodthunder and Maggie Brass), and Taopi and his wife lost children to lingering disease during the summer of 1862. Both families farmed. But protein energy undernutrition casts a mortality shadow into the future of children who experience it in the first three years of life by making them more susceptible to disease. Thus the deaths of older children in 1862 may trace back to an earlier "starving time" like the winter of 1855–56, exacerbated by increased exposure to diseases to which Dakotas had developed little immunity as the settler population in Minnesota mushroomed following statehood.

198. In 1863 Thomas S. Williamson was asked if the Dakotas, as widely rumored, were a dying race. In a written deposition he answered, "Up to the time of the outbreak in 1862 the Sioux or Dakotas were steadily increasing in numbers. Those in the immediate neighborhood of Forts or white settlements very slowly. Those on the prairies nearly or quite as fast as the white population of our country, omitting the increase of immigration." After their 1853 removal to the reservation, the Lower Sioux were increasingly landlocked by white settlement. That same year the government began constructing Fort Ridgley on the Lower Reservation north of the Minnesota River. In the same source, asked about the wisdom of placing forts near reservations, Williamson answered, "Indians near our forts become affected with Syphillis [*sic*] and this as well as intoxication is one of the principle causes which prevents such Indians from increasing in numbers. . . . Syphillis and intoxication have caused the destruction

of many of the Indians, that utter lack of security which makes life as well as every thing else of very little value among them is one of the chief causes of intoxication, and prevents them from making any proper exertions to provide for themselves and families and is I think the chief cause of their decay." "Answers to Questions proposed by the Hono. J.R. Doolittle by Thos. S. Williamson," 1863, James R. Doolittle Papers, MHS.

199. The absence of morbidity and mortality data is not peculiar to the Sioux Reservation in Minnesota. According to National Archives staff familiar with Office of Indian Affairs records across agencies, such data are not known to have been routinely collected for any reservation during this period. Presbyterian and Episcopal mission records provide an anecdotal barometer of sickness and death in the population of Dakotas under their purview. However, in 1862 most Dakotas were not associated with a church and, as non-farmers, also fell outside the publicity interests of federal observers.

200. In 1846 missionary Robert Hopkins hinted at one Dakota usage of the word English speakers translated as "starving" when he wrote after a stay at Sleepy Eyes's village, "if an individual [visitor] is dependent upon them, by their consent, he is not likely to be hungry if they have enough to eat. During my stay at Swan-lake their larders were empty. In their language they were starving. I was sometimes hungry, and had reason to believe that many of them were more so." Robert Hopkins to David Greene, 22 May 1846, NMM, MHS. On 6 January 1863 John P. Williamson wrote home to his father, Thomas S. Williamson, from Crow Creek, Dakota Territory, "It is not starving to death here yet, but it is starvation all the time, according to the definition Ahinyankewin made to me the other day. She said wicaakiran [*wicaakiȟan*] was when they hadn't enough to eat but akirantapi [*akiȟanatapi*] she supposed was when they hadn't anything to eat." Thomas S. Williamson and Family Papers, MHS. My thanks to Gwen Westerman for leading me back to this important source.

201. On Lower Dakota farmers feeding their traditionalist relatives, see Office of Indian Affairs, Special File 274, NARA. About 30 percent of the men living on the Lower Reservation and about 15 percent of those on the Upper Reservation are known to have been farmers before the war.

202. For example, Agent Joseph R. Brown summarized the Treaty of 1858: "The proceeds of the sale of one half of each of their reservations disposed of under their treaties with the government, in 1858, should be abundantly sufficient to place them beyond the fear of future want." Joseph R. Brown to W. J. Cullen, 10 September 1859, Office of Indian Affairs, *Annual Report, 1859*, 83.

203. Wabasha [Wabaśa] et. al., "We, chiefs and head men . . . to our Great Father the President of the United States," 18 December 1862, in *Congressional Globe*. In a 19 December 1862 cover letter endorsing the petition, reprinted in the same source, Sioux

agent Thomas J. Galbraith wrote, "The situation these men are in is a peculiar one. Not only are they generally *innocent*, but most of them have by their acts exhibited friendship for the whites, and moral and Christian fortitude, provocative of sincere admiration. They cannot go with the wild Indians again by any means, as such is the hatred their race engendered by recent atrocities, that our white citizens cannot be persuaded to allow them to stay among them."

204. See W. Wilson, *In the Footsteps*.

205. Holcombe, *Sketches Historical and Descriptive*, 53. Holcombe knew Heard and felt no qualms about challenging his fellow historians to explain themselves. See Return Ira Holcombe Papers, MHS. Heard's extended passages of direct quotation in his chapter 10, specifically attributed to eight named speakers, were worthy of verification. We also know that Heard and the Renvilles spent several days together at Camp Release and that Heard was actively gathering historical material for his book at the time. Although corroboration by another source is missing, the authenticity of the speeches Heard reported has never been challenged, in part because the views of the Peace Coalition are generally balanced by quotes from those who supported the war.

206. Quoted in Heard, *History of the Sioux War*, 145.

207. Mazakutemani to Ramsey, 2 September 1862, appendix A.

208. Quoted in Heard, *History of the Sioux War*, 152. In 1901, questioned whether the Sisseton and Wahpeton men who engaged in the Wood Lake battle had participated "of their own free will," Solomon Two Stars answered, "I think that they did; but they were the young men that had got scattered in among the rest and were not under the control of any of their own people. They had gotten out of the control of the chiefs." *Sisseton and Wahpeton Claims*, pt. 1, 92.

209. Ella Deloria explains the dynamics of these entreaties in her discussion of peacemaking at the beginning of "Law and Order," chap. 2 in *Dakota Way of Life*.

210. Quoted in Heard, *History of the Sioux War*, 159.

211. See Taṭaŋka Nażiŋ to Sibley, 19 September 1862, appendix A; and extensive testimony on this point in *Sisseton and Wahpeton Claims*.

212. In a later council Ḣdainyaŋka (Rdainyanka) repeated, "Before the treaties the old men determined these questions, but now I have no influence, nor have the chiefs. The young soldiers must decide it." Quoted in Heard, *History of the Sioux War*, 152. Ḣdainyaŋka, [trial no. 19] was executed on 26 December 1862. Bachman, trials transcription, copy in author's files. On Ḣdainyaŋka being Little Crow's spokesman, see deposition of Wicaŋhpinuŋpa (Solomon Two Stars), *Sisseton and Wahpeton Claims*, pt. 1, 77.

213. Quoted in Heard, *History of the Sioux War*, 145–46.

214. Mazakutemani, "Narrative," 86.

215. Quoted in Heard, *History of the Sioux War*, 157.

216. Mazakutemani, "Narrative," 85.

217. For the modern position, see W. Wilson, *In the Footsteps*.

218. Wabaśa to Sibley, 10 September 1862, appendix A.

219. Heard, *History of the Sioux War*, 152–53. Unfortunately, in the wake of the war Mazakutemani was proven wrong. Minnesotans did not exempt women and children as objects of their fury. See "Historical Introduction," 86–87, and notes 281–85.

220. Wabaśa to Sibley, 14 September 1862, appendix A.

221. Quoted in Heard, *History of the Sioux War*, 144. Modern scholars recognize that women and children were fair targets in the intertribal reprisals that constituted traditional warfare in the decades preceding the 1862 war. Traditionally, noncombatant men, women, and children among the enemy were either allowed to live or were killed, because taking and holding captives was logistically difficult. See S. Pond, *Dakota or Sioux in Minnesota*, 133. However, the practice of killing women and children was not universal. John Otherday reported, "Until I was forty years old I went on the warpath almost every year, and when I had made up my mind to stop and live like a white man, I had taken seventeen scalps of my enemies. . . . I never killed a woman or child. . . . Some of the war parties do kill women and children, but I would never allow it when I had charge, and tried to discourage it in others." "Jared Waldo Daniel Reminiscences," chapter 7, p. 4, Jared Waldo Daniel Papers, MHS.

222. Bachman is the author of "Colonel Miller's War," which develops the plots and cover-ups surrounding the attempted massacre of Dakota prisoners at Mankato in November 1862, and of "Deaths of Dakota Prisoners." Bachman uses the term "massacre" with care, writing, "Places at which 15 or more people were massacred during the 1862 war include: Milford (48 victims); Middle Creek (43); Beaver Creek (29); Sacred Heart (26); Leavenworth (23); Norway Lake (22); and Lake Shetek (17). . . . See, especially, Satterlee's 1919 victim list . . . which set forth known victims by locations of killings." Walt Bachman, "Northern Slave, Black Dakota" (forthcoming, 2012), chap. 4.

223. My database of named settler deaths in Renville County, 1862. Satterlee missed counting about 20 percent of the known (named) dead in Renville County.

224. At least 344 named mixed-bloods and settlers were taken captive in 1862. Forty-two settlers were released or escaped and three captive children died before the 26 September turnover of captives at Camp Release, reducing the number of white settlers freed there to about ninety. Sixteen more people were held captive (from days to years) beyond 26 September. Sources naming the settlers freed at Camp Release are collated in and discussed in Carrie R. Zeman, compiler, "Dakota War Captives Enumerated at Camp Release in 1862," MHS; and in my database of settlers and bicultural Dakota people reported in period sources as having been held captive.

225. *Papers Relating to Talks and Councils*, 93–94. "Wa-pa-sha" is Wabaśa.

226. Three examples of adoption/protection in the 1862 captivity literature are Mary Schwandt (Schmidt), Urania White, and Sophia Huggins. Schwandt was thirteen; White and Huggins were adults with children. Schmidt, " Story of Mary Schwandt"; and U. White, "Captivity." On Sophia Huggins, see "Mrs. Huggin's Story," in Heard, *History of the Sioux War*, 209–28.

227. G. Renville, "Narrative Account," 8. Mazakutemani felt the same way: "As I went from tent to tent in the [Lower] Dakota camp, I saw a great many white women and children captives. On that account my heart was very sad, and I became almost sick." Mazakutemani, "Narrative," 84. On the significance to Dakotas of wearing moccasins and therefore why it struck Gabriel as wrong that some captives were forced to march barefoot, see Deloria, *Dakota Way of Life*, 65.

228. The extensive first-person captivity literature from the 1862 war testifies to such treatment. On starvation, see Carrigan, *Captured by the Indians*, 31; Sweet, "Mrs. J. E. De Camp Sweet's Narrative," 370; and Amelia Ferch, "The Indian Massacre," Brown County Historical Society, Brown County, Minnesota, 4. On the threat to shoot, see Carrigan, *Captured by the Indians*, 20, 26, 27; Tarble, *Story of My Capture*, 32; Sweet, "Mrs. J. E. De Camp Sweet's Narrative," 366; Schwandt, "Story of Mary Schwandt," 472; and U. White, "Captivity," 409. On terrorizing propaganda, see Carrigan, *Captured by the Indians*, 33; Sweet "Mrs. J. E. De Camp Sweet's Narrative," 366; Ferch, "The Indian Massacre," 2–3; and U. White, "Captivity," 408, 413. On human shields, see Sweet "Mrs. J. E. De Camp Sweet's Narrative," 327; U. White, "Captivity," 418; Mazakutemani et al. to Sibley, 23 September 1862, appendix A; and Mazakutemani, "Narrative," 85, which reads, "You Dakotas are numerous and—you can afford to give these captives to me, and I will go with them to the white people. Then, if you want to fight, when you see the white soldiers coming to fight, fight with them, but don't fight with women and children." See also "Historical Introduction," note 220.

229. Heard, *History of the Sioux War*, 153.

230. Taṭaŋka Nażiŋ to Sibley, 19 September 1862, appendix A.

231. See, for example, G. Renville, "Narrative Account," 8 (quoted in "Historical Introduction," 50): "By this time Cloud Man, Mah-zo manne and all those of our people . . . were very much angered at what had happened and said: 'The Mdewankantons have many white prisoners, can it be possible they want to make the Wahpetons and Sissetons their captives too?'"

232. Sibley to his wife, 8 September 1862, as transcribed by Return I. Holcombe in 1893, Sibley Papers, MHS.

233. Mary Renville, letter to the editors, *St. Paul Weekly Press*, 5 March 1863, appendix B. Anton Manderfeld reported, "Joseph LaFramboise told me, also, that it was impossible for them to get through with their families, or else they would have been

gone long ago." "Narrative of Anton Manderfeld," in Bryant and Murch, *History of the Great Massacre*, 385. Stephen R. Riggs on wrote 8 September 1862, "Thomas Robertson says he could get away himself, but thinks that if he should do so, they would treat his Mother and the rest of the family badly on that account." Stephen R. Riggs to My Dear Wife, 8 September 1862, Riggs Papers, MHS.

234. Mazakutemani also complained that the Lower Dakotas had not shown themselves to be generous or trustworthy. "You have spoken, too, with false tongues. Two days ago you sent a massage by Sha-ko-pee, one of your chiefs, that you have laid aside for us half your plunder. We have come to get it and see nothing." This inducement had been offered to entice the young men of the Upper bands into joining in the war, and some had. Yet the Lower soldiers were not sharing the spoils they had promised. Heard, *History of the Sioux War*, 146. The underlying offense was that the Lower soldiers had looted the Yellow Medicine Agency warehouse of goods belonging to the Upper Dakotas, goods that might be essential to their survival through the coming winter.

235. The Lower Camp spread the story that the missing women had been shot for trying to escape. This is an example of the terrorizing propaganda mentioned in "Historical Introduction," note 228.

236. *A Thrilling Narrative*, chap. 6.

237. On soldier killing, see Deloria, *Dakota Way of Life*, 20–21.

238. For "whitewashed Indian," see William Crooks to Henry Sibley, 27 December 1862, Records of the Department of War, Indian Prisoners, NARA.

239. *A Thrilling Narrative*, chap. 6.

240. *A Thrilling Narrative*, chap. 4.

241. *A Thrilling Narrative*, chap. 6.

242. *A Thrilling Narrative*, chap. 6.

243. Derounian-Stodola, *War in Words*, 153.

244. Juni, *Held in Captivity*, 15.

245. Juni, *Held in Captivity*, 15. Other captive settler boys Juni's age orphaned by the war were August (Charlie) Buce (Busse), age ten; August Gluth, age ten; and Louis Kitzman, age twelve.

246. Gary Clayton Anderson cites the Renville narrative in his bibliographies. Mark Diedrich used it a as source in his 2010 biography of Mazakutemani, *Little Paul*.

247. See Wabaśa and Taopi to Sibley, 10 September 1862, appendix A; and Wabaśa to Sibley, 14 September 1862, appendix A.

248. Quoted in Heard, *History of the Sioux War*, 159.

249. *A Thrilling Narrative*, chap. 7.

250. *A Thrilling Narrative*, chap. 7. Anawaŋgmani fled, taking captives with him.

At the time of the Minnesota massacre, in 1862, Simon, with other Dakotas, nobly illustrated the power of Christian principle. In the soldiers' lodge and at the council fire he opposed the war, he pleaded for the whites, and, when the tempest broke, he befriended them at the peril of his life. Mrs. Newman and her children, taken captive by the Sioux of the Lower Agency, heard the voice of prayer from Simon's tent. She committed herself to his hands, and he, waiting until the Indians' camp was moved further north, stayed behind, and then placing her and her children in a one-horse wagon, he drove them in safety from Yellow Medicine to Fort Ridgely. ("A Converted Indian Brave," accessed 9 January 2011, books.google.com)

251. *A Thrilling Narrative*, chap. 7.

252. Wakiŋyaŋtawa's wife is the captive "Mrs. Lucy T." in *A Thrilling Narrative*, chap. 9. Before the war Wabaśa, Huśaśa, and Wakute's villages were adjacent to each other on the Lower Reservation.

253. G. Pond, "True History."

254. *A Thrilling Narrative*, chap. 8. See also appendix A, 203.

255. *A Thrilling Narrative*, chap. 10.

256. Mazakutemani to Sibley, second letter dated 15 September 1862, appendix A.

257. Exercising caution, Sibley crossed the Minnesota River in the shadow of Fort Ridgley, not upriver at the Lower Agency ferry crossing where Marsh's command had been ambushed on 18 August.

258. Mazakutemani to Sibley, 22 September 1862, *A Thrilling Narrative*, chap. 11, and appendix A.

259. Mazakutemani to Sibley, 22 September 1862, *A Thrilling Narrative*, chap. 11, and appendix A.

260. *A Thrilling Narrative*, chap. 12.

261. "True Facts about the Outbreak between the Sioux Indians and Pioneers in 1862, as Told to Me by George W. Crooks, 81 Year Old Sioux Indian," unpublished manuscript attributed to Crooks's granddaughter, 1937, Brown County Historical Society. The pits dug inside the tipis were four or five feet deep. Sapling poles were laid across the top and a buffalo robe—a typical floor covering in a tipi—was spread over the poles, disguising the pit.

262. Stephen R. Riggs to Mary Riggs, 22 September 1862, Riggs Papers, MHS.

263. Lower Dakotas knew Sibley had almost no cavalry and were planning to sneak inside his infantry picket line in the dark. They anticipated the white soldiers would leap to their feet to reach for their guns at first fire, as they had done at Birch Coulee. By concentrating fire on the army tents, Dakota warriors could decimate Sibley's soldiers before they stepped foot outside. On the Battle of Wood Lake, see Stephen Osman's authoritative essay "Audacity, Skill, and Firepower."

264. Paul Mazakutemani, Akipa, Mazamani, and the Three Chiefs to Henry Sibley, 23 September 1862, *A Thrilling Narrative,* chap. 12, and appendix A.

265. Stephen R. Riggs to Mary Riggs, 23 September 1862, Riggs Papers, MHS. Riggs, after settling his family in St. Anthony, joined Sibley's expedition as chaplain. In a letter dated the next day, 24 September 1862, Riggs told his wife, "When Simon Washichoontanka was brought into camp wounded, one of the field officers wanted to ask him how he'd like to be scalped. No one would interpret it." The comment may have needed no interpretation. Wašiçuŋtaŋka was one of the three Dakota boys who spent a year in Ohio in 1842 learning English.

266. Some stories say Mazamani was shot by Dakota soldiers while moving toward Sibley's line carrying a white flag. Descendants say Mazamani was hit by a cannonball fired by Sibley's troops, despite his display of a flag of truce.

267. Little Crow's last letter is not extant but is mentioned in *A Thrilling Narrative,* chap. 13. Campbell's daughter, Cecelia Campbell Stay, a fourteen-year-old captive in 1862, consistently credited her father with liberating "the captives" from the Lower Camp and turning them over to Sibley at Camp Release. Her claim is true but should be understood as being limited to those captives Little Crow turned over to Campbell on 23 September, like Sarah Wakefield and her children. See Alexander Seifert, "Notes on Committee Selecting Historical Data from New Ulm Minnesota August 5–6, 1924," Brown County Historical Society, and Cecelia Campbell Stay, "The Massacre at the Lower Sioux Agency August 18, 1862," copy of typescript from the Provincial Archives of Manitoba in the personal collection of Alan Woolworth.

268. *A Thrilling Narrative,* chap. 13. Obeying Little Crow's edict would have been in direct contradiction of Sibley's order to not approach his line.

269. Mazakutemani, Taopi, and Wakiŋyaŋtawa to Sibley, 24 September 1862, appendix A.

270. Sibley to Mazakutemani, Taopi, and Wakiŋyaŋtawa, 24 September 1862, appendix A.

271. Folwell, *History of Minnesota,* 2:183.

272. Stephen Osman, battle synopsis titled "The Battle of Wood Lake September 23, 1862," 2007, attachment to e-mail message from Stephen Osman to Carrie Zeman, 3 January 2010, in the author's project files for this book.

273. Wabaśa to the Indian Peace Commission, 15 June 1868, in *Papers Relating to Talks and Councils,* 93. Thomas A. Robertson agreed, recalling in 1901 that the Dakotas who surrendered understood Sibley to have said, "If they could get away get the prisoners if they could. . . . that he would assure them they would not be molested, excepting those who had been murderers in the outbreak, but all innocent people he would assure their protection." *Sisseton and Wahpeton Claims,* pt. 1, 139.

274. The estimate of seven hundred is based on a previously unknown document

that may be a census of Dakotas at Camp Release taken by Stephen Riggs around 27 September 1862 in the Sibley Papers, vol. 103, MHS. Previous historians have estimated about one thousand, following Folwell, *History of Minnesota*, 2:184n65. Over the next few days more Dakotas returned, for a total of approximately twenty-one hundred Dakota people at Camp Release. This means that more than four thousand of the sixty-five-hundred-plus Dakotas receiving annuities in Minnesota chose not to surrender. For almost all of them, that act cannot be equated with guilt. Rather, it reflected the fact that they had nothing to do with the war but feared being caught in the backlash of white retribution if they remained. Thus only those Dakotas who surrendered at Camp Release were subject to the overt race hatred that characterized Minnesota in the wake of the war. The abrogation of treaties in 1863 effectively prevented the return of the Dakotas who did not surrender.

275. Little Crow's followers took fifteen hostages west. Some remained in captivity for a few more weeks. Others were freed in the spring of 1863 and still others, not until 1865.

276. In 1865 Episcopal bishop Henry Whipple recommended monetary awards to members of the Peace Coalition because (among other reasons), "They had crops sufficient to support General Sibley's army for a number of weeks." Office of Indian Affairs, *Annual Report, 1866*, 237. Settler farmers whose crops were requisitioned by the army were compensated by the state. Dakota farmers were not.

277. *Berlin City Courant*, 25 December 1862, 1.

278. *Berlin City Courant*, 25 December 1862, 1.

279. *Berlin City Courant*, 25 December 1862, 3.

280. Thomas J. Galbraith to Clark Thompson, 19 December 1862, in *Congressional Globe*. See "Historical Introduction," note 288.

281. The *Stillwater Messenger*, whose editor, A. J. Van Vorhes, was held captive during the siege of Fort Ridgley, reported on 2 September 1862 that

a little band of us—the "Old Guard" of Fort Ridgley—mutually pledged ourselves upon the altar of the Eternal God that if either or all of us escaped from our then perilous situation, we would prosecute a war of utter extermination of the entire Sioux race;—that wherever a member of the race might be found, irrespective of age, sex, or condition, his blood should atone the untold outrages of the past fifteen days on our western frontier. We believe this should be the spirit which should actuate every white man. The race must be annihilated—every vestige of it blotted from the face of God's green earth.

Stories like this one might be dismissed as racist hyperbole if not for the significant fact that a month after this editorial appeared soldiers who survived the siege of Fort Ridgley were tasked with guarding the surrendered Dakotas at Camp Release (see

Thomas Watts, "Sight of Women, Children Rescued from Indians Fired Soldiers with Scheme for Revenge, Says Thomas Watts," *Minneapolis Tribune*, 15 July 1923) and later, in November, with escorting Dakota men, women, and children to Fort Snelling. Dakota oral history has long remembered persecution at the hands of white soldiers.

282. Thomas Watts, "Sight of Women, Children Rescued from Indians Fired Soldiers with Scheme for Revenge, Says Thomas Watts," *Minneapolis Tribune*, 15 July 1923.

283. See Glewwe, "Journey of the Prisoners"; and Bachman, "Deaths of Dakota Prisoners."

284. Walt Bachman marshals the evidence in "Colonel Miller's War."

285. See Wingerd, *North Country*, 312–38. The march and its route are extensively documented in Bakeman and Richards, *Trails of Tears*. Both routes are shown on map 4, this volume. On the internment, see Marz, *Dakota Internment Camp*. Plots to kill the members of the Peace Coalition and the family members of the prisoners continued throughout the winter of 1862 at Fort Snelling. See Thomas Rice Stewart, "Reminiscences of Service in the Minnesota Mounted Rangers, Company G," MHS. Dakota oral history about the march experience is collected in W. Wilson, *In the Footsteps*.

286. On children from the Fort Snelling internment camp, see "Historical Introduction," note 321.

287. Mary Renville to Stephen R. Riggs, 23 January 1863, appendix B.

288. Of the ninety one hundred captives historically classified as "white," only about seventy were ethnically European American; the rest were of mixed European American and Native or African American descent. However, all probably would have been considered "white" in a cultural sense. Pragmatically, it was in the best interests of whites to inflate the number of white captives, since there was comparatively less glory in liberating people of mixed blood. John and Mary do not appear on the first part of the list (counted as "whites"); they appear among the mixed-blood families at the back.

289. *A Thrilling Narrative*, chap. 13.

290. *Berlin City Courant*, 9 April 1863, 1.

291. G. Renville, "Narrative Account," 15. Gabriel's sentiments were shared by twenty Upper and forty-one Lower headmen interned at Fort Snelling who, on 18 December 1862, petitioned the President:

We did no harm and tried to do good. . . .We are farmers and we want that our great Father would allow us to farm again whenever he pleases, only we never want to go away with the wild blanket Indians again; for what we have done for the whites they would kill us. We of the Upper Sioux would like to go live on the Coteau des Prairies, fifteen miles west of Big Stone Lake, in Dakota Territory; and we of the Lower Sioux would like to go back on our farms, and live as white men, and farm as they do, if they would let us. (Wabasha [Wabaśa] et al., "We, chiefs and head men . . . to our Great Father the President of the United States," 18 December 1862, in *Congressional Globe*)

In a cover letter to Commissioner of Indian Affairs William P. Dole dated 24 December 1862 endorsing the petition, Superintendent of Indian Affairs Clark Thompson wrote,

> The Indians whose names appear on this petition have been true and loyal, and should not be punished for the sins of others. They are now without homes or means of earning a living. Their expectations, based upon the risk and danger they incurred in saving the whites in the late outbreak, have not been realized. They supposed the whites would be grateful and provide for them, and ask that their interests may be considered, and that they not be driven off with the wild or savage Indians, who would treat them as badly as they have treated the whites. . . . The matter in which they have acted toward the whites ought to entitle them to a reward over and above their benefits arising from their treaty stipulations. (*Congressional Globe*)

On 20 April 1863 Simon Anawaŋgmani, Paul Mazakutemani, Lorenzo Lawrence, Joseph Kewanke, and three other Upper leaders, hearing the rumor that the Dakotas interned at Fort Snelling were to be deported to the Missouri River, asked Sibley to be allowed to return to their old homes around Yellow Medicine. Records of the Department of War, Indian Prisoners, NARA. Instead, most of the men were drafted as scouts.

292. One of John and Mary's last items of business in Berlin was filing their claim for losses in the Dakota War, a privilege denied their full-blood Dakota neighbors at Hazlewood. John and Mary eventually collected about $1,000 in losses. The claims of their Dakota neighbors were disallowed by the commissioners charged with settling claims.

293. The scouts generally took their families with them. But this was not always possible. The Renvilles took in three-year-old Nona (Dora) Paul, daughter of Paul Mazakutemani. Nona's mother had died in 1860. On 11 July 1864 Mazakutemani informed Riggs that his son, whom he had taken to the Coteau, had just died. Of his daughters he wrote, "I am very sory [sic] for my two little Girls that their way from me I am very glad that got some money for my little girls that she is at school if there is anything happens to me on this expediedition [sic] I wish you will take good care of my children." Mazakutemani paid about 25 percent of Nona's support out of his scout salary. The ABCFM funded the balance. See Mary Renville to Stephen R. Riggs, 24 November 1864, Riggs Papers, MHS.

294. *A Thrilling Narrative of Indian Captivity* was typeset from clippings of the *Berlin City Courant* story, not the holographs, as evidenced by the typographical quirks that

carried over. For example, words hyphenated in the *Courant* due to the many line breaks in narrow newspaper columns retained those hyphens in the booklet form even if the word fell in the middle of a line. The few extraneous passages cut from the *Courant* edition and any meaningful changes are called out in notes to the 1863 text reproduced in this volume.

295. The *Minneapolis State Atlas* was founded in 1859 by Republican William S. King and survived until 1867, when competition with a new weekly paper forced a merger of the two into the *Minneapolis Daily Tribune*, a forerunner of the *Star Tribune*. See Hage, *Newspapers*, 73.

296. "Complimentary Notices," *Minneapolis State Atlas*, 10 June 1863, 2.

297. "Job Work," *Minneapolis State Atlas*, 16 September 1863, 2. On Taylor's Cylinder Press, see "Making the Magazine," *Harpers New Monthly Magazine*, December 1865, 23.

298. The Cunninghams left St. Anthony around 8 August 1863. Mary Riggs to Stephen R. Riggs, 11 August 1862, in M. Riggs, *Small Bit of Bread and Butter*, 256. See "Literary Introduction," this volume, for more on the publication history of *A Thrilling Narrative*.

299. Stephen R. Riggs, "Report of that part of the church among the Dakotas belonging to what is called the Scout Camp and others," n.d. [spring 1864], Riggs Papers, MHS.

300. Gideon Pond to Stephen R. Riggs, 9 February 1865, NMM, MHS.

301. *Minutes of the General Assembly of the Presbyterian Church of the United States of America*, n.s., 4, no. 2 (1904), 231, Presbyterian Historical Society, Philadelphia. John B. Renville was the first ordained Dakota pastor in the Presbyterian Church but not, as is widely repeated, the first Native to be ordained Presbyterian. That honor belongs to a Mohegan, Samson Occom, ordained in 1757. See Love, *Samson Occom*.

302. Stephen R. Riggs to Selah B. Treat, 11 May 1865, NMM, MHS; "What Civilizes," *Iapi Oaye*, 4 December 1876, 48.

303. Thomas S. Hughes to William W. Folwell, 21 April 1922, Thomas S. Hughes Papers, Southern Minnesota Historical Center, Minnesota State University, Mankato MN.

304. Mary Renville to Stephen R. Riggs, 10 March 1866, contained in a letter dated 7 March 1866, Riggs Papers, MHS.

305. On the Dakota experience at Crow Creek, see Hyman, "Survival at Crow Creek."

306. The U.S. Congress passed "An act of Congress for the relief of certain friendly Indians of the Sioux Nation, in Minnesota" on 9 February 1865. Bishop Henry Whipple was charged with gathering affidavits supporting the nominations of the thirty-five Dakotas (or their survivors), who shared the $7,450 award. John Otherday received

$2,500; others, from $50 to $500. John B. Renville received $100 under the act in 1866. Office of Indian Affairs, *Annual Report, 1866.*

307. On the Dakota scouts, see Samuel J. Brown's 1921 correspondence with Doane Robinson in the Doane Robinson Papers, South Dakota State Archives; Schuler, *Fort Sisseton*; and Johnson, *Chilson's History*, based on Herman P. Chilson's unpublished research in the Chilson Collection at the University of South Dakota, Vermillion.

308. John B. Renville to Stephen R. Riggs, 13 January 1868, NMM, MHS.

309. *A Thrilling Narrative*, addenda.

310. John B. Renville, sermon preached to a synod meeting at Mankato, Minnesota, 1878, paraphrased in "What Civilizes," *Iapi Oaye*, 4 December 1876, 48. Emphasis in original.

311. Mary Renville, "Reminiscences," Iapi Oaye, April 1881, 38.

312. John B. Renville to Selah B. Treat, 10 August 1869, NMM, MHS.

313. John B. Renville to Selah B. Treat, 10 August 1869, NMM, MHS. In *Creating Christian Indians*, Bonnie Sue Lewis considers the broader phenomenon of Native ordination in the Dakota and Nez Perce nations. John B. Renville is one of Lewis's subjects.

314. U.S. Federal Census, 1870, Beaver Creek, Renville County MN.

315. John B. Renville to Selah B. Treat, 6 February 1871, NMM, MHS. Thomas S. Williamson and his family were living at St. Peter. Williamson had been Mary's physician before the war.

316. John B. Renville to Selah B. Treat, 6 February 1871, NMM, MHS. John believed that Gabriel Renville was behind the action. The same letter continued,

> The Ruling Chief (my own cousin) a man of mixed blood although its understood at Washington that he is of a full blood Dakotah, is a man opposed to all religious movements and adheres to heathen practices I don't mean by this that he has Medicine dances but that he has three wives can it be expected that he will favor his Cousin in the Ministry for otherwise, I don't think such a man should be the leader of a Nation unless he leaves off those things. No excuse for his ignorance for he has been taught the Scriptures from his youth up besides he is naturally an able man and might lead the people right but he chooses his own way.

317. [Selah B.] Treat to John B. Renville, 31 March 1871, NMM, MHS. Emphasis in the original. Salaries noted on a scrap headed "Salaries" by Selah B. Treat, 1867, Riggs Papers, MHS.

318. Ella was enrolled in the English academy and then the preparatory school at Ripon College, Ripon, Wisconsin, from 1877 to 1881. Andrew Prellwitz, Ripon College archivist, to Carrie Zeman, 14 June 2010. Ripon, fourteen miles south of Berlin, was on the Milwaukee–St. Paul Railroad. The Milwaukee Road Depot in Morris was the train station closest to Ascension.

319. In her retirement Ainslie was determined to keep the wider presbytery abreast of the needs of home missionaries and the people they served. The year before this article appeared *Iapi Oaye* informed its readers,

Mrs. M. E. Ainslie of Rochester, Minn., certainly has a very effective way of putting things. She has been a missionary among the Indians, and her heart is brimming over with sympathy for the red man. In one of last summer's *Word Carriers* there appeared a short editorial on the devastations of the "Grasshoppers" on the Sisseton Reservation. Mrs. Ainslie entered into at once the prospective want and suffering that must be the result of this visitation, and gave the little notice a setting of her own, and through the columns of the *Presbyterian* and the *Evangelist* sent it through the Presbyterian churches. In answer to that appeal . . . a score of boxes and barrels of clothing [was] sent from church and ladies' societies and Sabbath schools to our native pastors [for distribution]". ("Rescue the Perishing," *Iapi Oaye*, April 1877, 16)

320. It seems "Aunt Jenny" was fictive, the name perhaps calling out the woman's unfailing generosity to causes espoused by Ainslie. "Aunt Jenny" was married to "Uncle Napton," who was regularly roused from complacence by Ainslie's appeals for donations to missions.

321. In April 1877 a short article called "The Children" appeared in *Iapi Oaye* with preamble by editor Alfred Riggs. It read:

One of the most varied and complex experiences of our missionary work has been in the line of educating Dakota children. Mrs. John B. Renville, the wife of the pastor of Ascension Church, who has given her life to the Dakotas, writes a little chapter which she heads "The Children." After the Outbreak of 1862, Mr. and Mrs. Renville, with their own baby daughter Ella, and little Belle Martin spent the winter with friends in Illinois [*sic*]. In the spring following, they returned to Minnesota, and made their home in St. Anthony, now East Minneapolis. With the consent of their parents, they took from the camp at Fort Snelling, Peter LaBelle and his sister Madeline, Susan Spotted Hawk, and Nona Paul. Mary Martin, older sister of little Belle came down from Fort Abercrombie soon afterward. This made a half dozen, besides their own, which, without Mission aid, they continued, not without difficulty, to support and educate the next four years. Mrs. Renville says: "Spotted Hawk (the father) came to St. Anthony and urged Susan to walk home with him, a distance of 180 miles. To this we could not consent. Afterwards, he sent for her. She begged with tears in her eyes to remain but finally yielded and went. Peter, at the age of fourteen went from us to live with his parents, and we took Joseph in his place." What has become of these children? Three have grown up and married. "Mary Martin spent a year at Rockford Seminary, then married Peter. Madeline married Spencer LaCroix. She has buried a child, and recently, her husband, and has a pair of twins left. Peter and Mary have two beautiful boys, Alfred and Philip. Belle buried her darling Julia, and Joseph his little one. The wayward Nona has had much trouble, only living with her husband now and then. The dear children! Affliction has laid its heavy hand upon them. They all come to us in their sorrow, but have learned that none but Jesus can comfort them."

322. Ainslie, "Dakota Mission," accessed 30 May 2009, books.google.com.

323. See *Iapi Oaye*, February 1879, 8; March 1879, 12; and May 1879, 20.

324. Ainslie, "Dakota Mission."

325. "Notes from Good Will," *Iapi Oaye*, September 1880, 71.

326. "Ehkahuen Cunwintku Ṫa," *Iapi Oaye*, March 1882, 18.

327. "Ehkahuen Cunwintku Ṫa," *Iapi Oaye*, March 1882, 18.

328. *Iapi Oaye*, April 1879, 16.

329. Mary Renville, "Mary Alice Bird," *Iapi Oaye*, October 1881, 79. The piece was a memorial upon the death of Mary Alice Bird, daughter of John's brother Antoine Renville.

330. The text of Wyllis K. Morris's address at Ella's funeral, along with the text of "Mine by Choice," were reproduced in the April 1882 edition of *Iapi Oaye*, 31. Morris was the husband of Martha Riggs Morris, who as a teenager at Hazlewood had found "Mrs. John B." consistently irritating. Wyllis and Martha were stationed at Good Will on the Sisseton Reservation. Very little is known about burial practices at Ascension during winter in this period. The road to the cemetery may have been impassable in mid-February; certainly, the ground was frozen. The mention of white flowers on Ella's casket and the publication of funeral details in April, two and a half months after her death, may indicate that her body was not buried until spring.

331. Mary Renville, "Trying to Overcome," *Iapi Oaye*, October 1882, 80; appendix B.

332. *A Thrilling Narrative*, chap. 7.

333. Mary Renville, "Trying to Overcome," *Iapi Oaye*, October 1882, 80; appendix B.

334. *A Thrilling Narrative*, chap. 6.

335. Mary Renville, "Trying to Overcome," *Iapi Oaye*, October 1882, 80; appendix B. "Daily Food" may be a reference to the Bible.

336. "[L]arge outdoor poor house," is from "Indian Reservations," *Iapi Oaye*, July 1877, 28.

337. Mary Renville to Stephen R. Riggs, 7 March 1866, Riggs Papers, MHS. On Isabella Riggs Williams, see Williams, *By the Great Wall*.

338. *Word Carrier*, October–November 1897, 30.

339. Creswell, "Prince of Indian Preachers."

340. John B. Renville, in "Voices from the Field: Rev. John B. Renville, a Sioux Indian," *Home Missions Monitor*, July 1897, 206, Presbyterian Historical Society, Philadelphia.

341. *Sisseton and Wahpeton Claims*. See, for example, Cecilia Campbell Stay's story about her father mentioned in "Historical Introduction," note 264. The contest between Presbyterians, like Riggs, and Episcopalians, like Whipple, over the claim of whose Christian converts acted most heroically in 1862 clouds the written record to this day.

342. Taṭaŋka Nażiŋ to Sibley, 19 September 1862, appendix A.

343. Members of White Lodge's band and Lean Bear's band were implicated in murders in the vicinity of Lake Shetek and in attacks on Fort Abercrombie. See, for example, Amos Ecetukiya's 1901 testimony in *Sisseton and Wahpeton Claims*, pt. 1, 125. The bands of White Lodge, Limping Devil, and Lean Bear were said, in 1862, to have been living on the Coteau apart from the Upper Reservation bands. *Sisseton and Wahpeton Claims*, pt. 2, 348.

344. For conversations that crystallized this analysis, I am indebted to historian Walt Bachman for challenging me to refine and to support arguments consistent with the body of primary source literature on the Dakota War.

345. When David Weston's testimony agreed in particular detail with Thomas Williamson's (Mdewankanton), who had testified a few hours previously, a lawyer asked Weston if he had discussed the case with Williamson. Weston answered, "I didn't compare notes with him, but there were matters that were being discussed. For the past thirty-nine years we have been talking over these things, and have since estimated the number of people who were there." The lawyer asked if Weston was certain. Weston repeated, "I have not compared notes with anyone in the last few days, but it is very common with us to talk about these things at any gathering, all along—anywhere—everybody." *Sisseton and Wahpeton Claims*, pt. 2, 315. See also Thomas Williamson's (Mdewankanton) testimony in *Sisseton and Wahpeton Claims*, pt. 2, 296.

LITERARY INTRODUCTION

1. Simon J. Ortiz, © 2009, reproduced with permission. E-mail from Simon J. Ortiz to Zabelle Stodola, 29 March 2010.

2. Susan Berry Brill de Ramirez, e-mail to Zabelle Stodola and to the Association for the Study of American Indian Literatures discussion list, 28 September 2009.

3. Diane Wilson, review of *The War in Words*, 42.

4. Mary Ann Longley Riggs, wife of John Renville's mentor, Rev. Stephen Riggs, wrote in a letter to her husband dated 11 August 1863, "Mrs. Renville is publishing her book in Minneapolis." Quoted in M. Riggs, *Small Bit of Bread and Butter*, 256.

5. The Indian captivity narrative is, in fact, only one manifestation of the larger taxonomy of the captivity narrative. The latter encompasses any story with a captor and a captive and accommodates an ever-growing list of distinct but overlapping forms, including the slave narrative, the spiritual autobiography, the convent captivity narrative, the seduction novel, the hostage account, and the UFO abduction story. See Kathryn Zabelle Derounian-Stodola, introduction to *Women's Indian Captivity Narratives*, and Derounian-Stodola, "Captivity, Liberty, and Early American Consciousness."

6. Take, for example, the poem "Captivity" in Alexie, *First Indian on the Moon*, 98–101; the poem "Captivity" in Erdrich, *Jacklight*, 26–27; and repeated references in Vizenor, *Fugitive Poses*. Also see the sections on the captivity narrative in Gregor, "From Captors to Captives."

7. Carroll, *Rhetorical Drag*. For an interesting examination of gender impersonation in Puritan captivity narratives, see also Toulouse, *Captive's Position*.

8. See Derounian-Stodola, *War in Words*, 77–93, for further discussion of the Indian captivity narratives embedded in these volumes.

9. For example, Mary Schwandt Schmidt, who was captured during the Dakota War and published several accounts of her experience, wrote in 1915, "I remember well after the outbreak the country was flooded with unscrupulous persons that wrote a lot of sensational stuf it mattered not if it was true as not just so they could sell thear books and the more lies they wrote the better they could sell thear books." Mary Schwandt Schmidt to Marion P. Satterlee, 19 December 1915, Marion P. Satterlee Papers, 1879–1937, MHS.

10. I am thinking here particularly of the marriages of Charles and Elaine (Goodale) Eastman, Elias and Harriett (Gold) Boudinot, and George and Elizabeth (Howell) Copway. See also Ellinghaus, *Taking Assimilation to Heart*.

11. Appendix B, 233.

12. *A Thrilling Narrative*, chap. 1.

13. Appendix B, 233 and 234 (emphasis in original).

14. "Evidence for the Claimants," *Sisseton and Wahpeton Claims*, pt. 1, 129.

15. Some of the information in the next few paragraphs originally appeared in Derounian-Stodola, *War in Words*, 279–83.

16. *A Thrilling Narrative*, chap. 8.

17. See Derounian-Stodola, *War in Words*, 282.

18. *A Thrilling Narrative*, chap. 8.

19. *A Thrilling Narrative*, chap. 3.

20. Ortiz, "Indigenous Language Consciousness," 2:144.

21. Deloria, *Speaking of Indians*, 24–25.

22. Rich, "Notes toward a Politics of Location."

23. Appendix B, 231.

24. Appendix B, 232 and 234.

25. Deloria, *Speaking of Indians*, 106.

26. Carrie R. Zeman, e-mail to Zabelle Stodola, 31 January 2010.

27. Ainslie, " Dakota Mission," 409, accessed 30 May 2009, books.google.com.

28. John B. Renville, "Obituary for Ella Renville," *Iapi Oaye*, March 1882, 18–19. Also of interest is Mary Renville's article "Reminiscences," *Iapi Oaye*, April 1881, 38, in which she describes the last days of Simon Anawaŋgmani's daughter Jennie, using the young woman's words as she approached death, "I shall be sorry for my father and mother, but I am anxious to go home to Jesus. I get very homesick here. They are very kind, but I had rather go home to Jesus."

29. Mary Renville, "Trying to Overcome," *Iapi Oaye*, October 1882, 80; appendix B (emphasis in original).

30. The most famous example of such a deathbed scene occurs in Harriet Beecher Stowe's 1852 bestseller *Uncle Tom's Cabin*, with the loss of the saintly Eva.

31. See especially Burnham, *Captivity and Sentiment*.

32. George, *Politics of Home*, 9.

33. *A Thrilling Narrative*, chap. 3.

34. *A Thrilling Narrative*, chap. 8.

35. *A Thrilling Narrative*, chap. 11.

36. *A Thrilling Narrative*, chap. 13.

37. *A Thrilling Narrative*, chap. 5. I was also interested to discover William Lloyd Garrison's use of the word "thrilling" in his preface to Frederick Douglass's *Narrative*. Recalling Douglass ascending the lecture platform for the first time, Garrison tries to convey the escaped slave's emotional power: "he proceeded to narrate some of the facts in his own history as a slave, and in the course of his speech gave utterance to many noble thoughts and thrilling reflections." See Douglass, *Narrative*, 35.

38. *A Thrilling Narrative*, chap. 13, chap. 2.

39. E. Lawrence, *Peace Seekers*.

40. *A Thrilling Narrative*, chap. 3.

41. *A Thrilling Narrative*, chap. 6.

42. *A Thrilling Narrative*, chap. 4.

43. Marcy Tanter, e-mail to Zabelle Stodola, 28 December 2009.

44. Letter to Zabelle Stodola from Bobbie Erdmann, president, Berlin Area Historical Society, 2 May 2010. It should be noted that even papers with larger circulations freely borrowed and reprinted stories from elsewhere.

45. Mary Riggs to Alfred Riggs, 30 March 1864, CWS.

46. Miller, *Luther Lee*. The only known copy of the poem is at the Wisconsin Historical Society, Madison.

47. See Staehlin, "History of Printing," 57, 232.

48. Receipt showing Clark Thompson, superintendent for Indian affairs for Minnesota in 1862, purchased a copy of *Six Weeks in the Sioux Tepees* at a stationer's shop for twenty-five cents. Clark Thompson Papers, MHS. Information from Carrie R. Zeman, e-mail to Zabelle Stodola, 1 October 2009. MeasuringWorth.com, a website from the Economic History Association, shows that$0.25 is equivalent to $4.48 in 2011 dollars.

49. See "Literary Introduction," note 9.

50. Florestine Kiyukanpi Renville, telephone conversation with Zabelle Stodola, 22 November 2010.

51. Dinesen, *Out of Africa*, 4. N. Scott Momaday refers to Dinesen's quotation in his essay "My Home of Jemez," in Evers and Zepeda, *Home Places*, 52.

52. hooks, *Belonging*, 18. See also Flinders, *Rebalancing the World*.

53. I thank Dakota scholar and Little Crow family descendent Gwen Westerman for this comment (and others) on an early draft of my literary introduction.

54. Grover, *Dance Boots*, 98, 60, 99.

A THRILLING NARRATIVE OF INDIAN CAPTIVITY

1. The title appears at the head of chapter 1 in the 1863 edition. See figure 11.

2. Chapter 1 corresponds to the first installment in the serial "The Indian Captives: Leaves from a Journal," *Berlin City Courant*, 25 December 1862.

3. The names are also omitted in the *Courant* story.

4. "Hazlewood" is often spelled "Hazelwood" in modern sources. The editors have privileged the author's spelling, which was widely used in contemporary primary sources.

5. The tableland is the Coteau des Prairies, commonly referred to as the Coteau. In 1870 the Renvilles settled permanently on the Coteau at Ascension (Big Coulee) on the Lake Traverse Sisseton and Wahpeton Reservation in South Dakota.

6. The Hazlewood Republic was organized by Christian Dakota farmers in 1856. John was a founding member. See "Historical Introduction," 15.

7. On the Dakota Reserve in Minnesota place-names often corresponded to a natural feature of the landscape or to the name of the band whose winter camp was located there. Hazlewood Republic was named after the band that had permanently settled near Hazel Run. This tributary of the Minnesota River was also known as Rush Brook.

8. Although the two messengers are not named here, Antoine Renville, John's brother, was the first to bring news of the outbreak to the Riggs home. Moses Adams, who knew the Riggses and the Renvilles personally, named Paul Mazakutemani as the second messenger. The Riggses were John and Mary's near neighbors. Office of Indian Affairs, *Annual Report, 1866*, 239; Adams, "Sioux Outbreak."

9. "Mr. Cunningham" was Hugh Doak "H. D." Cunningham, missionary at the Dakota boarding school at Hazlewood, who was born in Augusta County, Virginia,

in December 1822. In February 1857 at Traverse des Sioux, Minnesota, Hugh married Mary Beauford Ellison, born in May 1818 to James and Mary Beauford Ellison in Adams County, Ohio. The elder Mary Ellison was the half sister of Dakota missionary Thomas S. Williamson. In the spring of 1859 the Cunninghams were appointed assistant missionaries under the ABCFM at the Hazlewood Boarding School, where they served as house parents to Dakota children who boarded. The Renvilles appended the story of the Cunninghams' escape to the 1863 Atlas edition. See pp. 192–97, this volume.

10. Missionary Stephen R. Riggs, born in Steubenville, Ohio, on 23 March 1812, was educated at Jefferson College and Western Theological Seminary. He was ordained to preach in the Presbyterian Church in 1836 and the following winter was appointed to the Dakota Mission by the ABCFM. Riggs married Mary Ann Clark Longley in February 1837, who was born 10 November 1813 in Hawley, Massachusetts. The Riggses reached Minnesota in June 1837, serving at the Lac qui Parle and Traverse des Sioux mission stations until the spring of 1854, when they settled at Hazlewood.

11. Riggs was stabling a horse whose owner had enlisted to fight in the Civil War.

12. The Renvilles fled about a mile and a half to the Dakota farmers' settlement at Hazlewood.

13. The "Mission people" were the Riggses, the Cunninghams, and others associated with the mission at Hazlewood. This is the first time we see the Renvilles receiving different treatment than the missionaries (who were all of European American descent). While the missionaries were secluded on an inaccessible island in the Minnesota River, the Renvilles were hidden in plain sight at Hazlewood. Moreover, as made more explicit the following day, the Hazlewood leaders believed that the missionaries were safer without the Renvilles in their group.

14. "Messrs. R. and C." are Stephen Riggs and H. D. Cunningham. If not otherwise noted, "Mr. R." is Mary's husband, John Baptiste Renville. For Riggs's account see S. Riggs, *Tah-koo Wah-kan*, 279–303; and S. Riggs, *Mary and I*, 176–87. On Cunningham, see *A Thrilling Narrative*, note 9.

15. The wounded man was Richard Orr. Orr's trading partner, Peter Guilbault, was shot and killed at their post near Red Iron Village. Orr, stabbed in the shoulder and shot in the groin, lived to tell his story in Bryant and Murch, *History of the Great Massacre*, 270–71.

16. Chapter 2 appeared 8 January 1863 in the *Berlin City Courant*, two weeks after the first installment. There was no paper published on New Year's Day, which fell on publication day in the intervening week.

17. In the *Courant* version the second installment opens: "Our readers doubtless remember that on the last leaf committed to their perusal, we were making preparations to leave the camp, but were disappointed. Immediately after our friends left us, . . . "

18. Mary took refuge from the storm in an unfinished house being built by an unidentified Dakota farmer.

19. Wasuhowaśte (Enos Good Voiced Hail, Howaste) was an Upper Dakota farmer and member of the Peace Coalition's Soldiers' Lodge during the war. He subsequently became a scout. In 1866 Bishop Henry Whipple recommended Wasuhowaśte for a $250 award, commenting, "Saved the lives of Mr. McLaren, Mr. Walker and their families, and greatly aided Rev. Messrs. Williamson and Riggs, and was of the party that rescued Mrs. Huggins and children, going into the camp of the hostile Sioux for that purpose. He is dead, but leaves a wife and children. I recommend that the reward of their father's bravery be paid to the Rev. Dr. Thomas Williamson for their benefit." Office of Indian Affairs, *Annual Report, 1866*, 238.

20. The Riggs and Cunningham families, plus a newlywed couple from New Jersey, Mr. and Mrs. D. Wilson Moore, made up the party of fourteen hidden on the island. They are "our friends" in the paragraph below. "The Department people" were government employees and their families who lived in the agency town at Yellow Medicine. In August–September 1862 the rumor afloat in the captives' camp was that the residents of the town of Yellow Medicine had been massacred. In truth, after spending a harrowing night holed up in the government warehouse at the agency guarded by Gabriel Renville and his friends, on 19 August 1862 the white residents of Yellow Medicine were led away to safety by John Otherday.

21. The author here shows that she, like the Riggs family in their stories, credited the standard Indian captivity narrative trope that Indian men would rape white girls and women. "Those beautiful girls" were the Riggs's older daughters: Isabella, twenty-two; Martha, twenty; and Anna Jane, seventeen.

22. The Big Woods was a swath of hardwood forest north and northeast of the reservation, the former hunting grounds of the Lower bands. By 1862 the area was largely settled by whites, and little game remained. In white-authored histories of the war, this foray to the Big Woods is interpreted as an offensive move to clear the area of settlers and to loot or burn the settlements.

23. For the Renvilles' Christian readers, that the missionaries knew "in whom they have trusted" recalled the words of the Apostle Paul, who wrote from prison, "For which cause [preaching the gospel] I also suffer these things: nevertheless I am not ashamed: for I know whom I have believed, and am persuaded that he [God] is able to keep that which I have committed unto him against that day." 2 Timothy 1:12.

24. Mr. Gleason is George H. Gleason, government warehouse clerk and resident of the Lower Agency, who was driving Sarah Wakefield ("Mrs. Dr. W——d") and her two children when they were overtaken by two Dakotas on 18 August. Gleason was shot dead. Wakefield and her children were taken captive. Wakefield later told the story in what would become the best-known captivity narrative of the 1862 war, *Six*

Weeks in the Sioux Tepees. The first edition of Wakefield's story did not appear in print until ten months after Renville's installment ran in the *Berlin City Courant*.

25. The revised (1864) edition of Wakefield's *Six Weeks in the Sioux Tepees* reserves pointed spite for Mary Butler Renville. Renville's story of Gleason's murder beat Wakefield's version into book form by about one month in 1863. Worse than having a competing story published by the same publisher (the Atlas Press of Minneapolis), Renville's version of the story contradicted Wakefield's later contention that only one of the two Dakota men had murdered Gleason; the other, whom she called Chaska, had acted as her protector. Wakefield's testimony at Chaska's trial immediately following the war was much closer to the story Renville repeated here (first published three and a half months after Gleason's murder and about two months after the trial) than it was to the story Wakefield herself offered a year later in *Six Weeks in the Sioux Tepees*, where she vehemently defended Chaska as her protector throughout her captivity.

26. Renville refers to a cluster of four stores and the houses and tipis of the traders and employees licensed to trade on the Upper Reservation, located near the junction of the Yellow Medicine River with the Minnesota River. William H. Forbes was a licensed trader. William Quinn was Forbes's clerk. Quinn's wife, Angelique Jeffries Quinn, was taken captive along with their three children (Ellen, William, and Thomas) and Angelique's mother, Elizabeth Jeffries. They escaped on 2 September 1862 during the Battle of Birch Coulee and thus were not named among the captives enumerated at Camp Release. Joseph LaFramboise (see *A Thrilling Narrative*, note 29) was probably "the Clerk" who warned the residents of the traders' settlement to flee.

27. "Muzomony" is Mazamani (Mazomani, Iron Walker, Shade) (ca.1800–62), Wahpeton chief of the Little Rapids band. Mazamani was an Upper delegate to Washington DC for the talks that led to the Treaty of 1858, which ceded reservation lands on the north side of the Minnesota River. Mazamani joined his brother Akipa and Gabriel Renville among the Dakotas who guarded the families of agency employees at Yellow Medicine on 18 August and later helped negotiate the release of captives from the hostile faction to the protection of the Upper Camp. Mazamani was also the brother if Maza Śa, or Red Iron, who was allied with the Peace Coalition in 1862. Mazamani was fatally wounded at the Battle of Wood Lake while carrying a white flag toward Sibley's line and died two weeks later among his own people. See letter of 23 September 1862, appendix A.

28. Wakefield and Gleason also were travelling on the federal wagon road that ran the length of the two reservations when they were attacked. See Mary Renville's letter to the editor of the *St. Paul Press*, 5 March 1863, refuting the idea that main roads were passable as an escape route, appendix B.

29. Joseph LaFramboise (1831–1910; Sisseton), one of the two clerks who escaped, remained at the Upper Agency with his Dakota wife, Josephine Frenier, and their

children and became one of the five founding members of the Peace Coalition Soldiers' Lodge. In 1901 LaFramboise testified that there were five traders at Yellow Medicine in August 1862: Benjamin F. Pratt (for whom LaFramboise clerked), Stuart B. Garvie, Louis Robert, William H. Forbes, and Francois Patoile. (LaFramboise testimony, *Sisseton and Wahpeton Claims*, pt. 1, 145. According to agency licensing records, Patoile was actually Garvie's employee. Pratt and Robert were not on the reservation when hostilities erupted. Garvie, Forbes, and Patoile were killed.

30. The reference is to licensed trader Stewart B. Garvie, "Mr. G." below. In the *Berlin City Courant* version this sentence ends, "(this we believe to be true)."

31. In the *Courant* story the installment ends, "The space allotted to us in your columns will not permit us to say more of this energetic man at present. You may expect to hear about him in the next."

32. Chapter 3 appeared in the *Berlin City Courant*, 22 January 1863, 1. The previous week, on January 15, the Local Matters column of the paper ran a short notice: "The third chapter of the Narrative we are publishing did not reach us until too late for this issue."

33. Dakota farmers living in the vicinity urged white families to take refuge in the government complex at the Upper Agency. Gabriel Renville (Psin Ćinća; Tiwakaŋ), one of the Dakota protectors, later said, "Thirteen of us [Dakota] decided to go into and make a stand in the Agency buildings because they were brick buildings and were strong. In the Agent's house were Mahzomanne, Basswood, Shupayheyu, Clothed in Fire. Then in the doctor's house were Ahkeepah, Charles Crawford, Thomas Crawford, and Hanyokeyah. Then in the school building were myself, Two Stars, and Eneha. In the Farmer's building were Koda and Rapahu." G. Renville "Narrative Account," 7.

34. John Otherday (Ampetutokeça) led a party of sixty-two whites to safety. A number of narratives exist from members of the Otherday party, including: Parker Pierce in the *Mankato Weekly Record*, 23 August 1862; E. A. Goodell in the *St. Paul Pioneer and Democrat*, 24 August 1862; John Otherday in the *St. Paul Press*, 28 August 1862; and Nehemiah Miller in Bryant and Murch, *History of the Great Massacre*, 396–99. As punishment for this act, the warring faction burned down Otherday's house. See U. White, "Captivity," 411.

35. Thomas S. Williamson was called "The Doctor" by the Dakotas, or, as Mary Renville dubs him here, "The Dr." John Renville was an elder in Williamson's church at Pejutazizi.

36. Robert Hopkins, or Robert Hopkins Chaske (Chaskedon, Chaska), "now in prison," was on the council of elders of the Dakota Presbyterian congregation at Pejutazizi with John B. Renville. Hopkins was tried and convicted of murder. The missionaries defended his version of the event. Pardoned by President Abraham Lincoln in the fall

of 1864, Hopkins chose to remain in prison ministering to his fellow prisoners until the spring of 1865.

37. "Go and preach the gospel to all nations" was Jesus's parting command to his disciples (Matthew 28:19). Renville uses another Christian motif, characterizing Williamson as a good shepherd willing to lay down his life for the "little flock" of Christian Dakotas under his pastoral care (John 10:1).

38. While the text contains conflicting clues about the author's intended audience, some were likely contributors to "the Mission cause." Renville seems especially aware of these readers (readers like herself) in both the *Courant* and the Atlas editions of the story.

39. Gabriel Renville said that when counseled to flee, Williamson responded, "'I have been a long time among the Indians and I don't think they would harm me, my children have all gone and I am alone here with my wife.' Then I [Renville] said to him, 'It is reported that even the mixed bloods who are Sioux have been killed and the only thing for you to do is flee at once.'" G. Renville, "Narrative Account," 6.

40. The Williamson home was at Pejutazizi (Pajutazee, Pajutazi, Pehjihutazizi), about three miles south east of Hazlewood and only about two miles northwest of the Upper Agency at Yellow Medicine. The latter, because of the traders' stores and government warehouse, was a focal point of unrest in the early days of the war.

41. Paul Mazakutemani (He Shoots Iron as He Walks) (1806–85, Wahpeton), is called Paul, and Simon Anawaŋgmani (He Who Goes Galloping Along) (ca. 1810–91, Wahpeton), is called Simon throughout. Both men had (alternately) held the highest leadership position in the Hazlewood Republic before the war.

42. Jane Smith Williamson (1803–93) was born in South Carolina, the daughter of a Presbyterian pastor, Rev. William Williamson, whose life mission was to end slavery in America. Williamson took his family to West Union, Ohio, in 1805, where he legally freed the slaves he had inherited and helped establish the Underground Railroad there. Jane taught school in Ripley, Ohio, where she integrated the children of free backs into her white classroom. In 1843 Jane came to Minnesota to help her brother, Dr. Thomas S. Williamson, and sister-in-law with the education of their children but was soon called into ministry as a teacher to Dakota students. Jane escaped with the Williamson party on the night of 20 August 1862 with the help of Dakota friends. After the war she spent twenty years teaching in St. Peter, Minnesota, and ultimately joined her nephew, John P. Williamson, and his family at the Yankton Dakota Mission at Greenwood, South Dakota, where she died in 1893. I thank Lois Glewwe for sharing information from her manuscript "Jane Smith Williamson, Missionary and Abolitionist."

43. Andrew Hunter had married Elizabeth Williamson, daughter of missionaries Thomas S. and Margaret Poage Williamson. In a 29 August 1862 letter to the *St. Paul Daily Press*, Thomas S. Williamson wrote that he had sent his children (Nancy Jane,

Martha, and Henry) away with Andrew and Elizabeth Hunter and their children (Nancy and John Knox) the evening of 19 August 1862. Williamson, his wife, and his sister Jane escaped the following night. The Hunters and the Williamson children joined the Riggs party in time to be captured in the famous Ebell photograph *Breakfast on the Prairie*. Thomas, Margaret, and Jane Williamson caught up with the Riggs party on Friday, 22 August. (In his narrative in this volume, H. D. Cunningham recalled that the Williamsons joined them on 21 August.) This was the second time the Renvilles were prevented from leaving the frontier. The Williamsons were the last whites to flee, and with their departure, John and Mary's hope of escape among a group of settlers vanished.

44. Paul Mazakutemani lived in a house. But like most Dakota farmers, he also owned a tipi.

45. The Renvilles thus returned the same way they had come, through the wooded bluff tops and back to the mission station.

46. A panorama was a huge painted canvas that moved in front of the viewer, either revolving on a mechanical carousel or hand-cranked like an oversized scroll while a narrator read from a script. The author anticipated history. Several painters found the Dakota War a popular subject and toured after the war, exhibiting (for a fee) panoramas purported to represent it. Two former captives, Maria Koch and Lavinia Eastlick, helped John Stevens compose the best-documented Dakota War panorama, while Eastlick's son, Merton, performed as a narrator. On the Stevens Panorama, see the essays by Kirstin Delegard accompanying plates 119–125 in Wingerd, *North Country*.

47. Chapter 4 appeared in the *Berlin City Courant*, 29 January 1863, 1.

48. "Mr. R.'s house" refers to the Riggs house at Hazlewood. Mary Renville arrived on the Minnesota frontier in the late fall of 1858, a tumultuous time in the "civilization" experiment. During the winter of 1859–60 Dakota farmers carried loaded rifles in self-defense because of increasing persecution from traditionalists. S. R. Riggs to S. B. Treat, 24 August 1859, NMM, MHS.

49. "The Northerners" was a period term. Used by a member of the Lower bands, it often referred to the Sissetons and Wahpetons. (See testimony of Robert Hakewaśte in *Sisseton and Wahpeton Claims*, pt. 2, 362.) However, on the Upper Reservation "Northerners" generally referred to the Yanktonai bands of Lakotas, which is probably the usage here. A Yanktonai, "Ta-was-hmoo-doo-ta-ko-ke-pa-pa" was found not guilty by the Military Tribunal; see Bachman, trials transcription, trial no. 154, copy in my files.

50. "Katherine" is Catherine Tatidutawiŋ (ca. 1791–1888, Wahpeton) the first full Dakota convert to Protestant Christianity and mother of Lorenzo Lawrence. She appears again in chapters 6 and 7.

51. This supposed immolation of an effigy of Jesus Christ on Sunday, 17 August, is

the pinnacle story in the myth of "Godless New Ulm," an idea predating the Dakota War. New Ulm was founded in 1854 by German Turner atheists. Although no Christian houses of worship had been dedicated before the war ("their laws are strictly against selling lots to any person who will aid in supporting the gospel"), small Protestant and Catholic congregations were meeting in house churches in New Ulm under the guidance of itinerant clergy. On 17 August 1862, the New Ulm Turnverein (Turners' Club) held a mock funeral for a local labor boss, culminating with burning a straw effigy of the man. In postwar retrospect, this Sabbath-day fete birthed the myth of the burning of an effigy of Christ. In fact, one of the early names for the war, the "New Ulm Uprising," imagined a causal link between that town and the wrath of God supposedly unleashed via Indians on the Minnesota frontier. Renville returns to the myth (which she apparently credited) in the addenda in this volume.

52. At this point Mary Renville was one of only two white women in the region who the hostile faction knew were not under their control. (At least two other settler women remained lost on the prairie, undetected for the duration of the war.) Thus, like Sophia Josephine Huggins, in Wakaŋmani's care at Lac qui Parle (see *A Thrilling Narrative*, note 56), Mary spent the early weeks of captivity in hiding among the Upper Dakotas. In this paragraph she hints at a scene she described in more detail in her 5 March 1863 letter to the *St. Paul Weekly Press*: hiding in the woods, observing the main road, and assessing their chances of escape. See appendix B.

53. Gabriel Renville recalled that at the Upper Agency that night,

some of the people I met were drunk. . . . I saw they were drunk—because one of them had a bottle hitched to his arm. I . . . took the bottle away from the man who had it. [I] pulled out the cork and took a mouthful and swallowed some of it—but it burned my mouth and I threw the bottle away and then went on. The reason that it burned my mouth was that it was white liquor and had not been mixed with water. In a cellar under one of the agency buildings was a forty gallon barrel of alcohol for the use of the Agency physicians which was found by them and which created very much of a commotion in the people about the Agency. Every person had his gun, those that were drunk were preparing to shoot at one another, and those that were not drunk held them, and that was how it came that no one was killed. (G. Renville, "Narrative Account," 6–7)

54. "Miss Laframboi" ("Miss J. L. F." in the *Courant* edition) is Julia LaFramboise, "Miss L." below. LaFramboise, born 18 December 1842, was Dakota, the daughter of Joseph LaFramboise Sr. (who was Ottawa/French) and Hapistiŋa, the third daughter of Iśtahba (Sleepy Eyes). Taken under Wakaŋmani's protection along with Sophia Huggins, LaFramboise was claimed by her brother, Joseph LaFramboise Jr., and taken to live with her kin near the Upper Agency.

55. "Tuesday P.M." was 19 August 1862.

56. "Mrs. H" is Mrs. Sophia Josephine Huggins, Amos Huggins's wife. Amos was a second-generation Dakota missionary, the son of Alexander Huggins of Traverse des Sioux. Their children were Charles and Letta. The "Chippeways" were the Ojibwes of Minnesota, a traditional enemy of the Dakotas. The most recent episode in the ongoing intertribal feud had opened 23 July 1862, when an Upper Dakota and his son were killed by Ojibwes only eighteen miles south of Yellow Medicine. Dakotas had made several attempts to avenge the murders in the three weeks leading up to the war. Ojibwe reprisals were to be expected.

57. Twenty-four-year-old Sophia Huggins spent the duration of the war under the protection of Sisseton chief Wakaŋmani (Walking Spirit, or Spirit Walker) and his family. Huggins's captivity narrative, which first ran in the *Saint Paul Daily Press*, 3, 4, and 5 February 1863, was reprinted in Heard, *History of the Sioux War*, 209–28. In 1866 Henry Whipple recommended $100 awards to Wakaŋmani and to Rueben Tah-hop-wa-kan because "after Mr. Huggins was murdered, these men took care of her and her children during her captivity and evinced great kindness." Office of Indian Affairs, *Annual Report, 1866*.

58. In Military Tribunal trial 155, Tah-ta-ka-gay (Tatekaġe, Tatekagay), a grandson of Sisseton chief Wakaŋmani, was accused of "participation . . . in the murder of Amos W. Huggins on or about the 19th day of August 1862." Julia LaFramboise testified that although she did not see Huggins murdered, Tatekaġe was one of the three armed men who left the house just before she heard the two gunshots that killed Huggins. Tatekaġe denied firing his gun at Huggins. Found guilty, Tatekaġe was executed at Mankato 26 December 1862. See Bachman, trials transcription, copy in author's files.

59. As the English-language amanuensis, or scribe, for Paul Mazakutemani, Mary Renville may have retained draft copies of the letters she included in *A Thrilling Narrative*. See "Historical Introduction," 78–84.

60. See chapter 5 for Paul's plan to send this letter to Governor Ramsey by helping a "French Family" (Madeline Robidoux and her children) escape.

61. Mazakutemani's 2 September 1862 letter to Ramsey is the earliest known utterance of a supposed prewar plot to renew the 1859–60-era assassinations of Dakota farmers. "Government" without an article affixed is a period usage.

62. The majority of the Sisseton Dakotas were off the reservation hunting buffalo in Dakota Territory when the war began.

63. The variant stories about the treatment of trader Andrew Myrick's body after his death reflect something Myrick is alleged to have said or done. In this version, Myrick's head is stomped into the dust; in the next paragraph Myrick is said to have blustered that "he could chew them all up as fine as dust." In the most widely circulated story, Myrick's mouth was stuffed with the grass he told the Dakotas they could eat

when he refused them food. Yet another holds that Dakotas broke open his safe and stuffed his mouth with gold, since he valued wealth above kinship. Dakotas are also said to have expressed their contempt by kicking his corpse—quite literally kicking him when he was down—just as Myrick had abused them by refusing credit when they were hungry. See also "Historical Introduction," note 185.

64. "[T]he trader told them they could not fight" may refer to Governor Ramsey's 1861 refusal to allow a group of Lower Dakotas led by Philander Prescott to enlist for the Civil War. See Philander Prescott to Alex Ramsey, November 16, 1861, Letters Received, Indian Agencies Military Posts and Units, January 1860–July 1862, State Archives, MHS. In other instances Native men were permitted to enlist in Minnesota regiments.

65. It isn't surprising to find Mazakutemani, a farmer and leader in the democratic Hazlewood Republic, praising "Hon. Agent" Thomas J. Galbraith. Federal policies on the Sioux Reservation after the Treaty of 1858 heavily favored farmers; Mazakutemani was a direct beneficiary. The phrase "his volunteering about that time" refers to Galbraith's recruiting efforts, which were tied to his own desire to enlist to fight in the Civil War. At the time of the Dakota War Galbraith had agreed to hold his formal resignation as Sioux Agent until after the delayed annuity payment was made. The kernel of truth inside the rumors "exasperated" some Dakotas, who feared Galbraith's intent signaled that the federal annuity payment he administered would not be made at all.

66. Sioux agents had repeatedly petitioned the Department of War (via the Department of the Interior) to permanently garrison troops at Yellow Medicine for the protection of the Upper farmers' bands. The farmers at the Lower Agency were not similarly exposed. Their reservation was landlocked by white settlement, and the troops garrisoning Fort Ridgley were just across the river. The Upper Reserve stretched into Dakota Territory in the as-yet sparsely settled west-central part of the state, exposed to Ojibwe raids from the north, Lakota bands on the west, and internal opposition from Dakota traditionalists—all a two-day march for soldiers from Fort Ridgley.

67. "I have succeeded in getting one family" refers to Susan Frenier Brown and her children. Mazakutemani's 2 September 1862 letter is out of chronological order in the text. Renville tells the story of the Brown family in chapter 5.

68. Lorenzo Lawrence recalled,

Some days after the beginning of the massacre, I do not remember the day, week, or month, I determined that the only safety of the friendly and Christian Indians was to escape if possible from the hostile camp. I went and spent the night with Christian Indian named Anagmani [Simon Anawaŋgmani]. We talked about the matter all night, and determined to escape by the first opportunity. I went from there to the house of Mr. Cunningham where my wife and children were staying. I said to my wife, "I am tired of staying here. We can do no good. These Indians will ruin us. I want you to bake some bread as soon as possible for the journey." She said, "It is true, but I do not feel like running away. I am afraid we shall be killed." I said, "We must die anyway—we had better die now than with these bad Indians." She said, "I am not afraid to die, but I am afraid if we are taken by the soldiers they will kill our children also. I have pity on our children, and therefore I do not wish to go." I said, "No, the whites do nothing hastily; if we are taken they will not kill us until they council for some time, and at any rate they will not kill our children, they never make war like the Indians. It is better to go even if we die." (L. Lawrence, "Statement," 114–15)

69. Although this letter bears the names of Simon [Anawaŋgmani] and Lorenzo [Lawrence], it was clearly written by Paul Mazakutemani's amanuensis, Mary Butler Renville.

70. Chapter 5 appeared in the *Berlin City Courant,* 5 February 1863, 1.

71. "Gabriel" is Gabriel Renville, John B. Renville's cousin. Gabriel's father, Victor Renville, was the brother of Joseph Renville Sr. and the stepfather of Susan Frenier Brown. Gabriel's "sister's family" refers to Susan and her children with former Sioux agent Joseph R. Brown (who was out of the state when his family was taken captive).

72. The Browns lived on the north side of the Minnesota River near Patterson's Rapids, about seven miles below Yellow Medicine, and were headed to Fort Ridgley when they were overtaken. Susan Frenier Brown's son Samuel J. Brown recalled that when the Indians confronted his mother, she immediately demanded that her Dakota kinship ties be recognized. Buttressed by an appeal from a Dakota man whose life Susan had saved the winter before, her appeal to kinship worked; every person in their party escaped the scene of capture alive. Samuel J. Brown, "Claimant's Exhibit No. 1: In Captivity: the Experience, Privations, and Dangers of Samuel J. Brown . . . ," *Sisseton and Wahpeton Claims,* pt. 1, 43–45. For more on the Brown family see Derounian-Stodola, *War in Words,* chap. 7.

73. Charles Blair had married Lydia Brown. Taken to the Lower Sioux Agency as a captive, Blair was released by Little Crow and safely escaped to Fort Ridgley.

74. Susan's brother Gabriel Renville went to her rescue, accompanied by Joseph Akipa Renville, Susan's stepfather via her mother's third marriage. Samuel J. Brown dated their rescue to "Friday or Saturday," 22 or 23 August 1862. Gabriel and Akipa took the Browns to the Upper Agency at Yellow Medicine, where they lived for the next week. When Little Crow ordered the agency vacated, Gabriel and his relatives joined the nascent Peace Camp at Hazlewood. *Sisseton and Wahpeton Claims,* pt. 1, 27.

75. "Mrs. A. B." is Mrs. Angus (Elizabeth Fadden) Brown, a white woman who, like Mary Butler Renville, had married into a mixed-blood family (in Fadden Brown's case,

in early 1861). She gave birth to her first child in captivity and died in 1865 at the age of twenty-two.

76. Renville attributes the Browns' familiarity with the Dakota language to "having lived in the Indian country a long time," obscuring the obvious: that they were as bicultural as Renville's husband. Although Susan Frenier Brown understood English, she, like her brother Gabriel Renville, spoke only Dakota, and her children grew up speaking Dakota and English. Attributions like this helped underline Renville's thesis about her own family and her work as a teacher: that opportunity and desire, not genetics, determined cultural identity.

77. "Big Amos" is Amos Ecetukiya (He Who Brings about What He Wants) (ca. 1834–1901, Wahpeton), brother of Solomon Two Stars (see *A Thrilling Narrative*, note 141). See Ecetukiya's testimony in *Sisseton and Wahpeton Claims*, pt. 1, 120–29. Here, "below" refers to downriver, where the war commenced.

78. Angelique, Mary-Madeline, Rosalie, and Marguerite Renville were John's biological sisters. At least two of the women had married into Lower Sioux families and were probably living in that vicinity when they were taken captive in 1862.

79. See "Historical Introduction," 50–51. Samuel J. Brown recalled, "Right away the friendly Indians, those of them that were camped there [at Hazlewood] sent out for their friends, the Wahpetons, that were living all over the reservation. They came in there with blood in their eyes, with all kinds of weapons—some with guns, and others perhaps with hatchets and other things to defend themselves against the encroachments of the Lower Sioux. . . . They decided to resist. . . . This Soldiers' Lodge was for the purpose of defending themselves and to protect their prisoners [captives] that were camped with them." *Sisseton and Wahpeton Claims*, pt. 1, 28.

80. The principal officers, according to Gabriel Renville, were: speaker, Paul Mazakutemani; chief soldier, Gabriel Renville; and soldiers, Joseph LaFramboise, Henok Mahpiyahdinape, and Wakpayuwega. G. Renville, "Narrative Account," 8. Joseph LaFramboise recalled the officers as himself, Gabriel Renville, Wakpayuwega, and Padinikuwapi. LaFramboise, *Sisseton and Wahpeton Claims*, pt. 1, 148.

81. Two weeks into the war, the coalition that would become known as the Peace Party was only beginning to emerge. See "Historical Introduction," discussion starting on p. 42.

82. Dakotas in the Lower Camp hid their cattle and horses to keep the Upper Soldiers' Lodge from repossessing livestock that had been confiscated from the mixedbloods, because killing the animals was common punishment for those who did not obey the commands of a soldiers' lodge. See chapter 7 for another incidence of Dakotas remaining "perfectly quiet"—showing no fear—when confronted by soldiers: when the Lower Lodge visited the Upper Camp to punish the Lower Dakotas who had defected to the Peace Coalition.

83. Jannette DeCamp and her children, ages nine, four, and two. She was seven months pregnant when taken captive and gave birth four weeks after escaping. See Derounian-Stodola, *War in Words*, chap. 5. It is no coincidence that this scene follows immediately after that of the Upper Soldiers' Lodge making its first appearance in the Lower camp. That visit signaled to as-yet-undeclared peace-leaning Lower Dakotas, and to captives like DeCamp, that the Upper Camp offered a haven for any who would take the considerable risks of fleeing to them.

84. Samuel J. Brown said the captives were closely surveilled by Little Crow's scouts. *Sisseton and Wahpeton Claims*, pt. 1, 34.

85. It had been two weeks since the last of the Renvilles' missionary friends had fled the frontier. During that time Mary had seen only two white women: Elizabeth Fadden Brown and Jannette DeCamp. They were the first of nearly ninety female settlers who, over the next four weeks, came under the protection of the Upper Camp, providing a measure of the increasing power of the Peace Coalition as the war progressed.

86. In Sweet, "Mrs. J. E. De Camp Sweet's Narrative," DeCamp wrote that the mother of chief Wakute (Wacouta) warned her to flee, thus bringing her under Wakute's protection. Wakute was one of four Lower chiefs who, exiled from their homes on the Lower Reservation by Little Crow, wrote a letter to Sibley on 10 September 1862 seeking terms by which they could return home in peace. See Appendix A.

87. The author here describes DeCamp's twenty-five-mile journey from the Lower Sioux Agency to the Upper Reservation during Little Crow's first retreat from Sibley. Little Crow went into camp within a few miles of Hazlewood.

88. These young women were Mattie Anderson, Mary Anderson, and Mary Schwandt. On Mary Anderson, see Leaf, "Family Ties." On Schwandt, see Derounian-Stodola, *War in Words*, chap. 4. The subject of the rape of captives during the war is controversial. It is clear that white men expected that the captives had experienced rape even before Sibley's troops reached Camp Release and heard their stories. However, only a handful of Dakota men were tried for rape after the war, and only three were convicted of it. Further, Mary Schwandt, whose earliest biographer declared that she had been raped, spent her later years disclaiming it. Cultural assumptions further complicate the subject. Although integral to the idea of Indian captivity propagated in the popular literature, rape as torture was never part of traditional Dakota warfare. Sometimes a captive woman was adopted as the wife of the man who captured her. Yet if, as DeCamp suggests, the woman was unwilling, the act would have been condemned even by Dakotas. That rape was quickly proscribed by the war's leaders may be indicated by the fact that only one credible allegation of captive rape exists (the case of Mattie Williams) after the evening of the first day of the war, 18 August 1862. For a discussion of how Minnesotans propagated the idea of rape for political ends in the wake of the war, see Dean, "Nameless Outrages."

89. Mary Anderson. See Leaf, "Family Ties."

90. DeCamp recalled that a Dakota woman named Lucy helped her escape to Lucy's uncle in the Upper Camp, where she was temporarily sheltered by "Catherine." Catherine Tatidutawiŋ was the mother of Lorenzo Lawrence, who helped DeCamp and her children escape to Fort Ridgley (see chap. 6), and the maternal grandmother of Lucy Wikmankewastewin, Lorenzo Lawrence's niece. Thus Lorenzo's family kept DeCamp in the family. Sweet, "Mrs. J. E. De Camp Sweet's Narrative," 370, 371; Affidavits supporting the claim of Lucy Wikmankewastewin, 14 April 1860, Record Group 75, Entry 529, Misc. Sioux Reserve Papers, Unfilmed Records, NARA. DeCamp said that at the Upper Camp, among the Christians, "John Renville was in charge after the escape of Dr. Riggs' and Dr. Williamson's families." Sweet, "Mrs. J. E. De Camp Sweet's Narrative," 371. She made no mention of Mary Renville, possibly because Mary was bedridden at the time.

91. The "French family" was Madeline Dumerce (Mrs. Magliore) Robidoux and her four children. Robidoux's mother was Sisseton. Sioux Affidavits, Roll of Mixed Blood Claimants (microfilm), Claim 372, Record Group 75, Entry 529, Misc. Sioux Reserve Papers, NARA. Magliore Robidoux was a Renville Ranger.

92. Chapter 6 appeared in the *Berlin City Courant*, 12 February 1863, 1.

93. The Civil War, in its seventeenth month in August 1862, was going poorly for the North. Although historians have made much of the recruitment of the Renville Rangers days before 18 August ("when Government called for men at Yellow Medicine"), Renville's dating the Dakotas' "opinion" that "they have all gone South" to "about a year since" is significant. In April 1861, at the onset of the Civil War, the government closed its artillery and cavalry school at Fort Ridgley, on the north side of the Minnesota River, which occupied forty-five square miles that had been part of the Sioux Reservation before the Treaty of 1858. The Department of War sent the regular army battery to the Southern front and replaced the garrison at Ridgley with a fraction of its former troop strength in the form of untrained, ununiformed, volunteer infantry recruits whose officers were reduced to riding mules. The army was by law a fixture of Dakota reservation life; they were the Soldiers' Lodge of the federal government and, after 1861, were a sorry-looking group of warriors indeed. Hence the recruitment of more of the same in 1862 (the Renville Rangers) is said to have reinforced Little Crow's opinion that "none but old people and little children are left at home."

94. John B. Renville, among the elders "detained as captives," held nightly prayer meetings in his tent.

95. Lorenzo Lawrence wrote that he "hired" someone to help him bury the books. After Lawrence arrived at Fort Ridgley, Riggs wrote home, "He says they put up a box of our books—and put them in a cache by John Renvilles—but he is afraid they did

not cover them well." Stephen Riggs to Mary Riggs, 16 September 1862, Riggs Papers, MHS.

96. "Mr. Renville" is "Mr. J. B. R." in the *Courant* edition. The "Dr.'s church" was the Presbyterian Church at Pejutazizi, where John Renville was an elder.

97. The *Courant* edition elaborated, "The book gave us insight into the past Administration, especially the number of teachers employed by the Manual Labor School. Wonder if they have all received their salaries but us." Mary had discovered an old government ledger recycled for Riggs's use the previous winter (1861–62). The winter was so harsh and the snows so deep that the Upper Dakota could not get out to hunt and had exhausted their stored food supplies. Agent Galbraith purchased food for them from the traders. Riggs was charged with distributing it to more than nine hundred Upper women, children, and elderly men enrolled in a ledger Riggs called, tongue in cheek, the "Book of Life." Stephen Riggs to Alfred Riggs, 10 February 1862, CWS.

98. The government owed the Renvilles about eighteen months' worth of back pay, dating back to J. R. Brown's administration.

99. "Mr. R.'s" here is Mr. Riggs's.

100. Fort Ridgley was attacked twice, on 20 and 22 August 1862. Failing to take the fort, the Dakotas placed it under siege until the arrival of Sibley's advance guard on 27 August.

101. Renville refers to a tipi as a "tent" throughout. Many Dakota farming families who lived in a house also had a tipi to use as a spare room when family visited and to use on hunting trips. But the Renvilles did not own a tipi. Dakota tipis were traditionally made of tanned buffalo skin but by this period cotton canvas was widely used as a substitute.

102. "Mr. R." is "Mr. J. B. R." in the *Courant* edition.

103. See "Historical Introduction," 70–71.

104. "Bascom" is a correction of "Bascan" in the *Courant*. Frank Bascom, a grandson of Sleepy Eyes, was "one of Mrs. Renville's boys. He had sore eyes last summer and is now completely blind. He can read, knows the multiplication table, and could write." Martha Riggs to Alfred Riggs, 27 February 1861, CWS. In February 1862 Sioux agent Galbraith had secured permission and funding to send Frank Bascom to a school for the blind in Wisconsin. Office of Indian Affairs, St. Peter's Agency, Letters Received, Schools 1862–63, NARA.

105. Lillie's father was Nathaniel Brown, brother of Sioux agent Joseph R. Brown. According to a letter reprinted in appendix B, Nathaniel owed the Renvilles fifty dollars for Lillie's board. Lillie must have joined the Renville family shortly after Mary and John's marriage; they had been married only three and a half years in 1862.

106. There is both truth and trope in this statement. Mothers and children were violently separated from each other in the Dakota War. Yet the motif of mothers torn

away from children is also a staple in the captivity literature. For a discussion of the latter (as well as other tropes of female captives), see Derounian-Stodola and Levernier, *Indian Captivity Narrative*, 112–66.

107. Also "Neuman" and "Neumann." Before the war Mrs. Newman and her children were living in Renville County near the German settlements at Sacred Heart and Beaver Creek. Her husband, John Newman, is not listed among the dead and thus is presumed to either have escaped or been absent from home on 18 August. On Thursday, 11 September 1862, Riggs wrote to his wife,

> This morning when we were all shivering around the fire on account of the rain and cold, word was brought to camp that a team was coming from above. I immediately went out with others to meet them and lo! There was Simon and his son Thomas with Dr. Williamson's horse and wagon. They were bringing in a woman and three children who had been captured. They were almost chilled to death. We brought them into camp and got them to the fire and gave them some food. They ran off from Yellow Medicine Tuesday night. . . . Simon would have brought his wife and other children with him but she was afraid the white people might kill her, since the Dakotas have killed so many white people. (Riggs Papers, MHS)

108. Chapter 7 appeared in the *Berlin City Courant*, 19 February 1863, 1.

109. This story was propaganda from the pro-war camp, circulated to intimidate other captives after Helen Carrothers escaped. The story covered the truth that with the aid of peace-leaning Dakotas a young woman encumbered with a baby and a toddler successfully eluded her captors and escaped to Fort Ridgley.

110. Those "having more reason for fear than we had" refers to DeCamp and Newman, who had escaped the Lower Camp, whose Soldiers' Lodge was making the demonstration; John and Mary Renville were never under the direct the control of the Lower Camp.

111. For several speeches attributed to Mazakutemani, see Heard, *History of the Sioux War*, chap. 10, "The Captives"; and Statement of Paul Mazakutemani et al., 29 July 1856, in Diedrich, *Little Paul*, 55–56.

112. Renville may have been alluding to a story captive Sarah Wakefield told her. In the 1864 edition of *Six Weeks in the Sioux Tepees* Wakefield wrote,

> This reminds me of how frightened the Indians were just before leaving [the Lower Agency]. They said that an old woman every night came to that (Mr. Reynolds') house, made a bright light, and they dared not go near there. They thought it the spirit of some one, for after a little some of them said they would burn the building, which they did; but they continued to see her every night, sitting on the walls of the cellar. . . . The light they saw was the moon's rays on the glass; but the poor

superstitious beings thought they had offended some of their Gods, and this was the mark of their anger. (Wakefield, *Six Weeks in the Sioux Tepees*, 89)

113. The datebook had been lost or planted by a member of Sibley's campaign. It is significant that the 2 September 1862 dispatch was addressed to Ramsey. Until this datebook was discovered, it is not certain that anyone in the Upper Camp knew Sibley had been sent out on a rescue campaign. The first extant letter addressed to Sibley was written by Wabaśa on 10 September, three days after this daybook was found.

114. Catherine Tatidutawiŋ, mother of Lorenzo Lawrence.

115. The question for the Renvilles at this point was not whether to remain in captivity or attempt to escape. Rather, they debated whether to try to stay on the mission grounds at Hazlewood and await Sibley's arrival or to allow themselves to be relocated again, pushed farther west by the insurgents who were making plans to retreat to the Red River.

116. Joseph Napeśni or Napeśniduta (ca. 1800–70, Wahpeton), the son of John Renville's maternal aunt, was the first "Full blooded Dakota man, baptized and gathered into the Church of Christ" at Lac qui Parle in 1840. Napeśniduta was a farmer and an elder in the Zoar Church, the Presbyterian congregation at the Lower Sioux Agency, in 1862. T. Williamson "Napehshneedoota."

117. This realization must have informed Simon Anawaŋgmani's decision to try to escape; it seemed likely he was risking his life no matter what he did.

118. Wearing a bonnet would distinguish Mary as a white woman, endangering their survival strategy of hiding in plain sight among the Upper bands.

119. The "hill of difficulty" and the "Slough of Despond" are obstacles that the character Christian overcomes in John Bunyan's classic spiritual autobiography *The Pilgrim's Progress*, first published in 1678. It was translated into the Dakota language by Stephen Riggs and appeared in an American Tract Society edition as *Ćaŋte Techa: Maȟpiya ekta oićimani ya* in 1858.

120. In the *Courant* edition "happy effect" is "exhilarating effect."

121. At this point the Renvilles believed they were being forced out onto the prairie in Dakota Territory for the winter. Besides food for themselves, the dried corn would provide feed for their cattle and horses when snow covered the prairie grass. They were keeping their cattle alive as a food source to hedge against starvation.

122. In Dakota culture a woman, not her husband, was the owner of the family's tipi, and erecting and maintaining it was her responsibility. The Renvilles did not have a tipi because Mary did not own one and had no idea how to set one up. Having married an acculturated Dakota man, it was a skill she apparently never thought she would need.

123. In 1901 Joseph LaFramboise testified, "Little Crow's Soldier's Lodge came around in our camp and said that we must form a camp together with them, and

made threats that if we did not do so they would injure us. We did not do as they told us to do, and they came around the second time, and that time commenced pushing down our tents." LaFramboise, *Sisseton and Wahpeton Claims*, pt. 1, 148. This appears to have been an injunction of "Soldier Killing" directed against the Lower Dakotas who had defected to the Peace Camp. On soldier killing, see Deloria, *Dakota Way of Life* 20–21.

124. Chapter 8 appeared in the *Berlin City Courant*, 28 February 1863, 1.

125. For an extended treatment of Dakota death and mourning rituals, see Deloria, *Dakota Way of Life*, chap. 7.

126. Ellen Brown, or "Nellie," age twenty, daughter of Joseph R. and Susan Frenier Brown, was home for the summer from finishing school in Washington DC. Ellen's younger brother Samuel, seventeen in 1862, later told the story of the family's captivity, discussed in Derounian-Stodola, *War in Words*, chap. 7.

127. Pettijohn, a former ABCFM missionary and recently unemployed government schoolteacher, was moving his family from the Upper Agency to St Peter. See Pettijohn, *Autobiography*. "Mary," the fluent Dakota speaker who accompanied Mary Renville in this wash day story, may be Mary Martin. On Martin, see appendix B, note 19.

128. The next sentence in the *Courant* story was omitted from the book: "We were rather afraid to have Mr. R. leave us, but knowing it was very necessary, for him to get some corn stalks for the horses, and potatoes to save flour."

129. The *Courant* edition reads "about half a mile" rather than "about a mile."

130. Dakota women did not routinely participate in warfare. But beliefs abroad in popular culture like Renville reports here demonized Dakota women. While the Renvilles did not support the expulsion of Dakota people from the state in the wake of the war, demonizing rhetoric like this was used by others to justify removal. By early 1863 the *hausfraus* of New Ulm had a reputation of literally Teutonic proportions. Besides the rumor Renville repeated, the women of New Ulm were said to have led the attack on the wagon party of Dakota prisoners passing by New Ulm in November of 1862 en route to winter prison quarters at Mankato. Lois Glewwe discusses the latter attack in "Journey of the Prisoners."

131. This is one of two letters Wabaśa wrote to Sibley on 10 September 1862. The second appears in appendix A.

132. Wabaśa, Huśaśa, and Wakute were all Lower chiefs. In this letter these Lower representatives declare their political separation from the hostile Dakotas. Although the latter were retreating from Sibley toward the open west, these Lower chiefs wanted to move toward Sibley and return to the Lower Reservation, while rightly being concerned whether it was safe to do so. Returning to their former homes would physically place them on the "white" side of the frontier—and on the white side of war politics—east of the Redwood River, close to Fort Ridgley, with Sibley's army between them and the open west.

133. Wabaśa's fears were well founded. Heard, who accompanied the Sibley campaign, wrote that by the time the expedition reached the Lower Agency they had buried the bodies of so many settlers that "a flag of truce would not have saved the murder[er]s had they made their appearance on that scene of inhumane butchery." Heard, *History of the Sioux War*, 236.

134. Chapter 9 appeared in the *Berlin City Courant*, 5 March 1863, 1.

135. See Sibley to Little Crow, 8 September 1862, appendix A.

136. The federal wagon road traversed the length of the reservation, roughly paralleling the Minnesota River. In the summer of 1862 the government built eighteen bridges spanning the waterways that crossed the federal road. Office of Indian Affairs, *Annual Report, 1863*, 273.

137. Other sources refer to this as the Soldiers' Lodge, which traditionally was the central meeting place of the band's soldiers. "Plundered from the department" suggests the flag was formerly displayed on the agency warehouse at the Upper or the Lower Agency. Dakotas had captured and were flaunting the enemy's colors.

138. In a more typical Indian captivity narrative extended description, like this one of the Soldiers' Lodge, served as "authenticating ethnography," or proof to the reader that the non-Native author/captive actually had spent time in a Native culture. Mary's husband, however, was Dakota and came by this information from firsthand experience. As the main author, Mary was familiar enough with the captivity narrative genre to know that ethnographic observations were expected. While she never disclosed that John was Dakota, this extended passage, with its oral structure and syntax, tells us that John was, at least at times, intimately involved in composing the story. It reads as if John spoke and Mary recorded his words in writing, which was, in fact, a pattern in their relationship evident in their letters to Stephen Riggs.

139. This practice is commonly labeled "soldier killing."

140. Cornelia Whipple wrote that a Buffalo Dance had been held on the Lower Reservation the day before she arrived at the agency, or on about 30 June 1862. Cornelia Whipple to My Dear Children, 27 July 1862, Whipple-Scandarett Family Papers, MHS. On Saturday, 5 July, her husband, Bishop Henry Whipple, commented in his diary that buffalo had been sighted near the reservation but had retreated west before Lower hunters could reach them. Henry B. Whipple diary, vol. 4, 5 July 1862, Protestant Episcopal Church Diocese of Minnesota Papers, MHS. The event would have been a coup for the Lower traditionalists who had summoned the spirits of the bison via the Buffalo Dance, asking some to sacrifice themselves as food for the *oyate*. Evidenced by incidents like this, Dakota traditionalists would have argued that the people need not turn to Christianity or nuclear-family agriculture to have their needs met; traditional lifeways were still effective and robust. For a description of the Buffalo Dance, see Oneroad and Skinner, *Being Dakota*, 82–83.

141. "Two Star" is Wicaŋhpinuŋpa, Solomon Two Stars (Wicanunropa, We-cah-hpe-no-pha) (ca. 1827–1914, Wahpeton). "Mrs. Lucy T.," "Lucy" below, is Lucy Tate (Lucy Taunt), wife of Little Crow's head soldier, Wakiŋyaŋtawa.

142. This describes a traditional food cache: foodstuffs and the implements necessary to prepare them. This was a practical way for Dakotas to store food along routes they frequented. Although cached food like potatoes or dried corn could be eaten raw in an emergency, it was more digestible when soaked or cooked.

143. Mazakutemani wrote two letters to Sibley dated 15 September. The second letter, reproduced in appendix A, mentions a letter written earlier in the day that could not be gotten out of camp. The letter reprinted in *A Thrilling Narrative* may be Renville's copy of that earlier letter.

144. Colonel Sibley was promoted to the rank of general on 29 September 1862. While he was a general at the time this installment appeared, he was not yet a general on 15 September, when the letter was written. It is common in histories of the U.S.-Dakota War to find Sibley referred to as "General" before his promotion.

145. Sibley countered their offer to come to his command by instructing the chiefs to make a separate camp on the open prairie under a flag of truce and to await his arrival.

146. The "Cin-ci-ti-wans" are the Sisseton bands of Dakota. In the Janet Pond copy of *A Thrilling Narrative*, held by the Minnesota Historical Society, the word "scouting" is heavily crossed out and the word "hunting" written in below. In the newspaper version this sentence reads, "The Cin-ci-ti-wans came down today; they have just returned from a scout, and have had nothing to do in the Rebellion." *Berlin City Courant*, 5 March 1863, 1.

147. "[T]hen we will try to show how much we honor our great Father at Washington" may be a direct response to Sibley's closing line in his 12 September reply to Wabaśa and Taopi: "I sign myself the friend of all who were friends of your great American Father." See appendix A.

148. Chapter 10 appeared in the *Berlin City Courant*, 12 March 1863, 1.

149. On Simon, see *A Thrilling Narrative*, note 41, and letter of 2 September 1862, appendix A. Simon Anawaŋgmani and his son and Mrs. Newman and her three children arrived at Fort Ridgely on 11 September 1862.

150. Lorenzo Lawrence and the DeCamp family arrived at Fort Ridgely on 16 September. The other family he overtook was Madeline Robidoux and her children, presumably carrying the dispatch from Paul Mazakutemani to Governor Ramsey mentioned in chapter 4. Lawrence explained,

A half-breed woman, Mrs. Rebardo, and three children joined us; but as we were starting their hearts failed them. . . . The first night we went as far as Hop River.

We went ashore, and it rained and blew very hard. I made a shelter of boughs for the women and children, and went out onto the prairie to kill some game. I had not gone far when I heard a cry. After searching, I found a woman and three children crowded under boughs of a tree they had bent down to hide them. It proved to be Mrs. Rebardo and her children; she had followed us down. (L. Lawrence, "Statement," 116–17)

151. The same soldiers who were sympathetic to DeCamp's plight wanted to kill the man who led her to freedom. In 1892 DeCamp said that Lawrence refused to enter Fort Ridgely the night they arrived but insisted they wait for daylight. "He said to me: 'I been a good brudder to you; I save you; but if I go into fort tonight they kill me. We go in morning early, when see officer: you tell him I good Indian and not let them kill me.' He was genuinely afraid to venture, and, as it afterward proved, he was right. Even after had explained the noble part he had played it was all the officers could do to keep the soldiers from killing him on sight, so enraged they were at every creature having the appearance of an Indian." DeCamp, "In the Hands of the Sioux," Brown County Historical Society.

152. Renville was mistaken. A few Renville Rangers deserted when the battle commenced on 4 September 1862 and joined their relatives on the Dakota side, where, it is said, they were shot. Sibley heard of the attack when the repercussions from the gunfire at Birch Coulee were detected in the ground sixteen miles away at Fort Ridgley.

153. Eyewitness descriptions of the battlefield at Birch Coulee echo God's judgment on Israel recorded in the Old Testament: "'I sent among you a pestilence after the manner of Egypt; I killed your young men with the sword, and carried away your horses, and made the stench of your camp go up into your nostrils; yet you did not return to me,' declares the Lord. . . . 'Therefore thus I will do to you, O Israel . . . prepare to meet your God!'" Amos 4:10, 12.

154. See Ecclesiastes 12:1–6.

155. Being generous with food was a hallmark of good kinship and council hospitality. At this phase of the war the Upper Camp was holding councils with the Lower Camp, trying to win the release of hostages, and also with their near relatives the western Sissetons, hoping to persuade them to side against Little Crow.

156. Ella was two and a half years old during their captivity.

157. The *Courant* edition says the apples were supplied by "Miss Williamson"— Thomas Williamson's sister Jane.

158. Captive Urania White described how her Dakota "mother" made bread. "She mixed bread in a six-quart pan by stirring flour into about two quarts of warm water, with one teacupful of tallow and a little saleratus, bringing it to the consistency of biscuit dough. She then took the dough out of the pan, turned [the pan] bottom side

up on the ground, placed the dough on the pan, patted it flat with her hands, cut it in small pieces, and fried it in tallow." U. White, "Captivity," 406. Saleratus was a bicarbonate leavening ingredient used like baking soda.

159. Chapter 11 appeared in the *Berlin City Courant*, 19 March 1863, 1.

160. "Mrs. Crothers" is Helen Carrothers, age twenty-one. She was taken captive with her two children near their home at Beaver Creek on 18 August 1862, and they were taken to the Lower Sioux Agency, where she escaped. Carrothers's story was published as "Narrative of Mrs. Helen Carrothers of Beaver Creek" in Bryant and Murch, *History of the Great Massacre*, 283–97. The best-known version of her story was written later, after she had divorced Carrothers, under her married name Helen Mar Tarble, *Story of My Capture*. See Derounian-Stodola, *War in Words*, chap. 5.

161. Urania Fraser White had two children, Julia, age fourteen, and Frank, age six months. On White, see Derounian-Stodola, *War in Words*, chap. 5.

162. "Mrs. Adams" is Harriet (Hattie; Mrs. John) Adams of Hutchinson, McLeod County.

163. The author shows awareness of another trope in nineteenth-century American popular culture, the figure of an "Indian Hater." The idea held that some who witnessed loved ones' deaths at the hands of Native people took on an alter ego that compelled them to kill Indians on sight. The most famous Indian Hater in fiction, drawn by Herman Melville in his 1857 novel *The Confidence-Man*, was based on the historical Colonel John Moredock (?–ca. 1830) of Illinois, a member of the Illinois Territorial legislature who witnessed the massacre of his family as a child "and, it is supposed, never in his life failed to embrace an opportunity to kill a savage." See Hall, *Sketches of History* 1:74–84, quote on p. 81; and Pearce, "Melville's Indian-Hater."

164. Tom Robertson and Tom Robinson were the envoys to Sibley.

165. Chapter 12 appeared in the *Berlin City Courant*, 26 March 1863, 1.

166. The adjutant general tallied 1,619 soldiers under Sibley's command at Wood Lake. Folwell, *History of Minnesota*, 2:177.

167. See Mazakutemani's letter of 22 September 1862 at the close of chapter 11.

168. "Muzo-mo-my" is Mazamani. Although "Wa-ke-an-no-pa" is a phonetic spelling of "Two Thunder," no Dakota by that name is mentioned in the literature. A man whose name is reproduced as "Wake-wan-wa" signed a 24 September 1862 letter to Sibley (see appendix A). He may be Wakinyaŋtawa (His Thunder), Little Crow's former head soldier, whose stature fits the description of the mysterious Wa-ke-an-no-pa (Two Thunder) here. Yet due to the confusion in Anglo spellings of Dakota names ("Wake-wan-wa" is further mangled into "Wa-ke-nan-nan-te" in the published version of Sibley's 24 September letter of response), the identity of "Two Thunder" may remain obscure.

169. The battle referenced came to be known as the Battle of Wood Lake.

170. On 22 September 1862 Riggs wrote to his wife, "Simon Washechoontanka was wounded [at the Battle of Wood Lake] and brought in to die. He says he was forced into the fight—that some of the Mdewankantons stood behind them with guns threatening to shoot them." Mazamani, one of the authors of this letter, was also fatally wounded. Samuel J. Brown, a captive and a relative of Mazamani, told historian William Watts Folwell that Mazamani "was a hard worker for the prisoners [captives] during the outbreak and was wounded at the battle of Wood Lake and died from the effects of it at Yellow Medicine a few days after the general surrender [at Camp Release]. . . . He was shot in the leg, either by Indians or soldiers, while endeavoring to reach Sibley during the fight. He carried a piece of white cloth attached to a stick in accordance with instructions from Sibley to the friendlies." Samuel J. Brown to Folwell, 25 February 1920, Folwell Papers, MHS. Descendant Gwen Westerman's family story holds that Mazamani was "shot by a cannon under a flag of truce." Westerman, personal communication. Sibley's men were the only soldiers using cannon during the battle at Lone Tree Lake.

171. See letter from Taṭaŋka Nażiŋ (Standing Buffalo) to Sibley, 19 September 1862, appendix A. However, the subject of the extant letter does not match this description, making it possible that Taṭaŋka Nażiŋ wrote another letter to Sibley that was not received or is no longer extant.

172. The place and date of writing are given in the *Courant* edition and are missing, probably accidentally, from the Atlas edition.

173. "Coming events" refers to the Battle of Wood Lake, 23 September 1862.

174. Chapter 13 appeared in the *Berlin City Courant*, 9 April 1862, 1.

175. The *Courant* edition begins, "We alluded in our last number . . . "

176. Trader and amateur ethnographer James Lynd wrote in 1862,

The deities upon which the most worship is bestowed, if, indeed, any particular one is nameable, are Tukan (*Inyan*) the *Stone God*, and Wakinyan *the Thunder Bird*. . . . the adoration of the former is an every-day affair. The *Tukan*, the Dakotas say, is the god that dwells in stones or rocks, and is the oldest god. . . . The most usual form of stone employed in worship is round, and about the size of a human head. The devout Dakota paints the *Tukan* red, putting colored swan's down upon it, then falls down and worships the god which is supposed to dwell in it or to hover near it. . . . Scarlet or red is the religious color for sacrifices. (Lynd "Religion of the Dakotas," 168–69)

Samuel Pond commented, "Dogs were offered in sacrifice, and also game killed in hunting. After being killed, dogs were thrown into the water, or were marked with paint and left lying on the ground, sometimes covered with a piece of cloth or a blanket. . . . Such offerings were often made or promised when the parties making them were about to engage in some hazardous undertaking, and they were often made just before the departure of a war party or just after its return" (S. Pond, *Dakota or Sioux in Minnesota*, 104).

177. After his family reached safety, missionary Stephen Riggs agreed to be a chaplain on Sibley's 1862 expedition.

178. By 23 September the peace chiefs had already taken under their protection the majority of the settler captives. After the Battle of Wood Lake Little Crow turned over those captives he had retained for the duration of the war, including Sarah Wakefield and her children. Of the fifteen captives taken west by Little Crow's followers, eleven were freed in 1862–63. One was not freed until 1866. The fates of the remaining three, all children, are unknown.

179. On 22 September 1862, in a letter to his wife, Riggs named Enos Wasuhowaśte [mistranscribed as "Wisoohowanaty"] and Joe Campbell as having brought messages into Sibley's camp and Simon [Anawaŋgmani] and John Otherday as having successfully crossed over to the ranks of Upper Dakota and back to Sibley's lines again during the Battle of Wood Lake. Riggs Papers, MHS.

180. The *Courant* edition's wording underscores which people were responsible for the unjust exile by elaborating: "are doomed by the Minnesotians to an exile."

181. The addenda did not appear in the *Berlin City Courant* edition. This article dates to the summer of 1863. The religious and missionary themes suggest it may have been written for a Presbyterian or Congregational periodical.

182. "[A]rticles" is plural, yet Renville included only one, labeled with the plural "addenda," in the 1863 edition. She was a fairly prolific writer during this period and in fact mentions subjects like the history of the Hazlewood Republic and the life of Frank Bascom that she did not return to in this text. She may have published other articles in this period that are yet to be discovered.

183. Peter Great Fire (Tapetataŋka, Big Fire), was a member of the Hazlewood Republic. Although the author references his orderly conduct in church, he does not appear on rosters of church members before the war. See Military Commission, trial no. 95, "Ta-pay-ta-tanka" (in Bachman, trials transcription, copy in author's files), where he admitted to taking plunder from a warehouse at Yellow Medicine; to being at the Battle of Birch Coulee, although "far off" with a loaded gun he did not fire; and to having started with a war party to the Big Woods but turning back. He was condemned to hang, but his sentence was reduced to prison.

184. On 29 May 1863 a white soldier wrote home of a recent visit to Camp Pope near the Lower Sioux Agency: "One thing I was sad to see was wherever there was a grave of an Indian the body was dug up and allowed to rot above the ground. With all our boasting of our civilization are we not almost as barbarous as they." Merrill Dwelle to Sister Carrie, 29 May 1863, G. Merrill Dwelle and Family Papers, MHS. The

author thanks Stephen Osman for this reference. Thomas Rice Stewart of the Minnesota Mounted Rangers elaborated,

> One squad brought in several dead Indians they found that either they or other parties had dug up from their graves. Also, a coffin in which there were three papooses. . . . Whenever there was an opportunity to dig up an Indian, he generally came up and was seldom replanted. . . . [A]s we were riding along not far from our camp, there was a large smooth post set up in the ground close to the road. . . . [O]ne of the dead Indians brought into camp the day before was standing upright tied to the post. . . . [W]e were now in the country so lately devastated by the Indians and about half our company driven from our homes, most of the soldiers had friends or relatives killed or captured by the Indians, so there was little love shown for Mr. Indian, either dead or alive. (Thomas Rice Stewart, "Reminiscences of Service in the Minnesota Mounted Rangers, Company G," MHS, 46–47)

Recently deceased Dakotas were afforded no more respect by white soldiers. Benjamin J. Young, a teenage member of the Sixth Minnesota, Company A, who helped bury the Dakota soldiers killed at Wood Lake, recalled, "I remember the first man that was thrown into the ditch fell with his head down, gathered up in a heap. . . .We threw them in there pretty lively." *Sisseton and Wahpeton Claims*, pt. 2, 387.

185. On New Ulm, see *A Thrilling Narrative*, note 51.

186. The reference is to Thomas S. Williamson. After the war Williamson's wife, Margaret, and his sister Jane settled in St. Peter. At the time Renville wrote this, Williamson was living in a rented room in Davenport, Iowa, ministering to the Dakotas imprisoned at Fort McClellan.

187. The reference is to Stephen R. Riggs. The author here alludes to Riggs's multiple roles in the wake of the war: disburser of relief funds to settler refugees, chaplain on Sibley's 1863 military expedition, and author of letters defending Dakotas he believed had been unjustly accused. "[G]aining much popularity by some, and stripes from others (if not of many cords, of many words)" is an apt descriptor for Riggs. His conflicted views of "duty" and "justice" for Dakotas convicted in 1862 have been compounded historically by his tendency to take credit for the joint literary work of the Dakota Mission, like the Dakota Dictionary, making him increasingly unpopular in modern histories of the war.

188. The reference is to John P. Williamson, who went west with those exiled to Crow Creek in 1863 and spent the rest of his life as a missionary pastor to the Dakotas. The author depicts him here as an Old Testament Moses shepherding Israel though the wilderness. Tragically, as the author learned herself in the years to come, there was no earthly Promised Land awaiting those Dakotas who survived the journey.

189. "[I]n Missouri" is probably a typesetting error; the Crow Creek Agency was

on the Missouri River in Dakota Territory. The Cunninghams, along with Edward Pond and his wife, were on their way to Crow Creek to assist John P. Williamson.

190. The children at the boarding school were Dakota. Their Dakota parents reacted to the rumors of war by taking the children home.

191. On Pettijohn, see *A Thrilling Narrative*, note 127.

192. Zoe Hapa was identified as "an Indian woman, who at great risk brought provisions to the Island where Mr. Riggs and party were secreted" in Office of Indian Affairs, *Annual Report, 1866*, 238.

193. The Riggs party traveled overland from the Upper Sioux Agency to Hutchinson. Their path lay almost entirely within Renville County.

APPENDIX A

1. *A Thrilling Narrative*, chap. 4.

2. *A Thrilling Narrative*, chap. 4.

3. Order Book, vol. 103, Sibley Papers, MHS. See Heard, *History of the Sioux War*, 147. Sibley opened the correspondence with the Dakotas by leaving this note on a stake on the battleground at Birch Coulee. On Sibley, see Gilman, *Henry Hastings Sibley*; and Osman, "Sibley's Army."

4. Order Book, vol. 103, Sibley Papers, MHS. For variant reproductions, see Heard, *History of the Sioux War*, 147–48; and West, *Ancestry, Life and Times*, 263.

5. "Major" Thomas J. Galbraith was agent for the Dakota reservations in Minnesota in 1862.

6. "It is with the Traders that commence" is literal in more than one sense. Traders on the Lower Reservation were the first killed, on 18 August 1862. But as Little Crow goes on to outline, a generally accepted proximal cause of the war is that the traders (along with the federal government) provoked some Dakotas beyond endurance. See the discussion of this letter in "Historical Introduction," 55–61.

7. In November 1862 fourteen Hochunks [Winnebagoes] were tried for participation in the war; all were acquitted. For transcripts of the Winnebago trials, see Congressional Records, Records of the Thirty-Seventh Congress, House File 37A-E7.8, NARA.

8. Order Book, vol. 103, Sibley Papers, MHS. The first rendition in the Order Book reads, "You have murdered many of our people without any sufficient cause. Return me the Prisoners under a flag of Truce, and I will talk with you then like a man." The second, longer Order Book copy is supplied in this appendix. See also Heard, *History of the Sioux War*, 148; and West, *Ancestry, Life and Times*, 263.

9. *A Thrilling Narrative*, chap. 8.

10. *St. Paul Daily Press*, 16 September 1862, 1; Heard, *History of the Sioux War*, 149; West, *Ancestry, Life and Times*, 264. "Mayawakan" is Mayawakaŋ, or Red Iron Village.

11. George Spencer may have been the amanuensis for this letter. See testimony

of Maggie Brass, *Sisseton and Wahpeton Claims*, pt. 2, 380–81. Tom Robertson, who delivered the letter to Sibley, explained, "Some of those whom I knew were friendly came to me and said they did not like the fighting and murdering of the whites, but they were afraid to do anything or say anything openly, but wished, if I saw General Sibley, as they knew him to be their friend—always had been their friend—I would ask him what they could do in order to get back to the whites, and, if possible, to get the white prisoners, all the prisoners, back to the whites, if they would be killed or if they would have protection from the whites." Robertson testimony, *Sisseton and Wahpeton Claims*, pt. 1, 139. Whipple commented that "Wah-kin-yan-wash-te [Andrew Good Thunder] says that he signed Wabasha's name to the letter to General Sibley. He was evidently timid. His band was hostile and he could not act openly. His own son in law charged his death (he was hung) upon Wabasha. I am convinced of his fidelity." Whipple recommended Good Thunder for an award of $250; Wabaśa received $100. Office of Indian Affairs, *Annual Report, 1866*, 236–39. However, this assessment of Wabaśa is contested by sources like captive Jannette DeCamp, who recalled Wabaśa addressing his young men: "'Soldiers!' he said scornfully, 'You talk very loud. You talk of killing women and children. You are cowards, not braves. I know you. You are furious to kill, but you cannot kill these friends of mine until you kill me!' . . . He imperiled his own life over and again . . . by his determination to intercede for the whites." DeCamp, "In the Hands of the Sioux," Brown County Historical Society.

12. Order Book, vol.103, Sibley Papers, MHS; Heard, *History of the Sioux War*, 148; West, *Ancestry, Life and Times*, 264. Although undated, this letter was delivered on 10 September to Sibley with the letter from Wabaśa and Taopi dated 10 September 1862.

13. Order Book, vol. 103, Sibley Papers, MHS. See also Heard, *History of the Sioux War*, 149.

14. Order Book, vol. 103, Sibley Papers, MHS. See also *St. Paul Daily Press*, 16 September 1862, 1; and West, *Ancestry, Life and Times*, 265. West, Sibley's first biographer, believed Sibley's correspondence ended after this letter and another, also dated 12 September, to Little Crow. Documents reproduced in this volume show negotiation via correspondence continued until 24 September 1862, or about a day and a half before Sibley arrived at Camp Release. The Order Book copy is addressed to a third, unidentified Dakota.

15. Taopi described receiving the letter:

When they [Robertson and Robinson] returned from the fort (Ridgley) they brought an answer to my letter. I could not see it for some time as the Indians suspected something, and my tipi was always surrounded by their guns. A few of us went down into the Minnesota Bottom at midnight and concealed ourselves in the high grass and rushes. Mr. George Spencer, whose life was saved by Chaska [Wakiŋyaŋtawa,

His Thunder], read the letter to us. He drew a blanket over his head and lighted a candle under it and read the letter to us: He was covered with the blanket least the Indians on the hill should see the light. My heart was glad when I heard the letter. General Sibley said: "Save as many of the prisoners as you can. Get them into your possession as quickly and quietly as you can." (Taopi, "Statement," 112–13)

16. Minnesota Board of Commissioners, *Minnesota in the Civil and Indian Wars*, 2:229.

17. Simon Anawaŋgmani had reached Fort Ridgley with Mrs. Newman on 11 September 1862. Anawaŋgmani may have been considering returning to the Upper Camp, where his wife was, when Sibley wrote this letter. On 24 September Riggs wrote to John and Mary Renville, "I wrote to you [earlier] to send up by Simon but he did not go." *A Thrilling Narrative*, chap. 12.

18. Heard, *History of the Sioux War*, 163.

19. A few, like Helen Carrothers and her children, had literally escaped. Others had fled to the Upper Camp for refuge.

20. Heard, *History of the Sioux War*, 163–64.

21. This letter was written on Monday, 15 September. Sibley did not arrive at Camp Release for eleven more days.

22. With the camps combined there was protective ambiguity for the peace-seeking Dakotas and the captives in their care. If they made a separate camp on the open prairie, as Sibley suggested, the intentions of every family would be perfectly clear. Thus it was important that they not create a separate camp long before Sibley arrived.

23. *A Thrilling Narrative*, chap. 9. Mazakutemani wrote two letters to Sibley dated 15 September 1862. The previous letter, reprinted in Heard, mentions a letter written earlier in the day that could not be gotten out of camp safely. This letter, reprinted in *A Thrilling Narrative*, may be the Renvilles' copy of the earlier letter.

24. Heard, *History of the Sioux War*, 164.

25. See "Historical Introduction," 61–68, for excerpts of speeches attributed to Mazakutemani at these councils.

26. Renville signed her maiden name, presumably believing that if the letter was discovered and her role as amanuensis for Mazakutemani became known, her life would be endangered. A century later, when Marion P. Satterlee was compiling his lists of captives at Camp Release, this letter misled him to note Mrs. Mary Renville and M. A. Butler as two unique individuals.

27. Heard, *History of the Sioux War*, 164.

28. Heard, *History of the Sioux War*, 164–65. In 1901 Joseph LaFramboise described delivering this letter, which had been penned for Taṭaŋka Nažiŋ by Joseph's sister, Julia LaFramboise:

I went from the camp in the night with the letter. There were others with me. Myself and three others started with the letter toward where General Sibley was and it was daylight on the way. Shortly after daylight we saw a man riding after us. We stopped and let him come up to us. It was Gi-ci-ye-ce-ya [Ziciyeya?] meaning He who paints himself yellow [sic], and he said that after we had left camp it had got out that we were going to deliver this letter, and Little Crow had ordered that we should be stopped, and for that reason he was sent to notify us. This man returned from there, but we went on to Yellow Medicine, and in the rear of the timber overlooking a knoll toward where General Sibley was, we stopped there to rest and take a smoke. The other three who were with me were very anxious about what might be going on at the camp we had left, thinking perhaps all there had been killed in the meantime; I then told them it would be no use to turn back from there on account of any such fear and that I was going on, and I got onto my horse and started toward General Sibley's command. When I got near General Sibley's picket line I saw two of the pickets standing close together. I had a small flag with me, but in the excitement had forgotten about it, and was holding it so it could not be seen. After these pickets had started toward the camp then I thought of my white flag and raised it up, and seeing it, one of them came to where I was, and this was John Otherday. The other picket went inside of General Sibley's line and a short time after that a guard came out and took us into General Sibley's camp. (LaFramboise testimony, *Sisseton and Wahpeton Claims*, pt. 1, 151)

29. Samuel J. Brown testified that Taṭaŋka Nażiŋ said "that he was going away soon and would come down in two weeks with a force large enough to take us [away from the lower Dakota] by force if necessary. The battle of Wood Lake occurred before Standing Buffalo got back." *Sisseton and Wahpeton Claims*, pt. 1, 30.

30. *A Thrilling Narrative*, chap. 11.

31. *A Thrilling Narrative*, chap. 12.

32. *War of the Rebellion*, 13:664. Although this letter is addressed to no one, the content suggests Little Crow was the intended recipient.

33. Heard, *History of the Sioux War*, 165–66.

34. It is not clear who "the writer" is: the amanuensis or Heard.

35. Minnesota Board of Commissioners, *Minnesota in the Civil and Indian Wars*, 2:249–50.

36. Joseph Campbell is "A. J. Campbell" at the end of Little Crow's 10 September letter to Sibley.

37. Minnesota Board of Commissioners, *Minnesota in the Civil and Indian Wars*, 2:250. In 1901 Joseph LaFramboise testified that Sibley wrote his letter of reply in English and instructed LaFramboise to have it translated into Dakota. LaFramboise took Sibley's letter to the Peace Camp, where it was translated into Dakota by his

sister Julia LaFramboise. English and Dakota copies were placed in a single envelope and entrusted to Michael Paul (son of Paul Mazakutemani) for delivery to Taṭaŋka Nażiŋ, who by that time had returned to his hunting grounds in Dakota Territory. LaFramboise, *Sisseton and Wahpeton Claims*, pt. 1, 151.

38. Minnesota Board of Commissioners, *Minnesota in the Civil and Indian Wars*, 2:262.

APPENDIX B

1. John B. Renville to Stephen R. Riggs, 8 December 1862, Riggs Papers, MHS.

2. On Gilfillan, see appendix B, note 8.

3. See "Historical Introduction," note 291.

4. Mary A. Butler to Stephen R. Riggs, 10 January 1863, Riggs Papers, MHS.

5. "Ella" is John and Mary's biological daughter, who was nearly three years old at the time these letters were written. Ella was also held captive. "Belle" is Isabelle Martin Renville, daughter of John's sister Madeline, who had been a member of their family at Hazlewood. Mary Riggs to Alfred Riggs, 1 January 1862, CWS. Belle was living in St. Anthony in August 1862 and was not taken captive. She rejoined John and Mary's family after they were freed and traveled with them to Berlin, Wisconsin. "Lillie" was a young mixed-blood girl who boarded with John and Mary's family at Hazlewood. Lillie was the granddaughter of Bad Track, who reclaimed her near the outset of the war. On Lillie, see *A Thrilling Narrative*, note 105.

6. The Dakotas who were not tried and imprisoned after their surrender at Camp Release were interned at Fort Snelling, near St. Paul. This included the majority of the members of the Peace Coalition and John's siblings and their families. See Monjou Marz, *Dakota Internment Camp*.

7. In retrospect it is difficult to discern whether Germans distinguished themselves above the generalized fury in Minnesota directed against Dakota people in the wake of the war. Modern German scholars like Don Heinrich Tolzmann dispute that idea. Yet because German settlers were the ethnic majority in Renville and Brown Counties (the two counties with the most war deaths) and because New Ulm was the city nearest to the reservation, that idea quickly took hold. On 9 November 1862, outside New Ulm, German residents of that city attacked a wagon party of shackled Dakotas en route to Mankato, killing two men. A month later New Ulmers were ringleaders in a foiled attempt to lynch the same Dakotas in prison at Mankato. See Glewwe, "Journey of the Prisoners"; Bachman, "Colonel Miller's War"; and Bachman, "Deaths of Dakota Prisoners."

8. C. D. Gilfillan was a Minnesota lawyer who handled many settlers' claims for losses in the Dakota War. The "M.L. School" is the federal Manual Labor School at Yellow Medicine, where the Renvilles were employed as teachers.

9. She may refer here to the settlement due them from Joseph R. Brown, who, until May 1861, was Indian agent for the Sioux of the Mississippi. Brown left office without paying most of his employees' salaries. Brown's "books were not ready" because his agency accounts were being audited by the Second Auditor of the Treasury.

10. John B. Renville to Stephen R. Riggs, 22 January 1863, Riggs Papers, MHS.

11. These phrases appear in English within the Dakota letter.

12. John refers here to the story of the prophet Elijah and the widow of Zarephath in the Bible, I Kings 17. The widow was hospitable to Elijah even though she barely had food enough to keep her son alive. God blessed her by miraculously replenishing her supply of flour and oil so there was always just enough to feed her household. It was one of the stories John was translating into Dakota from *Precept upon Precept*. On *Precept upon Precept*, see appendix B, note 31.

13. Stephen and Mary Riggs were from Massachusetts. Aside from visits home, they had not been in Massachusetts since they came to the Minnesota frontier in 1835.

14. On proposed awards to "friendly" Dakotas, see "Historical Introduction," note 291.

15. On conditions in the Dakota internment camp at Fort Snelling, see appendix B, notes 17 and 18.

16. Mary A. Butler to Stephen R. Riggs, 23 January 1863, Riggs Papers, MHS.

17. Agnes, John B. Renville's half sister (daughter of Joseph Renville and his second wife, Therese Ermatinger [Armatender, Ermetinger]), was about fourteen when she died. Since Agnes died outside the camp, possibly at Mendota, she is not counted among the estimated two hundred Dakotas who died of disease during that winter at Fort Snelling. Since historians have not previously understood that some initial internees, like Agnes Renville and the four children who went to live with John and Mary Renville (see "Historical Introduction," note 321), were later paroled to communities outside it, the full reduction in the camp census by the spring of 1863 has been incorrectly attributed to deaths in the camp. Future research may shed more light on the complexity of the question of the internees' fates. Henry Sibley investigated charges of negligence brought against Dr. John Wakefield (husband of captive Sarah Wakefield), the government-appointed Sioux physician at the internment camp.

18. Measles was rampant in Minnesota that winter, especially in communities overcrowded by the thousands of people displaced by the war. Monjou Marz traces the measles epidemic from a few infected soldiers at Camp Release and Yellow Medicine in October 1862 through an estimated 134–166 Dakota deaths from measles at Fort Snelling by May 1863. See "Epidemic," chap. 4 in *Dakota Internment Camp*.

19. "Mary" is Mary Martin, born in August 1848 to John's sister Madeline (Magdaline) Renville and her husband, Louis Martin. The letter refers to Mary Martin as "Mamie" at the end of the same paragraph. Her 1856 Pepin Scrip affidavits claimed

she was being raised by Alex Duncan Campbell. Mary Martin was the older sister of John and Mary's adopted daughter Belle. See Jonas Pettijohn to Samuel Pond, 16 May 1846, and Thomas S. Williamson to David Greene, 12 June 1846, both NMM, MHS; John and Mary Renville to Riggs, 13 February 1863, appendix B; and "Historical Introduction," note 321. By 1865 John and Mary were acting as Mary Martin's guardians while she was in school at Rockford, Illinois. See Mary A. Renville to Stephen R. Riggs, 1 December 1865 and 7 March 1866, Riggs Papers, MHS.

20. Madeline's mother, Therese Ermatinger Renville (the widow of John's brother Joseph Renville III), married John Otherday in January 1863 in the Fort Snelling camp. Otherday's white wife, Rosanne [Roxanne], left him shortly after their August 1862 escape from the frontier. *St. Paul Pioneer*, 31 January 1863.

21. The reference is probably to Albert Barnes, *Notes on the New Testament* and/ or *Notes on the Old Testament*. These volumes were a popular Bible reference at the time. See "Biography of Albert Barnes," Christian Classics Ethereal Library, accessed 31 January 2011, http://www.ccel.org/b/barnes.

22. "Un. Sol." was Solomon Brown, brother of Joseph R. Brown, whose wife, Susan Frenier, was a stepsister to John's Renville's half brothers. Solomon lost his job at the Sioux Agency with the 1861 turnover of the Democratic regime. John and Mary Renville owed Solomon Brown for household goods he had consigned to them for sale when he left the agency.

23. Nathan Myrick was the older brother of trader Andrew J. Myrick, who was killed at the Lower Sioux Agency in 1862. Their trading firm was in bankruptcy before the war broke out and had been consigned to the ownership of Stewart B. Garvie, who died of wounds received at the Upper Agency. After the war Nathan Myrick resumed control and, in 1885, had to settle for considerably less compensation for 1862 business losses than he had claimed.

24. Written in the margin at the conclusion of the letter.

25. Mary A. Butler to Stephen R. Riggs, 30 January 1863, Riggs Papers, MHS.

26. The word "Gov." is overwritten here with "Gen." Sibley was governor of Minnesota from May 1858 until January 1860.

27. John and Mary Renville to Stephen R. Riggs, 13 February 1863, Riggs Papers, MHS.

28. The foregoing section of this letter is in John's handwriting. The remainder is in Mary's.

29. There is no evidence that Riggs's daughter Isabella complied. But Mary may have made the same request of the Cunninghams; their story appeared at the end of the Atlas edition.

30. John and Mary A. Butler to Stephen R. Riggs, February 21, 1863, Riggs Papers, MHS.

31. *Precept upon Precept*, first published in English by Mrs. Favel Lee Mortimer in 1859, was a popular book of Bible stories selected from the historical books of the Old Testament, in which God allowed rebellious Israel to be taken captive by foreigners before restoring his people to Jerusalem. Upon its appearance in 1864 John Renville's translation, *Wooŋspe Itakihna*, spanned a gap in Dakota-language Bible literature. The corresponding books of the Old Testament were not available in translation until 1878.

32. John B. Renville to Stephen R. Riggs, 24 February 1863, Riggs Papers, MHS.

33. Dakota Christians were raising money to reprint the Dakota hymnbooks lost in the war.

34. John refers here to his translation work on *Precept upon Precept*. Apparently an earlier translation, begun by the missionaries, was lost in the 1862 war.

35. Letter to the editor of the *Saint Paul Weekly Press*, 5 March 1863, 4. "Mr. Frenier" was mixed-blood Antoine Frenier, who before the war was an elder, along with John B. Renville, in the Dakota congregation at Pejutazizi. Frenier was a member of the Renville Rangers and thus escaped being taken captive. Mary Renville was responding to a letter (unidentified) that Frenier had written disputing the idea that mixed-bloods were captives.

36. Sibley wrote to his wife on 8 September 1862, "The half-breeds, whom I know, say that the mixed-bloods are not permitted to leave the camp and are virtually prisoners, as most of them are believed to sympathize with whites." Sibley Papers, MHS.

37. Mary Renville, "Trying to Overcome," *Iapi Oaye*, October 1882, 80.

BIBLIOGRAPHY

MANUSCRIPT COLLECTIONS
American Philosophical Society, Philadelphia, Pennsylvania
   Franz Boas Papers
Brown County Historical Society, Brown County, Minnesota
Carnegie Library of Steuben County, Angola, Indiana
   Butler Family Collection
Center for Western Studies, Augustana College, Sioux Falls, South Dakota
   Oahe Mission Collection, Riggs Family Papers
Dakotah Prairie Museum, Aberdeen, South Dakota
   John P. Williamson Papers
Minnesota Historical Society, St. Paul, Minnesota
   Alan R. Woolworth Papers
   Clark Thompson Papers
   Dakota Conflict of 1862 Manuscript Collection
   Fort Ridgley State Park and Historical Association Papers
   Fort Ridgley Post Administration Records (microfilm)
   G. Merrill Dwelle and Family Papers
   Grace Lee Nute Papers
   Henry H. Sibley Papers
   James R. Doolittle Papers
   Jared Waldo Daniels Papers
   Marion P. Satterlee Papers
   Minnesota Historical Society Institutional Archives
   Northwest Missions Manuscripts Collection
   Protestant Episcopal Church Diocese of Minnesota Papers
   Ramsey Gubernatorial Papers, State Archives

Return Ira Holcombe Papers
Samuel and Gideon Pond Papers
Stephen R. Riggs and Family Papers
Thomas S. Williamson and Family Papers
Whipple-Scandarett Family Papers
William Watts Folwell Papers
National Archives and Records Administration, Washington DC
    Records of the Department of the Interior
    Records of the Department of War
    Records of the Office of Indian Affairs
    Records of the Thirty-seventh Congress
Presbyterian Historical Society, Philadelphia, Pennsylvania
    Dakota Mission Collection
South Dakota State Archives, Pierre, South Dakota
    Doane Robinson Papers
    Riggs Family Papers
Southern Minnesota Historical Center, Minnesota State University, Mankato, Minnesota
    Thomas S. Hughes Papers

PUBLISHED WORKS

Adams, Moses N. "The Sioux Outbreak in the Year 1862 with Notes of Missionary Work among the Sioux." In *Collections of the Minnesota Historical Society* 9:431–52. St. Paul: The Society, 1901.

Adams, Moses N., John P. Williamson, and John B. Renville. "The History of the Dakota Presbytery of the Presbyterian Church from Its Organization to April, 1890." In *The First 50 Years of the Dakota Presbytery to 1890*, edited by Leslie B. Lewis. Freeman SD: Pine Hill Press, 1984.

Ainslie, Mary E. D. "The Dakota Mission—A Plea for Help." In *The Missionary Herald at Home and Abroad*, 408–11. Cambridge MA: Riverside Press, 1878.

Alexie, Sherman. *First Indian on the Moon*. New York: Hanging Loose Press, 1993.

Anderson, Carolyn Ruth. "Dakota Identity in Minnesota 1820–1995." PhD diss., Indiana University, 1997.

Anderson, Gary Clayton. "Joseph Renville and the Ethos of Biculturalism." In *Being and Becoming Indian*, edited by James A. Clifton, 59–81. Prospect Heights IL: Waveland Press, 1989.

———. *Kinsmen of Another Kind: Dakota-White Relations in the Upper Mississippi Valley, 1650–1862*. 1984. Reprint, St. Paul: Minnesota Historical Society Press, 1997.

———. *Little Crow: Spokesman for the Sioux*. St. Paul: Minnesota Historical Society Press, 1986.

Anderson, Gary Clayton, and Alan R. Woolworth, eds. *Through Dakota Eyes: Narrative Accounts of the Minnesota Indian War of 1862.* St. Paul: Minnesota Historical Society Press, 1988.

Atkins, Annette. *Creating Minnesota, a History from the Inside Out.* St. Paul: Minnesota Historical Society Press, 2007.

Bachman, Walt. "Colonel Miller's War." In *Trails of Tears: Minnesota's Dakota Indian Exile Begins,* edited by Mary H. Bakeman and Antona M. Richardson, 107–22. Roseville MN: Prairie Echoes Press, 2008.

———. "Deaths of Dakota Prisoners from the New Ulm Mob Attacks." In *Trails of Tears: Minnesota's Dakota Indian Exile Begins,* edited by Mary H. Bakeman and Antona M. Richardson, 179–80. Roseville MN: Prairie Echoes Press, 2008.

Bakeman, Mary H., and Antona M. Richardson, eds. *Trails of Tears: Minnesota's Dakota Indian Exile.* Roseville MN: Prairie Echoes Press, 2008.

Bieder, Robert E. "Scientific Attitudes toward Indian Mixed Bloods in Early Nineteenth Century America." *Journal of Ethnic Studies* 8 (1981): 17–30.

Big Eagle, Jerome. "A Sioux Story of the War." In *Minnesota Historical Society Collections* 6:382–400. St. Paul: The Society, 1894.

Black Thunder, Elijah, Norma Johnson, Larry O'Conner, and Muriel Provonost. *Ehanna Woyakapi: History and Culture of the Sisseton-Wahpeton Sioux Tribe of South Dakota.* Sisseton SD: Sisseton-Wahpeton Sioux Tribe, 1975.

Bordewich, Fergus M. *Bound for Canaan: The Underground Railroad and the War for the Soul of America.* New York: Amistad, 2005.

Bray, Edmund C., and Martha Coleman Bray. *Joseph Nicollet on the Plains and Prairies: The Expeditions of 1838–39 with Journals, Letters, and Notes on the Dakota Indians.* St. Paul: Minnesota Historical Society Press, 1993.

Brown, Samuel J. *In Captivity: The Experience, Privations and Dangers of Samuel J. Brown and Others While Prisoners of the Hostile Sioux during the Massacre and War of 1862.* Washington DC: Government Printing Office, 1900.

Bryant, Charles S., and Abel B. Murch. *A History of the Great Massacre by the Sioux Indians in Minnesota.* Cincinnati: Rickey and Carroll, 1864.

Burnham, Michelle. *Captivity and Sentiment: Cultural Exchange in American Literature, 1682–1861.* Hanover NH: University Press of New England, 1997.

Butler, Marvin Benjamin. *My Story of the Civil War and the Underground Railroad.* Huntington IN: United Brethren Publishing Establishment, 1914.

Carley, Kenneth. *The Sioux Uprising of 1862.* St. Paul: Minnesota Historical Society, 1961.

Carrigan, Minnie Busse. *Captured by the Indians: Reminiscences of Pioneer Life in Minnesota.* Buffalo Lake MN: Author, 1912.

Carroll, Lorrayne. *Rhetorical Drag: Gender Impersonation, Captivity, and the Writing of History.* Kent OH: Kent State University Press, 2007.

Clemmons, Linda. "Our Children Are in Danger of Becoming Little Indians: Protestant Missionary Children and Dakotas 1835–1862." *Michigan Historical Review* 25 (1999): 69–90.

Clifton, James A. *The Prairie People: Continuity and Change in Potawatomi Indian Culture, 1665–1965*. Lawrence: Regents Press of Kansas, 1977.

Congressional Globe. Eleventh Congress, Third Session, n.s. 33 (16 January 1863). Washington DC: John C. Rives.

"A Converted Indian Brave." *Foreign Missionary* 46 (1886): 55–56.

Creswell, R. J. "The Prince of Indian Preachers." In *Among the Sioux: A Story of the Twin Cities and the Two Dakotas*, 89–91. Minneapolis: University Press, 1906.

Curtiss-Wedge, Franklyn. *The History of Renville County*. Vol. 1. Chicago: H. C. Hooper Jr., 1916.

Dean, Janet. "Nameless Outrages: Narrative Authority, Rape Rhetoric, and the Dakota Conflict of 1862." *American Literature* 77 (2005): 93–122.

Deloria, Ella. *The Dakota Way of Life*. Rapid City SD: Mariah Press, 2007.

———. *Speaking of Indians*. 1944. Reprint, Lincoln: University of Nebraska Press, 1998.

Demos, John. *The Unredeemed Captive*. New York: A. A. Knopf, 1995.

Derounian-Stodola, Kathryn Zabelle. "Captivity, Liberty, and Early American Consciousness." *Early American Literature* 43 (2008): 715–24.

———. *The War in Words: Reading the Dakota Conflict through the Captivity Literature*. Lincoln: University of Nebraska Press, 2009.

———, ed. *Women's Indian Captivity Narratives*. New York: Penguin, 1998.

Derounian-Stodola, Kathryn Zabelle, and James Levernier. *The Indian Captivity Narrative, 1550–1900*. New York: Twayne, 1993.

Diedrich, Mark. *Little Crow and the Dakota War: The Long Historical Cover-ups Exposed*. Rochester MN: Coyote Books, 2006.

———. *Little Paul: Christian Leader of the Dakota Peace Party*. Rochester MN: Coyote Books, 2010.

Dinesen, Isak. *Out of Africa*. New York: Random House, 1937.

Douglass, Frederick. *Narrative of the Life of Frederick Douglass, an American Slave*. Edited by Houston A. Baker Jr. New York: Penguin, 1986.

Durand, Paul. *Where the Waters Gather and the Rivers Meet: An Atlas of the Eastern Sioux*. Prior Lake MN: Author, 1994.

Easton, Augustus B. *History of the St. Croix Valley*. Vol. 1. Chicago: H. C. Hooper Jr., 1909.

Edmunds, R. David. *The Potawatomis: Keepers of the Fire*. Norman: University of Oklahoma Press, 1978.

Ellinghaus, Katherine. *Taking Assimilation to Heart: Marriages of White Women and Indigenous Men in the United States and Australia, 1887–1935*. Lincoln: University of Nebraska Press, 2006.

Erdrich, Louise. *Jacklight*. New York: Holt, 1984.

Evers, Larry, and Ofelia Zepeda, eds. *Home Places: Contemporary Native American Writing from Sun Tracks*. Tucson: University of Arizona Press, 1995.

Flinders, Carol Lee. *Rebalancing the World: Why Women Belong and Men Compete and How to Restore the Ancient Equilibrium*. New York: HarperOne, 2003.

Folwell, William Watts. *A History of Minnesota*. Vol. 2. St. Paul: Minnesota Historical Society, 1924.

Fontaine, Harlam, and Neil McKay, eds. *550 Dakota Verbs*. St. Paul: Minnesota Historical Society Press, 2004.

Fowler, David H. *Northern Attitudes toward Interracial Marriage: Legislation and Public Opinion in the Middle Atlantic and the States of the Old Northwest, 1780–1930*. New York: Garland, 1987.

Gaul, Theresa Strouth. *To Marry an Indian: The Marriage of Harriett Gold and Elias Boudinot in Letters, 1823–1839*. Chapel Hill: University of North Carolina Press, 2005.

George, Rosemary Marangoly. *The Politics of Home: Postcolonial Relocations and Twentieth-Century Fiction*. Cambridge: Cambridge University Press, 1996.

Gillespy, John C. *History of Green Lake County*. Berlin WI: T. L. Terry, 1860.

Gilman, Rhoda. *Henry Hastings Sibley: Divided Heart*. St. Paul: Minnesota Historical Society Press, 2004.

Glewwe, Lois A. "The Journey of the Prisoners." In *Trails of Tears: Minnesota's Dakota Indian Exile Begins*, edited by Mary H. Bakeman and Antona M. Richardson, 79–106. Roseville MN: Prairie Echoes Press, 2008.

Goodman, Robert, and Nancy Goodman. *Joseph R. Brown, Adventurer on the Minnesota Frontier, 1820–1849*. Rochester MN: Lone Oak Press 1996.

Good Thunder, Andrew. "Statement of Andrew Good Thunder." In *Lights and Shadows of a Long Episcopate*, by Henry B. Whipple, 114. New York: Macmillan, 1902.

Graber, Kay, ed. *Sister to the Sioux: the Memoirs of Elaine Goodale Eastman, 1885–1891*. Lincoln: University of Nebraska Press, 1985.

Green, William D. *A Peculiar Imbalance: The Fall and Rise of Racial Equality in Early Minnesota*. St. Paul: Minnesota Historical Society Press, 2007.

Gregor, Theresa Lynn. "From Captors to Captives: American Indian Responses to Popular American Narrative Forms." PhD diss., University of Southern California, 2010.

Grover, Linda LeGarde. *The Dance Boots*. Athens: University of Georgia Press, 2010.

Hacker, Margaret. *Cynthia Ann Parker: The Life and the Legend*. El Paso: Texas Western Press, 1990.

Hage, George S. *Newspapers on the Minnesota Frontier, 1849–1860*. St. Paul: Minnesota Historical Society, 1967.

Hall, James. *Sketches of History, Life, and Manners in the West* Vol. 1. Philadelphia: Harrison Hall, 1835.

Heard, Isaac V. D. *History of the Sioux War and Massacres of 1862 and 1863*. New York: Harper and Brothers, 1864.

Hendrick, George, and Willene Hendrick, eds. *Fleeing for Freedom: Stories of the Underground Railroad as Told by Levi Coffin and William Still*. Chicago: Ivan R. Dee, 2004.

Hodes, Martha, ed. *Sex, Love, Race: Crossing Boundaries in North American History*. New York: New York University Press, 1999.

Holcombe, Return I. *Sketches Historical and Descriptive of the Monuments and Tablets Erected by the Minnesota Valley Historical Society*. Morton MN: Minnesota Valley Historical Society, 1902.

hooks, bell. *Belonging: A Culture of Place*. New York: Routledge, 2009.

Hyman, Colette. "Survival at Crow Creek, 1863–66." *Minnesota History* 61 (Winter 2008–9): 148–61.

Jacobs, Margaret T. "The Eastmans and the Luhans: Interracial Marriage between White Women and Native Men, 1875–1935." In *Frontiers: A Journal of Women's Studies* 23 (2002): 29–54.

Johnson, Norma. *Chilson's History of Fort Sisseton*. Pierre SD: ESCO, 1996.

Juni, Benedict. *Held in Captivity: Experiences Related by Benedict Juni of New Ulm, Minn., as an Indian Captive during the Indian Outbreak of 1862*. New Ulm MN: Liesch-Walter Printing, 1926.

Kenschaft, Lori. *Lydia Maria Child: The Quest for Racial Justice*. New York: Oxford University Press, 2002.

Kerber, Linda K. "The Abolitionist Perception of the Indian." *Journal of American History* 62 (1975): 271–95.

Lawrence, Elden. *The Peace Seekers: Indian Christians and the Dakota Conflict*. Sioux Falls SD: Pine Hill Press, 2005.

Lawrence, Lorenzo. "The Statement of Lorenzo Lawrence." In *Lights and Shadows of a Long Episcopate*, by Henry B. Whipple, 114–18. New York: Macmillan, 1902.

Leaf, Helene. "Family Ties to the Dakota Uprising." *American Swedish Genealogist* 27, nos. 2–4 (2007).

Lewis, Bonnie Sue. *Creating Christian Indians: Native Clergy in the Presbyterian Church*. Norman: University of Oklahoma Press, 2003.

Love, W. DeLoss. *Samson Occom and the Christian Indians of New England*. Reprint, Syracuse NY: Syracuse University Press, 2000.

Lynd, James. "The Religion of the Dakotas." In *Collections of the Minnesota Historical Society* 2:150–74. St. Paul: The Society, 1889.

Mazakutemani, Paul. "Narrative of Paul Mazakootemane or He Who Walks Shooting Iron." In *Collections of the Minnesota Historical Society* 3:82–90. St. Paul: The Society, 1880.

Meginness, John F. *Francis Slocum, the Lost Sister of Wyoming*. Williamsport PA: Heller Bros.' Printing House, 1891.

Miller, Otis A. E. *Luther Lee: An Episode of the Indian Massacre in Minnesota in 1862*. Minneapolis: Atlas, 1866.

Minnesota Board of Commissioners on Publication of History of Minnesota in Civil and Indian Wars. *Minnesota in the Civil and Indian Wars, 1861–1865*. 2 vols. St. Paul: Printed for the State by the Pioneer Press Company, 1890.

Monjou Marz, Corinne. *The Dakota Internment Camp at Fort Snelling 1862–64*. St. Paul: Prairie Smoke Press, 2005.

Morris, H. S. *Historical Stories, Legends, and Traditions of Roberts County and Northeastern South Dakota*. Sisseton SD: Sisseton Courier, 1975.

Office of Indian Affairs. *Annual Report of the Commissioner of Indian Affairs to the Secretary of the Interior, 1859*. Washington DC: Government Printing Office, 1860.

———. *Annual Report of the Commissioner of Indian Affairs to the Secretary of the Interior, 1863*. Washington DC: Government Printing Office, 1864.

———. *Annual Report of the Commissioner of Indian Affairs to the Secretary of the Interior, 1866*. Washington DC: Government Printing Office, 1867.

Oneroad, Amos, and Alanson B. Skinner. *Being Dakota: Tales and Traditions of the Sisseton and Wahpeton*. Edited by Laura L. Anderson. St. Paul: Minnesota Historical Society Press, 2003.

Ortiz, Simon J. "Indigenous Language Consciousness: Being, Place, and Sovereignty." In *Sovereign Bones: New Native American Writing*, 2:135–47. Edited by Eric Gansworth. New York: Nation Books, 2007.

Osman, Stephen E. "Audacity, Skill, and Firepower: The Third Minnesota's Skirmishers at the Battle of Wood Lake." *Minnesota's Heritage* 3 (January 2011): 24–40.

———. "Sibley's Army in November 1862." In *Trails of Tears: Minnesota's Dakota Indian Exile Begins*, edited by Mary H. Bakeman and Antona M. Richardson, 13–34. Roseville MN: Prairie Echoes Press, 2008.

Otherday, John. "Statement of John Other Day." In *Lights and Shadows of a Long Episcopate*, by Henry B. Whipple, 119–21. New York: Macmillan, 1902.

Papers Relating to Talks and Councils Held with the Indians in Dakota and Montana Territories in the Years 1866–1869. Washington DC: Government Printing Office, 1910.

Pascoe, Peggy. *What Comes Naturally: Miscegenation Law and the Making of Race in America*. New York: Oxford University Press, 2009. Based on Peggy Pascoe. "Race, Gender and the Privileges of Property: On the Significance of Miscegenation Law in the American West." In *Over the Edge: ReMapping the American West*, ed. Valarie J. Matsumoto and Blake Allmendinger, 215–30. Berkeley: University of California Press, 1999.

Pearce, Roy Harvey. "Melville's Indian-Hater: A Note on the Meaning of the Confidence-man." *Publications of the Modern Language Association of America* 67 (1972): 942–48.

Pearsall, Fred. *Short Stories and History of the Dakota People.* Privately published, 1983. (In the Minnesota Historical Society collections.)

Pettijohn, Jonas. *Autobiography, Family History and Various Reminiscences of the Life of Jonas Pettijohn; Among the Sioux or Dakota Indians.* Clay Center KS: Dispatch Printing House, 1890.

Pond, Gideon H. "True History of the Indian Outbreak in Minnesota: The Real Perpetrators of the Massacre Not Yet Taken." *Evangelist* 33 (5 March 1863): 10. (In the Northwest Missions Manuscripts Collection, Minnesota Historical Society.)

Pond, Samuel W. *The Dakota or Sioux in Minnesota as They Were in 1834.* St. Paul: Minnesota Historical Society Press, 1986.

Red Owl, Ed. "Traditional Man: Gabriel 'Ti Wakan' Renville." Pts. 1–8. *Ikce Wicasta* 1, no. 3 (1998)–3, no. 10 (2000).

Renville, Gabriel. "Narrative Account of the Sioux Massacre in Minnesota in 1862." *South Dakotan* 11 (November 1903): 4–17.

Renville, Mary Butler. *A Thrilling Narrative of Indian Captivity.* Minneapolis MN: Atlas Company's Book and Job Printing Office, 1863.

Rich, Adrienne. "Notes toward a Politics of Location." In *Blood, Bread, and Poetry: Selected Prose, 1979–1985,* 210–31. New York: Norton, 1992.

Riggs, Maida Leonard, ed. *A Small Bit of Bread and Butter: Letters from Dakota Territory, 1832–1869.* South Deerfield MA: Ash Grove Press, 1996.

Riggs, Stephen R. *A Dakota-English Dictionary.* Reprint, St. Paul: Minnesota Historical Society Press, 1992.

———. *Mary and I: Forty Years with the Sioux.* 1880. Reprint, Minneapolis: Ross and Haines, 1969.

———. *Tah-koo Wah-kan; or, the Gospel among the Sioux.* Boston: Congregational Publishing Society, 1869.

Robinson, Doane. "A Sioux Indian View of the Last War with England." *South Dakota Historical Collections* 5 (1910): 307–401.

Rosa, Joseph C. *Wild Bill Hickok, the Man and His Myth.* Lawrence: University Press of Kansas, 1996.

Ruoff, LaVonne, ed. *Life, Letters and Speeches of George Copway (Kahgegagahbowh).* Lincoln: University of Nebraska Press, 1997.

Schmidt, Mary Schwandt. "The Story of Mary Schwandt." In *Collections of the Minnesota Historical Society* 6:461–74. St. Paul MN: Pioneer Press, 1894.

Schuler, Harold. *Fort Sisseton.* Freeman SD: Pine Hill Press, 1996.

Seaver, James. *A Narrative of the Life of Mrs. Mary Jemison.* Canandaigua NY: J. D. Bemis, 1824.

Siebert, Wilbur H. *Vermont's Anti-Slavery and Underground Railroad Record*. Columbus OH: Spahr and Glenn, 1937.

Siems, Monica L. "How Do You Say 'God' in Dakota? Epistemological Problems in the Christianization of Native Americans." *Numen* 45 (1998): 163–82.

Silver, A. I., ed. *Introduction to Canadian History*. Toronto: Canadian Scholars' Press, 1991.

Sisseton and Wahpeton Bands of Dakota or Sioux Indians v. the United States [*Sisseton and Wahpeton Claims*]. 1901–1907. U. S. Army Court of Claims no. 22524. Washington DC: Government Printing Office, 1905. Bound testimony in the Minnesota Historical Society reference library.

Sleeper-Smith, Susan. *Indian Woman and French Men: Rethinking Cultural Encounter in the Western Great Lakes*. Amherst: University of Massachusetts Press, 2001.

Smits, David D. "'Squaw men,' 'Half-breeds,' and Amalgamators: Late Nineteenth-Century Anglo-American Attitudes toward Indian-White Race Mixing." *American Indian Culture and Research Journal* 15 (1991): 29–61.

Staehlin, Robert H. "A History of Printing in Minneapolis and Saint Paul, Minnesota, with a Bibliography of Imprints 1866–1876." Master's thesis, University of Minnesota, 1951.

Sweet, Jannette DeCamp. "Mrs. J. E. De Camp Sweet's Narrative of Her Captivity in the Sioux Outbreak of 1862." In *Collections of the Minnesota Historical Society* 6:354–80. St. Paul: Pioneer Press, 1894.

Taopi. "Statement of Taopi." In *Lights and Shadows of a Long Episcopate*, by Henry B. Whipple, 111–14. New York: Macmillan, 1902.

Tarble, Helen Mar Carrothers. *The Story of My Capture and Escape during the Minnesota Indian Massacre of 1862*. St. Paul MN: Abbott Print, 1904. Reprint, Garland Library of Narratives of North American Indian Captivities, vol. 105. New York: Garland, 1976. Citations refer to the 1904 edition.

Taylor, Daniel. *Tell Me a Story*. St. Paul: Bog Walk Press, 2001. First published as *The Healing Power of Stories*, New York: Doubleday, 1996.

Toulouse, Teresa. *The Captive's Position: Female Narrative, Male Identity, and Royal Authority in Colonial New England*. Philadelphia: University of Pennsylvania Press, 2007.

Turner, Glennette Tilley. *The Underground Railroad in Illinois*. Glen Ellyn IL: Newman Educational Publishing, 2001.

U.S. House of Representatives. *Executive Document no. 58*. 38th Cong., 1st Sess., 1864. Reprint, Fairfield WA: Ye Galleon Press, 1974.

U.S. War Department. *The War of the Rebellion: A Compilation of the Official Records of the Union and Confederate Armies*. 70 vols. in 128 parts. Washington DC: Government Printing Office, 1880–1901.

Vizenor, Gerald. *Fugitive Poses: Native American Indian Scenes of Absence and Presence.* Lincoln: University of Nebraska Press, 1998.

Wakefield, Sarah. *Six Weeks in the Sioux Tepees: A Narrative of Indian Captivity.* Edited by June Namias. Norman: University of Oklahoma Press, 1997.West, Nathaniel. *The Ancestry, Life and Times of Hon. Henry Hastings Sibley.* St. Paul: Pioneer Press, 1889.

Whipple, Henry B. *Lights and Shadows of a Long Episcopate.* New York: Macmillan, 1902.

White, Bruce M. "A Mouthful of Grass." In *Ringing in the Wilderness: Selections from the* North Country Anvil, edited by Rhoda R. Gilman, 259–67. Duluth MN: Holy Cow! Press, 1996.

White, Urania. "Captivity among the Sioux August 18 to September 26, 1862." In *Collections of the Minnesota Historical Society* 6:395–426. St. Paul MN: Pioneer Press, 1894.

Williams, Isabella Burgess Riggs. *By the Great Wall: Letters from China.* New York: Flemming H. Revell, 1909.

Williamson, John P. "The Dakota Mission Past and Present AD 1886." In *The First 50 Years of the Dakota Presbytery to 1890*, edited by Leslie B. Lewis. Freeman SD: Pine Hill Press, 1984.

———. *An English-Dakota Dictionary.* Reprint, St. Paul: Minnesota Historical Society Press, 1992.

Williamson, Thomas S. "Napehshneedoota." In *Collections of the Minnesota Historical Society* 3: 188–91. St. Paul: Minnesota Historical Society.

Wilson, Diane. Review of *The War in Words: Reading the Dakota Conflict through the Captivity Literature*, by Kathryn Zabelle Derounian-Stodola. *Minnesota History* (Spring 2010): 41–42.

Wilson, Waziyatawin Angela, ed. *In the Footsteps of Our Ancestors.* St. Paul: Living Justice Press, 2006.

Wingerd, Mary Lethert. *North Country: The Making of Minnesota.* Minneapolis: University of Minnesota Press, 2010.

Woods, Karen M. "A 'Wicked and Mischievous Connection': The Origins of Indian-White Miscegenation Law." *Legal Studies Forum* 23 (1999): 37–70.

Woolworth, Alan R. "Biography of Mazomani." In *Trails of Tears: Minnesota's Dakota Indian Exile Begins*, edited by Mary H. Bakeman and Antona M. Richardson, 173–76. Roseville MN: Prairie Echoes Press, 2008.

INDEX

Page numbers in italic refer to illustrations.

Lower Soldiers' Lodge (*continued*) 45; planning last stand, 80; raid on Hazlewood by, 50; razing of Hazlewood by, 68–69; recruiting young men, 111; and traders, 57–58, 268n188; and treatment of bicultural Dakotas, 41; violation of Dakota war conduct by, 62–63; visiting Upper Camp, 163–64, 299n82, 303n110. *See also* Lower Dakota Indians; Soldiers' lodges

Lucy Wikmankewastewin. *See* Wikmankewastewin, Lucy (niece of Lorenzo Lawrence)

"Luther Lee; an Episode of the Indian Massacre in Minnesota in 1862" (Miller), 132

Lynd, James, 310n176

Maȟpiyahdinape, Henok, 12–14, 19, 157, 250n39, 252n56, 299n80

Mah-zo manne. *See* Mazamani (Mazomani, Mahzomanne, Iron Walker, Shade)

Maine, 29–30, 257n101

malaria, 258n118. *See also* illness

malnutrition, 58–60, 268n190, 269n193. *See also* protein energy undernutrition; starvation

Manderfeld, Anton, 274n233

Mankato MN: attacks on Dakotas at, 86, 107, 273n222, 305n130, 317n7; Chaska executed at, 133–34; licensing of John B. Renville in, 94–95; Tatekaġe's execution at, 296n58; Thomas Williamson at prison in, 189–90; transcripts of trials in, 263n156

Mankato Weekly Record, 292n34

Marquette County WI, 22

marriage, 5, 18, 26, 247n9, 251n50, 255n85, 300n88. *See also* interracial marriage; polygamy

Marsh, Capt. John, 276n257

Martha's Vineyard, 20

Martin, Isabel "Belle" Renville (niece of John Baptiste): Alfred Riggs's article on, 283n321; background of, 317n5; in Berlin WI, 222; as boarder, 33; noisiness of, 229, 235; at school, 38, 87; scrip of, 233; sister of, 319n19; in St. Anthony, 92

Martin, Louis, 318n19

Martin, Madeline Renville. *See* Renville, Mary-Madeline Martin (sister of John Baptiste)

Martin, Mary, 92, 169, 170, 228, 231, 233, 283n321, 305n127, 318n19

Mascoutin city (Berlin WI), 22

Massachusetts, 12–13, 20, 104, 225, 252n58, 289n10, 318n13. *See also* Boston MA

Mayawakaŋ. *See* Red Iron Village

Mazakutemani, Paul (He Shoots Iron as He Walks) (Wahpeton): on acculturation, 47; in Battle of Wood Lake, 81; biography of, 275n246; and brother (Wambdiokiya) of, 8; on Brown family's escape, 154–55, 297n67; on burning of Rush Brook camp church, 164; on captive-taking, 66–67; on captivity, 72; children of, 280n293; on conduct of war, 67, 275n234; correspondence of, 51–53, 122, 153–55, 170, 174–75, 182–84, 199–201, 207–8, 211–14, 296n59, 307n143, 307n145; and daughter (Nona) of, 94, 280n293; death of, 81, 277n266; family history of, 247n11; feast planned by, 160–61; as founder of Hazlewood Republic, 19; and Harriet Adams, 180; on Hazlewood Republic members, 252n53; on helping Robidoux family, 158, 296n60; on Henry Sibley's advance, 76–78, 208–9; identity of, 260n137;